The Late Lord

The Late Lord

The Life of John Pitt
2nd Earl of Chatham

Jacqueline Reiter

PEN & SWORD
HISTORY

First published in Great Britain in 2017 by
PEN AND SWORD HISTORY
an imprint of
Pen and Sword Books Ltd
47 Church Street
Barnsley
South Yorkshire S70 2AS

ISBN 978 1 47385 695 0

Printed and bound in England
by CPI Group (UK) Ltd, Croydon, CR0 4YY

Typeset in Times New Roman by
CHIC GRAPHICS

Pen & Sword Books Ltd incorporates the imprints of Pen & Sword
Archaeology, Atlas, Aviation, Battleground, Discovery,
Family History, History, Maritime, Military, Naval, Politics, Railways,
Select, Social History, Transport, True Crime, Claymore Press,
Frontline Books, Leo Cooper, Praetorian Press, Remember When,
Seaforth Publishing and Wharncliffe.

For a complete list of Pen and Sword titles please contact
Pen and Sword Books Limited
47 Church Street, Barnsley, South Yorkshire, S70 2AS, England
E-mail: enquiries@pen-and-sword.co.uk
Website: www.pen-and-sword.co.uk

Contents

Acknowledgements

I am grateful to His Grace the Duke of Rutland for permission to consult, and quote from, manuscripts in his possession. Many thanks are also due to Jonathan Pledge of the British Library; Ben Fellows of the National Army Museum; Kate McQuillian of St George's Chapel Archives; Vanessa Wilkie and Anne Blecksmith at the Huntington Library, California; Janet Bloom and Diana Mankowski of the William L. Clements Library; Peter Foden and Emma Ellis at Belvoir Castle; and Anthony Pitaluga and Gerard Wood at the Gibraltar National Archives.

Sir Charles Hoare Bt has been incredibly generous with his time and assistance. Richard Selwyn Sharpe has been of great help piecing together the Townshend side of the story. Many thanks to June Lobanov-Rostovsky, who kindly permitted me to reproduce the portrait of Georgiana Townshend. Thank you, also, to Judith Edwards and the Trustees of the Chevening Estate for permission to reproduce the portrait of Lord Chatham by George Romney, and to Ian Davies and Sergeant Gary Chapman of the Royal Marines for permitting me to reproduce the portrait of Lord Chatham by the studio of John Hoppner.

Tim Pinches and Mark Chichon arranged for me to visit the Convent in Gibraltar, where Pepe Rosado was the perfect guide, full of anecdotes. Lec Pretlove and Hazel Jackson of TWI showed me round Abington Hall near Cambridge. At Cheveley Park Stud, Chris Richardson answered my questions and took me on a drive around the estate. Tim and Ellen Schroder went out of their way to help answer my questions about Burton Pynsent, inviting me into their house for lunch and a tour.

Carl Christie and Martin Howard have answered many of my questions regarding the Walcheren campaign, and were kind enough to look over my own chapters. John Bew has kindly answered some of my questions about Castlereagh, and Gareth Cole helped me track down some Ordnance material.

Therese Holmes has, as ever, been beyond amazing, reading the entire manuscript and giving me the benefit of her in-depth, expert feedback. Many thanks also to Maggie Scott, Jay Fedorak, and Margaret Porter: the final product is so much better for your input. Christopher Sorensen and

Paul Waite shared their considerable knowledge of naval history with me, and reassured this landlubber that she was not entirely 'out of her element'. Helen Pinches and Alice Grice have both been of great help in tracking down newspaper resources. Stephenie Woolterton has always been around for lengthy chats about our 'Pitt boys', and has been most generous in putting useful material my way.

A particular thanks to Jan Spoor, for persuading me that a biography of Lord Chatham was both viable and desirable; to Kate Bohdanowicz and Sarah Murden, for introducing me to Pen & Sword; to Alison Miles, for her patience and attention to detail in editing the manuscript; and to Heather Williams, for being an informative, approachable and tolerant point to contact.

For all my other friends and family, who have seen this project go from inception to the research and writing stage, and had to live with Lord and Lady Chatham the whole time – I'm so sorry. But thank you.

*   *   *

Abbreviations

BL	British Library
CC	*Chatham Correspondence*
CUL	Cambridge University Library
GNA	Gibraltar National Archives
HCJ	House of Commons Journal
HLJ	House of Lords Journal
JRL	John Rylands Library
NAM	National Army Museum
NLS	National Library of Scotland
NMM	National Maritime Museum
NRS	National Records of Scotland
PD	*Parliamentary Debates*
PRONI	Public Record Office of Northern Ireland
TNA	The National Archives

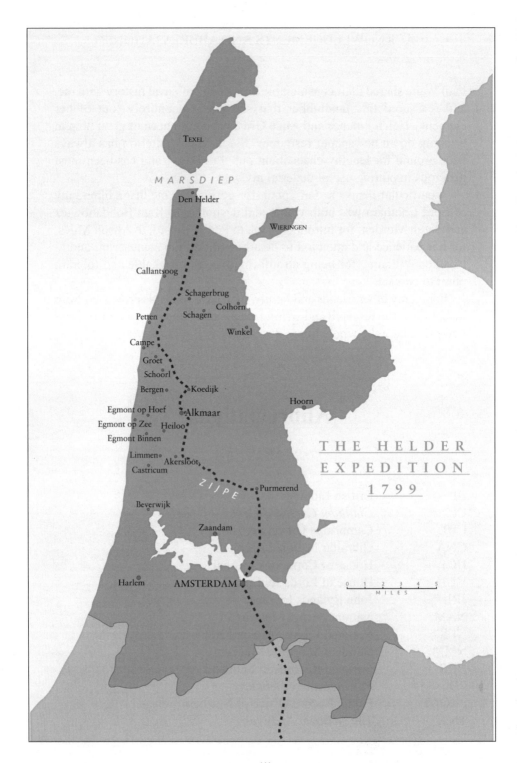

TEXEL

MARSDIEP

Den Helder

WIERINGEN

Callantsoog

Schagerbrug

Colhorn

Petten

Schagen

Winkel

Campe

Groet

Schoorl

Bergen

Koedijk

Hoorn

Egmont op Hoef

Alkmaar

Egmont op Zee

Heiloo

Egmont Binnen

Limmen

Akersloot

Castricum

ZIJPE

Purmerend

Beverwijk

Zaandam

Harlem

AMSTERDAM

THE HELDER
EXPEDITION
1799

0 1 2 3 4 5
MILES

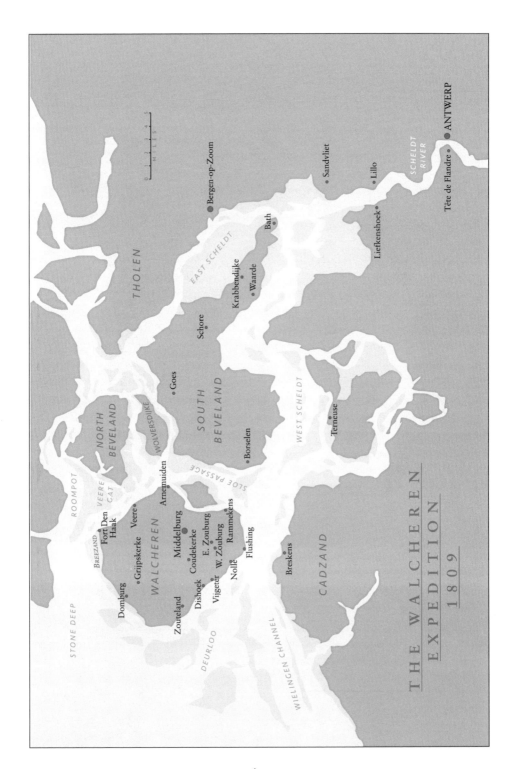

THE WALCHEREN
EXPEDITION
1809

ANTWERP

Tête de Flandre

SCHELDT RIVER

Lillo

Sandvliet

Liefkenshoek

Bath

Bergen-op-Zoom

THOLEN

EAST SCHELDT

Krabbendijke

Waarde

Schore

Goes

SOUTH BEVELAND

Borselen

WEST SCHELDT

Terneuse

SLOE PASSAGE

WOLVERSDIJKE

NORTH BEVELAND

VEERE GAT

ROOMPOT

BREEZAND

Fort Den Haak

Veere

Gripskerke

Arnemuiden

Middelburg

Coudekerke

E. Zouburg

W. Zouburg

Rammekens

Domburg

Zouteland

Dishoek

Vligeter

Nolle

Flushing

Breskens

WALCHEREN

CADZAND

STONE DEEP

DEURLOO

WIELINGEN CHANNEL

0 1 2 3 4 5
MILES

ix

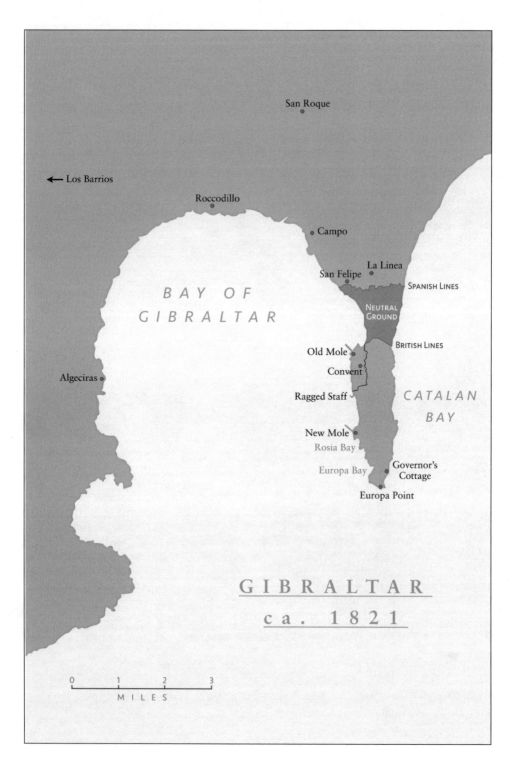

San Roque

← Los Barrios

Roccodillo

Campo

La Linea

San Felipe

SPANISH LINES

BAY OF
GIBRALTAR

NEUTRAL
GROUND

BRITISH LINES

Old Mole

Convent

Algeciras

Ragged Staff

CATALAN

BAY

New Mole

Rosia Bay

Europa Bay

Governor's
Cottage

Europa Point

GIBRALTAR

ca. 1821

0   1   2   3
MILES

Chapter 1

Lord Pitt
1756–78

The beginning of October 1756 was wet and stormy. A hurricane ripped through England from Newcastle to Bath, causing 'extraordinary' damage: 'Houses unroof'd, Stacks of Corn and Hay swept entirely away, large Oak Trees broke off at their Middles, and many other astonishing Effects'.[1] The wind blew just as hard in Kent, but for William Pitt in Hayes Place it was of no importance. He was 'in the joy of his heart', for close to midnight on the 9th his wife, Lady Hester, had given birth to a son and heir.[2]

In marked contrast with the child's later reputation for tardiness, his entry into the world was rapid. '[Lady Hester] had a sharp time, but not longer than two hours and a half,' the delighted father gushed to his brother-in-law. '. . . The young man meets with general applause for stature and strength . . . He is, however, as they flatter me, without appearance of heaviness, notwithstanding his size'.[3]

It was just as well Pitt could not peer into his son's future. The little boy, baptised on 7 November with the name of John, would spend twenty years holding Cabinet office, acquire a number of honours, including the Garter, and end his days as Governor of Gibraltar; but Pitt the Elder's hopes for his eldest son were not realised. Despite youthful promise, John suffered from life-long comparisons with the more famous members of his family. His career was blighted by his easy-going temperament and sheer bad luck. He fought as hard as he could against the hand he had been dealt, trying to overcome his many public and private disappointments, but he was ultimately the victim of his own family's success. His name became synonymous with one of Britain's worst military disasters.

All this lay in the future. For Pitt the Elder, his son's birth was a good

1

omen. He had been out of office for a year, following nine years as Paymaster-General of the Forces. This post was notoriously corrupt: its holders creamed off a percentage of the considerable funds passing through their hands by way of perquisites, and Pitt's ostentatious refusal to do so had earned him a reputation as an honest man. After publicly criticising his government's war effort in North America against France, Pitt was stripped of his office; but by the time of John's birth, the end of Pitt's exile was in sight. The war in America, which had spread to Europe, lurched from disaster to disaster. The prime minister, the Duke of Newcastle, needed more ministerial clout, and Pitt's reputation and powerful oratory made him the obvious choice.

In December 1756 Pitt took office as Secretary of State, and spent the next five years until his resignation in 1761 turning the war from a run of defeats into a series of victories. His strategy was to fight France on two fronts, by subsidising a large Continental force under Frederick the Great of Prussia and deploying British naval and military might in the colonies. The taking of Louisbourg and Quebec, victory at Quiberon and Minden, and successes in the West Indies all cemented Pitt's reputation as a war leader. 'Our bells are worn threadbare with ringing for victories,' Horace Walpole reported, and Pitt was widely credited with masterminding them.[4] But he never regained the dizzying heights of the 1750s. He was called to form a new government in 1766, but his decision to take the Privy Seal, a minor post without responsibilities, and a peerage as Earl of Chatham damaged his public standing. He lost support in the City of London, which cancelled celebratory illuminations in his honour when news of 'Lord Cheat'em' spread.[5] By the time his ministry fell in October 1768, his political reputation had been permanently compromised.

For little John, learning to walk and talk during his father's most glorious years, Pitt the Elder must have been a living legend. He and his four siblings (Hester, Harriot, William and James Charles) caught some of their father's reflected glory themselves. Whenever they travelled they were greeted by 'Croud[s] assembled . . . Bells and every kind Welcome'.[6] When a group of Mohecannuk Native Americans came to England to petition the King in a territorial dispute, they made a point of paying their respects to Pitt's eldest son and treating him as the representative of his absent father.[7] John had Pitt the Elder's name and political principles instilled into him from the cradle, and grew up with the conviction that being a Pitt was something special.

John's importance within the family as the eldest son was never in doubt, and he never forgot that he bore the weight of his father's expectations. He was, however, unlikely to follow Pitt the Elder into the House of Commons: at the age of 5 he became the heir to a peerage. In 1761 Pitt the Elder accepted a pension of £3,000 per annum for three lives and a Barony for his wife. Lady Hester Pitt was created Lady Chatham in her own right, and on her death John would become Baron Chatham. When his father formed his ministry in 1766 and accepted the Earldom of Chatham, John's status grew still further, and brought him the courtesy title of Viscount Pitt – 'Pitt' for short to his family.

Like his siblings, Lord Pitt was not particularly robust. He never outgrew his childhood tendency towards frequent fevers and digestive troubles, and even as an adult he was described as delicate. When he was 13 his parents talked of sending him to Eton, but in the end he and his four siblings were educated at home – Hayes Place in Kent, and Burton Pynsent in Somerset – by a private tutor, Edward Wilson.[8] Whenever they were separated Pitt wrote to the others in terms of great affection, although his lax writing habits were satirised by his brother William: 'I have told Pitt that I will not suffer him by any means to get off without giving me the History [of his travels] . . . tho' if it might be held in a nutshell it would hardly be worth the trouble of taking the inside out'.[9] Pitt was two-and-a-half years older than William, four-and-a-half years older than James, but he had no other companions even close to his own age. When Lady Chatham took Pitt and her daughters to London in April 1772, leaving William and James at Burton Pynsent due to ill-health, she wrote that 'Pitt does not know how to do as yet without' his brothers.[10]

Pitt's character was beginning to emerge. His 'boisterous' spirits and 'fly[ing] about' were recorded on more than one occasion by his mother, and he loved being outdoors.[11] His father described him at 18 months old, '[figuring] in his Green Surcoat, among the daizies [*sic*] and blossoms, in great vernal delight'.[12] He never lost his fascination with nature, boldly exploring Cornish underground rivers and showing his mother the aurora borealis above Hayes Place, but his first loves were riding and hunting.[13] 'Pitt lives much abroad, and grows strong,' Lord Chatham wrote in November 1771. 'The hounds and the gun are great delights, without prejudice to literary pursuits'.[14] 'I face frost and snow every day with my gun on my shoulder to the no small terrour of the larks and thrushes,' Pitt reported to his tutor with obvious satisfaction, and at 14 he received a

Spanish gun-barrel as a gift from one of his father's friends.[15] When he was 20 his mother apologised for his not writing letters to family because 'He is following the Fox Hounds, for the first day this season'.[16]

This reflected Pitt's lifelong tendency to put pleasure before obligations. Unlike William, who had to be restrained from working too hard, he required encouragement to succeed. He was undeniably intelligent: Mr Wilson's records of the children's performances in the schoolroom prove that Pitt often outstripped William in the Classics and Mathematics. (This superiority gave William occasion to note, cuttingly: 'Your Greek was excellent, and (I think) with practice you may become a Thucydides'.[17]) Pitt's parents, aware of their eldest son's tendency to rely on his abilities, pushed him to excel, and he responded well to their encouragement. Lady Chatham's sister-in-law noted Pitt's 'fresh ardour . . . upon commendation[;] a mind so well turn'd as his will ever feel the utmost satisfaction in being approv'd'.[18] Lady Chatham lavished praise on her eldest son in letters to her husband, knowing he would show them to Pitt:

> Your charming Boy cannot be enough admired in the sweet combination of his Talents, and the indearing [*sic*] manner in which they have been exerted with so much Propriety. I must love Him better for it, if I can. I long to tell him the infinite satisfaction I feel from your account of him, and that I am in debt to him both on your account, and His own, for his Winning Behavior.[19]

As for Chatham, he was quick to point out Pitt's superior performance in a play put on by the children for their parents in 1773: 'William is certainly very correct [in his speech], but Pitt will be *the* orator'.[20] Pitt's grace and gentlemanly attitude, indeed, seemed to point him towards a successful public career.

Yet Pitt never shook off a degree of sloth. Later he was notorious for it, but it sprang from a sense of inferiority rather than self-satisfied belief in his abilities. Chatham's biographer Brian Tunstall notes, shrewdly, 'He seems to have received rather less attention than he deserved'.[21] As an adult those closest to him noticed a surprising vulnerability beneath the surface. Mr Wilson's obvious amazement, and Lord and Lady Chatham's pride, at William's growing intelligence cannot have been easy to watch. There are few hints that comparisons were made in family circles between the two boys to Pitt's detriment, but outsiders did, and Pitt must have been aware that, although loved, he was not the favourite child.[22]

Whether Mr Wilson or Chatham planted the suggestion in his mind is unclear, but by the age of 16 Pitt aspired to join the army. In April 1773 Chatham wrote to his friend, the political philosopher Thomas Hollis, regarding a retired engineer named Captain Kennedy of Lyme Regis. Hollis had introduced Kennedy to Chatham the previous summer and Chatham wanted to know whether Kennedy might teach his eldest son engineering. He vouched for his son's eagerness in terms that suggested a military career was Pitt's own choice: 'His mind is strongly bent on the pursuit, and I am sure he will be a diligent disciple.'[23] The arrangement was made, and in June 1773 Pitt accompanied his father and brother William to Lyme Regis. They stayed in the building known locally as the 'Great House' on Broad Street, close to the beach, and here Pitt learned the basics of military engineering from Captain Kennedy.[24] Chatham was delighted with Pitt's clear enthusiasm:

> Pitt, whom I cannot too much applaud, sticks close to Mr Kennedy, *morning* and *after-dinner*, and is ardent in the *nobler Chace* of future Fame, from Sieges to Come, and Trenches to be yet open'd. . . . Nothing cou'd be more fortunate than falling into the acquaintance of Mr Kennedy, who is just, in all respects, the thing to be wish'd for our young Militaire to frequent. Such society . . . tends to put our *Boy*, on his *Man's legs*.[25]

Not everything was about work. The 'Militaire', or the 'young Vauban', was permitted a few afternoons off to bathe in the sea with (and splash water over) his brother William. They took tea with local society, and Pitt, already a keen social animal, 'danc[ed] all night with Lyme-Regis misses, and gay Matrons, till almost two'.[26]

At 17 Pitt was comparatively old to join the army, and he was anxious to be commissioned as soon as possible. Taking his father's advice, he sought an ensigncy in the 47th Regiment. Its colonel was General Guy Carleton, the Governor-General of Quebec. This held strong appeal for Chatham, whose most glorious hour had been the fall of Quebec to General Wolfe in 1759, and Carleton readily agreed to appoint Lord Pitt one of his aides-de-camp. Although a vacancy in the 47th did not exist, the Secretary-at-War, Lord Barrington, persuaded an existing ensign to transfer to a vacancy in the 29th, and the King waived the usual fees for purchasing the place.[27] By mid-November 1773, Ensign the Lord Pitt's future course was set.

In the summer of 1774, Lord and Lady Chatham travelled with their eldest son to London. Pitt had never been further from home than Cornwall, but he embraced this new adventure with enthusiasm. On 6 July he appeared at court, where he took official leave of the King, and on 20 July he sailed with General Carleton for Quebec.[28] He left England, and childhood, behind him.

*   *   *

Pitt arrived in Quebec in September 1774. He left no record of his impressions, but for a boy who had never seen anything more imposing than the Bristol Channel and the Welsh mountains Quebec was a strange but awe-inspiring place. The Chateau St Louis, Carleton's residence as Governor where Pitt lodged, looked out over a town that was both literally and figuratively divided. Perched on the edge of a tall cliff, Quebec's Upper Town, filled with wealthy homes, convents, churches and government buildings, spilled down into the narrow streets and dockyards of the Lower Town on the banks of the St Lawrence. The province contained about 80,000 inhabitants, a small proportion of them in Quebec, Montreal and Trois-Rivières, the rest scattered across small settlements.[29] Most of these *habitants*, as they were known, were of French Catholic origin, and co-existed uncomfortably with the English-speaking merchants.

General Carleton recognised that the majority of Quebec's citizens were French Catholics, and was reluctant to impose a British system too quickly. Cold and aloof to those outside his closest circle, he was respected but mistrusted by those who worked with him. He had spent most of the early 1770s in London advising North's government in the framing of the Quebec Act, which established a Governor's council of both British and Quebecois delegates and sanctioned the continuation of French customs and religion. There was scope for revision, although Carleton flat-out disapproved of establishing troublesome American-style elected assemblies, and the French-speaking *habitants* were pleased with the results. Predictably, the English-speaking merchants were outraged by what they saw as a consolidation of despotic control. Their economic

6

links with the southern colonies acquired a political complexion. Tension had been growing for some time between Britain and her colonies over heavy taxes to pay for the expensive Seven Years War, and Lord North's government had passed several Acts designed to tighten British parliamentary sovereignty over America. Secret committees were set up in Montreal and Quebec to correspond with the American disaffected.[30] Despite these signs, Carleton failed to see the southern troubles coming until it was nearly too late. In September 1774 the British army in Quebec was about 1,800 strong, but Carleton immediately sent 2 of his 4 regiments to Boston in response to the Commander-in-Chief General Thomas Gage's request for reinforcements. It was an astonishingly short-sighted move that left him with 800 regulars, a scattering of Indians and Scottish emigrants, and an unreliable militia.

For now, Lord Pitt's life in Quebec reflected this astonishing lack of urgency. No letters of his from this time survive, but others wrote home on his behalf to reassure Lord and Lady Chatham that their son was happy and well-treated. His day began with studies between 7 and 9, followed by breakfast with General Carleton and his wife. At 11 he attended Carleton at the mounting of the guard, and the rest of the day was his to spend as he pleased: reading, fencing or practising musket drill.[31] This leisurely life ended in April 1775 with the outbreak of rebellion in America. Carleton, at last aware of his exposed position, begged the Secretary of State for 10,000 reinforcements, but all available troops were diverted to Boston. By the time the government sent five regiments north the weather had turned icy, and only one regiment managed to land. Meanwhile, American eyes were turning northwards. In May 1775 the Continental Congress, America's revolutionary legislative body, ordered an invasion of Canada. General Benedict Arnold took possession of the British forts of Ticonderoga and Crown Point on Lake Champlain, then moved inland and laid siege to Fort St-Jean.

Under these dramatically changed conditions, Pitt's position as Carleton's aide-de-camp became embarrassing. Lord Chatham's sympathy for the American cause was well-known, and the Americans immediately recognised the benefits of capturing his eldest son. Chatham was a powerful politician and Pitt would have been a significant pawn in American hands. American officers were provided with his physical description to make sure he was not killed in action, and his treatment as a prisoner-of-war had been planned down to the last detail.[32] There were plenty of opportunities to capture him while he and Carleton moved between Quebec and Montreal over the summer of 1775, overseeing the raising of the militia. At one stage Carleton and Lord Pitt were allegedly 'within a quarter of an hour of falling into the hands' of the Continental Army, and narrowly escaped.[33]

Pitt soon discovered he had no control over his career in such politically charged circumstances. Around the time America was plunging into conflict, Lord Chatham suffered a relapse of the same mental illness that had crippled his ministry in 1766–8. At the end of June 1775 Lady Chatham wrote Pitt a long letter to remind him of his obligations to his father's political identity. As Chatham's heir, any actions Pitt took would reflect back on his father. Lady Chatham put pressure on him to return to England before he was forced to fight the American colonists against Chatham's wishes:

> I can . . . venture upon no advice to you, but that of entreating you to be sure in every part of your conduct to take care that your Actions shou'd be consistent with your Honor. That They may be so determine nothing without the Advice of Those Persons whose Knowledge whose Honor and whose Heart are chiefly to be trusted.[34]

Lady Chatham told a friend that she had given Pitt 'a *free power* to decide upon his own situation', adding to her son William: 'He will be the Judge, circumstanced as he is, what will be consistent with his Honor.'[35]

But Pitt, reading his mother's letter, knew his 'free power' was a nonsense. The decision to send him home had already been made. He dutifully sailed for England at the beginning of October carrying dispatches, and arrived in London on 2 November 1775.[36] For a few months his military future was in doubt. Having left Canada, he could not well serve anywhere else in the rebellious Colonies. Matters came to a head in February 1776 when his leave expired: there were, as Lady Chatham observed, 'strong objections to his remaining in the Army, and declining to serve'.[37] Since her husband was still ill, Lady Chatham took it upon herself to make Pitt's decision to resign his commission for him.

Pitt knew he was being used as a political weapon to reaffirm Chatham's opposition to the American war. The circumstances of his leaving the army may have seemed honourable to Lady Chatham, but others disagreed: 'Lord Chatham has been censured exceedingly on all sides . . . in letting his son Lord Pitt embark with the King's forces, for the subjugation of the Americans, and after such permission for recalling him so abruptly, and making him throw up his commission'.[38] Even Pitt's uncle, Lord Temple, 'was sorry the young man was thrown out of the army . . . Had *not his father determined for him*, he ought to have gone [back to his regiment], as an officer was to obey orders without enquiring the fairness of them'.[39] But the young man was more than an officer: he was a Pitt, and his first duty, as his mother emphasised, was to his family. Reluctant though he was to abandon his career before it had properly begun, it never crossed his mind to do anything but subordinate his interests to theirs. It was the first time he was required to abandon his ambitions for the sake of a close relative. Unfortunately for him, it would not be the last.

*   *   *

Now that he was a civilian again, Pitt began his political apprenticeship. He had a guaranteed seat in the House of Lords as the heir to his father's Earldom and, while Chatham remained incapacitated, he was expected to act as head of the family. Throughout 1776 and 1777 he attended debates in the House of Lords, listening to speeches by Chatham's protégé, Lord Shelburne, from behind the Throne.[40] He attended court functions, appeared at dinners held by prominent members of the Chathamite opposition, kept family and friends abreast of Lord Chatham's health, and acted as a scribe for his gout-stricken father.[41] Pitt's public profile, in fact, was so high it led to rumours that he meant to stand as a candidate for Westminster in the next general election.[42]

By this time Lord Chatham's health was improving, but the American situation was deteriorating fast. In July 1776 the Americans declared their independence, an act Lord Chatham deprecated. America was 'the great source of all [Britain's] wealth and power': 'I will as soon subscribe to Transubstantiation as to Sovereignty (by right) in the Colonies,' Chatham fulminated to Lord Shelburne.[43] A year later General Burgoyne's army was destroyed at Saratoga. Not only was a large proportion of the British army in North America lost at one stroke, but the defeat showed that the rebellious colonials were a force to be reckoned with.

In February 1778 France allied with the rebels and declared war on

Britain. Pitt could finally rejoin the army without the certainty of being sent to fight his American brethren, and he gladly seized the opportunity. He had, as yet, no regiment to join, but the newspapers reported him taking the rank of lieutenant as a gentleman volunteer. By the middle of April his destination – Gibraltar – was widely reported, but it was not until mid-June that the *London Gazette* noted his appointment to the 39th Foot.[44] By then Pitt's circumstances had changed yet again, this time permanently.

On 6 April, Lord Chatham received news that the Duke of Richmond intended to propose a motion in the House of Lords to acknowledge American independence. Richmond's argument was simple: while Britain warred with France, she could not afford to fight on two continents. Although suffering from gout, Chatham resolved to attend the debate and resist Richmond's motion, and – as he often did – he brought Pitt and his two younger sons with him. Chatham was clearly unwell, although he did utter some powerful lines:

> Shall we tarnish the lustre of this nation by an ignominious surrender of its rights and fairest possessions? Shall this great kingdom . . . fall prostrate before the House of Bourbon? . . . Shall a people that seventeen years ago was the terror of the world, now stoop so low as to tell its ancient inveterate enemy, take all we have, only give us peace? It is impossible! . . . Let us at least make one effort; and if we must fall, let us fall like men![45]

But it was Chatham who collapsed, only a short time later, felled by a stroke. Pitt never recorded his feelings on seeing his father drop, but the shock must have been immense. When John Singleton Copley commemorated the event in *The Death of the Earl of Chatham*, he portrayed Chatham surrounded by his three sons, William gesturing in alarm, James weeping and Pitt, in his military uniform, clutching his dying father's arm.

Lord Chatham recovered from his seizure enough to be carried to his house at Hayes, but over the next few weeks he slipped away. His reputed last words were to Pitt: 'Go, my son! Go whither your country calls you . . . spare not a moment, which is due to her service, in weeping over an old man, who will soon be no more.'[46] In fact Pitt had already left for Gibraltar, and was summoned back to Hayes from his ship at Portsmouth, where he had just embarked with General Robert Boyd.[47] He arrived just in time to witness his father's death on 11 May. The new Earl of Chatham was given a short time to settle his father's immediate affairs before returning to Portsmouth and sailing to Gibraltar, bearing one of Britain's most celebrated titles.

All his life he had been reminded at every turn of his obligations to his father, his family and his country, in that order. His father was now dead, and he was expected to act as head of the Pitts himself. His duty to his country still remained to be fulfilled. That he must live up to his new title was never in question. A few days after his father's death he wrote to his friend Lord Granby, the future Duke of Rutland, trusting that he 'inherit[ed] his father's opinions, principles, and love of his country'.[48] This was more than a desire to emulate his father's patriotism. It was a measure of the burden the Earldom of Chatham placed on his shoulders, and which he was never allowed to forget.

Chapter 2

'The Child of the Publick'
1778–88

'The present Lord Chatham is about 22 Years of Age, of a very delicate, tender Constitution, which he inherits from his Father,' the *Public Advertiser* reported, with evident curiosity. 'He has been bred up . . . principally in the House, in a very domestic way'.[1] As private as his upbringing had been, the new Earl was semi-public property because of his parentage. 'One looks upon him as the Child of the Publick,' Lord Grantham, Britain's ambassador to Spain, told his brother, who agreed Chatham had 'a difficult part to act' to balance the expectations revolving about him.[2]

Chatham's position was unusual. As an Earl and an automatic member of the House of Lords, he had an expected political and social role. Although family networks and connections still drove British politics, Chatham was very much an anomaly. At a time when acreage was directly correlated to importance he had comparatively little land, and eventually sold the little he had. His earldom was new, his ancestors had been accountants, lawyers and freebooters. Chatham's political importance was defined by who he was: penniless and landless, his name was his only asset.

It was, however, a powerful one, and, with the first Earl looming large in public consciousness, Chatham might have stepped into the void his father's death had created. Why, then, did Chatham not establish himself as an influential figure? One possible reason was his military career, which meant he was abroad for long stretches until mid-1781. Another obstacle was Chatham's personality. Physically, he was tall, thin and very dark-haired, with a pronounced downward slant to his nose which, along with the shape of his face, put acquaintances strongly in mind of his father.[3] But the same people who found his appearance so imposing were disappointed to find he had not inherited his father's character. Grantham thought him 'rather prim' and 'reserved', which he ascribed to Chatham's ·'very private Education'.[4] The *London Evening Post* noted 'the appearance of much mildness in his countenance' in 1779, and two years later the philosopher Jeremy Bentham saw 'a kind of reserve, tempered with mildness, but clouded with a little dash of bashfulness'.[5] In any case, by the time he settled permanently in England in 1782 Chatham had missed his opportunity to stand forward as his father's political successor. That role passed to his brother, William, and Chatham never regained it.

Chatham stayed just under a year in Gibraltar, before securing six months' leave to address some of his more pressing responsibilities as head of the family.[6] He began the long journey home in March 1779 with two friends, Hugh Conway (later Seymour) and a Scotsman named Adam Colt. The travellers spent a fortnight in Madrid with the British ambassador, Lord Grantham, who took time out from the deteriorating diplomatic situation to show them the sights and introduce them to Spanish high society. In early April Chatham went north through France to Paris, carrying dispatches detailing the collapse of relations with Spain. He arrived in London on 7 May and, just over a month later, took his seat in the House of Lords for the first time. He used the occasion to draw attention to his patriotic status as a military man defending his country, appearing in the scarlet and green regimentals of the 39th Regiment. The stratagem worked, and the newspapers enthused over Chatham's 'very elegant, manly, and graceful figure'.[7]

He took his seat at a critical time. Lord North's government had been in power for nine years, but by mid-1779 the strain of war with the American colonies was beginning to tell. The opposition was nominally headed by the Marquis of Rockingham, a powerful northern magnate, whose following included an impressive array of Whig landed aristocracy as well as able orators and administrators such as Edmund Burke and Charles James Fox. The Rockinghams differed in their approach to the American war from the Chathamites, now led by Lord Shelburne. Both factions deplored the struggle and insisted it could not continue, but the Rockinghams proposed granting unconditional independence, whereas the Chathamites preferred a federal union based on reciprocal commercial advantages. This subtle but significant difference had so far prevented the opposition working harmoniously to unseat North's government.

Chatham's name and military identity made him a valuable addition to opposition ranks, and his few political acts showed his determination to follow his father's line of politics. He took his parliamentary duties seriously, attending whenever the House of Lords discussed the American war or other military issues, and putting his name to two official Protests entered into the Lords' Journal. The first was in February 1781, against Lord George Germain's elevation to the House of Lords as Lord Sackville, on the grounds that Germain had been cashiered for disobeying orders at the Battle of Minden in 1759. The second was in June 1783, on the Lords' rejection of the Public Offices Regulation Bill, a measure proposed by Chatham's brother.[8] Despite these moments of prominence, Chatham kept a low profile. He offered his presence and vote when required, wielded the proxy votes he was entitled to cast for up to three other absent lords and helped manage the occasional conference between the Lords and Commons, but made no speeches. This no doubt suited his inclinations.

His social circle was predictably limited to Whigs of unimpeachable Chathamite pedigree. He visited Lord Shelburne in London and at his Wiltshire house of Bowood, dined with Thomas Townshend, who headed the Chathamites in the Commons, and consolidated a connection with Charles Manners, 4th Duke of Rutland. This friendship, deep and sincere on both sides, was a defining feature of Chatham's life, and his connection with the Rutland family lasted well beyond Rutland's premature death in 1787. Rutland had started his career under Rockingham's auspices, but placed his extensive political and financial networks at the Chathamites' disposal in the mid-1770s. His expansive good-humour complemented Chatham's quiet, serious character perfectly, and they shared a love of hunting and aristocratic splendour. The correspondence between the two men was frank, open and affectionate. Rutland opened almost all his letters to Chatham with 'My dearest Friend' and signed off in a variety of touching ways: 'I am ever the most attached & Sincere of your Friends', 'God Bless you my dear Friend & love you as much as I do', or simply: 'Ever unalterably yours'. Chatham, normally extremely restrained in his correspondence, was similarly effusive: 'with the truest affection, your ever attached friend'.[9]

Chatham might have established himself with Rutland's political backing as a political force to be reckoned with, but, even had he wanted this, he did not get the opportunity. Parliament was prorogued two weeks after he took his seat, did not sit again till the end of November, then rose again for Christmas. By the time Parliament reassembled in January 1780, Chatham was no longer in England. He had transferred out of the 39th Regiment over the course of the summer, and in the autumn Rutland gave him a captaincy in the 86th, a new regiment he had raised. In the new year Chatham received news his regiment had been ordered on foreign service. For a long time nobody knew where it was to be sent. America was a distinct possibility, and Chatham breathed a little easier when it was ruled out. His relief lasted only until the actual destination was confirmed: the Leeward Islands, where, according to the newspapers, 'near thirty were buried every week' from yellow fever.[10] 'I felt excessively sorry that military Ideas could not suffer him to attend to all the various Motives which might . . . have inclin'd him to avoid going out, in *such* a manner and at *such* Time,' Chatham's brother William regretted, but Chatham had sacrificed professional considerations to private necessities before and refused to do so again.[11] In fact he did not remain in the West Indies long. He was on leave from September 1780 to January 1781, and before he could return evidence of the climate's dangers arrived all too devastatingly in the form of news of the death of his youngest brother James in Antigua. As the head of the family Chatham's life was too important to waste and he did not return to his regiment. In December 1782 he left the 86th altogether and purchased a commission in the London-based 3rd Foot Guards.[12]

By this time, Chatham's political importance had declined sharply. While he had been in the West Indies, his brother William had been elected for the parliamentary constituency of Appleby-in-Westmorland. He took his seat in the House of Commons on 23 January 1781, made his maiden speech a month later to rapturous acclaim and spent the following year fully living up to this spectacular debut. Accordingly, when North fell in March 1782 and Lord Rockingham formed a coalition government with Lord Shelburne, it was William Pitt and not the Earl of Chatham who was offered a minor government post. Pitt declined, but accepted the Chancellorship of the Exchequer in July when Shelburne became First Lord of the Treasury after Rockingham's death.

Pitt's meteoric rise put an end to Chatham's time in the spotlight. Although he might have resented Pitt's success, Chatham was probably delighted to find the pressure to perform removed from his shoulders, and he gladly took advantage of it to focus on his family responsibilities. This was not exactly the easy option. His father had never demonstrated much interest in finance, and died deeply in debt. Parliament had voted £20,000 to pay the most pressing obligations and settled an annual pension of £4,000 on the Earldom to help relieve the new Lord Chatham from embarrassment, but these huge sums, in the 5th Earl Stanhope's words, merely enabled Chatham 'to maintain – and no more than maintain – the family honours'.[13]

Chatham had inherited two estates: Hayes Place in Kent and Burton Pynsent in Somerset. Burton theoretically provided an income of £3,000 a year, but actually represented an annual loss.[14] Both estates were mortgaged to the hilt, Burton for £13,175 including interest and Hayes for £10,000.[15] By 1778 the first Earl had tangled his estate in so much debt one creditor refused to agree to any more loans unless Chatham informed his children of the obligations secured on their inheritance, 'that they be [not] alarmed at it hereafter'.[16] Further complicating the situation was Pitt the Elder's will, which divided the money raised by the Hayes and Burton mortgages between his eldest daughter and three younger children.[17] In practice, this meant the second Earl had to sell his inheritance to provide his siblings with theirs.

By the time Chatham returned permanently to Britain the need to sell Hayes was pressing. The effects were auctioned off in November 1784, and the house itself sold the following year for £8,500. The proceeds were divided according to the terms of Pitt the Elder's will, but Chatham himself saw less than £1,000 of the final sum.[18] He could have done with more, for by 1785 he was in considerable debt on his own account. In December 1780 Chatham and Pitt paid a lump sum of £3,500 to the Duke of Rutland in return for an annuity of £300 derived from three of Rutland's Cambridgeshire estates – a lump sum acquired partly through two separate loans for £1,500, secured on two chambers at Lincoln's Inn, themselves purchased by the brothers with two further loans.[19] In 1785 Chatham borrowed an additional £3,150 through three moneylenders secured on the earldom's £4,000 pension.[20] Over the years this pension was further mortgaged out to Chatham's banker Thomas Coutts, the Jewish moneylenders Asher and Abraham Goldsmid, and various private creditors, until the security the sum offered must have worn exceedingly thin.

Chatham did not learn from his father's impressive disregard for his personal finances. The 4th Duke of Rutland put his hunting lodge of Cheveley Park at his disposal from August 1787. After Rutland's death in October, Chatham was allowed to continue using Cheveley as a country seat during the minority of the 5th Duke. He made full use of the privilege until 1798, and Cheveley's proximity to Newmarket drew Chatham into the ruinous world of horse breeding and racing, in which he had already shown interest in 1780.[21] While in town, he frequented card-tables more than was safe on his slender funds. He was a member of several clubs, including White's and Brooks's, and there were accounts of his sitting 'up all night' gambling, or 'cut[ting] in and out' at whist.[22] By the time Chatham was middle-aged, he was said to have 'totally ruined Himself by Play'.[23] Although such stories come second- or third-hand, there are enough of them to suggest they were not ill-founded. Whatever the truth, Chatham followed the same pattern for the majority of his life: spending, borrowing and using his pension and an assortment of often hastily contracted life-insurance policies to secure his enormous loans.

Unlike his father, Chatham had no heir on whom to inflict his difficulties, although he demonstrated a clear intention to continue the dynasty. His choice of bride was dutifully determined by politics, but also by love. During Chatham's stay in Madrid on his way home from Gibraltar, the British ambassador Lord Grantham noticed something singular about his guest. Chatham's travelling companions 'found out new Acquaintances [prostitutes] at Madrid, but Lord Chatham never went with them, & I would not swear that he is not in possession of a most precious Jewel'.[24] Some weeks later, Grantham's brother Frederick Robinson met Chatham at a dinner held by Thomas Townshend, later Lord Sydney, a former political associate of Chatham's father. By the end of the evening Robinson had solved the riddle. 'If [Chatham] has a mind to set that Jewel which you suppose him possess'd of very beautifully,' he told Grantham, 'he might consult Miss Mary Townshend'.[25]

Robinson was right: Chatham had fallen in love with Townshend's second daughter. Mary was already considered a beauty, elegant, dark-haired and quietly intelligent. She was the perfect match for the reserved, highly private Chatham, but at 16 she was too young for him to press his suit seriously, and his departure for the West Indies the following year slowed down their courtship. Still, he never forgot her, and once he settled permanently in Britain he renewed his attentions. By the summer of 1782 the fashionable set was full of Chatham's attachment to 'the beauty in Albemarle Street' (Townshend's London residence).[26] Chatham played it cool, dismissing such gossip as 'Stock Jobbing Reports', but he fed the rumours himself by visiting the Townshends over the summer.[27] By May

1783 the match seemed certain, and Chatham's sister Harriot wrote excitedly to her mother of the couple's very public '*amicable*' behaviour at a ball.[28]

Harriot had reckoned without the streak of schoolboy bashfulness in Chatham that made him miss nearly every opportunity to bring his suit to a point. Although he came '*very near*' proposing on a trip to Frognal, the Townshend family's country estate, he did not do so, and by 6 May Mary was 'not a little fidgetty [*sic*]'.[29] 'I think in this sort of way all sides may be likely to get *Frampy*,' Harriot grumbled, but Chatham did not screw up the courage to propose until 5 June.[30] The marriage contract, dated 5 July 1783, settled £5,000 on Mary as a dowry, and the wedding took place five days later.[31] The match cemented a close alliance between two strongly political families and, despite its fitful start, it was very happy. Although there were posthumous rumours that Chatham never travelled without a mistress, he and his wife remained close throughout the thirty-eight years of their marriage, despite the many difficulties and outright tragedies that beset it.[32] They made a handsome young couple, and Chatham did not hesitate to use the occasion of his wedding to make a typically ostentatious display of rank. Following a short honeymoon at Hayes, he and his bride were presented at court for the first time as a married couple on 31 July, riding the short distance from Albemarle Street to St James's Palace in an extravagant cavalcade of carriages and sedan chairs.[33] The new Countess of Chatham turned heads in her 'white sattin [gown], richly trimmed with silver fringe &c. Her head-dress was elegant, and she looked very beautiful'.[34]

For now, the newly wed Earl of Chatham was kept from domestic bliss by the memorable political events in which he was closely involved through his brother. Pitt resigned the Chancellorship of the Exchequer when Shelburne fell over the question of peace with America. Former prime minister Lord North had joined his considerable following with that of Charles James Fox, scion of the Rockingham party and formerly North's bitterest political enemy. Many found the blatantly pragmatic nature of their junction repellent, but the coalition tipped the numbers definitively against Shelburne. His resignation in February ushered in several weeks of uncertainty as the King fought against the likelihood of a Fox-North ministry headed by the Rockinghamite Duke of Portland. Chatham's brother was one of the men to whom the King offered the Treasury as a stopgap. Although still only 23, Pitt had shone during the debates on the peace and was carefully building a reputation as a champion of moderate economic and electoral reform; but, faced with the near-certainty of heading a minority government, he refused.

Fox and North took office at the beginning of April 1783. Despite an embezzlement scandal, they maintained their solid parliamentary support till the end of the session. Pitt, however, kept in touch with the King over the summer through his cousin Earl Temple and Lord Thurlow, who had been Lord Chancellor until Fox and North came to power. In October, word reached him that an opportunity to attack Fox and North had offered itself in the shape of their East India Bill. The Bill proposed to vest Indian patronage in the hands of a fixed term, politically nominated Board of Control, and could be interpreted as an attempt to entrench the government in office independent of the King's pleasure – an infringement of the King's prerogative to choose his ministers. Once Pitt was certain the King would throw his authority behind a new ministry he agreed to act. The King allowed his name to be circulated by Earl Temple in opposition to the India Bill, and, as a result of this constitutionally dubious course of action, it was thrown out of the House of Lords on 17 December 1783. Portland, Fox and North were dismissed, and Pitt installed in their place.

Chatham was not directly involved in the plotting that preceded his brother's elevation to power. He dutifully attended the Lords debates on the India Bill on 15–17 December and continued regularly attending throughout January and February, but otherwise kept his distance from the political manoeuvring.[35] When Lord Temple unexpectedly resigned the Secretaryship of State on 22 December 1783, throwing Pitt's fledgling government into temporary chaos, Chatham wrote to his mother with a hint of disapproval:

> You will have so far seen, by my last letter, conveying to you what had taken place, that my mind was not perfectly at ease . . . I had but too much reason for it . . . With what hopes of Success we stand I know not, but, in any case, as we now stand on ye most *unquestionable* ground, whether we go on or are beat, we can risque no loss of Caracter [*sic*] with the Publick, and in making a stand for the King and ye Constitution, my Brother's Caracter must I think rise whatever may come.[36]

Pitt soon got over the upset of losing Temple. He started out in a significant minority, but held firm, deciding against an immediate parliamentary dissolution to give time to deploy the influence of the Crown to its fullest extent. His defiance in the Commons worked its magic on public opinion, and by the end of February the King was receiving a stream of pro-government petitions. The City of London and the Corporations openly supported Pitt, as they had done his father, and on 28 February Chatham accompanied his brother to a banquet at Grocer's Hall to celebrate Pitt's receiving the Freedom of the City. On the way home they were attacked outside Brooks's Club 'by a body of Chairmen armed with bludgeons, broken Chair Poles &c (many of the waiters, and several of the Gentlemen among them)', and Chatham later remembered 'endeavouring to cover him [Pitt], as well as I cou'd, in his getting out of the Carriage'. He remained convinced the attack had been premeditated, but, if so, it was a sign of the Foxites' desperation.[37] In March Pitt found himself in a minority of one, and next day managed to pass the Mutiny Bill unopposed. The dissolution of Parliament followed immediately. The ensuing general election was a comprehensive Pittite triumph: over a hundred Fox-North supporters lost their seats.

Pitt now began reconstructing his ministry to his personal tastes. This might have led to rapid advancement for Chatham, but, by the time of his brother's victory, he had lost the ability to focus on politics. He was as delighted as anyone with the outcome of the crisis, accompanying his brother to celebratory balls and dinners held in the triumphant prime minister's honour, but his attention was almost entirely consumed by a sudden and distressing domestic calamity. In the spring of 1784 Chatham's wife Mary collapsed with a severe rheumatic illness. For some months she was completely crippled by it, and her health remained seriously affected for years after. She had shown signs of it before her marriage, but its savage return was sudden and unexpected.[38] At the beginning of the year Mary had been attending court events and representing her husband and brother-in-law at City Corporation dinners. By the dissolution of Parliament she had taken to her bed, and the doctors did not declare her life out of danger for several months.[39] Mary's sister Georgiana Townshend wrote to Chatham's mother that it was 'really quite horrid to think how much she has suffered'. Mary experienced agonising pain in her knee and hip, which was managed with a combination of bed rest and opiates. 'What would I give to see her walk again,' Georgiana fretted.[40] But this was just the beginning, and Mary did not walk again for a long time. She did not even stand for eight months, and, when she did, remained permanently lame on one side.[41] Her recovery was painfully slow. By January 1785 she was being pushed around the house in a wheeled 'Merlin chair', and two months later she received electrical treatment from the surgeon Miles Partington.[42] But in the summer she was still ill, and Chatham cancelled travel plans to take his wife to Buxton for the waters instead.[43]

Lady Chatham's illness threw Chatham's life into disarray. The task of nursing her engrossed so much of his time he was forced to resign his commission yet again from 1784 to 1787. Although he returned to the Army List as a lieutenant colonel in 1787, he did not resume an active military career until 1798.[44] His family anxieties were increased by the death in childbirth in September 1786 of his sister Harriot, who had married Edward James Eliot.[45] Two months later an unexpected glimmer of hope pierced the Chathams' domestic gloom. 'We have been seasonably chear'd with a piece of news that was communicated to me last Sunday, from the very highest Authority, respecting Lady Chatham,' Edward Wilson congratulated Chatham's mother. '. . . Besides the welcome prospect of increase we hope it will be a means of restoring her Ladyship's health'.[46] At long last Mary was pregnant, and the pregnancy had advanced far enough that Chatham felt safe informing close friends. But Mary miscarried, and she never fell pregnant again.

As the years passed and the Chathams continued childless, this private tragedy transformed into a considerable dynastic blow. Mary's failure to carry a pregnancy to term pointed to the possible extinction of the family title, but it also drew attention to Chatham's frustrating position within the Pitt family. His political importance had risen again since Pitt's coming to power, but negatively, for Pitt's remaining prime minister depended, in a very literal sense, on Chatham's life. Chatham ought to have been the most important member of the family; on the contrary, his role was limited to keeping his brother (and heir) out of the Lords and in the Commons, where he could best preserve the family's political pre-eminence. Pitt believed administrations were best led from the Lower House, particularly as the opposition had so much oratorical talent there in Fox, Burke and Sheridan, whom Pitt alone was capable of matching in debate. Leading ministries from the Lords was not impossible, but Pitt the Elder's disastrous stint as Lord Privy Seal in the 1760s was not exactly an encouraging example. Few contemporary political commentators expected Pitt's government to survive if he became third Earl of Chatham. Chatham was still young, but 'of a middling constitution . . . frequently ailing', and so long as he remained childless his recurring 'indispositions' provoked ripples of interest.[47] In June 1788 the newspapers reported 'the Earl of Chatham has been confined to his room these two months, owing to the kicking of his buckle against his ancle [*sic*] bone'.[48] The wound became infected and left Chatham lame and feverish. 'The Opposition are now busy in sending up Mr Pitt to the House of Lords ... by *the tongue of a buckle*,' tittered the *World*, but it was no laughing matter.[49] Three years later, when Chatham broke his leg, the newspapers ran amok again, so much so that Chatham's friend Lord Westmorland cheerfully advised more circumspection: 'I am most extremely sorry . . . to have ye account confirmed of your Blow on yr. Shin, pray remember my old advice, "Keep your Mouth Shut".'[50]

With Pitt confidently laying claim to the Chathamite inheritance, the second Earl's role was reduced to that of an onlooker. Nobody imagined this state of affairs would last long. The newspapers confidently predicted his appointment as aide-de-camp to the King, Chamberlain in the Queen's Household, equerry to the Prince of Wales and even Governor-General of Bengal ('He spends half his day at the toilet. Who would not laugh to hear that the side curls of the Governor General of Bengal were drest six times in a forenoon!').[51] Many of the articles were derisive in tone, as befitted commentary on an elder brother eclipsed by his younger sibling. Chatham was sufficiently irritated by the following piece, playing on Pitt's official title of First Lord of the Treasury, that he issued a rebuttal:

The office of Treasurer to the Queen, now held by the Earl of Guilford, has been promised to the Earl of Chatham . . . His Lordship and several other gentlemen were in a fruit shop in St James's-Street, when Mr Townshend, son to Lord Sydney [and Chatham's brother-in-law], came in, and said he was just informed of the death of the Earl of Guilford. Lord Chatham instantly exclaimed, then hail me Treasurer to her Majesty! This discovery has not a little mortified the disappointed peer, as all his acquaintances ever since call him in mirth, *my Lord of the Treasury*.[52]

This was as awkward for Pitt as it was for Chatham, and Pitt tried to groom his brother to take a more prominent role. Chatham co-operated as much as he could, watching Commons debates from the member's gallery and considering his brother's proposal of November 1787 that he move the Lords' Address to the Throne.[53] At the same time Chatham was able to acquire experience of political management through his friend Rutland, who had gone out to Ireland as Lord Lieutenant in early 1784. While he was away, Rutland asked Chatham to act as the official liaison point for the half-dozen Members of Parliament returned under his influence. Distracted by his wife's illness, Chatham was a chaotic point of contact: Daniel Pulteney, MP for Rutland's borough of Bramber, complained that 'through Lord Chatham we have no sort of plan, or system, or discipline', as a result of which he often had to guess how to vote.[54]

Still, these arrangements raised Chatham's profile and hinted at future employment. Although he did not actively seek it, he was keen enough for political advancement, and when a suitable opening offered itself in the summer of 1788 he jumped at the chance. This opening came with the resignation of Lord Howe, First Lord of the Admiralty. The vacancy at the Admiralty was an ideal solution to Pitt and Chatham's problems. In mid-July Chatham was confirmed as Howe's successor, embarking on a career in high politics that spanned nearly twenty-two years.

Chapter 3

First Lord of the Admiralty
1788–93

Chatham's appointment as First Lord of the Admiralty caused surprise and, predictably, derision. He was a 'landsman' with no prior government experience, and not quite 32 years old, although the startlingly young age at which his brother became prime minister robbed that objection of its power. The Admiralty was 'a department entirely separate from all others', with a huge amount of patronage attached, as well as the superintendence of one of the two branches of Britain's military force.[1] The Royal Navy was vital for national defence and prestige, and in 1785 Pitt had publicly identified naval reform as a priority.[2] Chatham had jumped from being the prime minister's unemployed elder brother to one of the most important men in the government.

Pitt himself questioned 'whether the public may not think this too much like a monopoly'.[3] He was gambling in bringing Chatham forward, and at a basic level the arrangement did look like a 'job'. The Admiralty came with a combined salary of £3,000 and the use of the newly built Admiralty House, a compact thirty-room mansion arranged over three floors and overlooking Horse Guards Parade. But the appointment was no sinecure, and Pitt expected his brother to knuckle down. Chatham's brief was clear: to connect 'the department of the Admiralty with the rest of the Administration, which has never yet been the case under Pitt's Government, even in the smallest degree'.[4] Chatham knew Pitt had encountered problems with Howe, who had strong opinions and was unwilling to compromise. Howe had opposed a government measure to improve the defences of Plymouth and Portsmouth in 1786, and had deployed the votes of MPs elected under the Admiralty's auspices against his own ministry. He had strongly resisted change in his department and frequently argued with his civilian underlings.[5] Chatham, by contrast, could be relied on not to push his agenda. He was fully aware that his closeness to the prime minister was his greatest asset: as late as March 1794 he spoke of 'the impossibility, I must always feel of resisting any anxious wish of my Brother's'.[6] In theory, also, his non-naval background reduced the likelihood of bias towards any part of the service in dispensing patronage.

As First Lord, Chatham presided over the Admiralty Board, which consisted of six Lords Commissioners in addition to himself.[7] The Board, an explicitly political body that changed in composition depending on who was First Lord, existed mainly to ratify strategic decisions made at a higher level, and to handle promotion and patronage. It acted as a link between the Cabinet and the professional Boards that ran the everyday business of the navy: the Navy Board, the Victualling Board and the Sick and Wounded Board. The Navy Board was the most important of these three. It dealt with manpower, equipment, the running of the dockyards and other essential financial and technical business, to ensure the navy operated smoothly and efficiently.[8] At the head of the Navy Board was the Comptroller of the Navy, the formidable evangelical Sir Charles Middleton.

Middleton, a naval officer who had been actively employed till the mid-1770s, was more comfortable in administration than on the quarterdeck. 'Narrow-minded, intolerant, priggish', he was a difficult man to get on with.[9] As his kinsman Henry Dundas remarked, 'He has very great official talents and merit, but . . . he requires to have a great deal of his own way of doing business in order to do it well'.[10] Middleton did not try to conceal his wish to be a 'Master of all the Detail'.[11] He had strong ideas about the need for reform in the Navy Board, and had gone through Pitt to get his way, thus making an enemy out of Lord Howe.[12] But Howe was gone, and Middleton expected much from the appointment of a civilian like Chatham. Pitt trusted Middleton and appeared like-minded in his approach to economy and administrative reform. Chatham's closeness to the prime minister could only augur well.

Middleton wanted Chatham to implement the recommendations of the Commission on Fees and Perquisites in Public Offices, set up by Pitt in 1785 to suggest ways of rendering government departments more efficient. Middleton saw the Commission as his chance to streamline the decision-making process of the Navy Board and clarify the way it interacted with the rest of naval administration. Middleton's proposal, echoed in the Commission's final Report, was to fix the Board at ten members divided into three separate branches. Different duties, pertaining to Stores, Accounts and Correspondence, would be delegated to each branch, with the Comptroller of the Navy in charge of the whole.[13] Giving Middleton such power had been something Howe had been unable to stomach, but Middleton had hopes Chatham would be better disposed.

Chatham was certainly willing to listen, and he met frequently with Middleton over the summer of 1788 to acquaint himself with the duties of his new department. Despite this promising start, two circumstances intervened to interrupt the momentum behind reforming the navy's administration. Chatham's health was still seriously affected by the leg injury he had received in late spring. A recurring infection kept him a 'Prisoner' in his house until September, when he borrowed the Wimbledon house of the Treasurer of the Navy Henry Dundas to recuperate.[14] At the end of the month he 'was attacked with a pretty considerable fever and St Anthony's fire which confined me very much to my bed for a week or ten days', while the newspapers speculated about his 'much impaired' health.[15] Although Chatham tried to work through his illness, missing a handful of Admiralty Board meetings even when otherwise kept in bed, his leg stopped him getting fully to grips with his new post and continued intermittently to lay him low throughout the winter.[16]

While Chatham recovered slowly, a second, much more serious, setback to naval reform appeared in the form of the King's mental illness. The King spent the summer of 1788 in Cheltenham for his health, but returned to business agitated and barely in control of himself. At the end of October, he physically attacked the Prince of Wales at dinner before collapsing with a high fever. The fever ebbed but the King did not regain his senses: he talked incessantly about Hanover, flooding and his dead children, and terrified the Queen half out of her own wits. British politics were plunged into instant confusion. A regent would have to be appointed if the King remained incapacitated, and the obvious candidate was the 26-year-old Prince of Wales, who favoured Pitt's political opponent Charles James Fox. Between October 1788 and March 1789, the government Chatham had just joined fought for its survival. While the King's doctors desperately sought to cure their patient, Pitt stalled the passage of a Regency Bill through Parliament as long as he could. Thankfully the King made a full recovery in the spring of 1789. Only now was Chatham able to take on his full duties as a Cabinet minister, for his appointment to the Privy Council had been delayed by the King's illness. He was finally sworn in on 3 April.[17]

As Chatham settled into his new role, he discovered Middleton at his elbow pushing reform less and less subtly to the forefront of the Admiralty agenda. After a year of Chatham's inaction, Middleton feared the time for action had passed. His anxiety turned to alarm when Chatham showed signs of wanting to set the subject aside:

> It will be desireable to trouble the King for some time with no more business than is absolutely necessary . . . Add to that, that in the unsettled state of things none of ye Lords of ye Council, not even [the] Ld. President, have looked into [the reports], and during the sitting of Parliament there will not be much leisure, and I shou'd think . . . that a *recess* is the most favorable time for considering them.[18]

Chatham appreciated Middleton's skill and application, but the man's single-mindedness had begun to irritate him. The recess came and went, but the Commissioners' Report was not laid before the Privy Council. At this point Chatham told Middleton that, rather than adopt the full extent of the proposed Navy Board reforms, the Privy Council was unlikely to go further than giving the Comptroller an extra Secretary and a professional assistant. This, relying on the Comptroller's 'superior ability and . . . confidential intercourse with Government' to make up for any shortcomings in the arrangement, might be enough for Chatham, but it was not for Middleton.[19] He continued pressing Chatham and Pitt to return to the Commission Reports, but, when it became clear that he was effectively talking to himself, he resigned in March 1790.[20]

Why did Chatham fail to pursue Middleton's reforms? He was on record as supporting reform in public offices: he had signed his name to an official House of Lords protest following the rejection of his brother's Public Offices Regulation Bill in 1783. Clearly he had changed his mind about the urgency of addressing 'gross Abuse and Mismanagement', in his department at least.[21] Historians have interpreted Chatham's lack of support for Middleton as evidence that his notorious laziness represented a 'dam' to reform, but to second-guess his motives based on his personality is unfair.[22] 'If Chatham had thrown his weight behind

Middleton – if Chatham had had more weight – Pitt might still perhaps have decided to go ahead,' Ehrman writes.[23] Chatham was relieved when the Commission's suggestions fell quietly by the wayside, but Ehrman's point works both ways. Chatham had been brought to the Cabinet to buttress Pitt's position, and he would have followed his brother's lead had Pitt required him to implement the reforms. The question is not why Chatham failed to take up reform, but why Pitt allowed it to drop. Perhaps, as Ehrman suggests, the favourable moment had passed; perhaps, as others have argued, he meant economic reform to happen on his terms and in his own time.[24]

Chatham's failure to reform Navy administration did not mean he was a weak, bumbling First Lord who filled a place between Howe and the more effective Spencer.[25] Throughout his career Chatham demonstrated a strong desire to avoid tinkering with the departments under his command, but this owed more to his innate conservatism than it did to laziness. He was never a man to promote change for change's sake, and his cautious nature (and lack of imagination) made him less likely to push for a peacetime shake-up at the Admiralty. Although reform was undoubtedly required, the urgency was not yet there; when war did come, his Admiralty was far from static. The creation of the Impress Service in 1793 and the Transport Board in 1794 took place under Chatham, and Middleton's return to office and his elevation to the Admiralty Board in May 1794 suggested a willingness to face a piecemeal implementation of the reforms he had long been advocating.[26] For now at least the navy's performance gave little cause for concern. Pitt's lavishing of money on the navy and dockyards had paid off. Shipbuilding and repairs went on at a rate sufficient to match both the Spanish and French fleets, Britain's nearest competitors. By the end of the decade Chatham presided over a fleet of over 140 sail of the line (the largest vessels, designed to bear the brunt of a battle), 90 of which were ready to sail at short notice.[27]

From Chatham's point of view, reform was less immediately pressing than the prickly question of patronage and promotion. This was an important part of the First Lord of the Admiralty's duties, and Chatham hated it: 'You have no idea of the persecution I experience every day on the subject'.[28] Promotion to lieutenant was largely regulated by examination, but picking the lieutenants who would become captains was harder. Battles were a good way for officers to distinguish themselves, but in peacetime well-connected men could all too easily find a great man to plead their cause.[29] Finding suitable commanders for ships involved both political and professional considerations, and Chatham, as a political First Lord, struggled to strike an appropriate balance. His hesitations drove his professional colleagues to distraction. Lord Hood complained in December 1790 that Chatham had 'been, for the last three weeks puzzling himself about who he should make . . . Not untill last night did he deliver his List to Stephens, & every name as it stood when he first showed it me a month ago'.[30]

Hood, part-time politician though he was, did not appreciate Chatham's problem. Even with an impeccable service record, a lieutenant's elevation to captain was uncertain, and with the best will in the world, Chatham's choices were bound to lead to disappointments: 'The list is so large already, that I fear, even in an extensive war many a brave and active Officer must be left on shore'.[31] Many naval men viewed the civilian First Lord as a placeman and 'jobber', intent on milking all he could out of the lucrative post he held, as demonstrated by this fictional account: 'Lord Chatham being requested to promote a *Lieutenant* who had fought nobly at the Dogger Bank, and being told that he distinguished himself, *purely for the love of his country*, his Lordship, with much *neatness* replied – "Well, then, he has had his reward! WE only serve those who can serve US!"'[32]

Accusations of Chatham's political bias were most marked after the polarising experience of the Regency Crisis, following which several officers felt they had been ignored because they had chosen the wrong side in the House of Commons. Sir George Collier, one of the few naval officers to emerge from the American war with a half-decent reputation, fretted that his anti-Pittite voting record had contributed to Chatham's 'Inattention': 'my Sins have arisen out of my political Character . . . I am passed over . . . as the Beacon to deter others from venturing to have an Opinion in future'.[33] Others, too, felt slighted. 'Lord Chatham told me there was a *line* drawn & he was sorry to say I was the wrong side of it,' one officer complained in 1793 after missing out on a promotion. 'I suppose I *crossed it* at the last county election.'[34] Part of this was, no doubt, a disappointed officer making excuses to himself, but Chatham's closeness to the prime minister exposed him to such accusations.

Chatham was acutely aware of the way he was viewed, and this contributed to his prolonged head-scratchings over who to send where.

The 'persecution' of promotion led him on one occasion to lose his temper in public:

> He wished, most earnestly, that he could employ every flag, & indeed every other officer, who is capable & willing to serve his country, but . . . if Gentlemen in general who happened not to be employed, conceived that the omission was to be attributed to any reference either to their Political, or Naval Conduct, they equally wronged him & themselves; & they ought, he said, to consider the number of Admirals as well as Captains to whom it was impossible to give commands.[35]

Chatham was right: applications for commands exceeded vacancies. Prior to 1795, only 30 per cent of navy captains were employed, and as late as 1800 half remained unemployed.[36] Nor did promotion under Chatham result in blocking true talent. Men such as Edward Pellew and Horatio Nelson both made good headway with Chatham's patronage. Politics almost certainly played a part in many of Chatham's choices, but he did not rigidly block opposition sympathisers, acquiescing in Edmund Burke's wish to provide a family member with a command, and he often denied his own connections.[37] 'The getting a Lieutenant on board a Flag Ship is by no means an easy thing, and it is an object, which as yet I have never been able to attain, though I have been in pursuit of it frequently,' Lord Sydney remarked. 'Lord Chatham has uniformly refused me on that head, though I have every reason to believe, that he wished to oblige me.'[38] This, from Chatham's own father-in-law, suggests Chatham was trying not to lay himself open to charges of favouritism.

He was the more vulnerable because his poor reputation as First Lord increased his unpopularity. He was not universally disliked, and his easy-going nature, his 'politeness and affability', and 'the great popularity of [his] manners' charmed many.[39] The King, particularly, was won over – a surprising champion, perhaps, given George III's famous dislike of Chatham's father and difficult relationship with Chatham's brother. The King had opened his professional correspondence with Chatham on an anxious note, hoping the new First Lord would keep to established procedure and 'not let any person whoever able in the Service gain too much of his ear'.[40] A year later Chatham had ingratiated himself at St James's, and he remained a much more enthusiastic and visible courtier than his brother. He had always been elegant (in his teens his father called him 'the powdered beau'), and his Cabinet status gave him added reason to show off. In 1789 his 'corbeau and blue striped' coat was acclaimed as 'one of the handsomest dresses at the Drawing room'; four years later his 'carmelite [light brown] coloured velvet coat and breeches . . . very richly embroidered with silver' provoked similar admiration.[41]

Chatham's court profile was certainly raised by his wife's enthusiastic assistance. Lady Chatham was already a familiar face at court: her mother and aunt, Lady Courtown, were both Ladies of the Queen's Bedchamber, and Mary often accompanied them on official business. Her sister Georgiana had been close to the Princess Royal, and Mary herself formed friendships with Princesses Augusta, Elizabeth and Mary. In the late 1780s, after her health had recovered from its mid-decade collapse, Lady Chatham's prominent presence at court events transformed her into a fashionable figure. Like her husband, she was something of a trendsetter, and her gowns were often complimented in the newspapers. She took her duties as a Cabinet minister's wife seriously and was well aware of her political influence, canvassing on behalf of government candidates in parliamentary elections, hosting official galas and Admiralty ship launches, and bringing a much-needed feminine touch to the upper echelons of government with her youth and beauty.

Outside court circles, Chatham's reputation was more mixed. He may have been diplomatic and beloved by the King, but his inexperience showed. This greenness would have mattered less had Chatham been a more active First Lord, but 'his indolence in office . . . [was] so notorious that he was nicknamed by the Navy ... *The Late Lord Chatham*'.[42] Reports were much exaggerated. Chatham's Admiralty Board attendance averaged between 55 per cent (1794) and 74 per cent (1789), with jumps of over 80 per cent during the Nootka Sound scare in 1790.[43] He did take regular holidays in the autumn and winter for hunting, but always came back to London promptly if summoned. The newspapers noticed if Chatham was away from his desk for lengthy periods. When he broke his leg in the summer of 1791, the *Star* remarked that 'His Lordship has not attended the Admiralty Board this fortnight'.[44]

This is not to say Chatham's reputation for sloth was undeserved. As time passed, he became more and more relaxed in his post, perhaps considering himself secure because of his closeness to the prime minister. His ebbing enthusiasm for his duties was obvious well before the beginning of the war in 1793. His superintendence of the Admiralty was chaotic at best. The super-organised Middleton bemoaned that 'when I first came to the Admiralty Board [in May 1794], I found no regular time fixed for beginning business nor any . . . dependence whatever in anything being carried into execution'. He blandly stated that 'Lord Chatham's ministerial concerns did not allow of a regular attendance in office hours'.[45] According to Admiral Gardner, a Lord of the Admiralty, Chatham's working day started at 11.30, and ended with supper at midnight and bed at 2.[46] Nor was this slackness restricted to his Cabinet duties. On one occasion in 1791 he did not appear at an official court event until 4.30, 3½ hours after it had begun.[47] None of this would have been difficult to change had he put his mind to it, but all his life he did not care in the least what people thought. 'An intimate friend of L[or]d Chatham has spoken to him on the inconvenience attending his laying in bed till the day is advanced, as officers etc were kept waiting,' a contemporary noted. 'L[or]d Chatham said it did not signify[,] it was an indulgence He could not give up'.[48] This was hearsay, but with a flavour of truth to it. Fifteen years later, Chatham's late rising and retiring – and his complete lack of care for the inconvenience it caused to others – remained prominent features of his behaviour.

Despite this, up until the outbreak of war with France in 1793, with Middleton's influence behind him and a much-strengthened navy under his command, Chatham's record in office was surprisingly good. Britain teetered on the brink of war twice between 1789 and 1793, and in neither situation did Chatham display incompetence in his post. At the beginning of 1790, the Spanish invoked a fifteenth century papal bull laying claim to Nootka Sound on what would later become Vancouver Island, where British settlers were building a trading settlement. The Spanish captured several British ships and sparked a diplomatic fracas that very nearly ended in conflict. Since any struggle with Spain would be fought largely at sea, the brunt of the preparations for conflict fell on the navy. Chatham knew it was his opportunity to prove his two years at the Admiralty had been well spent. 'I am, under all circumstances anxious to hear of ye Fleet being at Sea,' he wrote to a friend, 'and I am sure we shall derive great advantage, in settling the points still at Issue between the two Courts, by shewing a respectable force in readiness to act if necessary'.[49] He pulled his weight, regularly attending Cabinets and Board meetings and communicating with the admirals tasked with assembling the fleet, then overseeing the dismantling of the whole operation when the expected war did not come about. He found the whole experience thrilling, but also exhausting: 'My excursions this summer have been, as you will suppose, very much confined, never beyond Hollwood [Holwood, Pitt's country house], from whence I returned last night having passed Sunday there, which for me is a long stay in the Country'.[50]

Thanks in no small degree to the preparations of Chatham's Admiralty, Pitt's government came out of the business with an enhanced reputation.[51] When Lord Howe put to sea in the late summer of 1790, he did so with a fleet of nearly 50 ships, 29 of which were of the line, a number that had grown to 33 within 6 months.[52] Chatham had good reason to feel proud, and he did not go long unrewarded. In December 1790 the King disposed of three ribbands of the Order of the Garter that had become vacant over the course of the year. One went to the Duke of Saxe-Coburg, but the King intended the other two 'as a public testimonial of [his] approbation' for the outcome of the Spanish crisis.[53] The second ribband accordingly went to the Foreign Secretary, the Duke of Leeds, and the King offered the third to Pitt himself. Pitt was not one for accepting honours and declined, but requested that the King bestow the Garter on his brother instead. Chatham, whose love of pomp and status grew with age, was delighted, and the King expressed himself perfectly happy to 'give this public testimony of approbation which will be understood as meant to the whole family'.[54] Chatham remained proud of his Garter for the rest of his life, applying the insignia to his crest, his carriage and his cutlery. His niece Lady Hester Stanhope described him travelling like 'a Prince' with 'his led Horses, his carriages, his dress, his star & Garter, all of which he shews off in his *quiet way* with wonderful effect'.[55]

The year 1791 was less glorious for Chatham, although once again his Admiralty met its challenges promptly and well. Early that year Pitt nearly blundered into war. Russia and Austria had been at war with the Ottoman Empire since the late 1780s, and by 1791 Russia's territorial gains on the Black Sea threatened British Continental trade. Russia's capture of the fort of Ochakov, particularly, endangered important timber trading routes. This was a major consideration for a predominantly naval nation, but British interests in the struggle were much less clear-cut than during the near conflict with Spain. War with Russia would mostly have favoured Prussia, allied to Britain since 1788, which disapproved of Russia and Austria's encroachments on Poland. In terms of policy, also, Russia had always been a traditional British ally. From the outset war with Russia was a hard sell to the British public. Nevertheless, Chatham once again swiftly mobilised the navy, and in March 1791 Pitt sent an ultimatum to the Russian empress, Catherine II, threatening to send 35 ships to the Baltic, and 12 to the Black Sea, if she did not evacuate Ochakov. But the government was divided over forcing a question in which Britain seemed too obviously led by Prussia. Following a series of acrimonious Cabinets over March and April, and a harsh vote in the House of Commons, which showed he was unlikely to have public support for a Russian war, Pitt recalled the Russian ultimatum.[56]

Chatham had been a supporter of Pitt's hard-line policy, and he was unhappy with his brother's sudden change of heart. The reasons he gave in May for not sending a fleet to the Black Sea reeked of ambivalence:

> The undertaking would be rather an arduous one, the navigation being so little known . . . [In addition] the sailing of a squadron for the Black Sea would be considered, as tending to immediate hostility, and would renew all those alarms and discussions which have to a degree subsided, only from the persuasion that the business was in a train of negotiation. It is also feared that it might discourage at present, the favourable dispositions that seem to manifest themselves in the Court of Spain, and the old objection besides of expense recurs.[57]

This sounded like a man reeling off arguments with which he was not entirely in accordance, but he kept his misgivings quiet. The navy, indeed, had not emerged badly, and it was just as well it had so much practice in emergency mobilisation. Within eighteen months, Russia and Spain would be locked in alliance with Britain against a new common enemy: revolutionary France.

Like Pitt, Chatham was initially unimpressed with the French threat, but in the summer of 1792 the Revolution turned violent with the imprisonment of the French royal family and the September massacres in Paris. Despite these developments, the autumn saw both Chatham and Pitt peeling off to their respective country estates, Chatham to Cheveley and Pitt to Walmer Castle, acquired following his appointment (at the King's insistence) to the sinecure of Lord Warden of the Cinque Ports.[58] It was the brothers' last holiday. Chatham was soon convinced by increasingly bloody events in France that the Revolution posed a serious threat to monarchical order. He never lost his conviction that Britain was the last aristocratic bulwark against democratic anarchy, and remained one of the more hard-line members of the ministry whenever the question of peace or compromise with the republic came up. For Chatham, the war was a question of survival: he was, after all, an aristocrat with a direct stake in the social order, as well as a man whose instinctive conservatism revolted at the idea of fundamental change.

By 1793 the French invasion of Flanders, and the execution of Louis XVI, guaranteed British involvement in the Continental struggle. On 1 February 1793 the French declared war. Chatham was soon able to report that, thanks to the recent naval armaments of 1790 and 1791, over a hundred ships of the line were ready for service. In the first year of the war 56,337 extra seamen were raised to man them, 69,824 in the 'not quite two' years up to September 1794. As Chatham proudly pointed out, the next best figures from previous wars were 32,000 men raised in any single year, and 56,000 in any 2.[59] The numbers were undeniably impressive, but the picture was not as rosy as Chatham made it look. The Admiralty was about to be tested to its limits by a war which ultimately lasted nine years. As Middleton had long ago identified, the division of power between the Admiralty Board and its subsidiaries did not make for efficiency when speed of reaction was of the essence. Conditions on board ship needed addressing, from pay to provisioning. The navy in the 1780s had also prioritised the bigger warships at the expense of frigates and smaller vessels, all very well for glorious fleet engagements but less useful in a war where blockading enemy ports and protecting trade convoys were vital.[60] After less than a year of hostilities, all these shortcomings – and more – were clamouring for attention.

Unfortunately for Chatham, sixteen months of frustration intervened between the declaration of war in 1793 and the battle that became known as the 'Glorious First of June' in 1794. His navy's failure to engage the French, its inability to support Continental military operations effectively, and the enemy's occasional, much-publicised attacks on British mercantile convoys, drew criticism towards the way the Admiralty was run, and onto the head of the First Lord in particular. None of this would have mattered if Chatham had had the support of his colleagues, since nearly every government department was blamed at one time or another for the many wartime failures. But Chatham was, as John Ehrman notes, 'expendable', and his enemies picked up on his weakness.[61] His closeness to Pitt, which had once been an asset, made him vulnerable, and the blood connection with the Prime Minister made Pitt more cautious about defending him. By the time the navy beat its French counterpart, Chatham's political position was too shaky to withstand a challenge. He knew this, but when the anticipated assault occurred, he was entirely unprepared for the quarter from which it came: from the heart of the Cabinet, and men he trusted, admired and loved.

Chapter 4

'A Fatality of Temper'
1793–4

Chatham's wartime preparations were soon put to the test. On 25 February 1793, jubilant crowds gathered in Greenwich to watch 1,800 Foot Guards, under the command of the Duke of York, embark to join the Prince of Coburg's Austrian and Prussian army in defence of Holland and Flanders. A few months later 1,800 was increased to 6,500, bringing York's forces to a total of 34,500 men, including Hanoverians, Hessians and Dutch. While the diplomats put the finishing touches to a military coalition between Britain, Austria, Prussia, Sardinia, the Two Sicilies, Portugal and Spain, the Allies laid siege to several forts along the French border. These fell over the course of June and July, opening the way for a march on Paris, but instead of marching promptly on the French capital the Duke of York laid siege to the coastal town of Dunkirk.[1]

The move made sense. Dunkirk would offer a base for provisioning Allied forces and assisting the French counter-revolutionaries on the coast, and give the British more bargaining power at a peace table which, in the summer of 1793, looked like it was not far away. But Britain's allies remained uncommitted, the Austrians preferring to pursue their own strategic aims, and last-minute planning in London meant siege supplies had to be provided at short notice. Inevitably, the result was a shambles. There was insufficient artillery available, and when the supplies were gathered an error in the Admiralty's tide calculations delayed their sailing and forced the transports to anchor too far up the coast from York's army. Meanwhile, instead of the small, rag-tag army York had expected, he faced 45,000 seasoned troops under the command of Generals Houchard and Hoche, which defeated Britain's Hanoverian and Austrian allies at Hondschoote and threatened to drive the rest of York's force into the sea.[2]

Two days later, the siege supplies finally arrived, far too late to make a difference to the campaign's outcome.

Dunkirk was the first major blow against Chatham's Admiralty administration. The press, which reflected broader public condemnation of the way the Cabinet had botched the campaign, was scathing. Chatham and the Duke of Richmond, Master-General of the Ordnance, were particularly singled out for criticism. 'If the gun boats and floating battery had been ready,' the *Morning Chronicle* roared, '. . . there is no doubt but Dunkirk would have fallen on the first attack'.[3] The immediate effect of these accusations was to put Richmond on the warpath. He defended himself in the obvious manner by heaping the blame on the First Lord of the Admiralty. Chatham was aghast. Embarrassing mistakes had been made, but he had done his best on a very tight schedule. The majority of the blame had to be borne by the ministers responsible for spreading British resources too thinly in too many places: Pitt, the prime minister, and Henry Dundas, the Home Secretary, fast becoming Pitt's most trusted strategic adviser. But Chatham could not defend himself publicly on those grounds, and the effect of his silence, and Richmond's vigorous attempt to capitalise on Chatham's poor reputation, rapidly became obvious. Rumours spread of Chatham's 'indolent habits and indulgences. He is said to get drunk every evening, to sit up all night at a club, and to lie abed all day'.[4]

A victory might have neutralised the impression that Chatham was slacking, but, frustratingly, none was forthcoming. Naval actions were restricted to encounters between enemy ships and merchant convoys going to and from the East and West Indies. The convoys were defended well enough, but some inevitably fell victim to French attacks, and the lack of a spectacular victory to offset these episodes increased the Admiralty's poor reputation. Chatham was well aware of the impact of the fleet's impotence on public opinion. Lord Buckingham 'found him full of complaints and of ill humour' at the end of summer 1793 when Lord Howe's Channel fleet came in early for provisioning, having failed – again – to engage the French.[5] Chatham complained that 'the Enemy . . . shunned the Contest, and sheltered themselves behind ye Rocks and ye Shoals' of their own coast, robbing Britain of a glorious victory to justify her enormous naval armament, and the First Lord of the vindication he badly needed.[6]

That vindication looked, briefly, like it might be within Chatham's reach after all following an unexpected turn of events. In mid-September Chatham was having a late dinner with Pitt and Dundas in Wimbledon when a special messenger arrived with astounding news. At the end of August the port of Toulon, in southern France, had turned its back on the radical Jacobin government and sought the protection of Admiral Lord Hood, who was blockading the town.[7] Without firing a shot in anger, one of the most important French dockyards, and half the French fleet, had fallen into Allied hands, and Britain suddenly found herself with a toehold on the French mainland.

This was a potential turning point for the war, and one in which Chatham and the Admiralty might expect to play a primary role. But the opportunity was squandered. The Cabinet could not decide whether to focus on the war in Flanders and trap the revolutionary forces between two fronts, or use Toulon as a base for assisting the counter-revolution in Brittany (Chatham's preferred option). At least one Cabinet member had a different strategic approach altogether: Dundas was planning an expedition to attack France's West Indian possessions, and Toulon was a distraction from what he considered to be one of the most important economic spheres of the war. The result of this three-way strategic tug was, in Michael Duffy's words, 'a rather messy compromise' that suited nobody.[8] The decision to concentrate forces came at Toulon's expense, on the assumption that Britain's allies would make up the manpower shortfall. But the Austrians were much more concerned with the war in the north, and the Spanish were deeply suspicious of any attempt to establish British maritime supremacy in the Mediterranean. Although Naples did provide 6,000 men and 11 ships, Austria failed to send a single man of the 5,000 she promised. Sardinia committed to 20,000 men but produced 2,000. By December, the Allies had 18,700 troops in all, mostly Spanish and Neapolitan. Only 2,000 troops were actually British.[9]

By contrast with Allied confusion, the French response to the enemy presence on their soil was swift and focused. Having reduced the other counter-revolutionary centres of Lyons and Marseilles, and reinforced with soldiers freed up from Mainz, Condé and Valenciennes, 30,000 revolutionary troops surrounded Toulon in mid-December. Starved of troops and saddled with allies who distrusted him, Hood's position in Toulon was unsustainable. Two-thirds of the town's panicking population crowded aboard the British and Spanish ships, while Hood hesitated about destroying the French fleet and dockyards. In the end many of the ships were merely damaged, rather than rendered completely unfit for future service.[10] Within days the French swept back into Toulon, executing thousands of the remaining townsmen without trial.

Instead of cancelling out the Dunkirk disaster, Toulon underlined Chatham's weakness within the Cabinet. He tried to make the best of a bad situation, persuading himself there had been no point wasting lives in fighting for Toulon: 'ye sooner it cou'd be abandoned (with good faith) the better'.[11] But his voice as First Lord of the Admiralty meant nothing in determining strategic priorities; he later recalled, bitterly, that his 'opinion was treated with no great respect' when he tried to point out Hood's vulnerability. He was disgusted with his colleagues, Dundas in particular, who had 'constantly promised' Hood reinforcements but always let him down.[12] Being expected to watch while Dundas planned extravagant expeditions to the West Indies at the expense of campaigns in which the navy had a strong stake was too much for Chatham to bear.

His resentment was sharpened by the awareness that his job was under threat. In November or December 1793 Pitt decided to remove his brother from the Admiralty altogether, but changed his mind after a sharp warning to Chatham to bestir himself.[13] Instead of sacking his brother, Pitt arranged a chaperone for him: Dundas, the very man whose strategic decisions Chatham felt had damaged his reputation so much. Dundas's role as Home Secretary gave him some control over colonial naval deployment, and as Treasurer of the Navy he was closely involved with the Admiralty. His influence over Chatham was already great, and the frequency with which Chatham could be found at Dundas's house in 1793 reflected the degree to which the Secretary of State had established himself as an Admiralty adviser.[14] Now Pitt insisted Chatham submit himself to Dundas's direction in all matters. As Dundas put it to Pitt, he was '*while the War continues* . . . a Puisne Lord of the Admiralty', an unofficial position he felt he had adopted as a favour to Chatham.[15] P.K. Crimmin has assumed this unusual arrangement suited Chatham's lazy nature, but she misses the very obvious tension growing between Chatham and his supposed mentor.[16] There had been ripples in their relationship since preparations for the West Indies in September 1793 had threatened to upset arrangements for reinforcing Hood in Toulon, and in the autumn of 1793 Chatham and Dundas clashed openly over the use of naval vessels as troop transports.[17]

A storm was brewing at the heart of the Cabinet between the First Lord of the Admiralty and the Home Secretary. To Chatham's dismay, he quickly discovered his colleagues were unlikely to back him up in the event of a rupture. This sense of isolation made him prickly and impulsive, conscious that he had nothing left to lose. In March 1794 he confronted Dundas in a remarkably defiant letter. What called it forth is unclear, but by this time he viewed the Home Secretary as an enemy and intended to make his feelings clear. After referring in a pained manner to 'the confidence and friendship I always flattered myself subsisted between us', he issued a thinly veiled challenge:

> I had certainly much rather look to the future, than to the past, but, it is with unaffected regret I must confess, my prospects are not very sanguine. . . . You are not unacquainted, I know, with the circumstances under which I undertook the situation, I now hold, liable certainly to the charge of considerable imprudence, but to which my best endeavours have been devoted. Be assured, My Dear Sir, that no conduct of mine (whatever may be insinuated) shall ever bring any disgrace either on the Government or the Country, but I will never disgrace myself by acquiescing, in any conduct of others, which I may feel it neither becoming me nor my situation to permit.

Chatham was usually reluctant to commit anything self-incriminating to paper, but he could barely restrain his rage. 'I have already said more than I intended, tho' little compared with what I feel,' he finished.[18]

Chatham's anger graduated to open alarm when a government reshuffle increased Dundas's consequence. In July Pitt came together with the Duke of Portland and his followers, who formed a third party since the French Revolution had driven an ideological wedge between them and Fox. The Duke of Portland replaced Dundas at the Home Office, Lord Fitzwilliam became President of the Council, Lord Spencer Privy Seal and William Windham Secretary at War, a post elevated to Cabinet rank.[19] Dundas, meanwhile, took the new post of Secretary of State for War. He had even more of an excuse to interfere with Admiralty requirements, and Chatham was outraged enough to protest against the arrangement. But in locking horns with Dundas, he had picked the strongest enemy possible, as Pitt's firm, threatening slap-down must have proved:

There is no assignable Reason, why every Thing should not go on between Dundas in his present Department, and the Admiralty, exactly in the Train in which It has done hitherto. I am so convinced that on Consideration you must see this as I do, that I do not like to press it farther, or to say any Thing of the Embarrassment which would otherwise arise; and which, both for my sake and for the Service, you must I am sure wish to avoid.[20]

Pitt was deeply worried by Chatham's dislike of Dundas's new role, particularly as he had explicitly planned it to be sure Dundas would continue controlling Admiralty strategy despite the new arrangements:

I feel it quite impossible to venture the experiment of leaving the War Department in the Duke [of Portland]'s hands. You know the difficulty with *other* Departments, even with the advantage of Dundas's turn for facilitating business, and of every act of his being as much *mine* as *his*; and, therefore, if all the details of the war (particularly in one line which I need not mention) were to be settled by communication with a person new both to me and *to others*, I am sure the business could not go on for a week.[21]

The 'other' departments and individuals Pitt was reluctant to name may have been his brother at the Admiralty. Chatham was no fool. He may not have known the full extent of Dundas's role, but he had guessed much of it, and it cannot have been easy to swallow.

The least painful solution would have been to remove Chatham upon coalition with Portland. Chatham probably expected this to happen, but, by the time negotiations ended, his position had strengthened. On 9 June, he received news of the naval victory for which he and the public had been anxiously waiting. For some weeks, Lord Howe had been hunting down a grain convoy bound from the West Indies to Brest. France was undergoing a nationwide famine, and preventing the grain from reaching Paris would strike a vital blow to French morale and political stability. At the end of May Howe finally sighted the French fleet under Villaret de Joyeuse, gave chase and drew the enemy into a spectacular engagement which resulted in the French losing seven ships – the greatest British naval victory in over a hundred years. Typically, even Chatham's moment of triumph was imperfect: Villaret de Joyeuse's engaging Howe allowed the West Indian convoy to evade the vigilance of Admiral Montagu, who had been detached to obstruct its approach.[22] Nevertheless, Chatham breathed a sigh of relief. He was now safe in the Pitt-Portland reshuffle – or so he thought.

The victory was a much-needed boost to morale. Working with Pitt and Dundas, Chatham devised a week-long royal gala in Portsmouth to promote the natural connections between King, Navy and People. Like the battle, the celebrations were a mixed success. Chatham's old nemesis, patronage, reared its ugly head when he insisted Howe name the captains who had most distinguished themselves during the battle, offending many who did not make the list.[23] Ugly questions also abounded about the success of the French grain convoy in reaching Brest. Nobody was ready to undermine the celebrations by making a fuss, but Chatham never forgave the admiral responsible for allowing the convoy to escape, George Montagu, coldly informing him at the end of July that 'I am really not aware of the possibility of any other employment arising [for you], even if it were an advisable thing for you to accept of any other'.[24] Nearly ten years later, Chatham still represented 'an insuperable bar' to Montagu's employment.[25] With hindsight, Chatham probably felt the Admiral's failure was partially responsible for what happened next.

* * *

Following the Portsmouth gala Chatham was very ill with a recurring stomach complaint, and in August Pitt ordered him to the country to recuperate.[26] Pitt was not just worried for his brother's health. Keeping Chatham away from London also had a political motive, for Pitt was keen to maintain some distance between his First Lord of the Admiralty and Secretary of State for War. 'Have you yet fixed the day of your Return?' Pitt asked on 22 September, when Chatham had been away for nearly a month. 'The longer you can contrive to stay the better.'[27]

Pitt's efforts to keep his brother and Dundas apart failed. While Chatham was at Cheveley, eight French ships of the line were spotted in the Atlantic making for an unknown destination. Dundas, at the War Office, decided the French must be reinforcing their troops in the West Indies. Although British forces in the area had initially done well defending British holdings and seizing enemy islands, over the summer the French had retaken Guadeloupe and secured St Domingo. General Sir Charles Grey requested a reinforcement of 6,000 men, at a time when Britain's disposable force was already spread too thin.[28] A fresh draft of French troops might finish the British forces, devastated by the impact of yellow fever. Persuaded of the urgency of the need to send troops as quickly as possible, and faced with a shortage of available troops at home, Dundas made the snap decision to send British marines instead. He wrote immediately to pressure Chatham into sending them, and enough ships to relieve the Leeward squadron. If the French turned their full attention to the West Indies before British reinforcements arrived, the results would be disastrous, for 'our troops are worn to a Skeleton'.[29]

Chatham was unimpressed. Emboldened by the recent naval victory, he made the mistake of trying to assert himself. He reminded Dundas Lord Hood needed reinforcing in Corsica, where Hood had captured Bastia and Calvi and helped establish an Anglo-Corsican government. Hood had only 15 sail of the line on which to rely, against 18 of the enemy.[30] Because of this, since Howe's victory, Chatham had decided to prioritise sending reinforcements to the Mediterranean, where Dundas's plans had 'never allowed us that commanding Superiority . . . which the nature of the present War above all others seems to require'. Chatham had been waiting for the convoys to return at the end of September, but Dundas was ordering him to send those precious ships to shore up a tottering military exercise in the West Indies instead.[31] Dundas, who had clearly expected prompt co-operation from the First Lord of the Admiralty, replied stridently:

My Urgency on the subject of a Reinforcement being sent to the West Indies does not proceed from any Idle and unfounded Anxiety . . . The utmost exertions are making to send out an adequate force, but the impossibility of sending old and seasoned Regiments for that service, and the cruelty of sending out Regiments who have scarcely as yet had arms in their hands baffles every attempt to do it as speedily as the service requires. . . . I had no reason to calculate on the very unusual and Calamitous Mortality, which has so totally cut up the Army under Sir Charles Grey . . . Our Security in the West Indies for many months to come depends entirely on a commanding and extensive Naval Force.

44

Dundas concluded with a nudge: 'I have sent even the Official Dispatch to your Lordship, because the Messenger can return from you with any Directions you may have to give time enough to find Sir Charles [Middleton, since May 1794 on the Admiralty Board] when he comes to the office tomorrow morning'.[32]

Dundas's bullying tone infuriated Chatham as much as using navy personnel to cover the War Office's inability to provide sufficient troops. His anger at being dictated to was obvious in a letter to the naval commander in the West Indies, Sir John Jervis, informing him his naval force was 'very ample, and I shall think sufficient for Naval Objects'.[33] There the matter rested, as far as Chatham was concerned, but when he returned to London at the end of September he was horrified to find Dundas had overridden him in his absence. Six ships intended for Hood in the Mediterranean had been ordered to the West Indies, 'against my opinion, on account solely of ye want of Land Troops'.[34] 'I made another effort [to reinforce Hood], in October or November,' Chatham later recalled, 'and five sail of ye Line . . . got under weigh but were obliged to put back by contrary winds'.[35] By the time the wind changed, the political scene had changed also.

At the end of November, the simmering resentment between Chatham and Dundas boiled over in Cabinet. The immediate cause of the explosion was probably Chatham's attempt to exert control over his department in making further military arrangements for the West Indies. On 9 November Chatham wrote lamenting 'that fresh demands are likely to be made upon us . . . at the expense of some other Service', and warned Dundas it would be his 'duty to submit, whenever the measure in question comes under the consideration of the Cabinet . . . that, it is not practicable to afford the same certain protection, to two embarkations proceeding from different Places, that it wou'd be to one sailing from Spithead'.[36] Dundas probably interpreted Chatham following through with his warning as obstruction. Whatever happened, Dundas went straight to Pitt and offered his resignation.

Faced with a choice between his most trusted colleague and his much-criticised brother, Pitt did not hesitate to choose Dundas. Chatham's fate was further sealed by the need to preserve ministerial unity. The Duke of Portland had joined the Cabinet under the impression that Lord Fitzwilliam, currently President of the Council, would go to Ireland as Lord Lieutenant, but Pitt was reluctant to send Fitzwilliam on such a delicate posting, knowing his connections with pro-Catholic, pro-reform and anti-government interests in the sister island. A quarrel between Dundas and Chatham gave Pitt the opportunity to show his dedication to the alliance with Portland, despite this hesitation over Fitzwilliam. On 28 November, with Chatham happily oblivious, Pitt and Dundas agreed with Portland that the Admiralty would pass to the current Lord Privy Seal, the Portlandite Earl Spencer.[37]

Pitt now faced the task of breaking the news to his brother. Chatham had been living on borrowed time for a year, but there had been no naval disasters, no destroyed convoys, no parliamentary censure. The only reason for Chatham's dismissal could be that he was not up to the job. Pitt knew Chatham would not leave without a fight, but his attempt to avoid the inevitable worsened the impact of his decision. He retreated to the safe distance of his country villa at Holwood and dithered for three days before sacking his brother by letter. Pitt stated forthrightly that his decision sprang from long-standing communication problems, and although he did not specifically name Dundas he referred to him in a way Chatham would find unmistakable:

> I foresee too evidently the utter impossibility that business should permanently go on between you & those with whom, in your present department, you must have continual intercourse . . . I therefore trust you will think that I consult my affection to you as much as what I owe to other considerations in telling you fairly tho' reluctantly my perfect conviction that the time is come when it will be the best for us both as well as for the Public Service if you will exchange your present situation for one of a different description. I must ascribe it to some fatality of temper (in whom it is not material to enquire) that the attempt to prevent the unfortunate quarrel should have been in vain.

Pitt suggested Chatham take Spencer's post of Privy Seal, effectively a 'ministry without portfolio'. Having offered Chatham a meaningless office without responsibility in exchange for one of the most important positions in the Cabinet, Pitt dropped his final bombshell: 'I have preferred telling [this] to you by letter to a conversation, which must be unnecessarily distressing to us both, and to which I really do not feel myself equal'.[38]

At Admiralty House, just 15 miles away, the *fait accompli* of his dismissal dealt Chatham a stunning blow. 'You certainly judged right in thinking that in every point of view your letter must come most unexpectedly upon me, and I really hardly know what to think or what to say,' he spluttered. Close behind the shock came the self-righteous anger: 'You will, I am sure, recollect that I undertook the situation I am in by your desire and advice, and that I have sacrificed to it every other consideration, and I am not conscious, in the discharge of it, of having failed in my duty to the public, and less in anything towards you'. Convinced there was something Pitt had not told him, he begged for a meeting to discuss the matter when Pitt returned to town.[39]

It was the most embarrassing reaction Chatham could have had, at a time when Pitt needed his government to show a united a front. 'It gives me more pain than I can express to decline a conversation with you,' Pitt wrote, but 'I really can see no possibility that explanation or discussion can be of any advantage'. A change at the Admiralty was merely a matter of convenience: 'The successful exertions wh[ich] have been made & the general state in wh[ich] you w[oul]d leave our naval Force . . . are the most convincing proofs of the manner in wh[ich] you have provided for the most essential objects of the Service'. In the same breath as he told Chatham he had done his job well, Pitt refused to back down: 'Neither these circumstances (however creditable) nor the conviction of the attention wh[ich] you have given to the business of the Admiralty, & the compleat knowledge wh[ich] you have acquired of it, can . . . alter the opinion wh[ich] I have been obliged to confess'. Hoping to end the argument, Pitt hid behind his authority: 'I sh[oul]d not do my duty to you or to the Public or to myself, if I yielded to y[ou]r wishes or to any private feelings of my own. In one word, I ought not to remain in my present situation . . . if I were disposed to shrink from any part of my duty however painful'.[40]

By this time Chatham knew he was making no headway. He wrote of 'the pain wh[ich] y[ou]r Letter . . . has given me' and repeated his desire for a face-to-face interview, as 'I must meet my Colleagues in Office, & I must attend the King'.[41] Pitt reluctantly agreed. The brothers met on 4 December, but the meeting was inconclusive, and on the 5th Chatham begged for more time to consider. 'If it had been required of me, for the service of the Country, to sign my own death I sh[oul]d have taken as few minutes to consider as I have now done days,' he told Pitt, 'but when I reflect, that without attention, I may be signing my own disgrace, I know that all the feelings you possess, will not make you think the worse of me, if I pause again, & again in a situation, wh[ich] I never thought I w[oul]d have to look at, & for wh[ich] I am so little prepared'.[42] Knowing it was the one weapon left in his arsenal, he played on Pitt's sense of obligation to the head of the family:

> I am aware in our conversations I have said nothing of my personal feelings towards you, wh[ich] I can assure you arose only from finding myself unequal to doing it, as the recollection of the affection wh[ich] has uninterruptedly subsisted between us from our earliest days makes me feel the present circumstances doubly painful, to what w[oul]d have been the case if our connexion, of however old a date, had been purely political. I will only add, that whatever may be my fate in life, I shall sincerely wish for your honor & prosperity.[43]

The appeal did not work. Pitt, desperate to bring matters to a point, persuaded the King to press Chatham to receive the Privy Seal 'as a mark of . . . approbation of his past conduct'.[44] Faced with a direct order from his sovereign, Chatham had no choice.

He left an Admiralty battered and bruised by criticism. Much of this was due to his temperament, his lack of understanding of the naval profession, and his reliance on Middleton and the Navy and Admiralty Boards for advice. The war showed him his position was not invulnerable and he took his role as a wartime First Lord seriously, but he did not have the confidence to face a growing stagnation within the navy. He suffered from the fleet's inability to engage the French, and from a government strategy lacking in focus. The ambivalence of the victory of the Glorious First of June reflected all too well the pressures under which Chatham's Admiralty operated, and the shortcomings of its chief.

Chatham's biggest problem by far was his reduced standing in Cabinet. In peace, being Pitt's brother was an asset: officers and civil servants were reassured by the First Lord's ability to command the prime minister's attention. In war, Chatham was a liability. The less successful he was, the more censure focused on his occupying his position by virtue of his relationship to the prime minister:

48

Get a *birth* [*sic*] more secure for yourself and the crew,
Where the wages are high, and there's *nothing to do*;
For where *nothing's to do*, you'll perhaps be called wise,
And remain – 'till your brother's official demise.[45]

Instead of removing Chatham, Pitt chose to exercise more control. Chatham thereby retained his office and nominal importance, but (as he was himself well aware) he lost his main asset as First Lord of the Admiralty: his ability to argue the navy's case at the highest levels. By the time Pitt removed him in December 1794, Chatham's impotence, not his incompetence, had left the deepest mark.

The timing of Chatham's demotion reinforced the impression that he was dead in the water. He was painfully aware that removing him after a well-publicised victory, a few months after a major Cabinet reshuffle, at a time when there was no pressing strategic need for change, did not look good. Stung by over a year of buffeting in the press, his pride exploded into anger. He was affable and easy-going most of the time, but, when he felt himself injured, he held onto his grudge. In this case the betrayal came from his own brother, and the fact Pitt had been pressured into his decision by Dundas only made matters worse. It took Chatham years to forgive; and he never forgot.

Chapter 5

'He Can Never Set It Right'
1795–1801

Chatham knew his drop from Admiralty to Privy Seal would never be interpreted as anything but a vote of no confidence. 'The situation in which this arrangement puts me, is perhaps the most distressing in which any man was ever placed,' he wrote to his friend Camden.[1] Pitt's protestations of regret and affection meant little when he had forced Chatham to trade his reputation for government stability. Chatham's worst fears for his public standing were swiftly realised. On 7 January 1795 the opposition took the opportunity of the routine voting of military supplies to open their campaign against him. As Chatham had expected, Fox, Sheridan and others simply concluded his dismissal was an overdue recognition of incompetence.

To Chatham's dismay his colleagues, distracted by military disasters in Flanders, the furore over the continued suspension of habeas corpus and the failure of the treason trials against reformist radicals, did little to contradict this. Hamstrung by the closeness of their relationship, Pitt refused to defend his brother. He left the speechifying to Dundas, the man immediately responsible for Chatham's removal. Unsurprisingly, Dundas barely touched on the injured character of the former First Lord and focused on vindicating government naval strategy. All he said on Chatham's account was to 'defy any man breathing to say there had been a fault in any one part of the naval exertions of this Country'.[2] It was not exactly the world's most robust defence.

Chatham had suspected this might happen, and had made sure to recruit some professional naval men to his cause. His main support fell on the shoulders of two backbenchers, Captain George Berkeley and Admiral Alan Gardner. Berkeley's case was undermined by friendship with Chatham, and by Fox's forcing him to admit he owed his commission to the former First Lord. Gardner, a Lord of the Admiralty who knew Chatham's work habits well, argued more cogently. He gave his professional opinion that Chatham had done his duty, and well. Significantly, he concluded by demanding an official inquiry to rebut accusations of negligence: 'Nothing, he was assured, would give the Noble Lord greater pleasure, than an enquiry into his public conduct'.[3]

These words came directly from Chatham himself, and he was feverishly gathering evidence for such an inquiry. He collected statistics of mercantile insurance premiums as evidence that British convoys were not as vulnerable as the opposition alleged, and composed long memoranda detailing his department's arrangements for balancing home defence with active operations against the French fleet.[4] He compiled such detailed notes during the March 1795 Lords debate on the state of the nation, led by oppositionist Lord Guilford, that he must have had thoughts of answering the accusations launched against the naval conduct of the war, either by speaking himself or (more likely) putting his words in the mouth of another. 'The Navy itself perfectly satisfied,' he fulminated. '. . . The system of Opposition to disgust the Country with ye war, to raise of course discontent on ye subject of ye Navy'. He robustly – if over confidently – defended his record protecting trade: 'All our Convoys have returned safe. *Not one capture* with convoy.'[5]

Despite all these preparations, Chatham did nothing. Apart from Berkeley and Gardner, nobody spoke on his behalf; nothing was published in his defence. If his intention had been to make a public fuss, he was almost certainly pressured into changing his mind. His defence relied on incriminating Dundas, and this made any attempt to exculpate himself potentially embarrassing for Pitt. In private, Chatham did not stop justifying the strategic decisions made on his watch. His plans, he argued with increasing desperation, had been thwarted at every turn, his hands comprehensively tied by the Home and War Departments:

> At ye beginning of ye war, Adm[ira]l Gardner sent to ye West Indies . . . Mr Dundas pressed it . . . Expedition as early as September in great force to ye West Indies (where ye Enemy had none . . .) . . . The detention of our Naval Force in ye West Indies after our expedition had succeeded on account of our want of Troops . . . Opportunity lost of beating the French Fleet by ye same Influence . . . General Obstruction to ye Naval Service.[6]

Diverting ships from the Mediterranean, where the enemy was found in force, to the West Indies had not been Chatham's choice, but he had been constantly overridden by the Cabinet and by Dundas in particular.[7] He had a point, but making it public would stab at the heart of Pitt's illusion of Cabinet unity, the very thing Chatham had been sacrificed to safeguard. In any case, an inquiry would change nothing. Chatham's demotion would have happened sooner or later anyway, 'for the voice of the publick was against him, and that is reason enough'.[8]

In public, Chatham tamely swallowed his humiliation. In private, the story was very different. Chatham's fury at Pitt's treatment of him was painfully obvious to all. He spent most of the summer and autumn sulking at Cheveley and, although he and Pitt maintained a cold, stilted correspondence, they made sure not to overlap their summer visits to their mother. Nor did time help. While Chatham seethed openly, Pitt, typically, seemed to 'forg[e]t what has passed', an affected insouciance that failed to mend any fences.[9] When Lord Camden, recently appointed Lord Lieutenant of Ireland, made a tentative attempt at mediation, Chatham reacted violently:

> I never had a full and decided conversation, with my Brother . . . because he has very cautiously and constantly avoided it. . . . I am sorry I cannot agree with you, in looking forward to it, with a prospect of finding in it much relief or satisfaction. It may be a little better or a little worse, but that is all, for the mischief done me, is irreparable, and tho' my Brother, whenever he gives himself time to reflect, must (if he possesses any of the feelings which I always believed him to have) regret the step into which he was surprised, he can never set it right.[10]

Eighteen months on, the rift looked permanent.

In the end it was Pitt, not Chatham, who made the first overt step towards rapprochement. Lord Mansfield, who held the Lord Presidency of the Council, died in September 1796, and Pitt persuaded the King to offer the resulting vacancy to Chatham. The Lord President of the Council was a highly important Cabinet member, with the prestige of chairing Privy Council meetings and managing all Privy Council business. It was not as active a position as First Lord of the Admiralty, but it was several steps up from the Privy Seal in salary and significance. Chatham was not fooled by the King's offer, knowing very well whose idea it was. He toyed with rejecting it, as, 'having a great deal of uninteresting business attached to it, [it] is not perhaps . . . a much more desirable office than my present one'; but he was as sick as Pitt was with the stand-off, and agreed to accept what was clearly intended as an olive branch. Still, although promotion 'certainly afforded some relief to a wounded mind', Chatham was quick to point out his acceptance of it did not erase what had happened: 'The past, I can never bear to think of'.[11]

For now, Chatham kept a tight lid on his rancour. He visited Pitt at Holwood for the first time in two years, and it looked like things were returning to normal. 'It is very pleasant to see Lord Chatham quite happy, & in a situation which becomes him,' Lord Mornington told Camden with undisguised relief. '. . . All the disagreeable appearances between him & Pitt are quite over'.[12] But although Chatham agreed to pretend all was well, beneath the surface nothing had changed. December 1794 left deep scars. For the rest of his life he remained suspicious of colleagues, alert to challenges and quick to take offence. Lord Bathurst, more perceptive than Mornington, thought that although Chatham and Pitt were 'less uncomfortable together than they were', Chatham had 'recover'd his Spirits; but not his humour'.[13]

In reality, the brothers' relationship had been fatally undermined, and this was the most devastating effect of Chatham's humiliation. Although they continued to sign themselves off 'affectionately', this owed more to convention than genuine feeling. There was a marked lack of empathy between them, as though they were no longer comfortable sharing emotion. When rumours spread in December 1796 that Pitt was to wed, Chatham was sardonic: 'I cannot conceive what cou'd induce Bathurst, to write you word, *seriously*, that my Brother was to marry Miss Eden. I do not believe a word of it'.[14] Similarly, when their brother-in-law Edward James Eliot died suddenly in September 1797, Chatham was amazed at how quickly Pitt recovered from losing one of his closest friends:

My Brother was, as you will naturally suppose, much afflicted at the loss we have sustained. I am happy however in being able to tell you, that he is much better in health than when you saw him. . . . He dined here on Friday and Lady Chatham and I both thought him astonishingly mended in so short a time.[15]

Chatham ought to have had a special insight into his brother's state of mind, but on the contrary he was entirely unaware of what was happening in Pitt's life. As friendly as they pretended to be, neither brother trusted the other again, with confidences, emotional insights or anything else.

Pitt and Chatham's brotherly tension was undoubtedly deepened by the gloomy international scene. Reduced to the purely ceremonial role of Lord Privy Seal, Chatham could only watch helplessly as the war lurched from disaster to disaster. Between 1795 and 1797 several of Britain's allies, including Prussia, Spain and Austria, made separate treaties with France. The more diplomatically isolated Britain became, the greater the prospect of a French invasion. Accordingly, 1797 opened with news that one had been attempted in Ireland, always a hotbed of unrest due to its strong divisions between Protestant and Catholic, and rich and poor. Only bad weather prevented a landing. A few weeks after this narrow squeak, the French actually landed in Wales. The invasion was tiny and abortive – the invaders were quickly rounded up by the militia – but the impact on British morale was devastating, and a run on the banks nearly tipped the country into bankruptcy. For the first time Pitt faced a serious lack of confidence from the merchants and country gentlemen who usually supported him. By the end of April the King had received 26 petitions for a change of ministry.

This atmosphere of political uncertainty had a strong effect on Chatham. Only a year or two previously he would have provided Pitt with unquestioning support; in the wake of December 1794, and with the war going so badly, he had few qualms about expressing his disapproval of Pitt's war policy. In the summer of 1797, when the Cabinet discussed making peace with France, Chatham disagreed with Pitt's pacifist line. One thing kept him from causing an open fuss by resigning, and it wasn't the desire to show a united front for his brother's sake: 'I really think we cou'd not withdraw consistently with our duty . . . In my conscience I believe the times so critical, that things hang together only by a thread, and that the relaxation only of a week . . . wou'd absolutely endanger the very existence of ye Monarchy and of the Country'.[16]

Chatham's emphasis on the King betrayed a significant shift in his primary allegiance. Whereas before 1794 he had often spoken of wishing to conform to his brother's wishes, after 1794 he aligned his opinions with those of the court, allowing the King to sway him when he had no strong opinion. He would never have blocked government-sponsored measures, but he was becoming a pro-court representative within the Cabinet, masked by his name and relationship with the prime minister. Pitt never openly expressed his anxiety that Chatham might follow the court line on a major government issue, but Dundas later hinted that Chatham had always trusted 'too much to mere Court favour and protection . . . Many times I have heard his Brother warn him that such an Idea was not one to be acted upon by any Publick Man'.[17]

Pitt was not the only one to have noticed Chatham's unquestioning loyalty to the person, as well as the institution, of the King. George III, too, was grateful for Chatham's willingness to accommodate his opinions and wishes. Chatham and his wife had been actively and prominently involved in court life since Chatham's appointment to the Admiralty, and there could be no doubt which of the two Pitt brothers the King preferred. Chatham's presence was personally requested for weekend visits to Windsor; the Queen sent Chatham cures for his headaches; the Princesses sought fashion advice from Lady Chatham; and the royal correspondence was full of flattering expressions of admiration and friendship.[18] The King openly professed 'the warmest affection' for Chatham, who became a master at playing his side of the courtly game.[19] Upon being given the Governorship of Plymouth in 1805, he told the King 'He shou'd not do justice to the feelings nearest his heart, were he not to assure Your Majesty that his most sensible gratification must be derived from indulging the hope that he may ascribe this mark of Your Majesty's favour to your gracious acceptance of his affectionate zeal and unalterable attachment and devotion to Your Majesty.' The King replied that 'everything that ever comes from him breathes the sentiments His Majesty has ever found rooted in the Earl of Chatham's breast'.[20]

Chatham knew what he was doing. In consolidating his connection with the court, he demonstrated his open dissatisfaction at his political redundancy. He never actually opposed government policy, but his lack of a concrete role made him unpredictable and, in Lord Bathurst's words, 'a great *frondeur* [malcontent]'.[21] It brought out a streak of pettiness in his nature; he seemed, a friend noted, 'ready to agree to whatever is said against the Admiralty'.[22] Chatham gleefully corresponded with aggrieved former colleagues Middleton and Gardner, both of whom lost their Admiralty Board seats within months of Chatham's departure. He continued keeping statistics on naval deployment, acidly noting perceived injustices and deficiencies in the Mediterranean, his favourite arena, which Spencer 'had abandoned'.[23] In Chatham's opinion, Spencer's laxity had obvious consequences. Between April and June 1797, the British navy mutinied at Spithead and the Nore. Chatham could hardly conceal his disgust: 'I have been almost overpowered by . . . the situation of our Navy. The Spirit of the Times has doubtless principally contributed to what has happened but the unfortunate management not a little. I cannot bear to think of it.'[24] There was no hint of acknowledgment that the Navy's difficulties might have gone on far longer than Spencer had been at the helm.

One wonders how Chatham would have reacted to the mutinies had he still been at the Admiralty in April 1797. If his response to the 1798 Irish rebellion is any indication, the answer is 'harshly':

> I am perfectly clear that there is no other salvation for Ireland, but crushing by force, a desperate faction acting in concert with a foreign enemy, and that all idea of concessions at this period wou'd be fatal to ye existing Government in Ireland and to the connexion between the two Countries . . . I see none that cou'd be made that must not inevitably lead to all the confusion and mischief of Parliamentary Reform.[25]

Ireland had long suffered from a toxic combination of poverty, religious sectarianism and political corruption. Open rebellion in 1798 was quickly and viciously suppressed, but widespread disaffection remained long after the revolt was over. In September 1799, a full fifteen months after the rebellion, *The Times* still feared renewed hostilities, and martial law remained in force in Waterford and Tipperary.[26] Pitt and his colleagues, particularly Dundas and Lord Grenville, the Foreign Secretary, were convinced of the need to bring Ireland closer under British control to prevent future trouble: 'The only remedy is union – union – union'.[27] Two years of political cajoling and lavish bribery later, the Irish Houses of Parliament were persuaded to vote themselves out of existence and on 1 January 1801 the United Kingdom of Great Britain and Ireland came into being.

Chatham had a long-standing interest in Irish affairs. Three of his closest friends (the 4th Duke of Rutland, the 10th Earl of Westmorland and the 2nd Earl of Camden) had been Lords Lieutenant. Partly from correspondence with them and partly from personal interest, by 1798 Chatham had become something of an expert on the sister island. He took a prominent role in the House of Lords when the Irish union was discussed, chairing joint Commons and Lords committees and reporting back on them to the House of Lords (possibly the only time he ever spoke in Parliament).[28] For a while it appeared Ireland might give new purpose to Chatham's derailed political career, and Pitt, encouraged by Camden, seriously considered sending his brother there as Lord Lieutenant.[29] Chatham, however, was not over-enthusiastic. He much preferred Pitt's second idea, which was to send him to Ireland as military Commander-in-Chief, but this plan foundered when the King objected to an arrangement that would require removing at least four senior generals from the Irish staff.[30]

The plan to make Chatham Ireland's Commander-in-Chief tied in with a fresh direction in Chatham's career. Rather than focus on politics, in which his damaged reputation limited his prospects, Chatham had decided to return to the army. In truth he had never properly left. He had not served since 1783, but seniority had propelled him up the ranks. In 1793 he had been promoted to colonel in a general brevet (the promotion of all officers of a certain seniority in one go), and a further general brevet in 1795 bumped him up to major general. He spent the autumn and winter of 1798–9 at Colchester on the staff of Sir William Howe in the Eastern District, reacquainting himself with the profession he had more or less abandoned for fifteen years.

Chatham's return to the army coincided with an improvement in Continental circumstances. Over late 1798 and early 1799 Lord Grenville's Foreign Office worked hard to persuade Austria and Russia into a new coalition. While the main fighting would take place in Italy and Switzerland, Britain and Russia agreed to open a joint second front in North Holland to overturn the puppet Batavian Republic and re-establish the exiled House of Orange.[31] Chatham was given command of the Seventh Brigade in the expeditionary force sent to Holland, comprising about 4,000 men from the 4th and the 31st Foot. Both these regiments were skeletons made up to full strength by healthy drafts from the militia. The 4th received more than 2,700 militia recruits, and was divided into 3 battalions; the 31st received 955.[32] In terms of experience, this 'militia brigade' perfectly matched their commander. Chatham had never campaigned before, and as he gathered his forces on Barham Downs, with comfortable headquarters at Bifrons House, he had little idea of what lay before him. Across the sea in Holland, 20,000 British troops were making their way slowly down the Helder peninsula towards Amsterdam. Chatham and his troops sailed to join them on 10 September with the Duke of York, appointed Commander-in-Chief of the Allied forces. They, and their Russian allies, reached headquarters at the village of Schagerbrug around the middle of the month, having been delayed by poor weather.[33]

The poor weather continued throughout the campaign. Chatham bore increasingly frustrated witness to this, as well as to the deterioration of relations between the British and Russians. The latter were far too foreign for their allies, who considered them 'repulsive and ferocious'.[34] The situation went from tense to downright hostile after the first major joint assault on the enemy on 19 September. The Russians, under the command of General Hermann, started marching earlier than anyone else – 'for no reason, apparently, except their own caprice,' wrote Sir John Fortescue, bitingly, but more probably due to the failure of York's high command to specify a starting time.[35] Hermann discovered the French at dawn, long before any British support reached him. After fierce fighting the Russians were driven back into the village of Schoorl, trapped between the French in the plains and towering, 200ft - high sandhills behind. The Russians suffered nearly 3,000 casualties, and Hermann and his second-in-command, Chercekov, were captured.[36] The British hardly got a chance to engage and Chatham never saw any fighting. Despite this, he shared the general British opinion that the defeat 'may fairly be attributed to the misconduct of the Russian General and the Russian Troops'.[37] The Russians had a different opinion, and the only result of the battle was a complete loss of goodwill between the two allied forces.

Heavy rain delayed further operations. 'The weather has been much against us,' Chatham told Pitt. 'Constant storms of wind and heavy rain, which has broke [sic] up ye roads terribly'.[38] Luckily, at the beginning of October the weather improved, and the Duke of York began planning another assault. One of the conditions imposed upon him by the British Cabinet, in order to reconcile the Russians to a British commander-in-chief and prevent the disasters that had plagued the Flanders campaigns, was to require York to consult a 'Council of War' consisting of the highest-ranking British and Russian generals. These included Sir David Dundas, Sir Ralph Abercromby, Sir James Pulteney and Hermann's replacement, General Essen. For some reason Chatham, although only an inexperienced major general, was added, presumably as government spokesman.[39] At least one fellow council member was taken aback. Abercromby admitted Chatham was 'most sensible', but thought his performance suffered from his inexperience: 'He has not had the time nor the habits of the others' of his rank.[40] Still, Chatham's appointment to the Council meant he was probably present when York decided to press on towards Bergen.

The battle took place on 2 October. Chatham's brigade was, this time, prominently involved in the fighting, which strongly pointed up the terrain difficulties facing the Allies. The Helder peninsula was criss-crossed with dykes and canals and fringed with enormous sandhills along the coast. Marching in formation across the sand was difficult, and maintaining communications almost impossible. Chatham's brigade was in reserve in the plains behind Schoorl, ordered to cover the Russian attack on the Dutch lines behind the Zijpe Canal at Schoorldam, clear the main roads and sandhills, and support a Russian assault on Bergen.[41] Again, miscommunication meant this plan rapidly fell to pieces. While Abercromby assaulted Egmont-op-Zee and Dundas pressed the advantage in the sandhills, Sir Eyre Coote, commanding the Third Brigade, became over extended along the heights above Schoorl.[42] The Russians were closest to assist, but, in Coote's words, 'they all lay down, officers and all, and declared they had no more ammunition'.[43] Chatham's brigade was ordered up into the dunes to do the Russians' work for them. He 'very much distinguished' himself, sending the 31st to flush the enemy from the heights and extending Coote's line with the 4th, a movement which, as the Duke of York reported in his official dispatch, 'was admirably executed'.[44] Together Chatham and Coote marched briskly across the beech-studded expanse of the Schoorl heights, forcing the enemy back up a steep hill and capturing a battery. By dusk they had secured the road between Schoorl and Bergen and awaited orders to advance.[45]

The orders never came. The fighting had been strenuous on the sandy ground, the troops were exhausted and the rain resumed overnight, making it difficult for the Allies to consolidate their advantage. Supply was also an issue. Despite predictions that the inhabitants would rise gleefully in support of the House of Orange, the Allies had encountered little but apathy, and even veiled hostility. The locals were disinclined to share provisions, so supplies came from the British fleet still moored off the Helder, several dozen miles from the new Allied headquarters at Alkmaar along boggy roads. The French and Dutch, by contrast, though forced back on Beverwijk, were much closer to their supply base.[46] Under the circumstances the Duke of York hesitated, and once again consulted his Council of War.

This time Chatham had no share in the planning. His brigade remained in the sandhills, tentless and exposed to the elements. He was not much enjoying his first campaign experience. 'I have had great fatigue, having passed the last two nights on the top of the sand hills without any cover whatever,' he complained to his mother. On the 3rd he was sent to reinforce Abercromby's column at Egmont-op-Zee, while the Russians advanced to nearby Egmont-op-Hoef and Coote's brigade entered Bergen.[47] Three days later, the Duke of York ordered another push to move the French back from their new front at Beverwijk. The plan was to take the French outposts of Akersloot, Limmen and Bakkum and then pause to reassess the situation, but the Russians chased the enemy to the town of Castricum, which they believed to be undefended. This turned out to be incorrect, and within hours a manoeuvre intended to move the Allied lines into a more favourable position turned into a lengthy, and extremely bloody, engagement.[48] The French fought fiercely, and before the battle ended, in the darkness of night, the British had been forced back across the broad, dangerous network of sandhills separating the towns of Castricum and Egmont-op-Zee.

The battle for Castricum took everyone by surprise. It was a Sunday, and many soldiers were at church when news of the fighting arrived. About noon it began to rain so heavily it was impossible to see far beyond Alkmaar's curtain wall.[49] One of York's aides, Colonel Bunbury, 'was carried up and perched on the top of the tall steeple of Alkmaar, with a spying-glass, to try to ascertain . . . what was the direction and where were the main points of the fight. But all was confusion'.[50] If the Duke of York had no idea what was going on, the divisions in the field, caught on the hop, were even worse off. Chatham, still attached to Abercromby's division at Egmont, was heavily involved in the fiercest fighting at the gates of Castricum in support of the Russian retreat.[51] His brigade suffered heavily because of its exposed position. The 4th alone, which 'principally sustained the shock of the enemy's horse', lost nearly 500 men killed, wounded and missing, nearly an eighth of the entire brigade, and an enormous 25 per cent of the total Allied casualties.[52] Possibly connected to the chaos experienced by the brigade as a direct result of encountering a cavalry charge, and confused by the rain and poor visibility, a significant portion of the 2nd and 3rd battalions of the 4th managed to get themselves captured by 'forc[ing] their way within the Enemy's Lines, without knowing at all where they were'.[53] The devastation may be deduced from the handwritten amendments to the 4th's entry in the Army List for 1799, and from the army extraordinaries for 1801, which recorded £1,081 9*s* 3*d* sent 'to the Earl of Chatham, for sundry Appointments, &c of the 4th Regiment of Foot, which were lost on Service in Holland in 1799' – nearly twice as much as amounts issued to other regiments in the same campaign.[54] Despite these heavy losses, Chatham was again very well spoken of in the official reports. He was himself wounded, although the circumstance did not appear in the dispatches, probably to stop the spread of rumours at home. He was struck by a spent musket ball, which bounced off his epaulette, 'forced away part of his coat and waistcoat' and left 'a great contusion on his shoulder'.[55]

Castricum effectively ended the Helder campaign. Although the British had technically achieved their objective of flushing the French and Dutch out of Beverwijk, the dreadful weather, the exhausted state of the troops, the extended lines of supply and the lateness of the season contributed to the Allied decision to cut losses and retreat. News, moreover, had arrived on 1 October of the Russian defeat at Zurich a few months previously. The Helder expedition, intended as a sideshow to distract from the Continental campaign, was now in danger of becoming France's main focus. The Allies accomplished the 30-mile retreat to Schagerbrug over the night of 7 October in the driving rain. Behind them, the French took less than 24 hours to resume possession of the lines they had recently been compelled to abandon.[56]

Once back in Schagerbrug, Chatham attended another Council called by the Duke of York to discuss Allied options. The situation was dire. On the 10th, 6,000 Dutch defeated Prince William of Gloucester at Winkel, opening the road to the British headquarters.[57] The rain, meanwhile, continued to fall: as Chatham remarked wearily to his brother, 'We have not hardly known [*sic*] what it is to be Dry for some time'.[58] Continuing the campaign was out of the question. The choices were to embark the troops under enemy fire, which would probably result in enormous casualties, or make terms. The Council opted for the latter on 18 October. The British and Russians were given 6 weeks to evacuate unmolested, in return for releasing 8,000 prisoners of war from England. Under the circumstances the terms were not overly harsh, perhaps because the

French were unaware the Allies only had three days of rations remaining.[59]

Chatham 'concurred entirely' with the Council of War in its advice to the Duke of York to retreat. As the ministerial representative on the Council of War, he was called on by Sir Ralph Abercromby to look over and approve the terms.[60] He disliked the 'condition imposed' by the enemy of releasing the French and Dutch prisoners of war, but, in a long, gloomy letter to Pitt, he recognised that York's back was against the wall. 'I cannot but feel much . . . for the Duke of York's situation,' he confessed, in defending his beleaguered Commander-in-Chief's decision 'to preserve . . . [the country's] only army'. It was a strikingly cold letter from one brother to another, which spoke, perhaps, as much for Chatham's reluctance to open up to Pitt as it did for his palpable disgust at the campaign's outcome. The only personal aspect of the letter came in three curt words, added almost as an afterthought: 'I continue well'.[61]

On 22 October the troops re-embarked at Nieuwe Diep, and on the 30th Chatham landed at Yarmouth after a stormy journey.[62] His first foray into Continental warfare had been an unmitigated disaster: the expedition had sailed too late, and done nothing but deepen the distrust between Britain and Russia. Hounded by the French in Switzerland, and deeply disgruntled by the slights offered to his generals in the Helder, the Russian Emperor soon withdrew from the coalition. Within the year Russia was one of the founders of an 'Armed Neutrality' of Baltic States (Russia, Denmark, Sweden and Prussia) designed to protect their trade against incursions from British warships, and flirting with an alliance with France.[63] At a more personal level, Chatham suspected that the Helder would be his last campaign for some time. The reaction of Pitt's friends and colleagues to Chatham's near-miss at Castricum was one of frank horror. With the collapse of its war aims and the ongoing business of Ireland, the government was in quite enough trouble without losing Pitt to the House of Lords. 'Depend upon it,' Dundas told Pitt, 'the general sentiment of the public, and the opinions of your most intimate and best friends, will concur . . . in reprobating the idea of Lord Chatham's going at present upon any foreign Service, and the King will be under the necessity of interposing to prevent it'.[64] As had happened twenty-four years previously, Chatham was forced to subordinate his personal wishes to those of his family – although at least this time he was allowed to keep his commission.

Without the freedom to serve abroad, Chatham's military career was considerably stunted. He swallowed his disappointment and returned to his ceremonial duties as though nothing had happened, commanding a division in the Duke of York's encampment at Swinley Down and exchanging campaign hardships for royal parades. Meanwhile, behind his back, his colleagues wondered what to do with him. Shortly after Chatham returned from the Helder, his former antagonist Dundas made a most surprising suggestion. Desperate to resign the thankless post of Secretary of State and knowing Chatham would not serve abroad again in Pitt's lifetime, Dundas wrote to Pitt with a solution he thought would please everybody. He proposed to restrict himself to the India Board and Treasurership of the Navy, and leave the business of the War Office to Chatham:

> By doing the Duties of the Situation which I have suggested, he in truth, commits himself more closely with Military Ideas and habits, than in any other Situation. His Income will be adequate to the Expences of his Situation, while the War continues, and, as in the meantime he will be going forward in the Profession of the Army, it is more probable than otherwise, that before that time (Peace) his Military Emoluments will be superior to any he enjoys as President of the Council.

Dundas had not forgotten the circumstances under which he had pressed for Chatham's removal from the Admiralty, and anticipated Pitt would remind him of them. He had an answer ready: 'You are certain, that this arrangement will be highly acceptable to the King, and as he [Chatham] will have constant opportunities of private intercourse with His Majesty, many things disagreeable in the conduct of business will be prevented, or immediately remedied'.[65]

Chatham had lost the Admiralty five years previously because of Dundas. Dundas was no longer an obstacle to his holding significant office, but Chatham probably never even found out about his old enemy's change of heart. Like Chatham, Pitt had never recovered from the experience of 1794. Trusting his brother with significant wartime responsibility had ended badly once, and Pitt's response to Dundas showed he was unlikely to make the same gamble ever again:

The Arrangement which you propose . . . is in the very first article of it, liable to such insuperable objections, that the Idea of it instead of furnishing an Argument in favor of the measure would strengthen tenfold all the other Arguments against it. You will believe I do not say this lightly, or without regret as to the Grounds on which my opinion is founded, but you must I am sure upon Reflection feel that they are just. Let me therefore entreat you for all our Sakes, to abandon wholly this Idea.[66]

Dundas, formerly responsible for Chatham's disgrace, found himself defending him to his own brother. 'I am really sorry my Proposition strikes you in the light it does,' he wrote. Chatham had learned his lesson:

Every Circumstance which occurred relative to your Brother leaving the Admiralty would now ensure perfect activity and exertion in another arduous Situation he might be called to. His talents for it are unquestionable, and if I am right in my belief that no symptoms of it would now appear, I say it without affectation of disparaging myself, he is under all Circumstances better calculated for it than the Person who now holds it.[67]

But Chatham's career stalled in his brother's shadow. There was no change in either his political or military position, and he was forced to make the best of his closely clipped wings.

This did not mean he was happy about the decline in his military prospects. He was forced to accept it, but he did not become a passive onlooker. Chatham took advantage of the Cabinet's unfocused war strategy to assert himself in an area where he – the only serving military member of the government save Cornwallis, who was in Ireland – could claim expertise. There was a three-way division between Dundas, who favoured colonial defence, Grenville, in favour of Continental intervention, and Windham, the Secretary at War, who preferred assisting the counter-revolution in France.[68] Pitt, distracted by the Irish question, domestic unrest and poor health, did little to control these bitter disagreements, and this lack of overall direction allowed Chatham an opening. In March 1800, the Cabinet decided to send 15,000 men to Minorca to cooperate with Austria in Italy. This last-minute proposal responded to immediate circumstances rather than to any long-term plan, and the Duke of York protested against the strain on Britain's overstretched forces. Chatham, like York, had no wish to see Britain's precious troops frittered away in badly planned sideshows like Dunkirk, Toulon and the Helder. The Minorca project involved cooperating with Austria or Russia: but Russia was in the process of pulling out of the coalition, and Austria was also wavering in her commitment to the alliance. Chatham therefore demanded an official discussion of York's objections, obliging Pitt to call another Cabinet which, after much debate, admitted the poor planning underpinning the Minorca expedition.[69]

Chatham's prominence in these Cabinet discussions, along with his return to military life and his keenness to serve, unexpectedly helped thaw relations between him and Dundas. The War Secretary had been feeling isolated in Cabinet, and, impressed by Chatham's professional arguments, jumped at the opportunity to acquire a knowledgeable and potentially influential ally. Experience had convinced Dundas the way to defeat France was not through Continental alliances but to wage economic war on her and her allies all over the world, in the West Indies, India, Egypt and even South America. He recognised Chatham agreed with abandoning the ad hoc approach of the 1790s for a grander, more structured strategy, and hoped to gain his Cabinet support, buttering him up by bombarding him with plans, letters and memoranda.[70]

Chatham was surprised and flattered by Dundas's willingness to share his thoughts, and the former enemies corresponded frequently over the spring and summer of 1800. This correspondence, however, soon showed Chatham that he and the Secretary of State were as far apart in opinion as ever. Dundas's 'blue-water' plans were too bold for Chatham, whose opposition to the Minorca expedition did not mean he was ready to abandon the conviction he had adopted while First Lord of the Admiralty of the Mediterranean's importance. He still hoped developments in Malta and Portugal might provide future opportunities there:

> ye opinion, which I had so strongly taken up, as to the best employment of our Force (with a view to every contingency) was certainly the result, of much reflexion, on the subject, and I must fairly own, I do not, as yet, see any reason to depart from it. At ye same time, I can assure you, that I shall come to the discussion of the proposed plan, whenever it may arise, perfectly open to conviction.[71]

As 'open' as Chatham was, Dundas failed to convince him. A separate peace between Austria and France seemed certain, and the ever cautious Chatham came down definitively against gambling on 'remote enterprize' when a French invasion seemed likely: 'Our *present* force, is *all* we have to trust to whether for peace or for war . . . [Even] the propriety of any attempts nearer home, must depend wholly on ye more or less well-grounded prospect of success'.[72] Reading such a letter, Dundas was doubtless glad his plans to elevate Chatham to the War Office had come to nothing.

* * *

As important as questions of long-term strategy seemed to be, Chatham's attention was almost immediately distracted from them by unexpected political developments. By the summer of 1800 Pitt was physically and mentally wrecked by Cabinet divisions, domestic troubles and the strain of implementing the Anglo-Irish Union. The Union had passed both the Irish and British parliaments, but Pitt was still undecided about how to deal with Ireland's predominantly Catholic population. Cornwallis, the Lord Lieutenant, had promised emancipation (extension of political participation to non-Anglicans) in return for Catholic support of the Union. Pitt faced the prospect of proposing an exceedingly divisive measure that did not have the unanimous support of the Cabinet and which was, most importantly of all, anathema to the King.[73]

Chatham spent the summer in close contact with the royal family, borrowing the royal lodge at Shrub's Hill, entertaining the King, Queen and Princesses for dinner, and conversing 'principally' with the King during evening walks on Windsor Terrace.[74] He was thus well aware of the King's opposition to removing the restrictions on the United Kingdom's Catholic population. Chatham's own views were ambivalent, but, as always, 'the inclination of his opinion was . . . of course favourable to his Majesty's view of the subject'.[75] Pitt, consequently, chose not to confide in his own brother, and Chatham left London in the autumn of 1800 under the impression Pitt had not 'in the least . . . made up his mind' about emancipation. In the new year disturbing rumours reached him that Pitt intended to force it through as a government measure. Chatham was 'a good deal perplexed what to do, as to staying here [with his regiment in Winchester], or coming up to town directly'. The fact he had not heard directly from Pitt worried him even more, knowing how unlikely his brother was to discuss a topic on which they disagreed: 'His silence is my only clue to his present opinion.'[76]

Chatham was too late. By the time he wrote this letter, Pitt's ministry no longer existed. On 25 January 1801 Pitt called a partial Cabinet, excluding well-known opponents of emancipation, and tried to make the informal gathering into a determination of action.[77] Word got out and reached the King, who fulminated publicly that he should 'look on every Man as my personal Enemy, who proposes that Question to me'.[78] On 31 January 1801, Pitt wrote a long letter to the King explaining his motivation in bringing forward Catholic relief. The Catholics had not been the British constitution's enemies for more than a generation: they had been replaced by the spirit of French revolutionary 'Jacobinism', and giving non-Anglicans a direct stake in the polity would guarantee their loyalty to it. Pitt hoped the King would consider the topic and change his mind, but, if not, wished 'to be released from a situation which he is conscious that . . . he could not continue to fill but with the greatest disadvantage'.[79] Perhaps Pitt had not expected the King to call his bluff, but his resignation was accepted. Pitt was succeeded by Henry Addington, a man considered by some as a professional-class upstart, but by others as a sensible man whose 11-year stint as Speaker of the Commons had earned him the respect of the backbenchers and country gentlemen.[80]

Chatham first learned of this from Pitt after the excitement had blown over. 'We have both had experience enough of times of difficulty not to be unprepared to encounter anything, however unexpected,' Pitt began. He explained he had not broached the topic sooner 'as you seemed from our last conversation to have no decided bias in your mind' – at best a naïve interpretation of Chatham's opinion.[81] Chatham could barely hide his frustration. If 'I cou'd . . . have contributed even to put off the extremity to which the agitation has led, I shou'd think I had done much,' he said, and recognised the deliberate nature of Pitt's silence: 'I consider myself as fortunate, in having avoided a discussion which cou'd only have been painful to me, in many respects'. Still, he recognised the delicacy of Pitt's position, and pledged to return to London as soon as possible.[82]

Pitt probably thought Chatham was hurrying to town to offer his brother his support. In fact, Chatham had not the slightest intention of following Pitt out of office. A day or so after the exchange with Pitt, Chatham wrote to Addington to lay his services at the new minister's disposal.[83] Chatham did not tell Pitt of his determination to stay on until 11 February, deliberately returning the compliment of failing to keep his brother in the loop.[84] Chatham's remaining surprised many when the news was made public, and several former colleagues, including Grenville, felt he should have retired with his brother.[85] 'If you can make anything out of all this, it is much more than I can,' Fox grumbled in February 1801, but Chatham probably felt his brother's resignation was his chance to show his political career did not depend on Pitt's goodwill.[86]

His commitment to remain certainly impressed the King, who correctly interpreted it as a declaration of allegiance. Not satisfied with verbal expressions of gratitude, he wanted to give Chatham a mark of recognition for his loyalty. Initially the King merely suggested Chatham take the lucrative sinecure of the Clerkship of the Pells.[87] But since the sinecure's incumbent was very much still alive, the King hit upon a better scheme. Knowing Lord Cornwallis, the Lord Lieutenant of Ireland, would probably resign with Pitt, the King wrote to Addington to suggest Chatham as a suitable successor.[88] Addington approved the suggestion in principle, and on the 18th the King officially offered Chatham the Lord Lieutenancy:

> The Manners, Integrity and Correct Line of Conduct of the Earl of Chatham certainly point Him out as the Person most proper for the Station; besides His having returned to His Military Profession, He as Lord Lieutenant must of course take the Supreme Command of the Troops stationed in Ireland, and the Commander-in-Chief only act under His Orders.[89]

Chatham was stunned, even though he had been considered for the Lord Lieutenancy before. The King thought he was making a splendid offer, but nobody yet knew the terms under which the Lord Lieutenant of Ireland would operate now that Ireland was part of the United Kingdom. Ireland's Catholics, disappointed of political relief, remained unhappy, and there were bound to be problems implementing the Union in a country still only three years from having rebelled. With all this in mind, Chatham had no hesitation in declining:

> Being firmly convinced, on considering all the circumstances of the present times, as well as on a review of the past, that he shou'd

be, of all others, the most unfit to advance (what must be always nearest his heart) Your Majesty's service, he presumes to hope that he cannot more strongly evince the sincerity of his attachment or the warmth of those sentiments which he must ever gratefully entertain towards Your Majesty, than by supplicating Your Majesty to permit him to decline a station to which Your Majesty's partiality has induced you to call him.[90]

Chatham had a point in blaming the King's 'partiality', but he could not mistake the significance of George III's taking such a personal interest at the same time as the King was writing to Pitt on what he believed to be the 'close' of his 'political career'.[91]

In contrast, Chatham's career was experiencing an unexpected renaissance. Unshackled from his brother's suspicious, restrictive influence, and basking in the King's favour, he and his wife were at the forefront of fashionable and political society, trading their house on Hyde Park Corner for one on St James's Square and hosting Cabinet meetings and dinners. Chatham did not have long to wait before he was offered an even better chance to restore his reputation. In the summer of 1801 Addington, about to open peace negotiations with France, sought to strengthen his government by bringing in Lord Pelham as Home Secretary and giving the Duke of Portland the Presidency of the Council. Chatham was moved to the Master-Generalship of the Ordnance, left vacant since May by Lord Cornwallis's resignation. The Master-Generalship was less prestigious than the Presidency of the Council, but it was a much more practical post. After 6 years of occupying posts with abstract duties, Chatham had returned to an office with real and vital impact. Pitt must have been horrified.

Chapter 6

Master-General of the Ordnance
1801–6

Chatham's well-meaning but haphazard period at the Admiralty seemed to indicate his unfitness for a post depending so strongly on interdepartmental communication. The previous Master-General of the Ordnance, Cornwallis, later lamented 'that so important a department should be placed in hands so incapable and improper'.[1] Retrospective assessments of Chatham's Ordnance have generally agreed that Cornwallis was right to worry. In the 1950s Richard Glover portrayed the Ordnance as sluggish, stagnating, even declining, under a Master-General who came very close to destroying his department at a crucial time, and his conclusions have been followed by most subsequent histories of the Napoleonic Wars.[2] Recent scholarship, however, points to the development of the Ordnance and its ability to meet the enormous expectations placed upon it during Chatham's Master-Generalship.[3] Departments were repartitioned, new arms depots created, fortifications improved and factories established – symptomatic of a reactive policy perhaps, but hardly signs of stagnation.

Chatham's new department was responsible for the manufacture, maintenance and issue of weapons, gunpowder and stores, as well as building and maintaining fortifications, batteries and other permanent works at home and abroad. It had depots at nearly every British base around the world, its own fleet of transports and employed nearly 900 people. It sponsored scientific experimentation for improving ammunition and explosives, engaged in mapping and surveying, and educated the 'scientific soldiers' in the Royal Artillery and Royal Engineers to a rigorous standard. Although strategy was decided by the Secretaries of State and the Admiralty, the Master-General was the Cabinet's main military adviser.[4] Chatham was in a position of influence with vast resources at his fingertips, although he had no direct control over their application.

The department consisted of the Master-General and the Board of Ordnance. The Board comprised of five officers: the Lieutenant General, Chatham's second-in-command; the Surveyor-General, responsible for the quality, storage and inspection of ammunition and stores; the Clerk of the Ordnance, who kept the accounts and copies of all commissions, contracts and other paperwork; the Principal Storekeeper, in charge of receiving and storing weapons at the Tower and main depots; and the Clerk of Deliveries, responsible for keeping records of all arms issues.[5] Each Board member headed his own department, and each department checked the activities of the others. This system made the Ordnance slow and bureaucratic. Military men in the field often found this command chain of Chinese whispers frustrating, but the Board's novel structure impressed Chatham, who felt that 'much more responsibility attaches . . . to the Heads of particular Departments, than could do to the Board collectively'.[6] Each officer was accountable to his colleagues, to the Board as a whole and to the Master-General, which theoretically increased efficiency.[7]

Chatham's duties as Master-General were less well defined.[8] Since the bulk of the Ordnance work passed through the Board, his post could be construed as an appointment with very few duties other than the dispensing of patronage. In practice, however, he was the ultimate Ordnance authority. The Board was explicitly subordinate to him, and his decision could override theirs. As the Duke of Wellington, a later Master-General, put it, 'The whole power of the Ordnance is, by his patent, vested in him, if he chooses to exercise it'.[9] Chatham was more moderate. He saw no reason to interfere more than necessary:

> During the arduous period I was at the Ordnance, and the very great increase of business consequently brought upon the Department, I found the Board fully competent to the discharge of all the functions appertaining to them; and the measures (as far as the Board was concerned) necessary to meet the exigencies of the Public Service, were conducted by them with great promptitude and ability.[10]

This easy-going attitude was typical of Chatham, but it did not mean Richard Glover was right to conclude he palmed all his tedious duties off onto the Board.[11] The looseness of the Master-General's role allowed him to devote time to his many other responsibilities, and his frequent absences from London were not a sign that he 'preferred to remain in the country potting pheasants'.[12] He was based in Chatham and Eastbourne in the Southern District until 1805, and from 1806 onwards he spent significant portions of the year in Colchester as Commander of the Eastern District. He was also Governor of Plymouth between 1805 and 1807, and of Jersey from 1807 onwards, although neither post occupied much (indeed any) of his time. Many of these positions overlapped, and Chatham's familiarity with the areas most likely to be affected by a French invasion helped inform the Ordnance's response to the threat.

The first eighteen months or so of Chatham's Ordnance tenure took place in peacetime, but with time he acquired a definite grasp of his department's importance. Peace preliminaries were signed in October 1801, and the definitive Treaty of Amiens was concluded in March 1802. Not everybody welcomed the suspension of hostilities: several of Chatham's former colleagues, including his cousin Lord Grenville, blamed Addington for what they saw as the surrender of nearly all Britain's hard-won wartime territory except for Trinidad, Ceylon and the Cape of Good Hope. Chatham stood by his government on peace, although he had opposed negotiation in the past and his private opinion on the subject was unclear. If he retained any doubts he hid them well, impressing the French ambassador with his politeness and grasp of the issues in question.[13] Lady Chatham, on the other hand, could hardly hide her relief at the suspension of hostilities (no doubt remembering what had happened the last time Chatham went campaigning). 'I'm no coward when needs must,' she wrote, 'but I believe I may as sincerely wish the Peace to last, as a friend to my Country, as I do as a Wife'.[14]

Lady Chatham's wish did not come true. War broke out again in May 1803, in part over Napoleon's continued encroachments in Switzerland and Britain's refusal to evacuate Malta.[15] Despite Addington's efforts to negotiate alliances with Austria and Russia, treaties were not signed with the Continental powers till after he fell in 1804 and Pitt returned to power. This diplomatic isolation contributed to Britain's inability to engage in sustained Continental warfare for some years, and Chatham's Ordnance was initially concerned with the threat of French invasion. This was at its height between 1803 and 1805. Faced with Napoleon's *armée d'Angleterre* ostentatiously camped on the Boulogne coast, Addington's government engaged in a drive to raise a large auxiliary force and strengthen the coastline.

This entailed a sharp, and unexpectedly heavy, increase in Chatham's burden. At the opening of hostilities in 1803 there were just under 280,000 muskets in store, more than 4 times the number available in 1793 and amply sufficient to arm Britain's 100,000 soldiers and 60,000 militiamen.[16] But the government had reckoned without the overwhelming response to a June 1803 circular calling on the counties to raise as many civilian volunteers as possible to fight invasion. By the end of the year, even after belated attempts to limit offers of service, there were 380,000 volunteers on the Home Office's lists expecting to be trained and armed by government.[17] The government also raised a new auxiliary body of 40,000 men to supplement army recruitment known as the Army of Reserve, replaced in 1804 by the 'Additional Force' (and later still by Castlereagh's 'Local Militia'). By 1 January 1805, counting militia, volunteers, regulars and other auxiliaries, there were over 590,000 men for the Ordnance to arm.[18]

By autumn 1803 the Home Office was forwarding increasingly urgent demands for weapons from volunteer corps all over the country. Chatham's slow response to this small arms shortage has been criticised, but the Ordnance was operating within an established tender process under very extraordinary conditions. Thanks to stopgap efforts such as paying volunteer companies to arm themselves or sourcing weapons from abroad (both designed as emergency expedients) the Ordnance was ultimately able to step up musket production to meet the massive increase in demand. By 9 March 1804, although several inland volunteer societies were still drilling with pikes, the Ordnance had managed to arm 213,903 men, rather more than half of the 380,000 raised at their peak. The number of muskets received by the Tower quadrupled in 1804 and remained at that level until 1808 when it jumped again following the opening of a government-sponsored factory in Lewisham.[19]

Chatham was fond of playing up the difficulties facing his department. Towards the end of his tenure, for example, he warned the Foreign Secretary that, 'with the utmost exertions that can be made, (and greater [exertions] cannot [be made] than have already) It will be matter of much anxiety and no small difficulty to keep pace with ye exigencies of our own Service in every part of the World'.[20] Nevertheless, that summer

(1809) he provided enough weapons for British troops in Portugal, for his own expedition to Walcheren, for insurgents in North Germany and for arming Britain's Spanish and Portuguese allies. By 1815, 350,000 small arms had been issued to the regulars, 59,405 to the militia, 151,969 to the Local Militia, 307,588 to the by then defunct Volunteers and 215,233 to the navy. These numbers were collated to prove the ruinous expense of the war, but they also testified to the Ordnance's successful efforts to adapt to new pressures – a process that had begun under Chatham's watch.[21]

While Chatham and his department struggled to arm as much of the nation as possible, the government was planning to fortify the coasts most threatened by France. The result was a significant change in the character of the south-eastern coast. Martello, or round, towers were constructed at regular intervals along the coasts of Essex, Kent and East Sussex, and later Ireland. There were plans for 86 towers (74 eventually built) between Folkestone and Seaford.[22] The Royal Military Canal was planned and begun in the Romney Marshes, 28 miles of zig-zagging waterway defended by dykes running in parallel.[23] Dover's Western Heights, and the communication lines at Chatham, were strengthened and the dockyards and magazines at Plymouth, Portsmouth and Cork reinforced and refortified. New artillery depots were set up at Warley, Sittingbourne, Sevenoaks and Sutton, and most notably at Weedon Bec, considered one of the furthest points from the coast.[24]

Chatham was much more involved in the decision-making over fortifications than he had been in small arms production, the detail of which fell mostly to the Ordnance Board. He was not only the military authority in the Ordnance Department; his appointments in the Southern and Eastern Districts gave him an on-the-spot appreciation of what was required in a field rife with divided responsibility. His department shared control over fortifications with the War Office, the Commander-in-Chief's Office and the Barrack Office, among others. 'Permanent' works of masonry were carried out almost entirely under Ordnance supervision, but temporary 'Fieldworks' (to strengthen the position of an army in the field or defend a stronghold from attack) fell under the remit of the Commander-in-Chief.[25] Because of this confusing conflict of interest, Chatham was not shy about declaring himself the ultimate power in *all* fortification matters:

> If the Works ... were to be *permanent* they cou'd only be undertaken by the Ordnance, when other Services wou'd permit; but if intended in ye first instance to be executed as Field Works, and to be converted afterwards into *Permanent* Works, they must equally come to me, in order that the Opinion of the Engineers might be taken upon them. And indeed strictly speaking all *Field* Works merely, shou'd be communicated to me, before the King's Pleasure is signified for their execution to the C[ommander] in C[hief], as involving great demands for Men, Guns, Stores &c &c &c.[26]

This was not merely departmental 'jealousy'. To save time and money, Chatham preferred to be kept informed of what was being done that might involve his engineers, surveyors and artillerists. This lesson had been learnt the hard way. Both Dover's Western Heights and Chatham's regenerated Lines began as fieldworks, but the earthworks collapsed and had to be converted to brick, as a result of which Ordnance involvement escalated rapidly and expensively.[27]

Despite this clear interest in fortifications, Chatham has been taken severely to task by historians for neglecting them. S.G.P. Ward and Richard Glover have blamed his notorious laziness for his reluctance to build Martello towers and his preference for more 'conventional' defence expedients such as maintaining existing sea batteries. Glover has even accused Chatham of deliberately blocking the towers because he felt the Commander-in-Chief's enthusiasm for them trespassed on his authority.[28] The implication is that Chatham, not the Commander-in-Chief, should have originated the proposal of towers, and that he obscured his embarrassment at not having done so by kicking up a fuss over trivialities. It is certainly true the towers were a long time building, and that Chatham was partly responsible for this, but to blame his laziness for his reluctance to undertake the work is both unfair and misleading.

Martello towers were first suggested in August 1803 by Colonel William Twiss, Commanding Engineer in the Southern District. Chatham instinctively disliked the idea of relying on a system of fortifications to repel a French invasion, and argued against Twiss's proposal. He was backed up in his opinion by the Committee of Engineers, which rejected the plan as impractical and instead suggested four 'circular batteries' to plug the gaps between existing defences. Unfortunately for Chatham,

Twiss's scheme found favour with General Dundas, the Southern District's commander, and the Duke of York, the army's Commander-in-Chief. Both men put pressure on Chatham to bring the expensive and resource-hungry plan to fruition. Rather than provoke controversy by arguing, Chatham's typical reaction to the problem was to ignore it. At first his tactic seemed to work, and in February 1804 he wrote, optimistically, that the necessity for the Martello towers was 'not so strongly felt at present by those who originally proposed it'.[29] But Twiss had not given up, and six months later he made a lengthy reconnaissance between Beachy Head and Dover and presented the government with a more detailed proposal for 59 towers. The project now caught the interest of the prime minister and, faced with a direct order to proceed from the top, Chatham had no choice.[30]

He had not changed his mind, and this unwelcome turn of events as a result of Twiss's 'hasty Journey along the Coast' profoundly annoyed him. He genuinely could not see the point of building fortifications for the sake of being seen to do something. He reminded Robert Morse, the sympathetic Inspector of Fortifications, that 'in most instances I have had the opportunity of personal inspection' of the District's defences as one of the highest-ranking generals on the Southern District staff, and still 'it is utterly impossible for me, without very detailed Reasons being given in support of it, to form any judgment of the propriety or necessity of [the system's] being carried into effect'. Despite this he gave Morse permission to source men and materials 'with the utmost dispatch', and suggested an order in which the towers might be built. Still, he clearly felt rushed into a decision from which he wished to distance himself as much as possible. Further details were for the government as a whole and not for the Ordnance to determine, he wrote, for 'I should not, without much more investigation, than the time will *now* permit, feel myself justified in ordering it'.[31]

Chatham's reluctance to begin building towers sooner was neither laziness nor jealousy: he simply did not agree with the principle behind them. He had two major reservations, apart from thinking they would merely duplicate the work of the existing sea batteries. The first was manpower. A total of 3,000 troops were required to garrison the new coastal defences, at a time when the government struggled to find enough men to field an army abroad.[32] Chatham had long been aware of a shortage of trained artillerists, who were easily lost and not so easily replaced.

How, then, were the new Martello towers to be manned? The Secretary of State for War suggested a second battalion of Artillerymen might be raised and used for the towers while in training, but Chatham disagreed, arguing that employing trainee Artillerymen so narrowly was no way to fit them for general duties later. His preference was to rely on the Veteran or Invalid battalions, who, 'being men who have seen service, might be relied on for an obstinate defence more than any other description of force'.[33] Chatham's idea was adopted: in Jersey and Guernsey, at least, towers were manned by a combination of the militia and two Invalid Companies of Artillery.[34]

Chatham's second objection was that the towers would interfere with other, in his opinion more important, work. 'I hope you bear in mind, that in getting materials for all these new Works, it will be necessary to reserve such a Supply as will enable us to proceed rapidly with completing the Works at Chatham,' he reminded General Morse. 'I fear a deficiency of Bricks is already felt there.'[35] This belief that the towers could never be anything more than an expensive distraction for his department was the main excuse Chatham gave the War Office in February 1804, when Lord Hobart wrote to find out why the original proposal submitted by the Duke of York six months previously had sunk without a trace. 'I lost no time in sending the same to the Inspector General of Fortifications,' Chatham replied, but 'other objects, upon which [the Committee of Engineers] were engaged, that appeared more immediately pressing' had taken priority. These were: strengthening Cork Harbour and Bantry Bay, where the French had previously attempted an invasion in 1796; improving the defences of the naval arsenal at Plymouth; and restoring the naval arsenal at Portsmouth. These measures had been recommended by the Commander-in-Chief himself, and Chatham could (and did) interpret this as permission to prioritise existing fortifications over building new, more expensive projects.[36] He certainly made no attempt to disguise his opinion that Martello towers 'must be a very secondary consideration' to the grand national concern of restoring existing fortifications.[37]

Chatham's opinion was based on sound, if conservative, military reasoning. He believed concentrating Britain's military power in easily defensible pockets of strength was the best response to an invasion. Plymouth and Portsmouth were his linchpin: restoring them ('this great, and in my judgment necessary work') would always take precedence over the coastal defences more generally, which, while Plymouth and

Portsmouth remained vulnerable, were little more than a distraction.[38] He was not alone in his distrust of novelty. A predecessor at the Ordnance, the Duke of Richmond, had also prioritised Portsmouth and Plymouth during his time as Master-General, and was delighted to find Chatham championing his old projects. Despite their chequered history, Richmond sent Chatham advice for transforming Portsmouth's forts and dockyards into a 'place of safety to which the Sovereign with the remains of His Army might retire and prevent any Force the Enemy might have, from at once over-running the whole Country'.[39] This was exactly what Chatham wanted to hear, and he never tried to keep his prejudices out of the decision-making process. The Ordnance Estimates show how much work went into fortifying Britain's great naval bases. Between 1805 and 1807, some of the largest sums in the Ordnance Extraordinary and Unprovided Expenses went to Chatham, Portsmouth and Plymouth, although the new Ordnance depots and Martello towers also made a sizeable dent in the budget.

Small wonder, then, that the Ordnance Estimates between 1803 and 1810 grew from £1.27 million to £5.31 million.[40] This was partly the effect of Chatham's being obliged to combine his traditional preferences with the experimental approach adopted by the government, which gave the impression of a lack of direction and control. While historians have accused Chatham of doing too little, his contemporaries reviewed these enormous sums and accused him of doing too much. The post-war Select Committee on Finance complained loudly about the vast amount of money spent on Ordnance services, apparently unchecked and unplanned. They firmly rejected the principle of a system of military fortifications, attacking Chatham's Ordnance by endorsing everything Chatham had been trying to say for years:

> A powerful fleet, and an unconquerable spirit pervading a numerous population, with the means of arming and training whatever proportion of that number may be required for any emergency, afford better security against foreign invasion, than can be derived from the most perfect system of lines and towers, which could be applied to every point of our extensive coast.[41]

Chatham cannot have appreciated the irony that his administration was being indicted for adopting the very measures he had tried so hard to resist.

The Select Committee's criticisms of Chatham's department were not all unfounded. The massive explosion in Ordnance spending was a symptom of the department's unfocused decision-making process. Although lessons were learned, the benefits of these became more obvious after Chatham left the Ordnance, when regular campaigning opportunities reopened on the Continent. A fundamental shake-up might have produced quicker results, but Chatham's record at the Admiralty showed he was perfectly happy leaving an existing system alone even if it cried out for reform. When asked in 1811 whether any change was necessary in the role of Master-General, Chatham characteristically replied he did 'not conceive that any alteration in the situation of the Master-General would be advisable; nor am I aware of any change in the formation of the Board, or in the conduct of the business in the higher branches of the Ordnance Department, that would be likely to produce any advantage'.[42]

Nevertheless, the Ordnance Chatham left in 1810 was very different from the Ordnance of 1801. How far Chatham was directly responsible for this change is debatable, but Roger Knight exaggerates in saying he deserved 'none of the credit'.[43] Chatham was not just a figurehead: he maintained an umbrella supremacy within the department and, as the fortification issue showed, stamped Ordnance policy with his personal preferences. Colleagues were impressed. His Secretary and, from 1804, Surveyor-General, James Hadden, thought 'the Country never had a more pure or able Master General', and considered 'the system of Lord Chatham's arranging' better than that of any other, including the Duke of Richmond, whom Hadden had served as Secretary in 1794.[44] Lord Eldon, who was Chatham's colleague as Lord Chancellor for many years, famously considered him 'the ablest man . . . in the Cabinet'.[45] Even George Canning, who disliked Chatham personally, thought he was 'a good officer in his department'.[46]

The looseness of Chatham's role obscured his centrality. Hadden perceptively noted its hidden nature: Chatham, he thought, 'never would come out and take the merit [for Ordnance measures] as truly his own'. This was partly because Chatham was often away from London or distracted by other things, but his inability to focus completely on the Ordnance was not his fault. His time as Master-General coincided with a period of great personal upheaval, and between 1801 and 1810 Chatham faced some of the most distressing public and private experiences of his life.

Chapter 7

'The Misfortunes of Late Years'
1801–7

Chatham was in a unique position after his brother's resignation in 1801. Remaining in government after Pitt's departure seemed odd, particularly to those unaware of the distance that had grown between the two brothers over the course of the war. At first this worked in his favour and boosted his importance within Addington's government. To outsiders, Pitt and Chatham seemed closer than they had been for a long time. For much of the summer of 1801 Chatham was unwell with recurrent gout, stomach troubles and jaundice, and Pitt showed appropriate brotherly concern by coming to visit him at Addington's country house when Chatham stayed there for a few days to recover.[1] Pitt and Chatham also came into frequent contact while Pitt assisted Addington in framing the peace terms with France. They were on at least one occasion spotted arm in arm, 'seemingly [in] very earnest and anxious conversation', which naturally led to the supposition that Chatham was one 'of the PITT party', and Pitt's representative at Cabinet meetings.[2] As the opposition *Morning Post* put it, crudely, he was widely perceived to be 'the breath of [Pitt's] nostrils'.[3]

But Chatham's relationship with Pitt was changing. By 1802 Pitt had become alienated from Addington, whose first peacetime budget seemed to repudiate nearly everything Pitt's wartime financial policy represented. Relations were not improved by Addington's receiving significant support from former oppositionists such as Richard Sheridan, Thomas Erskine and George Tierney, who actually became Treasurer of the Navy in 1803. Addington had plenty of enemies in Pitt's close circle of friends, notably George Canning, George Rose and Lord Grenville, who were keen to distance the former prime minister from his successor.[4] As a member of Addington's government, and with Pitt drifting towards open opposition,

Chatham had to be careful. He tried his best to keep neutral, turning down his brother's offer of Deal Castle (in Pitt's gift as Warden of the Cinque Ports) and deliberately snubbing George Canning's grand gala to celebrate Pitt's birthday in May 1802, but despite his clear efforts to stay away from politically embarrassing situations many of Pitt's friends thought him untrustworthy and Pitt himself seemed to agree.[5] In the autumn Pitt stayed away from London because of his 'great embarrassment' at the 'impossibility of avoiding to see some of the Ministers . . . particularly his brother'.[6]

Chatham continued to keep his distance, conscious of his difficult position and perhaps unwilling to try too hard to reverse their drift apart. Any desire to warm relations was in any case hampered by Addington's unpropitious attempt to separate Pitt from the 'new' opposition forming under Lord Grenville. Through Lord Melville (Chatham's old enemy Henry Dundas, elevated to the peerage in 1802) Addington proposed an arrangement by which he and Pitt would serve as joint Secretaries of State under Chatham as a figurehead First Lord of the Treasury. Addington thought he was being reasonable in proposing Pitt's own brother as a compromise prime minister, but, given the continuing fragility of his relations with Pitt, Chatham was an unfortunate choice. Chatham took no part in these discussions, and was probably unaware of the role Addington had in mind for him. Pitt himself gave Chatham the benefit of the doubt, writing 'I do not know whether you are apprised of the Conversation which Addington held with Lord Melville previous to his coming here, or have talked with the latter since his return'.[7] But the experience hardly helped reconcile the two brothers, and Chatham's disapproval of the way Pitt broke off negotiations with Addington did not help.[8] Although Chatham did visit Pitt at Walmer in October 1803 this reeked of duty more than affection.

Pitt and Chatham were indeed going separate ways. Even the death of their mother in April 1803 failed to reconcile them, and their public lives barely overlapped. Chatham had his Cabinet duties to distract him and, after the declaration of war in 1803, his military life as a general in the Southern District. For much of 1803 and 1804 he was based in Chatham, where he and his wife attended military reviews, socialised with the other officers and their families at plays, concerts and balls, and enjoyed country carriage rides *á deux*.[9] Pitt, meanwhile, emerged gradually into open opposition to Addington's government. In March 1804, he loosely joined forces with Fox and Grenville (themselves openly allied against Addington since January) in an attack on Addington's defence policy. At the end of April Addington's parliamentary majority had dropped to 37, and he resigned.[10] A few days later Pitt took office for the second time. The King forbade him offering government posts to Fox and his friends, and, since Grenville refused to join without Fox, the new government was very weak. This was one reason why Pitt felt obliged to keep his brother on as Master-General of the Ordnance despite his former doubts about Chatham's reliability.

Over the next eighteen months the new government, of which Chatham formed a part, fought for its life. At first there was good news in the formation of a new Continental coalition with Austria and Russia, although Prussia, hotly courted, held stubbornly aloof. With Continental prospects more optimistic than they had been for half a decade, Pitt (encouraged by Chatham) tried to reverse his political weakness by making amends with Addington, who joined the government as Lord President and took a peerage as Lord Sidmouth. But in April 1805, calamity struck. The combined opposition under Fox and Grenville scored a significant victory over Pitt by impeaching the First Lord of the Admiralty, Lord Melville, who was accused of embezzlement while Treasurer of the Navy. Melville resigned at the beginning of June, and Sidmouth followed three months later, following a broken promise of Pitt's to give the vacant Admiralty to one of his following.[11]

Pitt's battered government faced the prospect of Fox, Grenville and Sidmouth all acting in concert against it. To avoid disaster the ministry either needed to strengthen itself, or its Continental strategy had to start paying off. Since the King still refused to allow approaches to Grenville and Fox, good news from Austria and Russia was imperative, and the government pressed on with plans to send an expedition of 18,000 men to North Germany and a further 4,000 to the Two Sicilies. But the first Continental reports, in early November, were bad. Austria had been caught by surprise by Napoleon and defeated at Ulm on 19 October. There was one piece of good news: on 21 October Lord Nelson won an important naval victory over the combined French and Spanish fleets off Trafalgar. Although Nelson himself was killed, the battle much reduced the likelihood of a French invasion, and news of the victory put Pitt in a much better political position. Everything hinged on the Russians, and on finalising an alliance with Prussia. Rumours in mid-December suggested the Russians had won a great victory over the French and Pitt, wintering in Bath for his health, had grounds for optimism.[12]

Chatham, like Pitt, tried to put events on the Continent out of his mind. His military duties continued to engross most of his attention. At the end of 1805 he went down to Eastbourne, where he had his headquarters. His time was entirely taken up with Ordnance arrangements for the expeditions to Germany and Sicily, and in the everyday business of a district general, recommending promotions, breaking up camps for the winter and chivvying the Commander-in-Chief to attend to his men's allowances.[13] In December he was summoned back to London by the War Secretary, Castlereagh, to attend a series of Cabinet meetings to discuss the next Continental steps. But on 2 January 1806 the government received devastating news. The Continental reports of a Russian victory could not have been more wrong, and in fact the Russians had been resoundingly defeated by Napoleon at Austerlitz on 2 December. Both Austria and Russia were out of the war; Prussia had still not joined the Third Coalition and was unlikely to do so. The British expeditions to Germany and Sicily, intended to support the Allies, would have to be recalled. Pitt, still in Bath, despaired. He faced the new session of Parliament with his Continental strategy, like his health, in a state of collapse.

While Austria and Russia made armistices with France and Pitt returned by slow stages to London, Chatham had private troubles on his mind. Over the winter the Chatham household in St James's Square had been thrown into turmoil by Colonel William Pringle, an Irishman of a well-born but impoverished military family. Pringle had fallen in love with Chatham's orphaned niece and ward, Harriot Hester Eliot, who had been living with the Chathams since her grandmother had died in April 1803. Although the attraction between the couple was mutual, Chatham suspected Pringle of fortune hunting: Harriot Hester was fifteen years his junior and a considerable heiress, with £20,000 to her name inherited from her father.[14] The result was a battle of wills between Chatham and his niece, with Chatham refusing his consent to the match. When Harriot Hester threatened to elope anyway, Chatham reluctantly agreed to reconsider if the couple stayed apart for a month.

Distracted by the problem with his niece, Chatham failed to notice (or ignored) the signs that his brother was more ill than he had ever been. When Pitt arrived back at his suburban villa at Putney Chatham waited two days before going to see him, and when he did so his indifference scandalised everybody. 'And here is L[or]d Chatham arrived, as brisk, & bustling as if nothing was the matter, and saying he must speak with [Pitt] upon business,' George Canning, in the house at the time, wrote in disgust.[15] George Tomline, Bishop of Lincoln, who was staying with Pitt to make sure he did not over-exert himself, was horrified to find Chatham barging in 'rather abruptly . . . & accost[ing] [Pitt] in a manner & tone as if he had been sitting in Downing Street'. Pitt was seriously ill, but Chatham wrapped himself up in denial and refused to accept his brother was worse than usual. 'I think Lord Chatham is far less aware of Mr Pitt's situation than any other person,' Tomline recorded. 'He calls it mere weakness from Gout'.[16]

Over the next few days, Chatham's denial evaporated. Pitt was unable to keep anything down, and fainted after meeting with friends and colleagues. It was obvious that he was in grave danger. While this was sinking in Parliament met on 21 January, although it was immediately prorogued in deference to the prime minister's situation. Chatham was not present: he was at Putney, although he was not allowed to see his brother.[17] The next day Pitt worsened rapidly. Chatham again returned to Putney, knowing, now, that this was almost certainly his last chance to see his brother alive. According to an informed newspaper account he was allowed to Pitt's bedside at 5 in the evening, although at least one person thought Chatham was turned away.[18] He never saw Pitt again. Early on the 23rd Chatham learned that his brother had died at 4.30 in the morning.

The rapidity of Pitt's collapse had taken Chatham unawares. Relations between the brothers had not been good for some years, but this did little to lessen his grief. The Bishop of Lincoln dined in St James's Square the day of Pitt's death and found Chatham and his wife 'both much afflicted'.[19] At 49, Chatham had lost both parents and all four of his siblings. He was also shortly to lose his office. The Cabinet had already met on 19 January to discuss what to do if Pitt died. Chatham concurred with Lords Hawkesbury, Castlereagh and Camden in preferring a Cabinet reshuffle to coalescing with Fox and Grenville.[20] The day after Pitt's death, however, the remaining cabinet members – Chatham excepted, although he acquiesced in absentia – informed the King they could not continue. The King had little choice but to fall back on Fox and Grenville. For a while it looked as though Chatham might remain part of the new arrangement under his cousin. Both Tomline and Canning thought it possible, and at least one newspaper reported it as fact.[21] In the end he resigned with his colleagues, and handed the Ordnance over to Lord Moira.

'I certainly do not quit a department, to which I have so much reason to feel warmly attached, without considerable regret,' Chatham confessed to the Deputy Adjutant-General of Artillery.[22] Surprisingly, given Chatham's reputation, the sentiment was mutual. Hadden, the Surveyor-General, regretted Chatham's loss more than any other in the department, and some years later one of Chatham's District staff recalled that when Lord Moira proposed Chatham's health at an Artillery dinner, 'one general Sentiment seemed to pervade the whole Corps, & to such a degree, that would have proved highly gratifying to [Chatham's] feelings'.[23] It was a tribute to Chatham's popularity, and the extent to which he had quietly enmeshed himself in the department in the four-and-a-half years since his appointment.

* * *

Pitt's death hit Chatham hard, but his woes were far from over. Within days he experienced yet another domestic calamity. Lady Chatham became 'seriously ill . . . with a delirious Fever' and remained 'in bed & delirious' for weeks.[24] Although her life was never in danger, the doctors feared for her long-term sanity and Chatham could not even commit to attending his brother's public funeral as Chief Mourner until nearly the last minute. Mary's condition improved in mid-February, but she remained seriously unwell in mid-March, and her continued fragility added to the many pressures on Chatham in the wake of Pitt's death.[25]

These pressures sprang partly from Pitt's last wishes. Pitt had composed his will just hours before death, and had left Chatham and the Bishop of Lincoln as his executors. The will itself was exceedingly vague, specifying only settling the bill to Pitt's doctor, Sir Walter Farquhar, repaying a loan of £12,000 raised by Pitt's friends in 1801 and paying his servants double wages, but it was immediately obvious that even these terms could not be complied with. Pitt's debts, when he died, were enormous: £24,000 was owed in bills from the previous year alone.[26] Parliament followed the precedent set at the Elder Pitt's death by voting £40,000 to pay off his son's creditors, but Tomline estimated that the total owed would 'amount to between £58,000 & £60,000, & [Pitt's] Effects may be worth £10,000, including a Debt from Lord Chatham'.[27]

Chatham's position was delicate. There were considerable difficulties involved in his being executor for an estate in which he had a clear interest, both as a beneficiary of his brother's will and as a joint debtor in some of Pitt's financial transactions. Pitt had probably been too close to death to appreciate the subtleties of this point, but Tomline spotted it immediately: 'There is nobody to apply to or consult confidentially [on Pitt's affairs] but myself. Lord Chatham is out of the question.'[28] This was shown all too well by Chatham's behaviour over a debt into which he and Pitt had entered jointly with their banker, Thomas Coutts, for £10,000, of which about £7,500 was still outstanding in 1806.[29] Chatham later claimed the debt had been undertaken on his mother's behalf, but his repaying a large chunk of the original sum in July 1804 suggested at least some of it had been for his personal use.[30] Chatham, hoping to avoid paying the debt on his own, pressed Coutts to claim for the remainder of the sum out of the parliamentary grant. This caused a brief falling-out between the two executors and ended in Tomline's referring the matter to Spencer Perceval, the former Solicitor General. Perceval's legal opinion was based on the assumption that the joint debt had been 'advanced for your [Chatham's] use' alone. As such, Perceval informed Chatham in a remarkably patronising letter that any attempt to use the parliamentary grant to discharge it was 'neither more nor less than that of an application by [Tomline] and you of a part of the money which had been given by the Public for the payment of your *Brother's* debts to the discharge of your own'. This was not only 'an undue appropriation' of the grant, but Perceval told Chatham that, by bringing the matter to the notice of his co-executor, Tomline might be obliged to sue him on the estate's behalf if he did not immediately repay Coutts' debt.[31]

The Coutts affair strongly highlighted the fact that Chatham's finances were too bound up with his brother's for him to help Tomline effectively, or indeed ethically. Chatham was not indifferent, but, as time passed and the immediate distractions of grief passed, his easy-going nature made him happier and happier to leave the shiftwork to his colleague, limiting himself to providing occasional instructions or necessary pieces of information: 'I should certainly prefer as you were so good to undertake it, the not having any intercourse upon it'.[32] Tomline's alarm and irritation at Chatham's inactivity ('I have scarcely ever been engaged in any business which gave me greater uneasiness than this,' he complained) gradually faded as the years passed, even though probate was not granted till 1821 and the final settlement not formalised until 1822.[33] From mutual distrust, their relationship transformed into a strange sort of dependent friendship. Chatham needed Tomline's grasp of detail to settle the debts; but Tomline was also a last link to his brother, a man who had been close to Pitt for thirty years and had been present at his deathbed. For Tomline, friendship with Chatham placed a seal of respectability on his claim to intimacy with the Pitt family.

In the long run, Tomline undoubtedly benefited from Chatham's lack of application. In the 1810s he announced his intention to write Pitt's biography. Chatham's active involvement in 'that most interesting work', correcting drafts and allowing Tomline to keep hold of Pitt's correspondence, earned him the dedication of the final product.[34] This came at the expense of control over his family papers, and Chatham was probably unaware his fellow executor had gone through Pitt's papers and destroyed everything he felt did not conform to the sanctified image his biography was designed to create. More ominously, as it turned out, for Tomline possession was nine-tenths of the law. At the end of his life Chatham made a belated attempt to prise his brother's letters out of the hands of Tomline's son William, to deposit them in the British Museum. William Tomline's refusal to give them up must have made Chatham wish he had taken more interest in them in the past.[35]

*   *   *

Chatham's troubles in the dark period following Pitt's death went far beyond the pressures of executorship, and no doubt contributed to his eagerness to distance himself from the complicated business. Family squabbles and financial headaches combined to make Chatham's life thoroughly miserable, and the two years following Pitt's death were among the worst of Chatham's life. Whereas in sorting out Pitt's affairs Chatham could fob the majority of the work off onto the Bishop of Lincoln, he had no such luxury when it came to his many private afflictions. The most immediate problem was the need to deal with his unmarried nieces, Harriot Hester Eliot and Lady Hester Stanhope. Harriot Hester's situation was easily, and quickly, resolved. Her attachment to Colonel Pringle had not ebbed, and by March 1806 Chatham realised he could reasonably do no more to keep the pair apart.[36] On 20 May 1806 Harriot Hester married Pringle by special licence in Chatham's Dover Street house, Chatham signing the register as witness. Despite the difficulties he had thrown in the way of her courtship, 'Dear Mrs Pringle' (later Lady Pringle, when her husband became a Knight of the Bath) never forgot the years she spent under Chatham's roof. She, her husband and growing family were frequently found visiting Chatham until the 1830s, and her eldest son John Henry was named one of Chatham's heirs.

Chatham's other niece, Lady Hester Stanhope, was a different proposition. Lady Hester and her half-brothers Charles and James had fallen out with their eccentric father, the 3rd Earl Stanhope, whose wholehearted espousal of French revolutionary principles made him a highly embarrassing Pitt family connection. She had been living with Pitt since 1803 and now expected Chatham to offer her a home. When he did not, she never forgave him: 'We all despise him . . . Had *His* protection been *thought advantageous, we* s[houl]d have been recommended to his care'.[37] This showed a startling lack of empathy for a man who had just lost his brother and whose wife was dangerously ill, but Lady Hester's brothers naturally took her part, even though Charles had served his military apprenticeship with Chatham in 1802.[38] James Stanhope wrote scathingly in 1807:

> The immortal Chatham e'er he died
> These gifts he thus assigned
> Take then my *fortune John*, he cried
> Thou *William* hast *my mind*
> *This* son that Part improved with toil
> That 'twas his Country's *weal*
> The *former* Burton learnt to *spoil*
> To *shuffle, cut, and deal*.[39]

Pitt the Elder's 'fortune' was far from the glorious thing Stanhope imagined it must have been, but the point of the poem was clear.

The last lines of Stanhope's poem made spiteful reference to another aspect of Chatham's troubles: the straitened state of his finances. How much of this was due to gambling is unclear, but on paper, Chatham ought to have had plenty of money. He had the £4,000 pension attached to the earldom in 1778 and, since 1803, the £3,000 pension settled on his mother in 1761 for three lives, along with salaries of £2,500 as Commander of the Eastern District, £400 as Colonel of the 4th Foot, and (from 1807) £3,500 for the Governorship of Jersey.[40] In all, his annual income in 1807 amounted to about £13,500 gross – probably closer to £10,000 after tax and various fees, but an excellent income by any standards. But Chatham had always been extravagant, and he was still dealing with the obligations he had inherited from his father, as well as the considerable debts left by his mother. To deal with all this Chatham dug himself deeper into debt. The exact amount of his obligations is unknown, but if the size of the loans he negotiated to help relieve the immediate burden are anything to go by, he owed a great deal. Apart from the £10,000 borrowed from Coutts in the 1790s, he borrowed £3,000 from Lord Camden in 1797, and a further £8,000 in 1806. Various bonds in the Chatham Papers at The National Archives show Chatham was continually mortgaging out his £4,000 pension as security for loans, many of them dated 1806 and 1807, the period when he lacked the additional income and cachet of his Cabinet status.[41]

By 1806, he had no other security on which to rely. Chatham had come into sole possession of Burton Pynsent on his mother's death in 1803, by which time the 1,200 acre property was in a state of collapse. The older part of the house had been shut up for years, and as for the new wing, 'the Air [is] so Damp that the House except where there is Fire [is] almost as wet within as without'.[42] The house's fate had been decided long before the Dowager Lady Chatham died, and the estate was sold on 16 October 1804 by Messrs Skinner, Dyke and Co., at Garraway's Coffee House. A second sale of other parts of the estate took place on 2 April 1805. According to the newspapers the property fetched just over £43,000, although it did not do as well as expected.[43] The house itself sold to John Frederick Pinney, a local landowner, for £8,810 – which, given it was mortgaged for £13,000, was not nearly what Chatham must have hoped to receive.

Selling Burton was the easy part. As Chatham quickly discovered, getting the buyers to hand over the money was more difficult. Burton had been left jointly to Chatham and his mother in Pitt the Elder's will, and the estate placed in the hands of trustees. This was standard practice, but there was a complication: the trustees were all dead, and Lady Chatham had died intestate, so her property ought to be divided equally among her surviving relatives. Chatham had to prove he was legally able to sell his own house without permission from his four nieces. Possibly this was a matter of legal form which merely rubber stamped an existing agreement, but it forced Chatham to bring two cases to the Court of Chancery, one in April 1806 and one in October 1807, an expensive and time-consuming process at a time when he badly needed the money from Burton. These cases confirmed what everyone already knew: that Chatham was 'Heir at Law of his Mother the late Countess, who was Surviving Devisee in Trust of the late Earl, with power to sell'.[44]

Even when the money finally hit his bank account, Chatham had to untangle a number of legal problems dating back to his father's lifetime before accessing the funds. First there was the £13,000 mortgage to be written off, which took two years.[45] Once this matter was settled, Chatham had to divide the remaining proceeds among his nieces according to the terms of his father's will. Harriot Hester Eliot was owed £3,795 4s 5d plus interest by right of her mother, and the Stanhope girls were entitled to a third each of the portion that would have gone to theirs.[46] 'You know full well the manner in which my hands are tied up, and in which I was left, without the power of raising one single sixpence,' Chatham complained to his mother's old friend Mrs Stapleton in December 1807 in an uncharacteristically emotional history of his troubles. '... The whole life Interest I have in [Burton], is not worth much above half of what My Mother's debts amount to'.[47] For the first time in decades, perhaps ever, Chatham was forced to budget, and he did not like the experience: 'My finances are strictly appropriated, in order to get rid gradually of some incumbrances, which ye misfortunes of late years have brought, to press very heavily upon me'.[48]

These 'misfortunes' were not merely financial, and at the forefront of Chatham's mind was the 'sad distress' of his most serious domestic tragedy. Over the course of 1806, Mary Chatham's physical health continued to improve. Her mental health, however, declined sharply, and by the spring of 1807 she was what would now be termed clinically depressed. For a while the Chathams tried to pretend nothing was amiss, perhaps in the hope that the routine of fashionable life might shake Mary back to normality. She drifted from function to function, appearing at Lady Camden's 'rout', a concert in honour of Miss Johnstone, and at court drawing rooms at St James's. In June she accompanied Chatham on a summer trip to Ascot, and followed him on a shooting holiday to Newmarket in September.[49] But Lady Chatham was a very sick woman. Her *'violence'* and *'horrid* language' distressed everybody, including Mary herself, who was under no illusions as to the severity of her condition. 'My cold is better,' she wrote to her sister Georgiana in a heartrending cry for help, 'but I am *shocking horrible* in mind & Spirits &c. Oh Why, why write to write this so[?] Keep it to yourself . . . or rather burn it[.] Tell me I may be suddenly different'. Georgiana's helplessness in the face of the mental collapse of her 'suffering Angel Sister' was plain: 'May God spare her, & take her to himself!'[50]

Chatham's strategy of forcing Mary to lead a normal life was not working: on the contrary it made her worse. She did not get to bed until 2 and woke up late, 'exhausted with London hours & racket'.[51] She was obliged to take 'cordials' laced with opiates to support herself through the day, and her profound depression sought an outlet in physical violence. 'I leave you to judge in what state she must have been in, before she would attempt to strike me, which her L[ad]yship actually did on Tuesday at dressing time,' Lady Chatham's maid reported to Georgiana. 'Fear made me shrink fr[om] her, & she immediately became conscious of what she had done . . . She never struck me before, but has many times gone off in a very violent way'. Immediately after this episode Mary was propped up with yet more cordial and went out to dinner with her husband. Trapped in this never ending cycle of depression and concealment, Mary openly contemplated suicide: 'She could not live in this way, *she must put an end to it*'.[52] In October 1807 she may indeed have made the attempt. 'I have never got the better of one heavy calamity, which happened, when I thought all was going on well,' her sister Lady Dalkeith wrote.[53] After this, Mary disappeared from public life for some time.

Chatham's marriage had grown out of childhood friendship and he and his wife had always been close. Lady Chatham followed her husband on all his military district postings, and on the one occasion Chatham served abroad, at the Helder in 1799, she accompanied him as far as Ramsgate, where she waited until he returned. When he was based in Chatham in 1803–4, Mary 'never fail[ed] being present at the Sunday Reviews' held by her husband.[54] Her illness, and its nature, completely floored him. As with his brother's death, his strategy for dealing with his wife's madness was to pretend the problem did not exist. Georgiana noted, sadly: 'Nobody thinks her well, but him . . . [Lady Chatham] has regretted to me that poor L[or]d C[hatham] thought her getting better when she was as ill as ever, & alas! there is I fear too much truth in that'.[55]

Chatham's denial soon transformed into a profound despair at his inability to make any difference to Mary's state. Mary did not respond well to the attention from loved ones, and her husband became an obstacle to her recovery, particularly as Mary fretted his constant attendance on her distracted him from his duties. 'Doctor Vaughan pressed me much to go away for a time as he thought it better on many accounts, and particularly that the having kept me so long, from where I ought to have been is a source of great anxiety to her,' Chatham told his brother-in-law Sydney in October 1807. 'I shall therefore go in a few days to Colchester, where I shall be near, in case of any change.' He did not go into detail on the subject of Mary's condition, but closed with a few lines that must have given Sydney an idea of it: 'I am myself pretty well, but ye misery I have suffered the last fortnight or three weeks, has required all the fortitude I have left, to be able to bear up against.'[56]

Mary Chatham's illness stretched on for years. In May 1808 Chatham reported that 'Lady Chatham is I hope essentially better, but far from well yet'.[57] In November 1808 he hoped his wife 'is rather better than she was, tho' her amendment, I am sorry to say, has been very slow'.[58] Chatham was wrong. Mary's illness continued for nearly another year, but by summer 1809 it was on its way out. Three-and-a-half years on from Mary's initial 'delirious fever', her slow return to normality must have seemed like a miracle, but the dynamics of the Chathams's marriage inevitably changed. The danger of relapse was well known; Chatham found himself keeping bad news from his wife, taking important decisions alone and, in his words, 'mak[ing] everything appear to the best'.[59]

There was plenty to conceal. Even while Lord and Lady Chatham struggled to maintain a normal life against the odds, Chatham's public political and military career reached a critical point. In March 1807 Grenville saved the Pittites the trouble of unseating him by committing political suicide. He angered the King by reviving the spectre of Catholic Emancipation and trying to allow non-Anglicans to serve in all ranks of the army and navy, and was immediately dismissed. By the end of the month Chatham was back in government with the scattered remnants of Pitt's following under the Duke of Portland. But the Portland ministry was weak, leaderless and divided, unable to capitalise effectively on the Continental opportunities for military intervention against Napoleon, and Chatham's role in it was strangely uncertain. The next two years were a time of disappointments and missed opportunities for him. Because of this, by the time his wife was slowly recovering from her long illness in 1809, he was no longer able to pick and choose his opportunities for active employment. The result of this lack of flexibility was disaster.

Chapter 8

The 'Mischievous Intriguer'
1807–9

On 19 March 1807 Chatham was called upon 'by the King's express desire', along with the Duke of Portland and Lord Lowther, to form a new Pittite administration.[1] The process of cobbling together a new government took several days. Chatham was deputed to keep the King informed of the Pittite discussions, and his progress report of 23 March concluded with a reminder of his personal loyalty to the Throne:

> Lord Chatham will not trespass upon Your Majesty by offering any observations upon the critical situation in which Your Majesty's affairs are placed by the conduct of your Ministers. He only begs leave to express his hope that Your Majesty is convinced of his entire devotion to your service, and that Your Majesty will be persuaded that he is prepared to meet with firmness and energy whatever difficulties may present themselves, tho' at ye same time he is by no means insensible to their extent.[2]

Chatham was right: the Pittites faced significant challenges. The most obvious one was that there was no clear successor to Pitt, whose death had left his political following united by little more than devotion to his memory. The one thing they should all have had in common was the wish to oppose Lord Grenville's ministry, but even this caused problems, and many Pittites had preferred to recognise Grenville (Pitt's cousin and former Foreign Secretary) as their new leader, particularly after Fox's death in September 1806. Under these conditions Chatham might have played a unifying role on the scattered party. Many of Pitt's followers who otherwise had little in common with each other would happily have served together under his elder brother. The King, too, would have been happy with Chatham at the Treasury, and Chatham's enjoyment of royal favour continued to inflate his political importance. These assets, added to the fact he had 'cross'd seas, & served with distinction', seemed to point him out as the most likely candidate to unite the many competing political interests.[3]

And yet, despite the King's obvious preference for Chatham, the new ministerial arrangements saw Portland as First Lord of the Treasury, Lord Hawkesbury as Home Secretary, George Canning Foreign Secretary and Lord Castlereagh Secretary of State for War (with Spencer Perceval as Chancellor of the Exchequer). Chatham returned to his old post of Master-General of the Ordnance. For the next two years his profile remained low, surprisingly so given the prominent part he had taken in constructing the government. He took no part in defending his government in the House of Lords and spent much time away from London in Colchester, where he was still in command of the Eastern District. He was appointed High Steward by the Colchester Assembly in September of 1807, partly in recognition of his role in buttressing Portland's pro-Crown, anti-Catholic government, but also, no doubt, because he was such a familiar face on the Colchester scene.

Chatham's domestic woes were at least partly responsible for his near-invisibility. While Lady Chatham continued to be seriously ill, he could not commit to any long-term political prominence. Chatham's decision to step back was also, however, due to personality. As the King, who knew him well, observed when Chatham's name came up as a candidate for the Treasury: 'I believe he never had a thought of it. I don't believe he would take it.'[4] Chatham was not held back by any lack of self-confidence, as Wendy Hinde has insinuated.[5] Rather, he may have been reluctant to deal with the notorious instability of Portland's ministry: 'The Disputes amongst the members of the Government are incessant. They *all* think themselves qualified for the D[uke] of Portland's place which he has no thoughts of giving up to them, [and] they are all jealous of each other'.[6] Chatham probably had no wish to head this group of competing interests. Yet his name came up repeatedly as a possible replacement for the sick, elderly Portland, who had only volunteered his leadership from duty and whom nobody expected to remain at the Treasury for long. 'If a vacancy were now to happen . . . Lord Chatham would be the person,' Lord Bathurst informed the Duke of Richmond on 4 January 1808 during one of Portland's illnesses. 'Between you and me, he would, I am afraid, be far from being as practicable a man as the Duke, but he is upon the whole the best person to put forward, and one whom the King would prefer'.[7]

This lack of 'practicability' was perhaps another reason why Chatham remained in the background. He could be brusque to the point of rudeness, establishing the boundaries of his Ordnance influence and retaliating swiftly against any attempts to trespass on it. This reflected the unprecedented worldwide scale of the war: its ordnance requirements inevitably led to friction with the other departments involved in planning, particularly the three Secretaries of State and the Admiralty. The stress of dealing with his wife's mental illness almost certainly shortened his fuse, and his prickliness with his colleagues probably sprang from frustration and despair as much as anything else. But Chatham's paranoia after 1794 also played a role. He treated his colleagues with barely concealed suspicion, reacting aggressively in response to anything he believed to be a challenge. On one occasion Chatham irritated the Home Secretary, Lord Hawkesbury, to the point that Hawkesbury refused to be in the same room with him.[8] Hawkesbury had already warned a colleague to treat Chatham with caution, as he was very precise and pedantic – possibly a reminder that Chatham worked slowly, but almost certainly a warning to tread carefully around the proud, touchy Master-General.[9]

Chatham was, in fact, an anomaly in the Portland Cabinet. He was not really a Pittite, for his views had rarely been analogous with those of his brother. Apart from his private friends Camden and Westmorland, neither of whom brought much weight to the government other than their name and political influence, the one person with whom Chatham's name was most frequently connected by newspapers and political commentators was George Canning. The relationship between the two men was strange and mistrustful: Chatham barely tolerated Canning, who, for his part, considered Chatham selfish and unfeeling. Chatham's propensity for 'mischievous intrigue', or his habit of appealing to the King whenever he felt threatened, repelled him.[10] Still, Chatham's 'inefficiency' was counterbalanced by his connection with Pitt and the fact his coming to government was likely to satisfy the most people, particularly the King.[11] In 1809 Canning openly suggested Chatham as Prime Minister to both the King and the Duke of Portland, in the hope he would prove a sympathetic (and pliable) First Lord of the Treasury. He also consented to Chatham's appointment to the Walcheren command in the hope that success might reconcile the country to his elevation.[12] Chatham probably never knew of

Canning's plans. If he found out, it was unlikely to have endeared Canning to him, and it is clear from their awkward, impersonal correspondence that Chatham profoundly disliked his brother's brilliant young protégé. But then Chatham's relations with all his colleagues after Pitt's death were much the same: polite, but fringed with ice, and liable to tip into haughty passive-aggressiveness at the slightest hint of challenge.

And there were plenty of challenges. As foreign expeditions became more commonplace, and Continental developments (particularly in the Peninsula) called for Britain's greater military involvement, the Foreign and War Secretaries of State took more responsibility for the war effort. Since the end of the Third Coalition on the battlefields of Ulm and Austerlitz, Britain had devoted little effort to Continental warfare. Grenville, once a devotee of coalitions, had lost his trust in them and his administration focused on campaigns in the Mediterranean and intervention in South America. This policy had not endeared Britain to her abandoned allies, particularly Russia, which ended up in open concert with France following the Treaty of Tilsit in July 1807. The Portland government's reaction to Russia's attempt to form a new 'armed neutrality' of Baltic states against British trade was a pre-emptive strike on the Danish fleet in Copenhagen in August and September 1807, partly to show its determination to break away from Grenville's isolationism.[13] Not until Spain openly revolted against Napoleon in May 1808, however, was Britain able to find a foothold anywhere on the Continent other than Sicily and Sweden. British money and military aid was sent to the insurgents, and in the summer of 1808 an expeditionary force of 25,000 men was sent to take advantage of the unsettled state of the Peninsula.

All this meant weapons, which in turn led to departmental clashes between Chatham and the Secretaries of State. Their correspondence became little more than a series of large requisitions on the parts of Canning and Castlereagh, and protestations against their enormity from Chatham. His reluctance to meet these demands was less a reflection of his laziness and more an attempt to stop his department's resources being taken for granted. As Master-General of the Ordnance, Chatham had no direct influence over government strategy: by inflating the Ordnance's difficulties, he forced the Secretaries of State to take his opinion into account. Canning was especially disdainful of mere practicalities. He thought the war in the Peninsula had the potential to finish France once and for all, and was not averse to issuing Chatham with outright demands for guns, veiled in cheeky politeness. When Chatham expressed reluctance to send any more weapons to Spain in late June 1809, Canning came very close to saying that if the Spanish uprising failed through want of arms, it would be Chatham's fault:

> [Nothing I say has] the remotest tendency to blame or discredit your exertions . . . but the subject itself is of such immense importance, the calls upon us are so loud, and so frequent, the failure of the effort in Spain, if attributable to the want of *any* help that we *could* by *any* exertion furnish, would be so fatal and so disgraceful, that I cannot forbear bringing the subject under discussion.[14]

Chatham caved in, but he was not amused by Canning's barely concealed encroachment on his responsibilities.

Castlereagh, the Secretary of State for War, was less blatant than Canning in stepping on Chatham's toes. Nevertheless, his prominent role in organising Britain's overseas expeditions brought him into close contact with the Ordnance, and Chatham did not pass up the opportunity to underline his department's vital role in campaign planning. He was particularly insistent about Castlereagh's adhering to the proper form. 'Signifying the King's Pleasure' in requisitioning arms was not merely a statement of the War Office's superiority over the Ordnance in the Cabinet hierarchy.[15] It was an established phrase reflecting the decision of the whole Cabinet, providing accountability for a public department dealing with huge sums of money under the scrutiny of Parliament and the Treasury. It formalised in writing a decision that had already been made, either collectively, or in individual consultation between departments. It also allowed Chatham (the Cabinet's resident Ordnance expert) to 'suggest . . . Alterations or Additions that would benefit the Service', and thereby maintain some control over the resources under his command.[16] Omitting the 'King's Pleasure', or simply being vague about it, betrayed a lack of consultation and respect.

But Chatham's near pathological insistence on proper form was not just a way of asserting himself. He was always prone to getting bogged down in detail, a characteristic he demonstrated throughout his life. He spent considerable time picking on a lapse in Lord Liverpool's official style during the process of composing an official statement welcoming an inquiry in the Walcheren aftermath.[17] Much later, when Governor of Gibraltar, Chatham quarrelled with the Undersecretary of the Colonial Office over a tiny detail in a circular regulating the way in which official letters home were to be addressed.[18] This pedantry as a means of control stung Lord Mulgrave into calling him 'a jealous votary of formalities', but it was simply Chatham's style: rigidly formal and drenched in self-defensive etiquette.[19] Perhaps it was also a sign of the insecurity Chatham carried as the son and brother of much more famous men, exacerbated by the tragedies of his private life and the disappointments of his career. Whatever the reason, Chatham often wrapped himself in the dignity of his office to distance himself from his colleagues and deflect criticism. The Ordnance's nebulous but powerful bureaucracy was an excellent device for this.

*   *   *

The increase in Britain's Continental military involvement did not just mean more business for the Ordnance. It also offered Chatham the opportunity to revive his military career, dormant since Pitt's prohibition against his serving abroad. Pitt was dead, and Chatham, now a lieutenant general, might have been expected to angle for his first independent command. Surprisingly, his military experience continued limited to District commands, even though he had the pick of two prestigious military appointments. The first was an appointment to the court of Sicily at the end of 1807. Sicily was one of Britain's only remaining Continental allies, and 20,000 troops were stationed there to help defend the island. The current British minister, William Drummond, and the British military commander, Sir John Moore, were at loggerheads, and the Queen of Sicily disliked Drummond's attempts to interfere in Sicilian domestic affairs.[20] What was needed, Canning told Chatham, was a military man who could also embrace the role of a diplomat. 'He must be a person of high rank, both military and civil, and in the entire Confidence of this Government . . . [capable of] comprehending large, and intricate subjects'. Canning and Castlereagh had previously agreed that Chatham was the best man for the job. Chatham's immediate reaction was nevertheless to pass the responsibility to someone else: 'I think you cannot do better, if Sicily is to be retained, than to propose the Mission to Lord Wellesley'.[21]

There was never much doubt that Chatham would refuse such a

difficult posting, but the second military appointment offered to him was nearly accepted. It was the command of the expedition to Portugal in 1808, intended to assist the Spanish uprising against the French. At the beginning of the summer the government was planning 'a grand expedition' variously said to consist of 30,000 to 40,000 men, and for some weeks Chatham was identified as the commander.[22] Nor was the appointment mere rumour. Chatham himself briefly believed he would be sent out, and spent some time discussing strategy and logistics with fellow officers and War Office staff 'during the few days that I had any concern with the details of this Operation'.[23] In the end Sir Hew Dalrymple was appointed instead, although for a while it looked as though Chatham might still go out in a subordinate command. Dalrymple was recalled in disgrace after his appointment resulted in the Convention of Cintra, which squandered a British victory at Vimeiro by allowing the French to evacuate Portugal in British ships with their spoils of war. Once again Chatham was identified as his most likely successor. The *Morning Post* 'very confidently reported, that Lord Chatham had been appointed Commander-in-Chief of the British Armies in Spain and Portugal, and that he had left town to embark for Spain'. Nevertheless, two days later the *Morning Post* was forced to admit the rumour was 'utterly without foundation'.[24]

Why Chatham did not go to Portugal is something of a mystery. There were suggestions he withdrew his candidacy for the command when the Duke of York expressed interest instead, or that he decided the expedition was too small for a general of his seniority after it was reduced to 25,000 men. Alternatively, he may simply have been unable to travel to the Peninsula at short notice.[25] Eventually his name dropped out of reports completely, although no reason was ever given for his staying at home. As with Chatham's reluctance to take the Treasury, this was probably a matter of personal choice. Very probably his desire to stay in England was directly connected with his wife's serious illness, which at least one political commentator had identified as Chatham's main reason for not succeeding the Duke of Portland.[26] Chatham could not commit himself to a potentially lengthy campaign so far from home at a time when Lady Chatham's health was at its worst.

Whatever the reason, Chatham knew he could ill afford to let more campaigns pass by. Refusing to serve never looked good, particularly when there were precious few opportunities for active service. At the end of 1808 he was 52 and had served abroad only once, in a subordinate command. In 1809, however, came an opportunity for more extensive British Continental involvement. Austria took advantage of German uprisings and Napoleon's distraction in Spain to re-emerge into open conflict with France. While the Archdukes Charles and John marched across Italy and central Europe, forcing Napoleon's generals into temporary retreat, Britain agreed to provide Austria with a downpayment of £2 million, a further £400,000 a month and a military diversion in a sphere of Britain's choosing.[27]

For the first time since 1806 Britain had an active and powerful Continental ally. Thanks to Castlereagh's Local Militia Act, which created a balloted force of 200,000 men who were actively encouraged to transfer into the line, she also had a large disposable force. The question was where to send it. Austria preferred an expedition to northern Germany, but the government had tried committing troops there without a corresponding alliance with Prussia in 1805 and had no wish to do so again. Elevating Portugal from a sideshow into a major commitment was another option, but the government was reluctant to reinforce Wellesley's army after the embarrassment of the Convention of Cintra. After lengthy debate the Cabinet dusted off a plan that had been often considered since the late 1790s: an assault on the French dockyards in Antwerp, located on the Scheldt River in the French-controlled 'Kingdom of Holland'.

Antwerp was the second largest French naval centre after Toulon and destroying it would be a huge relief to the British government, perennially worried about invasion and French maritime power. A campaign in the Scheldt would not immediately assist Austria, but it would still provide a serious distraction, since Napoleon could not afford to ignore a threat so close to the French border. Furthermore, a campaign close to home was likely to be cheaper, and also popular, since its object touched on questions of British naval supremacy. If the campaign succeeded, opening the Scheldt would also pierce Napoleon's Continental System, which had closed Europe to British trade (with huge financial repercussions).[28] All the intelligence coming in suggested that Antwerp and Flushing, on the island of Walcheren at the mouth of the Scheldt, were in a crumbling state and that the area had been stripped of troops to fight the Austrians inland. The opportunity to strike a blow at the enemy fleet, consisting of 10 or 12 ships of the line and several smaller vessels, was too good to miss.

The moment the first draft from the Local Militia became available in May, Castlereagh pressed forward with preparations. The Commander-in-Chief was ordered to collect an army of just over 39,000 rank and file, and the Admiralty busied itself forming a fleet of 616 vessels of all sizes, including 264 warships. The Ordnance prepared 200 pieces of artillery, 10 million rounds of ammunition and over 100,000 shells (enough, as General Lord Cathcart observed, 'to produce an earthquake somewhere'), plus several thousand horses and 200 wagons and carts for transportation.[29] In Sir John Fortescue's words, 'It was incomparably the greatest armament that had ever left the shores of England.'[30] The only thing left was to appoint a commander.

Chapter 9

Walcheren
1809

May 1809 found Chatham recovering from illness in his Hill Street house. His health had not been particularly good recently. An extended attack of gout had kept him indoors for several weeks over Christmas, 'in bed till towards four or five o'clock every day' and unable to 'go out even in a carriage' until the middle of January, and he had been mildly unwell on and off ever since.[1] He was aware, as Master-General of the Ordnance and a member of the Cabinet, of the size and destination of the expedition in contemplation, but his military opinion had neither been sought nor offered. On 18 May, however, he received a letter from Castlereagh. No progress in planning the expedition could be made, Castlereagh said,

> till we have come to a decision who is to be Entrusted with the Execution of the Operation . . . nor indeed till this is fixed, can any of the Departmental arrangements be satisfactorily proceded [*sic*] on.
>
> Under these Impressions, and in the hope that the result may prove as honorable to the Commander, as advantageous to the Country, allow me to propose it for your acceptance.
>
> In expressing my own wishes, that it may be confided to you, I am authorized to add the Duke of Portland's, and I have no doubt those of all our Colleagues.[2]

Chatham's reaction was characteristically guarded:

> Of course, I shou'd be at all times, ready when called upon to obey His Majesty's Commands, but considering this proposal, as an Option given to me, confidentially on your part, I can only say, that

I shou'd be very anxious to have some further conversation with you on this subject, before I venture to give any decided answer to it.[3]

But Chatham did not really have 'an Option'. He had already refused the Peninsular command because of his domestic troubles, and any reservations about the distance from home and unpredictable length of such a mission did not hold for Antwerp, which was less than 24 hours from the English coast. As Castlereagh later made clear, Continental circumstances, particularly the inability to rely on an alliance with Prussia, did not allow for an extended foray on the Continent: 'The Expedition must therefore be considered as not in the first instance assuming any other Character than that of a Coup de Main'.[4]

Though not announced or even formally accepted for some weeks, Chatham's appointment to such an important command did not remain secret long. Contemporaries were mystified. Setting aside his reputation, Chatham lacked experience for an amphibious campaign in virtually unknown terrain. His District commands had brought him to the notice of the Commander-in-Chief, Sir David Dundas, at Horse Guards, and his reputation there was good; but although Dundas described Chatham's appointment as 'very proper', he was at pains to stress that it was not his responsibility: 'I was consulted in a certain degree . . . I knew he was meant to be appointed, but it was not my choice'.[5]

The 'propriety' of Chatham's appointment stemmed from his seniority. Martin Howard has concluded that 'the simplest explanation for the choice of Chatham is that he was the best senior military officer available', and certainly his proximity to the top of the Army List weighed heavily at the War Office in considering who to appoint to the largest military expedition of the wars so far.[6] But Chatham was still far from the top of the list. As the radical *Examiner* observed when Chatham's name had come up for the Peninsula in 1808, 'What mystery talked of the appointment of the Earl of Chatham as Commander-in-Chief, when such officers as Lord Cathcart and Lord Moira are not only known to be active soldiers, but what is infinitely more in these times, are actually *above him on the list*!'[7] This was even more pertinent in 1809, for both Cathcart and Moira had experience with amphibious operations, Moira in Ostend and Cathcart at Copenhagen.

Why, then, was Chatham picked for the Walcheren command, and by whom? Thomas Picton, who accompanied the expedition as a subordinate officer, had no doubt Chatham was selected because 'his fortune was embarrassed, and this lucrative command would improve it'.[8] Certainly Chatham must have welcomed the pay – £3,457 10s 0d a year, or £9 9s 6d per day – but Picton's remark was mere gossip.[9] More informed opinion suggested Canning might have pushed Chatham forward expecting him to return a hero, succeed the Duke of Portland at the Treasury and install Canning as effective Prime Minister.[10] By his own admission Canning 'agreed to the nomination of Lord Chatham as Comm[ande]r of the Expedition' because he hoped 'the Eclat of the Success' might reconcile 'the Country to his Succession to the First Lordship of the Treasury'.[11] But this was Canning defending himself against charges of over ambition by claiming he had never sought the Treasury for himself. Chatham had no need to bolster his claim to the premiership: he had been seriously considered for it in 1803 and 1807, and was still widely expected to succeed the Duke of Portland in the event of his likely retirement or death. Besides, Canning's precise wording was that he had *agreed* to Chatham's nomination, implying that nomination came from elsewhere. Was it from the King, who was, after all, notoriously fond of him? Historians have been quick to dismiss the King's influence, despite his undeniable prerogative to suggest military commanders.[12] No doubt Chatham's appointment pleased George III, and this doubtless played a role in choosing him. But Castlereagh's letter of 18 May clearly shows he had not yet consulted the King when he offered Chatham the command.

Chatham, therefore, was Castlereagh's choice. After the expedition was over Castlereagh's brother could hardly believe it: 'I never have understood how you came to appoint him of your own accord . . . You have been led into it to satisfy or give into the ideas of those who aimed at your overthrow'.[13] Yet Castlereagh's letter of 18 May shows he had consulted nobody but Portland in the matter.[14] Probably Castlereagh, like Canning, hoped Chatham would reflect glory on the government of which he formed a part, giving it a much-needed boost. Castlereagh's words to Chatham – 'the hope that the result may prove as honorable to the Commander, as advantageous to the Country' – were designed to tempt Chatham to accept, but they also hinted at the way Castlereagh viewed the expedition: as an operation likely to succeed and prove a decisive turning point in the war. This pointed to another significant advantage of appointing Chatham. Pitt had taken Britain to war in 1793 in response to French encroachments in Flanders and Holland. If a British army could strike a decisive blow against France in that very sphere, under the command of Pitt's own brother, the symbolic nature of the victory would be as important as the victory itself.

The problem, as Chatham well knew, was that the military men were less convinced than the politicians that the expedition would be a walkover. The Commander-in-Chief, Sir David Dundas, and four of his staff, were consulted on the feasibility of attacking Antwerp. They were given two options. The first was a landing at Ostend followed by an approach to Antwerp over land. The second was an amphibious assault from the Scheldt, under the protection of the navy's guns. The Staff officers unanimously rejected the Ostend plan, and were ambivalent about the Scheldt project, which required swiftness of execution, perfect co-ordination between army and navy, and a great deal of luck. Crucially, none of them ruled it out completely, and Castlereagh pressed ahead with the enterprise on the basis of their not entirely encouraging advice. Remarkably few general officers appointed to the expedition had any faith in it.[15]

As Chatham studied the (considerably outdated) maps provided by the War Office, he felt his doubts growing. Antwerp, the 'ulterior object', was situated some 20 miles from the mouth of the Scheldt. It was protected by a string of forts, the two largest of which, Lillo and Liefkenshoek, straddled the point at which the river widened towards the sea. A further 8 miles downriver, the Scheldt divided into two at the easternmost point of the island of South Beveland. On the left was the West Scheldt, or the Hondt. On the right was the East Scheldt, riddled with shoals and sandbanks. The basin beyond was filled with islands, the two largest of which were Walcheren and South Beveland. The entry to the West Scheldt was commanded by a large battery at Breskens, on Cadzand, 3 miles across from the fortified town of Vlissingen (or Flushing, as the British called it) on Walcheren. The East Scheldt was less well protected, but the Veere Gat channel between Walcheren and North Beveland was defended by Fort Den Haak and the town of Veere. Walcheren and South Beveland were separated by the Sloe, itself covered by Fort Rammekens to the south and Veere to the north. At the easternmost tip of South Beveland was the fort of Bath (then spelled variously as Bat or Batz), just over 3 miles of shallow water from the fort of Sandvliet (or Sandfleet) on the mainland.

The more the Cabinet firmed up its plan for an attack on Antwerp via Walcheren, the less Chatham liked what he was hearing. The aim of the expedition, as summarised in his official Instructions, was remarkably open-ended: 'The Capture or Destruction of the Enemy's Ships, either building at Antwerp and Flushing, or afloat on the Scheldt; the Destruction of the Arsenals and Dock Yards at Antwerp, Terneuse, and Flushing; and the Reduction of the Island of Walcheren, and the rendering if possible the Scheldt no longer navigable for Ships of War.'[16]

The plan for achieving these aims depended on the coming together of a number of favourable circumstances. Probably put together by Captain Sir Home Popham, an intelligent but controversial naval officer who had considerable experience in amphibious operations and extensive knowledge of Antwerp, the proposal was for the navy to sail down the West Scheldt and land Chatham's army at three locations: Cadzand on the mainland, Flushing on Walcheren and South Beveland.[17] Once Cadzand's Breskens battery had been disabled, Flushing blockaded and South Beveland was in British hands, the remaining 20,000 men under Chatham would proceed up the West Scheldt, land at Sandvliet, reduce Forts Lillo and Liefkenshoek, and march under the navy's protection to Antwerp to complete the mission. Speed was essential, for the plan hinged on the assumption that the French would not have time to reinforce or restore the supposedly crumbling defences of Flushing, Antwerp and nearby Bergen-op-Zoom. It also depended on the army and navy moving as nearly in concert as possible.[18] To save time the plan merely required Flushing to be 'masked', or blockaded, by land and sea. Its full surrender was not considered necessary to land the bulk of the army at Sandvliet, so long as the navy was able to move freely up the West Scheldt.

This emphasis on simultaneous operations, and all the variables this depended on, worried Chatham more than anything else. Since accepting the command he had been having frequent discussions with naval and military officers, and their almost uniform pessimism was rubbing off on him. In mid-June he had a significant conversation with General Alexander Hope, the author of one of the five military Opinions collected by Castlereagh on the proposed expedition. During this conversation Chatham was unsettled by Hope's obvious doubts about the chances of landing at (or re-embarking from) Sandvliet.[19] For the first time one of the essential components of the plan was being called into question. When the Cabinet met on 14 June Chatham, fresh from his conversation with

Hope, refused to commit himself to the possibility of his own expedition's success. Eventually Liverpool, the Home Secretary, 'pointedly' asked him whether he thought the expedition viable. Chatham, in his reply, gave vent to his fears:

> I felt no doubt, but that with a little more or less loss, according to circumstances . . . we shou'd certainly succeed in making ourselves Masters of Walcheren and of Flushing, but as to ye Ulterior Operations against Antwerp and the French Fleet, it seemed to me . . . that our business must be accomplished before the Enemy shou'd be able to collect in great force to interrupt our Operations, and which he wou'd doubtless attempt from all Quarters.

With Hope's doubts about Sandvliet still ringing in his ears, Chatham asked the First Lord of the Admiralty, Mulgrave, to state once and for all 'whether a Fleet of the magnitude which ours must necessarily be, cou'd at once proceed up the Scheld [*sic*], at ye same moment that the Operation against Walcheren was proceeding, and afterwards land the Troops, Horses &c &c at Sandfleet or such other Point above Batz, as shou'd be fixed on'.[20] This last point was Chatham's '*sine qua non*'. If Mulgrave could not guarantee that the fleet could proceed up the West Scheldt after Bath was taken, but before Flushing fell, then the whole deal was off.

Asking for more information at this late stage was typical of Chatham, who hated making a decision without mulling over all the available information in his head first. His cold feet could not have come at a worse time for Castlereagh. The Austrians were pressing harder for the promised British diversion because their campaign against Napoleon had been boosted by a victory on 21–2 May at Aspern-Essling. Now was the time for Britain to strike, when Napoleon would be distracted by the need to make up his losses on the Continent. Instead Castlereagh was forced to ask the King to 'postpone' giving his 'final Commands' until 'the practicability of a Landing at Sandfleet can be assured'.[21] Thankfully for Castlereagh, Mulgrave breezily swept aside Chatham's doubts. Chatham recalled him saying 'rather eagerly (I am quite positive as to ye words) "Well then if that is all your difficulty, I will bring you tomorrow, to the Cabinet, an *Opinion signed* by the three Naval Lords of the Admiralty, which shall settle this Point, of the practicability of the Fleet going up["]'.[22] The promised opinion, dated 19 June, was circulated among the ministers and discussed at a final Cabinet next day. Three Lords of the Admiralty responded to Chatham's concerns by committing 'to undertake that the troops shall be conveyed, when the Island of Beveland . . . is in our possession, to the Dyke between Fort Lillo and Sandfleet, and landed, as far as the question of Landing depends on the nature of the place, with relation to the approach to the shore of boats and other vessels capable of receiving troops'. The opinion was accompanied by papers from Home Popham and Captain Plampin, who had both been to Sandvliet in 1793, and agreed a landing there presented, in Popham's words, no 'obstacles . . . that the Navy will not devise expedients to remove'.[23] Curiously, the opinion was not as emphatic as Chatham later recalled, and did not state that the fleet could 'at once *land* the Troops . . . on either bank of the Scheld [*sic*], as might be required'.[24] The opinion's main purpose was nevertheless to confirm that operations could be conducted at Walcheren and Sandvliet simultaneously, and to address the important issue of Chatham's '*sine qua non*': the viability of a landing at Sandvliet. Arguably, it settled both points, and the Cabinet – and Chatham – gave the Scheldt plan full sanction.

The expedition now made progress. Rear Admiral Sir Richard Strachan was appointed naval commander-in-chief in early June. In contrast with Chatham, he had a long history of active service, almost all of it on the open seas, although he had acquired some experience of combined operations as a subordinate during an expedition to Belleisle in 1800.[25] Meanwhile, the various government departments, including Chatham's Ordnance, hurried to complete all necessary arrangements. The troops selected to take part were ordered to march to embarkation points in the Downs and at Portsmouth and Spithead (the latter locations were a feint designed to fool the enemy into believing half the troops were bound for Portugal).[26] While waiting for the necessary transports to arrive from Lisbon, however, Chatham was confronted with a bombshell.

Tension had been growing for some time between Castlereagh and Canning. After the disastrous Convention of Cintra and Sir John Moore's retreat to Corunna in January 1809, Canning had decided he could no longer work with Castlereagh and threatened resignation. In a choice between the unstable but brilliant Foreign Secretary and Castlereagh, who was intelligent and hard-working but unpopular, Canning was certain to carry the day. The Duke of Portland promised Castlereagh's office as Secretary of State for War to Canning's friend Lord Wellesley, although not until the next parliamentary recess in June. By this time plans for Walcheren were well underway and, when Canning's colleagues were informed of the plot, they insisted Castlereagh should not be replaced until the expedition was over, in the hope that the expedition's success would make it impossible for Canning to oust Castlereagh from the War Office.[27]

Chatham was one of the last of the Cabinet to find out. Edward Cooke, Castlereagh's undersecretary at the War Office, thought 'he, when he accepted the Command [of the Walcheren expedition], was in entire Ignorance; but after his Acceptance was inform'd of the case in strict Confidence', probably around the beginning of July. Chatham was shocked by the revelations and disagreed with concealing the state of affairs from Castlereagh, but (as Cooke noted) did not speak up against any of the arrangements. He nevertheless agreed to continue with the expedition, 'not from Inclination but from Duty'.[28] Indeed the plot changed everything, and completely overshadowed his relations with the War Minister, for Chatham knew his success or failure would determine Castlereagh's political fate.

The ease with which Castlereagh was protected from Canning's plotting contrasted sharply with the attempts to keep the Walcheren preparations secret. Putting together an enormous expedition of 40,000 men and 600 ships inevitably attracted attention. Information leaks via civilian observers was an ongoing problem for Chatham throughout the campaign, and it began well before preparations for the expedition had been completed. One civilian observer Chatham was obliged to keep close was Lord Lowther, the eldest son of the Earl of Lonsdale and one of a clutch of well-connected young gentlemen who accompanied the expedition 'to see *The Fun*'. Lowther sent frequent, gossipy letters home, which he occasionally entrusted to merchant vessels so as to bring his father and, no doubt, any intercepting parties 'the first intelligence' of Chatham's army.[29] Despite a self-imposed silence from many of the government-run papers, such as the *Morning Post*, the 'Grand Expedition' received plenty of coverage.[30] Not until mid-July did the newspapers release their opinion of the expedition's destination, but they got it in one: Walcheren.[31] Not that it had been difficult to guess. One of the Lords of the Admiralty, Lord Palmerston, thought 'the enemy certainly were ignorant of [the expedition's] destination till it arrived off Walcheren', but this was hopelessly optimistic. The French could read as well as the

English and were hurrying to repair Antwerp's defences and bring as many troops to the Scheldt area as possible.[32]

By 19 July, the majority of the men were embarked and ready, with the exception of some cavalry and many of the general officers. Chatham himself began the day in London. His departure had been delayed by private business. On 17 July he was with his solicitor, settling funds from the sale of Burton Pynsent on his niece, Harriot Hester Pringle, in the event of his death.[33] He also finalised arrangements for the care of Lady Chatham, whose mental state remained precarious. She left town a few days after her husband to stay with a friend.[34] Only after tying up these loose ends was Chatham able to depart for Ramsgate. His journey to the coast was characteristically unhurried. He left Hill Street at noon on 19 July, checked in at the Ordnance and War Office, and left town at 4. After sleeping at Sittingbourne, he reached Ramsgate in time for a quick meeting with Castlereagh on the 20th.[35] But his expedition had already been overtaken by events. On 22 July, Chatham received news that the Austrians had been defeated at Wagram a fortnight previously and signed an armistice. It was a devastating blow, and for a while it seemed there was no point sending out an expedition which had, after all, been intended to distract the French from attacking the Austrians. Still, because a Scheldt victory might keep Austria in the war, Chatham and Castlereagh decided not to suspend the campaign – even though it was sailing late, and the French were forearmed.[36]

Even without Wagram, Chatham's expedition assembled under a pall. The plan seemed too hurried, the embarkation was confused and there was too much cynicism in the highest echelons of command. One anonymous source reported from Deal: 'Lord Chatham at Ramsgate gets up late, and all the troops were shuffled in the wrong ships, and have been two days sorting by the men of war, like a pack of cards. [Admiral Sir Richard] Keats and [Home] Popham do not speak. Sir William Erskine [one of the brigadiers] dislikes the plans, and I think all will go to H[e]ll.'[37] Chatham knew he was viewed ambivalently by the men under his command. This was probably inevitable, given he was better known as a politician than for his military exploits, and his reputation for sloth did not fill his subordinates with confidence. Sir John Hope did not mince his words: 'I cannot think from any thing I see that L[ord] C[hatham] is equal to his task'.[38] Lower ranking officers were even more blunt. One called Chatham 'a d—d bad general'.[39] Lord Lowther scratched out the following assessment of Chatham from a letter to his father: 'The Lord knows what can be expected from such a – '.[40] The word he suppressed can easily be guessed at.

Not everyone was pessimistic. Superficially, an air of holiday greeted Chatham when he arrived at Ramsgate. Spectators flocked to the coast to see Britain's greatest armament sail. 'I saw the different divisions of the expedition file off in view of Ramsgate,' the Dutch diplomat Hendrik Fagel wrote to the Duke of Portland's secretary, 'which was a magnificent sight, particularly as the weather then was very fine. . . . There was absolutely no counting the number of Ships of all descriptions'.[41] Gathered in the Downs, 600 men of war, commandeered merchant vessels and flatboats waited for the signal to depart. As he viewed the enormous force under his command, Chatham must have felt exhilaration at the prospect of his first military action in ten years. If his initial doubts about the campaign's viability had not entirely been done away, he may also have felt a rising sense of trepidation, fed by the depressing news from the Continent, the reports of French preparations and the gloominess of his officers; but if he felt any such anxiety, he kept it to himself.

* * *

With the Commander-in-Chief present the expedition could sail, but a change of wind on the 21st kept the other half of the expedition at Portsmouth. While Chatham waited for the wind to change again, news arrived that the enemy fleet had emerged from the safety of Antwerp's guns and anchored off Flushing. The moment Sir Richard Strachan heard this he was itching to get underway. For some reason he believed the French would sit and wait to have their retreat cut off by a British invasion of South Beveland, or (even more incredibly) come out to sea to engage the British in a battle.[42] Unfortunately for Strachan, the Portsmouth fleet – carrying Chatham's second-in-command, Sir Eyre Coote, and the division of the army destined to besiege Flushing – was still pegged into harbour by contrary winds, and Chatham refused to leave without them.

It was the first of many clashes between Chatham and Strachan. The two men were in many ways polar opposites. Chatham was well-connected, cultured and aristocratic, more accustomed to the drawing rooms of London than the thick of battle. Strachan was brave, short-tempered and impulsive, prone to swearing on the quarterdeck and with a long record of active service. The two men disagreed over priorities. Strachan wanted to fulfil a part of his instructions by destroying the enemy fleet, but Chatham argued that sailing without the troops and ships for blockading Flushing – without which the fleet could not safely carry the rest of the expedition to Sandvliet – made little sense. Rumours circulated rapidly about Chatham and Strachan's coolness, forcing Chatham to offset the stories in a letter to Lord Camden:

> I can only however assure you that I have had on all occasions the most unreserved and confidential intercourse with Sir Richard Strachan, who is a man I particularly like, and as far, as I can judge, I should say that we are upon ye most friendly and cordial footing possible. I have always not only been ready to communicate with him, but have sought it on all occasions, and there is not a wish of his with respect to our movements, that I have not met.[43]

Castlereagh had closed Chatham's official instructions trusting 'that the utmost Spirit of Concert and Harmony will prevail throughout the whole of their Operations, between the respective Services'.[44] This already looked unlikely, and the armament had not even sailed.

By the time Chatham wrote to Camden the Portsmouth fleet had reached the Downs at last, and the whole force was ready to go. Chatham was now as keen to sail as Strachan, for a whole week had been lost waiting for the wind to change. 'I came on board yesterday,' he wrote on 27 July from Popham's vessel, the 74-gun *Venerable*, which Strachan was temporarily using as his flagship. 'The wind blows fresh, so that we shall sail most likely this evening.'[45] Chatham was wrong: a further minor delay kept the *Venerable* in port until between 6 and 7am on 28 July, when she weighed anchor in thick fog.[46] She was followed by Admiral Keats's division carrying Sir John Hope. Commodore Owen sailed with Lord Huntly's division at roughly the same time, bound for Cadzand with orders to disarm the Breskens battery and co-operate with the masking of Flushing to allow full access to the West Scheldt. The Portsmouth fleet, however, waited a further 24 hours for some essential equipment.

The *Venerable* anchored off the Stone Deep at 7pm, 10 miles off the broad beaches of Domburg, where the main landing was to take place. From here the flat, sandhill-fringed island could clearly be seen, stark against the horizon. But the carefully laid plans went wrong almost immediately. The wind changed yet again, 'blowing fresh' from the west, and soon turned into a gale. By the time the Portsmouth fleet carrying Coote's division arrived on the 29th it was clear that the Domburg landing would have to be abandoned.[47] An alternative landing place was selected at the northernmost point of Walcheren at Bree Zand. The enemy, relying on the difficulty of disembarking, was unprepared for a landing here, but the British would now have to march across the whole breadth of the island to reach Flushing. Nor was this all. The westerly gale threatened to throw the British fleet against Walcheren's shallow, dangerous sandbanks. Two gunboats were dismasted and one of the warships, the 80-gun *Caesar*, actually ran aground. Under the circumstances, Popham proposed to guide the fleet into a sheltered bay at the mouth of the East Scheldt known as the Roompot. Getting several dozen large warships and hundreds of transports through a narrow, unknown passage in unfavourable conditions was, to put it mildly, a difficult operation. Chatham later wrote to Castlereagh in 'the strongest Terms' of his 'Admiration of the distinguished Abilities with which the Fleet was conducted through the Passage into the Vere Gat'.[48]

Chatham's expedition was safe – but in the wrong place. Not counting Huntly's division destined for Cadzand, the entire force (including Rosslyn and Grosvenor's divisions, originally bound directly for Sandvliet) was in the narrow, difficult-to-navigate East Scheldt. Instead of masking Flushing and sailing directly up the West Scheldt, the armament was separated from the Cadzand force by Walcheren itself, and unable to pass through the intricate Sloe Passage into the West Scheldt until Veere and Rammekens had surrendered. Chatham played down this difficulty in his dispatch, but General Brownrigg later pinpointed the entry into the Roompot as the moment the entire campaign foundered: 'I consider the unfortunate necessity which obliged the whole armament to have been assembled in the Roompot, as fatal to the ulterior objects of the Expedition'.[49]

For now, Chatham and his men were just glad to be alive. Sir John Hope was sent on with Admiral Keats's division of the fleet to land on South Beveland, and Coote prepared to land at Bree Zand and take the nearby Fort Den Haak. Due to the weather and tide (and, according to one of Coote's aides-de-camp, 'the want of arrangement on the part of the Navy') nothing was done until 6 in the evening on 30 July, when the first wave of transports started for shore.[50] 'Lord Chatham,' the *Morning*

Post reported proudly, 'as might have been expected, was so anxious to be as prominent in example as he is high in command, that with a spirit worthy of the name of Pitt, he landed in the first boat'.[51] This is suspect from a ministerial newspaper, but the dry Proceedings of the Army recorded 'the Commander-in-Chief, with the Head Quarter Staff' joining the troops 'when the line of Boats was formed', and the log of the HMS *Venerable* reported him boarding the transport at 4.30pm, so Chatham probably was one of the first ashore.[52] He almost certainly was not *the* first, as it was not known what the enemy would do to repulse the landing, but in fact the French defended themselves minimally. While the rest of the 12,000 men in Coote's division were landed overnight, the light troops under Lieutenant Colonel Denis Pack of the 71st cleared the thick furze and heather topped dunes and took some prisoners. Eventually Fort Den Haak fell silent: its garrison spiked the guns and fled to Veere, pursued by Pack's men.

Having made a good impression by landing with the first wave, Chatham ruined the effect by failing to control his 'immense retinue'. He had seven aides-de-camp, although only three of them were official.[53] Coote's own aide was scandalised to see each of them 'giv[ing] his opinion, & insist[ing] before the face of the very Generals in command, that it ought to be adopted' while Chatham watched in silence. This embarrassing spectacle only ended when someone brought up the Commander-in-Chief's horses, to the astonishment of Coote's aide, who couldn't work out how Chatham had contrived to have them landed so swiftly, but also to his relief, for at 8.30 Chatham rode off along the beach to establish his headquarters in the captured Fort Den Haak.[54] He and his staff – and the civilian observer Lord Lowther, clearly disappointed with the enemy's lack of resistance – went 'quietly to bed about eleven', only to be woken two hours later by Popham, who advised Chatham to return to the landing place. Colonel Pack, who had followed Den Haak's defeated garrison to Veere with four companies of the 71st, had got too close to the town walls. He lost over 30 killed and wounded before retiring, but for a while it looked like the Veere garrison might attempt to retake Den Haak. With about 4,000 men landed, Chatham was in an exposed position. Just as he was readying himself to leave a note arrived from Pack informing him that the 'affair' was over, 'upon which L[or]d C[hatham] returned immediate [*sic*] to bed & was asleep again in two minutes, snoring'. He was no more bothered by the French than he was by the mosquitoes, which – ominously, given what happened later – 'half demolished' Lowther that night.[55]

Chatham was woken again 4 hours later, this time by Sir Eyre Coote, who informed him that deputies had arrived to surrender the town of Middelburg. Chatham and Coote arranged the capitulation of Walcheren's capital while the artillery and stores were disembarking and the 12,000 soldiers rearranged into 4 divisions.[56] That afternoon the army marched on Flushing in two columns. The first, under Generals Graham and Lord Paget, and followed by Coote and Chatham, moved to Grijpskerke. Here Chatham established his headquarters for the second night, before parting from the advancing column on 1 August and fixing himself in Middelburg Abbey while Coote went on to besiege Flushing. The second column under General Houston went to St Laurens, and General Fraser besieged Veere, which surrendered at dawn on 1 August, opening the Sloe Passage between the East and West Scheldt to British navigation as far as Fort Rammekens.[57] Meanwhile, Sir John Hope landed on South Beveland and took the town of Goes without a fight. Two days later, on 3 August, Rammekens surrendered to General Fraser, a day after Sir John Hope found the fort of Bath totally evacuated. The East Scheldt, and with it access to the West Scheldt, was completely in British hands.

Within four days of landing, Chatham's army had captured Walcheren and South Beveland with very little resistance. This swift progress was merciful as Chatham was hugely behind schedule. But he had never doubted the islands would fall sooner or later, and Flushing was already causing more trouble than anticipated.[58] Although it was invested on the landward side, the town remained open to French communication from the sea. Commodore Owen and Lord Gardner were both present in the West Scheldt, but neither was able to manoeuvre against the strong wind. Chatham and his men could only watch while the French got reinforcements into Flushing nearly every day in broad daylight. On 1 August 600 men came over from Cadzand, and a further thousand followed the next day. When the British tried to stop the empty boats returning, the wind pushed them too close to the enemy guns and several ships were raked. On 4 August, gale-force winds allowed the French to get 300 more men over virtually unmolested. By 8 August Coote begged Chatham for more reinforcements: 'There is no knowing where it will Stop if the Navy do not find means to prevent this arrival of Fresh Troops'.[59]

Chatham knew much depended on Lord Huntly's being able to disarm the enemy's battery at Breskens, cutting off French reinforcements and allowing the British fleet freer movement in the West Scheldt. On 3 August, however, he received bad news. After arriving off Cadzand on 29 July, Huntly and his 2,000 men had been prevented from landing due to the same gale that had driven the rest of the fleet into the Roompot. The weather was more favourable on the 30th, but Huntly hesitated. He had assumed, from conversations with General Brownrigg, that he was to land all 2,000 of the men under his command at the same time: but Commodore Owen informed him he only had boats for 600. Owen asked Lord Gardner, stationed some 12 miles away in the Deurloo Passage, to lend some of his boats to help, but Gardner replied he had no such orders. With Owen unable to commit to sending a second wave of 600 men for more than an hour after landing the first, Huntly scoured the coast for enemy movement. From what he could see – and he was restricted to what was happening on the tops of the dykes, which obstructed any further view – the French were preparing for an attack. Huntly thought he 'saw two distinct bodies, amounting together to eighteen hundred men at one time, in two different uniforms'.[60] From this moment the attack was pretty much abandoned, and Owen was directed to land Huntly on South Beveland instead.

Chatham and Strachan put a brave face on the failure – Strachan even suggested to Lord Gardner that Chatham would 'be glad' of it – but in reality the complicated failure of the Cadzand enterprise spelled the end of the expedition's rapid progress.[61] The fleet could not guarantee moving troops and supplies to Bath until Flushing fell, and success at Flushing depended on the navy's being able to establish an effective blockade, which it had so far failed to do. This was a sore point between Chatham and Strachan. Not only were the constant French reinforcements embarrassing and damaging to morale, but they were also ruining the plan (already undermined by the fleet's inability to run up the West Scheldt) for simultaneous operations at Flushing and Antwerp. Because the strength of the Flushing garrison could only be guessed at from the unreliable reports of deserters, Chatham had to reinforce Coote's besieging army with men from the force destined for Antwerp. On 2 August General Grosvenor's division of 5,000 landed to join Coote at East Zouburg. On 4 August, Huntly's 2,000 men and Lord Rosslyn's force were also stationed off Rammekens in case they were required, and on the 5th the Light Brigade of the King's German Legion was diverted from South Beveland.[62] Instead of 12,000 troops, 20,000 men lay before Flushing, with others holding themselves available to assist.

With so much of his army tied down before Flushing, Chatham could not simultaneously pursue the ulterior objective. The Navy's inability to blockade Flushing left the British reserve on South Beveland open to attack and threatened to close off any retreat from Antwerp. Even when the wind changed on 8 August and allowed the navy to close communications between Flushing and Breskens, Strachan made it clear to Chatham he could not guarantee a complete blockade when a further change of wind might return things to their pre-8 August state.[63] Chatham knew the taking of Flushing was now indispensable. But even had Flushing fallen immediately, the ordnance and supplies required to assault Antwerp still had to be brought from the East to West Scheldt through the complicated navigation of the Sloe Passage. On 8 August Chatham renounced his intention to proceed to South Beveland and declared he would 'remain [on Walcheren] until the Naval Arrangements were in forwardness for proceeding up the West Scheldt'.[64]

This enforced delay worsened the fraying relations between Strachan and Chatham, who had not forgotten Mulgrave's 19 June guarantee that the fleet could make a quick run up the West Scheldt to Sandvliet. 'You will recollect how lightly these matters were consider'd previous to our leaving England, and with how much ease it was said they could be effected,' Brownrigg wrote, ominously, adding two days later: 'We have been grievously disappointed in the co-operation we had hoped to have derived from the Navy'.[65] But Chatham's commitment to remaining on Walcheren also widened a breach with another colleague. The operations against Flushing were the responsibility of the second-in-command, Sir Eyre Coote. Chatham had never intended to set foot on Walcheren at all, but, with the fleet's unexpected entry into the Roompot, his proceeding immediately to Sandvliet had become impossible. Coote would have preferred Chatham go off to badger Sir John Hope on South Beveland, but this made little sense with British activity concentrated so much on Flushing. Chatham had instead chosen to remain until the intended advance on Antwerp could proceed, and Coote was horrified to find himself outranked in a command he had assumed would be left entirely to his discretion. He became convinced Chatham was following him on purpose:

He was put in orders as the Officer to whom the attack of Walcheren was confided, & he no sooner lands, than he finds the Commander of the Forces, with all his Staff, close at his heels; and the moment he moves on, he is followed, & tho' his measures are not exactly thwarted, or opposed, yet they are much impeded by the various opinions and advice forced upon him. It is altogether a most anomalous situation.[66]

While he had expected to move on any day Chatham had held back from direct involvement in the siege, but 'he could [no longer] remain . . . an idle Spectator' now he was committed to remaining on Walcheren until Flushing fell. He therefore took overall control as Commander of the Forces.[67] This was in any case justified by the 'really provoking' slowness of the engineers in erecting the six batteries designed to bombard Flushing into submission.[68] Ordnance supplies had to be landed at Veere and marched across the island, which hindered the building of the batteries, and poor relations between officers and men had further delayed their completion. On 8 August Chatham replaced Coote's chief engineer, Colonel D'Arcy, with his own man, William Fyers.[69] 'Things . . . are going on better,' Brownrigg wrote in relief on the 10th, but this progress came at the expense of good relations between Chatham and Coote.[70]

This tension reflected an increasingly serious deterioration of morale. As the so-called '*coup de main*' limped towards the end of its second week, the men – who, apart from those employed in building the batteries, had little to do but get rained on – were getting bored. The French enlivened matters by attempting an abortive *sortie* on 7 August, but after this brief excitement things resumed their course and the lack of action was making everyone edgy, including Chatham himself.[71] 'Nothing very material has occurred since my last Dispatch of the 3d Instant,' he wrote home on 7 August, and his private letter to Castlereagh on 11 August reflected his growing uneasiness:

I am in constant expectation of the return of some confidential Persons, sent into Antwerp and Bergen op Zoom, and on whose report if they succeed in the objects of their mission, I may be enabled to enter a little more into ye subject of our future prospects . . . but as yet our Intelligence is so vague and unsatisfactory, that any opinion, I cou'd now venture to give, must be formed on very

John Pitt, 2nd Earl of Chatham by George Romney (1783, Copyright: Trustees of the Chevening Estate). Romney's portrait, now at Chevening in Kent, was commissioned by Chatham's former tutor, Edward Wilson, along with a companion portrait of Pitt the Younger (now at the Tate).

William Pitt the Elder, 1st Earl of Chatham: print, after William Hoare (private collection).

Left: Mary Elizabeth Townshend, Countess of Chatham, possibly by Edward Miles (1789, private collection). Chatham married Mary Townshend in 1783 after a long, bashful courtship. Their marriage was happy, but childless.

Right: Georgiana Townshend, by an unknown artist (private collection). Georgiana was Lady Chatham's elder sister. She remained unmarried, and spent much of her life devotedly nursing Lady Chatham through her many illnesses.

Left: William Pitt the Younger, by the studio of Thomas Gainsborough (1787-9, Yale Center for British Art, Paul Mellon Collection). Chatham's brilliant brother became Britain's youngest prime minister in 1783 at the age of 24.

The death of the Earl of Chatham, engraved by Francesco Bartolozzi, after John Singleton Copley (1788, Yale Center for British Art, Paul Mellon Collection). The 2nd Earl of Chatham is depicted in his regimentals, holding his father's arm. Beside him is his youngest brother James Charles, in naval uniform. William, behind, gesticulates in alarm.

The crests of Lord and Lady Chatham, from a family pedigree (private collection). Chatham's crest is depicted surrounded by the Garter and surmounted by an earl's coronet.

Chatham's fob seal (private collection). Chatham's crest impales that of his wife, and is surrounded by a garter and surmounted by an earl's coronet.

Chatham's Garter star (private collection). As a Knight of the Garter, Chatham would have worn this regularly at court and on military duty.

Chatham's signature and handwriting (private collection).

The Admiralty (private collection). Chatham was First Lord of the Admiralty from 1788 to 1794.

'The Death of the Great Wolf', James Gillray (1795, Yale Center for British Art, Paul Mellon Collection). Gillray's composition parodies Benjamin West's famous 'Death of Wolfe'. Pitt, as 'the Great Wolf', is revived by a glass of port proffered by Henry Dundas. Chatham stands sorrowfully behind, holding the flag.

The sandhills behind Schoorl, looking out over the plains (photo by the author). The first major battle of the Helder campaign in which Chatham took part was fought on this terrain on 2 October 1799. Chatham and his men were in reserve in the plain before being called up to support Sir Eyre Coote in the sandhills.

Dunes between Castricum and Beverwijk (photo by the author). The second battle of the Helder campaign in which Chatham took part was the battle for Castricum on 6 October 1799. Chatham was wounded during the fight.

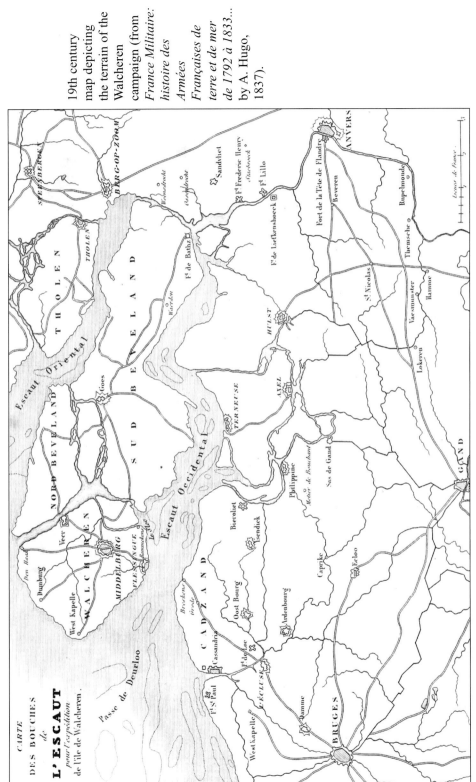

19th century map depicting the terrain of the Walcheren campaign (from *France Militaire: histoire des Armées Françaises de terre et de mer de 1792 à 1833...* by A. Hugo, 1837).

John Pitt, 2nd Earl of Chatham, studio of John Hoppner (1799, courtesy of the Commando Forces Officers' Mess, Royal Marines Barracks, Plymouth). This portrait shows Chatham around the time he re-entered the army.

Bree Zand, Walcheren (photo by the author). Chatham landed here with his army on 30 July 1809.

Flushing harbour, Walcheren (photo by the author). Now a peaceful seaside resort, Flushing was heavily bombarded by Chatham's army between 13 and 15 August 1809.

Middelburg Abbey, Walcheren (photo by the author). Chatham's headquarters for most of the time he was on Walcheren.

Cannonballs embedded in houses at Veere, Walcheren (photo by the author). The cannonballs date from the bombardment of Veere by the British on 31 July and 1 August 1809.

'Attaque de Flessingue' (from *France Militaire: histoire des Armées Françaises de terre et de mer de 1792 à 1833...* by A. Hugo, 1837). The siege of Flushing was the only major action of the Walcheren campaign.

The Bombardment of Flushing (from *British Battles on Land and Sea* volume 3, by James Grant, 1873). Nineteenth-century depiction of the naval bombardment of Flushing.

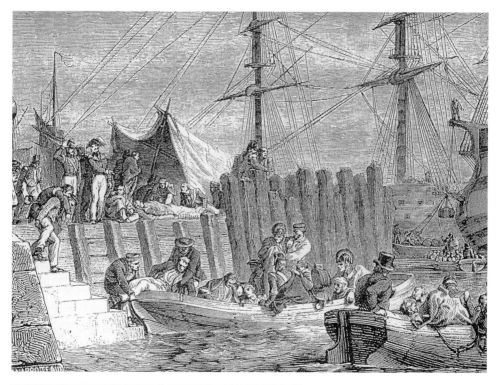

The evacuation of South Beveland, August 1809 (public domain via Wikimedia Commons). By the end of August thousands of Chatham's army had become sick with 'Walcheren fever', with hundreds more falling ill every day.

Spencer Perceval, by William Skelton after Sir William Beechey (Yale Center for British Art, Paul Mellon Collection). Perceval succeeded the Duke of Portland as prime minister in October 1809. Chatham felt let down by his handling of the Walcheren inquiry.

'Secret Influence, or a Peep Behind the Screen', Charles Williams (1810, Library of Congress Prints and Photographs Division, Washington DC). Chatham submitted a narrative to the King in February 1810 explaining his conduct during the Walcheren campaign. This narrative caused him more trouble than the campaign itself.

Abington Hall, Cambridge (photo by the author). Chatham rented Abington Hall from John Mortlock in 1816. He was responsible for whitewashing the exterior, as can be seen in this photograph. His time at Abington was full of misery.

Chatham's house in Hill Street, London (photo by the author). Now the Naval Club. Chatham lived here from 1808 until his departure for Gibraltar. Lady Chatham died here in May 1821.

View of Gibraltar by Charles Dyce (ca 1849, Yale Center for British Art, Paul Mellon Collection). Chatham became Governor of Gibraltar in 1820, although he did not go out until 1821. He returned to England in 1825.

The Convent, Gibraltar (photo by the author). Chatham's residence in Gibraltar as Governor. The exterior dates from the late 19th century.

Cathedral of the Holy Trinity, Gibraltar (photo by the author). Sir George Don originated the project for building Gibraltar's first Protestant church, but Chatham brought it to fruition. He laid the foundation stone just before departing Gibraltar in 1825.

Chatham was responsible for completing Gibraltar's Grand Casemates Square and for repairs to the Waterport Gate defences in 1824. (Photo by the author)

The 2nd Earl of Chatham in later life (detail from NPG 999, 'The Trial of Queen Caroline, 1820' by Sir George Hayter, 1820–1823, © National Portrait Gallery, London). This depicts Chatham about the time of his wife's death, when he was in his mid-sixties.

10 Charles Street, London (photo by author). Chatham died here on 24 September 1835.

insufficient grounds. . . . With regard to ye probable duration of the Siege [of Flushing], it is difficult to form any conjecture till after our Batteries open upon the place, and that their means of resistance are a little more ascertained.[72]

As pessimistic as Chatham was beginning to sound, he still restrained himself from setting down the full story. Brownrigg told Alexander Hope that the situation was much worse than Chatham felt at liberty to set down on paper, in the knowledge that his letters might be published in the *Gazette* and read by all interested parties in Britain (and France): 'Lord Chatham is fully aware of the obstacles that will be thrown in his way, and is by no means sanguine, in his Expectations to overcome them; but He does not feel the necessity of transmitting Home any part of the Intelligence He receives'. Brownrigg nevertheless had every confidence that the Commander-in-Chief's 'judgment and firmness' could be relied upon to avoid 'risking the safety of the Army'.[73]

But Chatham, although wise and firm in the opinion of his staff, could not reverse the impression of the forces that everything was going wrong. His style of command, to judge from the glimpse provided by Walcheren, was exactly what might be expected of a parade-ground general: distant and out of touch, with an over insistence on ceremony and etiquette. He lacked both the imagination to form viable alternative strategies on the spur of the moment, and the flair required to inspire devotion in his men. He made absolutely no effort to make himself visible, remaining at headquarters in the peaceful, prosperous town of Middelburg as much as possible. Nor did he make any change in his habits: he rose 'between 12 & one, not receiving Officers till 2 o'Clock', after which he took 'his morning ride, as far as the [Flushing] Lines'.[74] 'Everything goes on at headquarters as if they were at the Horse Guards,' one naval officer reported towards the end of the campaign. 'It did not signify what you wanted, you must call between certain hours, send up your name and wait for your turn'.[75] Under the circumstances, doubts about Chatham's fitness for command were expressed more loudly. 'Direct imputations are cast upon Lord Chatham's courage, as well as his generalship,' Lord Temple told his father, Lord Buckingham. '. . . In the luxury of a London kitchen, was he living within twelve miles of the enemy, whilst his army were living upon salt meat and biscuit, without tents or covering of any sort, and in water.'[76] The burghers of Middelburg gave Chatham two turtles as a gift, which backfired spectacularly, given his reputation and the glacial pace with which the siege of Flushing was advancing. Chatham became 'Turtle Chatham', the turtles a physical representation of his sloth and love of fine dining:

> Dialogue between Lord Chatham and a Friend:
> F: When sent fresh wreaths on Flushing's shores to reap,
> What didst thou do, illustrious Chatham? C – Sleep!
> F: To men fatigued with war, repose is sweet,
> But when awake, didst thou do nothing? C – Eat.[77]

Even the enemy nicknamed him 'Lord j'Attends'.[78]

Chatham's inactivity, at least until 8 August, was partly ascribable to his having nothing to do while the siege of Flushing remained Coote's responsibility. Nevertheless, his reluctance to do more than he absolutely had to deepened the impression that he was out of touch. Frustratingly, Chatham was capable of charming those who came into regular contact with him, such as the anonymous author of *Letters from Flushing*: 'Everyone seems to feel a lively regard for him; his manners are so gentlemanlike, and his temper so easy and affable, that he has at least won all our hearts'.[79] Even a little interest in the men under his command would have warmed them, and reduced the severity of the attacks later made upon him. But, either from a persuasion that the commander of an army ought to remain aloof, or because of a shy personality that thrived on the pomp and superiority of his rank, Chatham never did condescend to mingle with his troops. In return they made 'that *old wife Lord Chatham*' the focus of their frustration.[80]

*   *   *

Chatham's success now rode on the batteries encircling Flushing making an immediate impact. By 11 August they were ready to open but, in an instance of the sheer bad luck that dogged the entire expedition, their completion was further retarded by weather described by Chatham as 'the heaviest rains I ever saw'.[81] Morale was not improved by the discovery that the enemy had cut the dykes to try to flood out the British lines. This was countered by opening the sluices in Middelburg, but the rising water contributed to the troops' general misery.

Chatham was as frustrated as anybody else with the delay although, as he reported to Castlereagh, nothing further could be done against Antwerp until Strachan had managed to get the siege supplies into the West Scheldt:

> I am sorry to say, that the Division of Transports, with the Cavalry and Artillery Horses, the heavy Ordnance, and the Stores of all Descriptions, have not yet been brought through the Slowe [*sic*] Passage. The Moment they appear, it is my Intention to proceed towards Bathz [*sic*]; but, as till then no Operations can be undertaken, I have thought my Presence here [in Middelburg] was more useful.[82]

To make sure Flushing fell quickly, Chatham expected Strachan to provide assistance from his ships' guns. But Strachan had not yet managed to get any warships through the Deurloo Passage between Flushing and Breskens, although he had been talking about it since the end of July.[83] He put his plan into operation on 11 August, although the first Chatham knew of it was when the French opened fire on eight British ships passing through the Deurloo. 'Until we heard the firing yesterday evening we did not know, that the Passage of the Scheldt was then to be forced,' General Brownrigg complained. 'A co-operation from our Land Batteries would have been useful had they been ready'.[84] At least everything was ready for the reduction of Flushing to begin.

The bombardment began from five of the six batteries at 1pm on 13 August.[85] A total of 52 pieces of artillery of all sizes poured a constant barrage of fire on the town. Gunboats from the Scheldt also contributed. After the build-up of their dash through the Deurloo, however, Strachan's eight ships of the line did nothing for now: 'the wind being from the South West, prevented them getting under Weigh'. A party of Royals and soldiers from the 14th Regiment pushed the British lines forward through the sandhills before the battery at Nolle, meeting with little resistance. 'Soon after dark our Gun-batteries ceased firing, and the Gun-boats (their Ammunition being expended) drew off': but the three mortar batteries at West Zouburg continued firing and rockets were released, 'the combined effect of which succeeded in setting fire to the town at about Midnight, in a very considerable degree, and it continued to burn with great violence the whole of the Night'.[86] The author of *Letters from Flushing* waxed lyrical: 'Imagine a dark, gloomy, and almost tempestuous midnight, whilst the vault of heaven was rent by a most dreadful bombardment, and rockets, like meteors, hissed and blazed in the air'.[87]

The enemy fought back robustly, particularly against the barrage from the centre batteries. Overnight, however, they stopped their firing, and when daylight came all six British batteries opened again. At 10 Strachan's eight ships joined in with 'the most incessant & tremendous [cannonade] that ever was heard. The roar was terrific, & so much so, that in a very short time, the Enemy's sea batteries were almost altogether silenced'. Even though Strachan's flagship, the *St Domingo*, and Gardner's *Blake* ran aground – actively illustrating the perils of shallow waters – the effect of the naval bombardment was devastating: 'at the expiration of an Hour scarcely a Shot was return'd'.[88]

Chatham watched the bombardment from the Nolle battery, accompanied by his staff and Lord Lowther. He was impressed with its effect, exclaiming, 'What a noble spectacle!'[89] 'Had some shells thrown at us,' Lowther remarked laconically, but by now Chatham had noticed the beleaguered town was hardly responding.[90] At about 2 the enemy batteries fell silent completely. At 4.30pm Chatham, who had moved to the Vijgeter Battery, '[observed] the propriety of discontinuing the fire which was uselessly thrown away, or employed principally in demolishing the Town'.[91] A flag of truce was sent into the town at 6, giving Monnet, the French commander of Flushing, '*One Hour* . . . to surrender with his Garrison, Prisoners of War'. Monnet played for time, asking for permission to consult a council of war. At 9.30pm, therefore, the batteries resumed their fire, 'and a dreadful Bombardment it was, flights of 10 & 12 Shells being seen in the Air at the same time'.[92]

At 10.30pm Monnet requested a 48-hour ceasefire to deliberate. 'This he was immediately informed was inadmissible, and that no other proposals could be listened to, than what were founded upon the basis of the garrison of Flushing becoming prisoners of War'. While this was going on, General Fraser sent Colonel Pack and 150 light troops to attack the enemy positions on the right. They lost the element of surprise due to the brightness of the flames from Flushing, but they persevered, the British troops delighted to see some action at last: 'We could hear very distinctly the French Drums beating to Arms, which were answered by the chearful huzzaing of our Troops'.[93] The French were beaten back and 40 men taken prisoner. Shortly before 2 in the morning Monnet sent another flag of truce, this time to surrender. At 3am on 15 August 1809, the land batteries ceased fire. Half an hour later the ships of the line followed suit. After 36 hours of almost constant bombardment, the siege of Flushing was over.

*   *   *

The reaction in Britain to Chatham's success at Flushing was, generally, ecstatic. The *Morning Chronicle* reported Monnet's flag of truce as early as 18 August, although the victory was not officially confirmed until the firing of the Park and Tower guns on 20 August.[94] While the public celebrated, Chatham's colleagues, who had been despairing for some time over the increasingly taut dispatches from Walcheren, were delighted. Castlereagh's official dispatch rejoiced, without a trace of irony, that such a

> serious Obstacle to the vigorous Prosecution of the ulterior Objects of the Expedition, has thus been so seasonably overcome . . . His Majesty feels persuaded that those important Objects will be followed up without a Moment's Loss of Time, with the same Energy, Perseverance and Rapidity, which has hitherto distinguished the Course of your Lordship's Operations.[95]

Privately Castlereagh added his personal congratulations on the 'most brilliant Close of the first branch of your operations . . . God grant that you may find it practicable to terminate with equal Honor to yourself, and advantage to the Country the remainder of the arduous Task with which you have been charged'. Having given Chatham this much to mull over, Castlereagh closed with the hope that 35,000 men (including seamen) would soon be poised to advance on Antwerp.[96]

On Walcheren, Chatham was far from sharing Castlereagh's giddy predictions of glory. Flushing, which according to government predictions ought to have surrendered immediately, had tied half his army down for two weeks. Official reports from July 1809 that Flushing contained 2,000 men had been proven 'quite fallacious': thanks to the daily reinforcements from Cadzand, Brownrigg estimated the number of defenders had been 4 times as high, and nearly 6000 enemy were taken with the town.[97] Chatham could justify devoting so much effort to reducing the place: Cadzand's remaining in enemy hands made Flushing's fall vital for the British to command the West Scheldt, protect Hope's men in South

Beveland and cover a retreat from Antwerp. Nevertheless, the siege had revealed a serious disagreement between the military and naval commanders and laid bare a lack of cooperation between Chatham and Coote. Everything Chatham heard, moreover, suggested the window of opportunity to attack Antwerp was closed, if it had ever been properly open. The enemy had taken advantage of Chatham's slow progress to rush thousands of reinforcements to the Scheldt basin. Reflecting on the latest intelligence reports, Chatham must have wondered whether the siege of Flushing had been worth the effort.

For now, Chatham focused on what had been achieved rather than worrying about what was to come. The Flushing garrison marched out on 18 August, after several trivial delays. At 7 in the morning the British were assembled on either side of the Coudekerke road. A path lined by the 79th, 81st and 9th Light Dragoons led to a large field where the surrender was to take place. Everyone was ready for the enemy garrison to begin marching out at 8am – except for the British Commander-in-Chief. Chatham, 'not being a very early man' slept in, and the French and British troops had to wait under an increasingly hot sun until he made his leisurely appearance at a quarter to 9.[98] Military pageantry was something Chatham did well, tardiness notwithstanding, and he was immaculately turned out, his enamelled Garter star glinting in the sunlight as the enemy piled their arms. His French counterparts were less elegant. A junior officer attached to the 81st thought 'it was almost farcical to see these men received by their captors with the ceremonies performed, and I believe our Generals and Staff Officers (of which there was a great number splendidly attired) felt somewhat ashamed of the ostentation displayed when they discovered for whom it was done'.[99]

The surrender over, Chatham turned his thoughts back to Antwerp. Although his subordinates were more convinced than ever that the ultimate objective was out of reach, Chatham informed Castlereagh he intended to proceed to South Beveland as soon as possible.[100] He was nevertheless in no particular hurry, and remained at Middelburg an extra day to settle some financial difficulties that had arisen as a result of the Treasury's refusal to send more specie from Britain. By the time he reached South Beveland on 21 August, leaving a disgruntled Coote in command of Walcheren and a garrison of 12,000 men, 6 days had passed since Flushing's surrender. Castlereagh's lightning 'coup de main' had been lingering for three full weeks.

In truth Chatham did not need to move faster. Until the troops intended for Antwerp landed on the Continent, they remained at the mercy of the Navy, the difficult navigation and the changeable wind. The ordnance equipment required for siege work was still working its way between the East and West Scheldt, and General Graham's division had only just begun 'following [General] Grosvenor, who embarked two days ago but is still in the *Sloe*'.[101] Chatham correctly anticipated that neither troops nor supplies would overcome the considerable navigation difficulties of the Sloe Passage for some days. The day after establishing temporary headquarters at Goes he met with Sir John Hope, and asked him what he thought about the likelihood of reaching Antwerp. 'My Opinions I gave very freely,' Hope recalled.[102] He told Chatham bluntly 'that there was no probability of our success'. Latest intelligence reports estimated enemy strength at a little over 30,000 on both banks of the Scheldt, 11,000 in Antwerp alone and a further 12,000 immediately available between Bergen and Lillo.[103] Lord Rosslyn, who met Chatham later the same day, said the same thing.[104]

Both Rosslyn and Hope imagined the campaign was over. Chatham's opinion was less clear, but the slowness with which he had moved from Walcheren to South Beveland suggested he agreed. Brownrigg believed Chatham had privately given up on Antwerp even before leaving Middelburg, and had gone on to South Beveland because he thought 'it right to judge for himself, and to shew that nothing has been left untried'.[105] But Brownrigg, who had formerly expressed confidence in his commander's judgment, was beginning to wonder whether Chatham was only proceeding because he could not face going back. Brownrigg hoped some plan of action would be adopted once all the generals and naval men met at Bath, 'but I will not promise this, as we are unfortunately too slow in determining'. He hastily added that 'under all circumstances, we could not have acted with more rapidity', but it was the first sign in his correspondence that Chatham was growing indecisive.[106]

Sir John Hope shared Brownrigg's fear that Chatham had no real idea what to do next. 'What the Plans are I know not, or whether any plan Exists,' he wrote on 19 August, adding a few days later, 'Much indecision & irresolution prevails'.[107] He could not seriously believe Chatham meant to attack Antwerp, and yet every step further south brought more enemy reinforcements to the Scheldt basin:

I cannot but regret that more Troops, and so many large Ships of War, are pushed up the West Scheldt, because if there is not an absolute determination to persist at all hazards . . . [they will] embarrass us extremely, and the necessity of withdrawing them, without effecting our purpose, must give an air of failure, and disappointment to the whole, which would have been avoided, had our means been kept a little in the back Ground, until an ultimate determination had been made.[108]

Hope's protests made no difference. The Commander-in-Chief continued his slow progress across South Beveland. He concealed any doubts from his staff, and also Sir Richard Strachan, who met Chatham on 24 August and saw no reason to suppose the attempt on Antwerp would be abandoned.[109]

Chatham reached Fort Bath on 24 August. From here he could see the sight that had tantalised Sir John Hope and the Reserve ever since 3 August: 'We could plainly discover the fortification of Antwerp, and the cathedral was very plain as we could see the dial with the naked eye and count the number of large ships laying in the basin . . . likewise the great fort of Lillo was very plainly perceived'.[110] On 25 August the last troop transports arrived from the Sloe Passage. As the rains that had persisted, on and off, since the expedition began set in again, the whole force destined for Antwerp assembled at the furthest point of South Beveland. The time had come to decide whether to continue or turn back. While Chatham considered his options, Brownrigg and Popham made an unfortunate discovery while reconnoitring the planned landing point at Sandvliet. Although they were forced to retire by the appearance of some enemy cavalry, they saw enough to conclude that the beach at Sandvliet was unsuitable for landing, since the position of the dyke surrounding it left attackers vulnerable to enemy fire; nor was the hard sand suitable for cavalry.[111] Chatham had accepted the Walcheren command on Mulgrave's twin assurances that the navy could carry his men up the West Scheldt and land them at Sandvliet. Neither of those promises had come to pass, and the certainty that he had been led into a difficult situation under false pretences fed Chatham's growing anger at the Admiralty's handling of the naval side of the expedition.

But the Sandvliet discovery, although frustrating, was not enough to force him to turn back. What put a decisive end to Chatham's campaign was the sudden and violent appearance of sickness in his forces. Its first manifestation is difficult to establish. *Letters from Flushing* refers to fatalities in large numbers as early as 12 August, but on 8 August Brownrigg had reported 'We have yet no sick', and on 11 August Chatham thought 'the Troops upon ye whole continue healthy'.[112] The Inspector of Hospitals on Walcheren did not report any instances of illness on South Beveland until 20 August, and on Walcheren until the 24th.[113] By the time Chatham reached Bath, however, sickness was tearing through the army at a terrifying rate. By 25 August 3,000 men found themselves on the sick list, which on 27 August 'was increasing every Hour'. On 28 August alone there were 500 fresh cases.[114] 'Our men fall sick by Hundreds of a day,' Coote's aide despaired. '. . . This island [Walcheren] is a mere Hospital and an Inspector of Hospitals will shortly be a more useful officer than the General Commanding'.[115]

The planning for the campaign should have foreseen some illness, and Chatham himself had expressed fears about the effects of Walcheren's climate on his men before leaving England.[116] Despite this, the expedition's medical staff had been formulated with a force of only 30,000 men in mind. Although in mid-August Brownrigg considered Horse Guards had 'made ample provision for our Sick and Wounded', by the end of the month the provision for dealing with sickness was unable to keep pace with its spread.[117] 'Walcheren fever', as it was known, may in fact have been several illnesses exacerbating each other. Disembarked with a lightning campaign in mind, the men had neither tents nor greatcoats to protect them from the rain, and the stagnant water lying everywhere on the islands of Walcheren and South Beveland did not help. Malaria was, of course, present, carried by the mosquitoes flying about the wetlands, but typhus, typhoid and dysentery probably accounted for the illnesses recorded in mid-August before malaria had had the requisite two to three weeks to incubate. The result was, in Martin Howard's words, 'a lethal combination of old diseases . . . acting together in a group of men weakened by previous campaigning and a life of drunkenness and poverty in the lower reaches of society'.[118]

Faced with the devastating impact of disease on his forces, Chatham talked for the first time of 'retiring'. He knew what reaction he could expect if he returned home unsuccessful, with an army riddled with sickness: Strachan later remembered him being 'extremely hurt that circumstances had prevented him from proceeding on to the ulterior objects of the Expedition'.[119] But to press on in the face of all the evidence of enormous French reinforcements, with an army that was growing sicker and sicker every day, would have been madness. On 26 August Chatham spent the day with Hope, Rosslyn, Grosvenor, Coote, Huntly, Paget and Brownrigg, the remaining lieutenants-general (Fraser had been sent home sick some time before).[120] Strachan and his second-in-command Admiral Keats also attended. After a day of deliberation – one or two of the generals, particularly the Marquis of Huntly, may have opposed the abandonment of the expedition – Chatham asked Brownrigg to draw up a summary of the main points under discussion.[121] Brownrigg's memorandum was largely a matter of military mathematics. The enemy could call on a force of 35,500 men in the vicinity, 11,000 in Antwerp itself. The British, on the other hand, had 30,000 effectives, and only 14,000 of them would be available to march on Antwerp.[122] The cause was lost, as the generals told Chatham on the 27th:

Inundations are said to be effected around Lillo, in the country between Hulst and Liefkenshoek, and in front of the Tête de Flandre. The defences of Antwerp are stated to be restored . . . As a preliminary measure, the possession of forts Lillo and Liefkenshoek is considered indispensable . . . The probable time in which these objects can be accomplished, cannot be estimated at less than from three to four weeks, during which period the means the enemy will have of augmenting his force are incalculable. Our total effective force . . . is reduced by a rapid, and it is feared increasing sickness . . . We are of opinion that, under all the circumstances that have been laid before us, the undertaking the siege of Antwerp is impracticable.[123]

Faced with this unanimous opinion, Chatham reluctantly decided to evacuate South Beveland and retreat back to Walcheren. By 4 September all troops, supplies and transports were back on Walcheren, the South Beveland forts destroyed as far as possible, and Chatham had returned to Middelburg. Within 24 hours the enemy had retaken South Beveland.

* * *

Chatham announced the campaign's failure to Castlereagh in an official dispatch dated 29 August, while his officers wondered how to pack 35,000 men, many very ill, into cramped, damp and bomb-damaged accommodation. He excused the decision to retreat by suggesting it had been the inevitable end for the expedition even before the troops landed on Walcheren at the end of July, and ended on a defensive note:

> I had certainly understood on my Arrival at Walcheren that the Enemy were assembling in considerable Force at all Points, but I was unwilling to give too much Credit to these Reports, and I determined to persevere until I was satisfied upon the fullest Information that all further Attempts would be unavailing.
>
> . . . Under these Circumstances, however mortifying to me to see the Progress arrested of an Army from whose good Conduct and Valour I had every Thing to hope, I felt that my Duty left me no other Choice than to close my Operations here; and it will always be a Consolation to me to think, that I have not been induced lightly to commit the Safety of the Army confided to me, or the Reputation of His Majesty's Arms.[124]

But by 6 September, with the sick returns standing at over 8,000, he had still heard nothing in response: 'I have waited with much Anxiety for an Answer to my Dispatch'. When Castlereagh's mysterious silence continued, Chatham started sending men home ahead of War Office orders.[125]

By now whatever fighting spirit remained in Chatham's army had completely broken. Two weeks of inaction combined with increasing sickness to create an atmosphere of despair and near panic. Many sick officers, including Graham, Grosvenor, Rosslyn and Hope, secured Chatham's permission to return home, most under the influence of genuine illness, but Brownrigg thought others were malingering: 'A considerable degree of apprehension of Climate and Disease has prevail'd too generally, and there has been much anxiety shewn to get away from this Island as if it had been a second St Domingo'.[126] One British newspaper reported Chatham as being 'among the sick, considered dangerously ill'.[127] The paper was misinformed: Chatham was not ill, but he was almost certain to be called home to account for his actions. When he left, the duty of holding onto Walcheren would devolve on Sir Eyre

Coote, who was so incensed at seeing 'every other Lt. Gen. (all junior in rank) go home' before him that he came very close to threatening to leave Chatham to pick up the pieces. Chatham managed to calm Coote down and they parted in a friendly enough manner, but Coote remained unhappy.[128] He urged the need to provide a sizeable force to defend Walcheren, given the sickness of the army and the proximity of the French in Cadzand and South Beveland, but when he asked about Strachan's opinion of how Walcheren could best be defended Chatham could barely restrain his contempt: 'The Navy knew nothing of the matter'.[129]

The friction between Chatham and Strachan had broken into open coldness since Chatham's arrival on South Beveland. Relations broke down completely when Strachan rashly ordered Admiral Keats to co-operate with Lord Rosslyn in a joint advance on Antwerp before Chatham and his men had arrived from Walcheren. Chatham was furious when Rosslyn told him about this clear attempt to bypass his authority, and stopped communicating with Strachan almost completely.[130] The Admiral grew increasingly frustrated with Chatham's contemptuous silence, abusing the military commander in private letters. In London, Chatham's colleagues received Strachan's complaints in confusion and alarm. 'This want of communication in a joint concern is the last fault into which I should have imagined Lord Chatham would have fallen,' Lord Bathurst lamented.[131]

Chatham's natural taciturnity and Strachan's inability to express his thoughts coherently on paper or in person inevitably led to an atmosphere of miscommunication and misunderstanding. From Chatham's point of view, Strachan's failure to cut Flushing off from Cadzand during the siege, and the slowness with which he had brought the supplies and troops through the Sloe Passage, had decisively delayed the army's advance on Antwerp. Chatham was almost certainly taking out his frustration at the campaign's inglorious end on the most obvious victim available, and he did not make much allowance for the impact of the weather, wind and tide on Strachan's ships. Arguably, however, naval logistics were not his concern. His remit was strictly military, and it was up to Strachan to get round the obstacles in the way of full naval cooperation. A more experienced (and imaginative) military commander might have tried harder to mitigate the effect of the Navy's difficulties on the Army's advance, but Chatham could, and did, argue that he had done everything he could to get the army moving.

All Chatham could do was nurse his humiliation, await his orders to return, and anticipate the inevitable public backlash. The expected orders arrived on 7 September, and realised Chatham's worst fears. Castlereagh's official recognition of Chatham's 29 August dispatch was 'the coldest thing imaginable', merely acknowledging his decision to end the campaign without approving it:

> Under the opinion stated by Your Lordship that the ulterior Objects of the Expedition . . . are no longer practicable, in which Opinion the Lieutenant-Generals of the Army appear unanimously to have concurred, I have only to convey to Your Lordship the King's Commands that, after providing effectually for the Security of Walcheren, you do return with the Remainder of the Army to England.[132]

It was almost as discouraging as the clutch of newspapers received at the same time as the dispatches, which conveyed in no uncertain terms the country's disappointment and disgust at the news of the campaign's failure.

'When all comes out, & which must be the case when Parliament meets,' Coote thought, optimistically, 'the thing will speak for itself.'[133] Brownrigg was less sure: 'I can only upon the whole trust that the Publick will judge Lord Chatham fairly. He deserves well at their hands. A General with a mind less firm, might have risk'd, what to all appear'd so hazardous, rather than encounter the ill-natured Clamours of the Publick'.[134] But Chatham was returning to a country where the newspapers openly demanded his court martial, and to colleagues with a proven track record of stabbing each other in the back. He must have wondered whether staying to face the French might not be the better option.

Chapter 10

'The Clamour Raised Against Me' 1809–10

Chatham landed at Deal in the afternoon of 15 September 1809, and arrived back in London the following morning. The newspapers reported his return with evident curiosity. 'Lord Chatham came back – got in at Pit price,' the *Morning Chronicle* punned, referencing not only Chatham's name and the current 'Old Price' Riots over ticket hikes at Covent Garden Theatre, but also the widely held expectation that Chatham would escape scot-free: 'The nation, *la bonne nation*, is gulled, and Lord Chatham remains a General, and a Minister as before, ready to succeed to Premier until he shall think proper to resign, or when it shall please God or the King to remove him, as being unfit for the duties of the present, or ripe for the happiness of the next world'.[1]

Chatham's position was, however, far from secure. Robbed of what should have been an easy victory and presented instead with a tragic debacle, the infuriated public fastened on Chatham as the obvious scapegoat. He had commanded the military part of the Walcheren expedition; he was part of the government that had planned it; and his famous name, rather than protecting him, drew more attention to him. Ominously, also, Chatham had discovered the reason Castlereagh had taken so long to respond to his 29 August dispatch. News of the Portland government's swift, spectacular implosion had trickled across the sea to Middelburg during the second week of September. Portland had suffered a serious stroke in mid-August and, although he had recovered, his inevitable resignation had been hastened by the bringing of Canning's plot against Castlereagh into the open at last.[2] Castlereagh and Canning both promptly resigned. On 21 September they fought a duel on Putney Heath, a highly publicised event that brought the beleaguered, leaderless government further into disrepute.

Chatham had been expecting Castlereagh's resignation ever since

132

deciding to abandon the campaign. When Sir Eyre Coote privately complained that Castlereagh was neglecting him, Chatham quietly replied, 'Lord Castlereagh would not be for ever Secretary of State.'[3] The War Secretary's disgrace did not bother him, for Chatham held Castlereagh's shaky intelligence reports and blithe assurances of victory partly responsible for his current predicament. But, in this atmosphere of political chaos, Chatham could not be sure a new Secretary of State for War would be more favourable. Portland's chosen successor as First Lord of the Treasury was Spencer Perceval, the Chancellor of the Exchequer. He was a highly intelligent man, slippery in debate and a clever political strategist, and strongly aware that the failure of the Walcheren expedition put his weak government at a significant disadvantage. Although he would no doubt feel obliged to help Pitt's brother, and chose not to remove him from the Ordnance in the reshuffle that followed Castlereagh and Canning's departure, he made no secret of his disapproval: 'Lord Chatham had really left us so much in the dark as to material points that no judgment or opinion could . . . be given [regarding his actions on campaign] . . . There were material chasms that required to be filled up'.[4]

Under the circumstances, Chatham kept his distance from his colleagues. Virtually the first thing he did upon returning to London was to write to Perceval declining to attend a Cabinet meeting on 17 September: 'Under the circumstances in which I feel myself placed . . . I shou'd not consider it was proper in me, to do so'.[5] This must have told Perceval quite clearly of Chatham's dissatisfaction with his lack of support, but Chatham felt he had no choice. His caution was the more necessary because he had been warned by his friend Camden that he had another enemy in the ministry to contend with:

> You cannot doubt for a Moment that the most cordial disposition prevails amongst us to do you entire Justice, but it is felt that some Circumstances are not sufficiently explained in your public Dispatch accounting particularly for the necessity of your not going forward to S. Beveland after you had entrusted the Siege of Flushing to Coote.[6]

Camden did not specify who Chatham's enemy was, but Chatham was fairly sure he knew the answer: the First Lord of the Admiralty, Lord Mulgrave.

Mulgrave was one of the Cabinet members who had been most confident of the expedition's success. His brash assurances of an easy landing at Sandvliet, and the 19 June opinion signed by three Lords of the Admiralty, had been partly responsible for the Cabinet's endorsement of the campaign in the first place. Looking back from his vantage point at the beginning of September 1809, Chatham considered every single one of the promises the Admiralty had made him to have been broken. The Navy had not been able to make swift progress up the West Scheldt once the majority of Walcheren and South Beveland were in British hands; nor had it been possible to land troops at Sandvliet. On the contrary, Strachan took three weeks after the fall of Veere and Rammekens to get the British forces and siege supplies as far as Bath, giving the French time to garrison Antwerp and repair its defences. Chatham certainly thought part of this was due to Strachan's mismanagement of the forces under his command, but Strachan by himself could do Chatham little harm. With Mulgrave's protection, he became dangerous.

Chatham's suspicion that Mulgrave was preparing to throw the Admiralty's full support behind Strachan was increased by the contents of the *London Gazette* of 3 September. A week previously, on 27 August, Strachan had written Chatham a private letter emphasising the poor state of provisions and warning against proceeding to Antwerp: 'Really when I consider the reduced state of the provisions, the encreasing sickness, and the encreasing power of the enemy, little success can be expected from any operation'.[7] Chatham later stated he found this odd, given the manifest incorrectness of Strachan's assumption that provisions were a few days from running out, but took the letter as evidence that Strachan agreed with the decision to suspend operations.[8] His puzzlement turned to horror when the latest edition of the *London Gazette* arrived in Middelburg on 7 September, along with Castlereagh's 'cold' letter and Chatham's orders to return. The *Gazette* juxtaposed Chatham's dispatch of 29 August announcing the end of the campaign with an extract of a letter from Strachan to the Secretary of the Admiralty dated 27 August. Strachan complained that, although he had assembled the flatboats ready to carry the troops to Sandvliet prior to the meeting of the lieutenants general on 26 August:

I found them [the generals] decidedly of Opinion that no Operation could be undertaken against Antwerp, with any Prospect of

Success, at this advanced Season of the Year, and the Enemy encreasing in Strength, and our own Forces diminished by Sickness. . . . [I]t was also their decided Opinion, that the Army ought not to make any Attempt on [Lillo and Liefkenshoek]. I had already, in the most unqualified Manner, offered every Naval Assistance to reduce these Fortresses, and also in Aid of every other Operation of the Army.[9]

There was not a word on the scarcity of provisions or Strachan's apparent belief, expressed in his letter to Chatham of the very same day, that Antwerp was out of reach.

The effect of publishing both dispatches together was devastating. Chatham's dispatch explaining the urgency of suspending operations contrasted with Strachan's insistence that the navy had 'offered every . . . Assistance' in the teeth of opposition from the military men. The *Morning Chronicle*'s fulminations left Chatham in no doubt of the extract's impact on public opinion:

We are sure . . . that we are not singular in thinking that his letter will convey to most minds an impression of [Chatham's] total incapacity for business, whether civil or military. It is, indeed, a most delectable composition . . . a languid expression of drowsy dullness from a mind feeble by nature and rendered completely effete by habitual sloth . . . It is evident from Sir Richard Strachan's letter . . . that our naval commanders are most indignant at the way in which the service was conducted. . . . Sir Richard adds, that he had in the most *unqualified terms* offered every naval assistance for the reduction of the fortresses, an expression which plainly enough indicates, that *he* did not conceive any enterprize thus far to be impracticable.[10]

Brownrigg thought Strachan's 'strange and uncandid' letter 'must put them [Chatham and Strachan] in a state of Hostility, which cannot be easily removed'.[11] Brownrigg, however, was missing the point. Chatham was livid, but he was just as angry about the way the extract had come before the public as he was about its contents. The extract's publication convinced him Mulgrave intended to take advantage of the Navy's popularity as the 'constitutional' safeguard of the nation to transfer the

Admiralty's share of the blame for the expedition's failure onto the army and its Commander-in-Chief. He strongly suspected the extract's impact would have been blunted by printing 'the *whole* of Sir Richard Strachan's letter', which he thought must refer to the shortage of provisions Strachan had warned him about.[12] Nor was Chatham mistaken. The excised paragraphs spoke of the exhaustion of 'the Wells on the Island' and the 'sickly' nature of the troops, and concluded by predicting the French fleet would be well out of reach beyond Antwerp.[13] Removing these paragraphs completely altered the complexion of Strachan's letter, which appeared to have been 'ambiguously worded, so as to throw all the odium (which in England is not small) . . . upon the Comm[ande]r of the Forces'.[14] None of Strachan's other letters had been published in extract, which suggested Mulgrave's decision to publish this one had been carefully made to produce a particular impression.

By the time he returned to England, Chatham was certain Mulgrave would do all he could to undermine him. Still unsure of the new Prime Minister's intentions, he threw himself on the influence of the one man he knew would support him: the King. On 19 September Chatham requested permission to attend the next levee. The King agreed in terms that suggested Chatham had been right to place his trust in the Crown:

> His Majesty . . . feels perfectly sensible that, in the general Line of Conduct which Lord Chatham has pursued he has always been guided by the utmost Zeal for His Service, and, in his late Decision [to abandon the campaign], by a just Consideration of the Difficulties which occurred and of the Preservation of his Troops under the probable Effects of a most destructive Climate & Season.[15]

The levee took place at noon on the 20th. Chatham was presented, and in turn presented most of his staff, perhaps in a show of solidarity: his aides Captain Gardner, Major Bradford and Lord Charles Manners, his military secretary Colonel Carey, the Adjutant General Colonel Long and General Brownrigg.[16] He had got what he so badly needed: a public show of support from the King himself, who also made sure to tell Perceval of his support of Chatham's actions, and his conviction the campaign had been impossible from the start.[17] But the game had just begun.

* * *

An inquiry of some sort into the abject failure of the biggest expedition Britain had yet fielded during the war seemed inevitable. While he took care to be seen in possession of the King's confidence, therefore, Chatham also started building a case for his public defence as the expedition's military Commander-in-Chief. 'I doubt not you have prepared a Narrative of all the Events with their dates & I beg you will let me & others of your friends have it,' Camden wrote to Chatham soon after the suspension of the campaign.[18] Camden was not the only one whose thoughts turned in this direction. The King, too, wished to give Chatham the opportunity to defend his position. On 13 September the Commander-in-Chief, Sir David Dundas, wrote to General Brownrigg:

> the K[ing] desired . . . Lieut. General Brownrigg to advise Lord Chatham, That as he acted under the signed Orders of the K[ing] he should send a special report to His Maj[esty], of the reasons which during the siege of Flushing, and towards the close of it, prevented the Men of War from going up the Scheldt, and then undertaking a combined operation of the Troops and Navy against the Enemy, and that he should communicate a Copy of this Report to the Cabinet.[19]

Chatham set to work immediately. He checked dates and orders with his subordinates, began gathering his papers together, and made copies of all his campaign correspondence, particularly with Sir Richard Strachan.

This focus on Strachan was significant, for Chatham had discovered he was not the only party preparing a narrative. Like Chatham, Sir Richard Strachan had been summoned home to account for his actions and arrived in late September.[20] Almost immediately he tried to acquire copies of letters and orders from his immediate subordinates with the aim of writing an account of his own. Chatham later dismissed this as rumour, but his vagueness was deliberate to protect his source, Lord Gardner, the admiral whose assistance Commodore Owen had requested during the abortive Cadzand landing.[21] Gardner's evidence was unquestionably more than rumour: it was a letter from Strachan, dated 5 October 1809, asking Gardner for copies of their official correspondence 'as I have been suddenly called upon by the Admiralty to lay before their Lordships a Narrative of the Proceedings of the Fleet which I had the honor to command'.[22] Perhaps fearing Strachan would blame him for the Cadzand failure, Gardner wrote to Chatham warning him of the Admiral's intentions and enclosing a copy of Strachan's letter as proof.

The revelation that Strachan was also preparing a narrative put Chatham in a delicate position. He was close to completing his report, and put the finishing touches to it on 15 October. The King expected a copy of it to be delivered to him and to the Cabinet, until which time it could not be used as evidence in an official investigation. But Chatham did not want to give Strachan ammunition for his narrative by releasing his defence first. Chatham therefore requested both the King's permission, and Perceval's, to hold back from submitting his paper officially. He knew the minute it circulated through the Cabinet it would come 'into the hands of Lord Mulgrave', who would then pass it 'to Sir R[ichard] Strachan which I was anxious it should *not* untill he had given in some original statement by which he wou'd be bound to abide'.[23]

This was the more likely because Chatham's suspicion that Mulgrave and Strachan had agreed to blame the army for the Navy's shortcomings drove the contents of his narrative. Chatham always considered Strachan's 27 August letter had 'been the foundation of all the clamour raised against me in ye Country'.[24] His narrative consequently took Strachan's extract as the starting point for his defence, which merely 'explain[ed] the grounds of his own Proceedings' and left it to Strachan to answer for his actions.[25] Chatham focused on two questions: first, why an attack against Antwerp was abandoned, and second, why it took so long for the army to reach Bath. The first point he dismissed in a paragraph referring back to his 29 August dispatch reporting the end of the campaign. The second occupied the body of the narrative, and Chatham boldly placed responsibility for the campaign's delays at the Navy's door: 'Why the Army was not brought up sooner to the destination from whence its ulterior Operations were to commence, is purely a Naval Consideration, and . . . the delay did in no shape rest with me, or depend upon any Arrangements in which the Army was concerned'.

Chatham recalled the expedition would not have been undertaken without the Admiralty's assurance that an advance up the West Scheldt to Sandvliet was perfectly practicable, so long as Walcheren and South Beveland were in British hands. He pointed out that the military arrangements required to allow the fleet to pass from the East into the West Scheldt had been accomplished in good time. Following the fall of

Veere and Rammekens between 1 and 3 August and the taking of South Beveland by Sir John Hope, 'the Passage of the Sloe was open to the Transports and Gun Vessels . . . and I know of nothing, (but this, of course, is a point for the Admiral to speak to) to have prevented the Line of Battle Ships and Frigates from coming in, and passing up above Flushing'. With the West Scheldt apparently accessible to British ships, Chatham had expected Strachan to complete the seaward blockade of Flushing and run the part of the army destined for Sandvliet down to Bath. 'Unfortunately, however, this did not take place': on the contrary, 'I saw no Movement making to push forward a single Vessel up the West Scheldt', either to move the troops forward or cover their advance. Chatham pressed the necessity of 'bringing up the Cavalry and Ordnance Ships, Transports, Store ships, Victuallers &c &c in order that the Armament might proceed without delay to its destination . . . To this, and to the several Arrangements I explained to Him in detail,' Strachan 'fully assented', but nothing was done to send the ships of the line past Flushing till they forced the Deurloo on 11 August.

The remainder of the paper detailed the slowness of the advance of the transports, which began moving through the Sloe on the 18th but only arrived off Bath between the 22nd and the 25th. 'Notwithstanding every Effort on my part with the Admiral,' Chatham concluded, 'the Armament was not assembled at the point of its destination 'til the 25th and of course . . . the means of commencing Operations sooner, against Antwerp, were never in my Power'. The narrative's purpose, Chatham claimed, was to record facts, not judge:

I shall here close this report . . . by observing, that wherever it has been necessary for me to advert to disappointments experienced, thro' the Arrangements of the Admiral, in the Naval Co-Operation I had been taught to expect, I have confined myself to stating the Facts, abstaining, as it became Me, from all Comment . . . to bring under Your Majesty's view, the Circumstances which may have occasioned them; and, above all, to account for the difficulties which prevented the Investment of Flushing (a point never even doubted of before) as well as to shew the Obstacles which presented themselves to the early progress of the Armament up the West Scheldt, which Operation I had always looked upon as the primary Object of his Instructions, and on the Accomplishment of

which our best hopes of Success in any of the ulterior Objects of
the Expedition, principally, if not wholly, depended.[26]

Chatham's narrative was undeniably one-sided in its tendency to lay all
delays at Strachan's door. He showed a blinkered refusal to recognise his
failure to adapt the agreed plan of action to accommodate on-the-spot
circumstances. Taken out of context, as indeed it was, the narrative
appeared little more than a disgraceful attempt on Chatham's part to have
the last word by abusing his privilege of approaching the monarch as a
peer and Privy Councillor. This was emphatically not what Chatham had
intended. His narrative was a riposte to the publication of the 27 August
extract blaming the army for the campaign's failure, and designed to lie
alongside Strachan's own report. Nor did Chatham ever view his narrative
as anything but a public document, which he himself eventually brought
before the Walcheren Inquiry as evidence.

All this would have been more obvious had Chatham submitted his
narrative to the War Office rather than the King, but, as Chatham later
observed, 'a special Report . . . was *called* for by His Majesty, and none
was ever asked of me, by the Secretary of State'. Chatham had received
his commission under the Sign Manual, which theoretically made him
directly responsible to the King and not to the Secretary of State for War.
This argument was later attacked by Canning, who pointed out that all
foreign ambassadors 'received the same sanctions; but there was a clause
in [their] instructions, that they should conform to the orders and
correspond with the Secretary of State who appointed them'.[27] The precise
wording of Chatham's instructions, however, was that he was to
correspond with the Secretary of State '*during your Continuance on
Service*'.[28] As Chatham later observed, he had ceased to be in command
on 25 September.[29] By October he was theoretically at liberty to choose
whether to lay his narrative before the King (who was favourable) or
Perceval's Cabinet (which was not):

This Paper wou'd necessarily be to pass to the Cabinet, and I had
grounds at that time, but too well justified since, for thinking, that
it wou'd not be advisable, nor indeed safe for me, that this shou'd
take place, untill I saw a little what course, the business was likely
to take. . . . This caution was especially, imposed on me, in
consequence of what I had observed, and knew, of the disposition,

and conduct of Lord Mulgrave towards me, as well as from his Official, and private connexion, with those, adverse to me.[30]

Chatham expected Mulgrave to take his criticisms personally, and was understandably keen to avoid 'a second edition of Canning and Castlereagh'. All he had to do was make sure he kept his narrative back 'untill the time came when the whole Cabinet might see it . . . whenever Sir Richard Strachan gave in any Paper he wou'd be bound by'.[31]

But Strachan never did submit his report, and this made the timeline of Chatham's own report submission seem odd. The more Chatham asked the King 'to be permitted to defer presenting it' while he waited for Strachan to make the first move, the more secretive his behaviour appeared.[32] Why Strachan did not make his report Chatham was never able to ascertain, but he had his suspicions. Mulgrave and Strachan later claimed no report had ever been written, but Chatham thought they were lying. He believed Strachan's narrative, 'either the whole, or in part, was communicated at the Admiralty, but that not being approved of, it was altogether suppressed. But all enquiry into this, was carefully avoided'.[33] He concluded Strachan had made accusations against him that had been too strong even for Mulgrave to stomach: 'What charges or what Insinuations were contained in Sir Richard Strachan's Narrative prepared by order of the First Lord to be submitted to the Board in ye month of October but which was never brought to light, Lord C has no means of knowing'.[34]

*   *   *

As time passed Chatham was less and less blamed for the failure of the expedition. The consensus was that he had done his best in a task the government ought to have known was impossible from the beginning. The *Morning Chronicle*, three weeks after lambasting Chatham for his 'disgusting' dispatch of 29 August, backpedalled sharply and aimed its vitriol higher up: 'Lord Chatham . . . deserves praise for his manly determination to look the Ministers in the face, and stop in due season in the execution of impossible orders'.[35] Chatham was not comforted by this growing trend in his favour. He was still smarting from the earlier attacks on his bravery and capability, some of which had come uncomfortably close to libel:

It has required no small degree of patience and forbearance . . . to submit quietly to them . . . for what cou'd I do? I cou'd not stoop to a Contest with the News Writers . . . To prosecute them (the only notice to be taken of them) wou'd be hopeless, for sorry I am to say, not more on my own account than on that of the Country, that there is no law left in it, for the protection of Innocence, or of the honor and reputation of a publick man.[36]

For now he tried to put Walcheren out of his mind. He was more successful than, perhaps, he ought to have been. In mid-October Sir Eyre Coote reported 128 deaths from sickness in the past week alone, and 1,600 fatalities in the 7 weeks since the start of September, all while keeping a worried eye on the enemy troops entrenching themselves in South Beveland and Cadzand.[37] Chatham, meanwhile, went shooting at Cheveley Park with the 5th Duke of Rutland. He rode out daily with General Grosvenor, and wagered on foot races between Rutland's servants and his own.[38] His correspondence with the Duke revolved almost entirely around sport and racing:

I am sorry poor Salvator has come to disgrace, tho' I am willing to hope that it was not so much his fault, as that a little over fine riding of Chiffney [the jockey] threw away the race . . . Tho' we have not won much by Volvere's match yet his winning it, may perhaps assist us in finding a Purchaser for him . . . You say nothing of the shooting by which I fear that you have not as great plenty of birds as in former years.[39]

Perhaps Chatham occasionally devoted a thought to the sick arriving daily from Walcheren and overcrowding the military hospitals in Kent, Hampshire and Essex, or the tribulations of General George Don, who had sailed out to replace Sir Eyre Coote at the end of October, charged with evacuating the island once and for all. If he did, he left no sign.

As the session of Parliament approached, however, Chatham was less and less able to forget his experience. The government would almost certainly wish to placate Parliament's wrath with an inquiry of some kind into Walcheren, although Chatham still did not know whether it would be via select committee or military tribunal. Chatham was in no doubt which he would prefer: 'A Court Martial . . . was what, under all circumstances, I felt wou'd be most advantageous to me'.[40] But this became the least likely outcome following a meeting of the City of London's Court of Common Council on 5 December 1809. Radical Alderman Robert Waithman moved an Address to the Crown calling for an official investigation into the expedition.[41] The King's Answer, composed by Perceval, was predictably bland, but (instead of promising a court martial, as Chatham had hoped) it made Parliament responsible for collecting 'such information, or to take such measures upon this subject as they shall judge most conducive to the public good'. This was not what Chatham wanted, as it 'directly pointed' to a political 'Proceeding in Parliament' to be managed by Perceval's government on the King's behalf.[42] But the King's Answer was the King's Answer, and on 22 December 1809 Chatham wrote to the War Secretary, Lord Liverpool, expressing himself 'most entirely ready to submit every Part of my Conduct to such Military Investigation as His Majesty may be pleased to direct, and that I shall not be less so, whenever Parliament may assemble, to meet any Enquiry, which in their Wisdom they may judge it fit to institute into my Conduct'.[43]

Chatham's reluctance to pursue the political route was not just because he thought Parliament would be less likely to acquit him of negligence. He still doubted the goodwill of his Cabinet colleagues. This impression was increased by the draft of the King's Speech circulated in mid-January. The references to Walcheren were limited to detailing the purposes of the expedition and regretting that little more had been achieved than 'the Demolition of the Docks and Arsenals at *Flushing*'. Chatham immediately noticed the Speech held back from bestowing approval on what had passed. He feared the ambivalence of 'the manner in which the Expedition to Walcheren was mentioned' was a sign of 'the feeling the Cabinet have as to ye Services of the Army employed there', and suspected his colleagues might be preparing to saddle him with full blame for the expedition.[44]

By mid-January, however, Chatham knew he would have to place his fate in Perceval's hands if he wanted his narrative to be available to an inquiry. This could only be done by submitting it to the King and Cabinet simultaneously. The King was still waiting for the report he had requested in September, and had in fact been badgering Chatham about it for some weeks. Although he was not ready to submit his final narrative, Chatham felt obliged to show the King evidence of his progress. On Monday, 15

January 1810 he took the plunge and sent a draft of his narrative to Windsor, under the proviso that it was 'for his Majesty's information only' until he was ready to lay the final version before his colleagues. He intended to attend the levee on the 17th (his last opportunity before Parliament met on Tuesday, 23 January) to receive royal approval and pass the narrative to Liverpool, but became ill.[45] 'I am the more obliged to submit to remedies, and to take care of myself . . . as I must if it be possible endeavour to go to ye Levee tomorrow,' Chatham wrote to Perceval on 16 January, but his illness worsened.[46] Having missed the obvious opportunity to act, indecision almost certainly now prevented Chatham submitting his narrative. Within a fortnight of submitting his draft, also, the political scene had developed dramatically.

Parliament met on 23 January. The opposition was in a belligerent mood, scenting the new prime minister's blood. When Lord Porchester moved for the inevitable inquiry on 26 January, the form he chose took everyone by surprise. He called, not for a select committee, but for a committee of the whole House of Commons:

> I cannot consent to delegate the right of inquiry on this occasion to any select or secret Committee, by whom the course of investigation might be misdirected, or its bounds limited – before whom, possibly, garbled extracts, called documents, might be laid by ministers themselves, in order to produce a partial discussion . . . It is in a Committee of the whole House alone, we can have a fair case, because if necessary we can examine oral evidence at the Bar.[47]

Perceval moved the previous question (effectively an attempt to dispose of Porchester's motion) on the grounds that a select committee would be better suited to the task; but the prime minister was pretty much the only party trying to dodge the bullet. Castlereagh had already declared that 'he had more reason to court than to shrink from inquiry', and Home Popham, as the Member of Parliament for Ipswich, supported an inquiry on his and Strachan's behalf. General Thomas Grosvenor, one of Chatham's lieutenants general and his personal friend, likewise supported Porchester's motion.[48] Although Popham and Grosvenor both denied speaking from authority, Grosvenor had, as Lord Grenville put it, 'been L[or]d C[hatham]'s cabinet counsellor in this whole business'.[49] Chatham,

144

indeed, was himself on record supporting an inquiry with his previous month's letter to Liverpool. Under the circumstances the Treasury Bench's protests rang false. Castlereagh, Grosvenor and Popham all voted for Porchester's full House investigation, and carried the day by 195 votes to 186. Less than a week later, the inquiry Chatham had been anticipating (and dreading) for so long got underway.

Chapter 11

'Unconstitutional and Clandestine'
1810

Sir David Dundas, the Commander-in-Chief, opened the inquiry with a nervous and repetitive testimony on 2 and 5 February. Early questions focused on the aims of the expedition and, apart from a few comments on Chatham's inexperience, touched more on the planning than the conduct of the campaign. This changed on 9 February with the appearance of Commodore Owen and General Montresor (Lord Huntly's second-in-command), both of whom gave extensive evidence on the reasons for the Cadzand failure in July. Owen was also questioned on the reasons why the Navy had not succeeded in blockading Flushing until the second week of August. Owen laid the blame on poor weather but, when asked to explain why Strachan had not brought his ships through the Deurloo when he had first expressed a wish to do so on 2 August (before the bad weather began), he replied: 'I cannot'.[1]

So far, the evidence was largely going Chatham's way. But, as the inquiry progressed, Chatham became more and more concerned about the government's lack of firm direction. Astonishingly, Perceval made no attempt to impose control over a question that bore so strongly on his stability. The easiest solution would have been to remove Chatham from the Ordnance, but that would have looked like scapegoating. Perceval's solution was to hold aloof, neither condemning Chatham nor throwing government support unambiguously behind him. No Cabinet meetings were called to decide how to respond to the inquiry, and Chatham received no advice on how to handle questions. The War Office similarly failed to support him. Liverpool was too new to the office, and his predecessor, Castlereagh, had made clear his reluctance to help the men responsible for his political disgrace. The Commander-in-Chief's office at Horse Guards made more of an effort on Chatham's behalf, but it lacked the political influence of a government department. As Alexander Hope pointed out to General Brownrigg, the Navy had the Admiralty's backing and was much better organised in the Commons: 'The Secretary [of the Admiralty, William Wellesley-Pole] & Naval Lords are present upon the part of the Admiralty, and Sir Home Popham at once a planner & Actor . . . is perfectly qualified to protect the Executive part on the side of the Navy. The Army alone is unrepresented. Its interests are left to chance'. Chatham and his officers were kept almost completely in the dark in the midst of this highly politicised inquiry, to the extent of not even knowing in advance which witnesses were to be called on a particular day. Confused by deliberately obtuse questions, unbriefed officers fell headlong into traps and contradicted each other (and occasionally themselves) with 'defective or imperfect' evidence.[2]

Before any more structured approach could be adopted, notice was given that the naval and military Commanders-in-Chief themselves would soon be called before the inquiry, beginning with Strachan on 15 February. The appearance of such high-profile officers was sure to attract the most difficult questions, yet even now Perceval and Liverpool gave Chatham no overt assistance. Unsurprisingly, Chatham took his defence into his own hands. He was assisted by three men: General Grosvenor, his friend and subordinate; General William Loftus, MP for Tamworth, another friend and colleague from the Eastern District; and Chatham's military secretary, Lieutenant Colonel Thomas Carey. Together they devised a list of questions for Loftus to ask Strachan during the course of the interrogation. These mostly revolved around the 27 August extract in the *Gazette* and the circumstances under which Strachan had written it, since Chatham was certain this would form the basis of Strachan's evidence.

Chatham and his team now made the fateful decision to 'bring Matters to a Point' by finally releasing Chatham's explanatory narrative into the public domain.[3] Since sending the draft to the King on 15 January and failing to appear at the levee on the 17th, Chatham had taken no further action. He would later regret taking so long, but the lengthy pause seemed to play in his favour by allowing him to release his narrative close to the date of Strachan's inquiry appearance. It also allowed him to make some minor changes to the narrative's text. On 7 February, Chatham asked the King's permission to excise a few paragraphs 'which I . . . thought wou'd be better omitted'. On 14 February, the day before Strachan was due to appear, Chatham took the final narrative to the levee at St James's Palace and laid it officially before the Secretary of State for War. All he had to do was wait and see if Strachan's examination took the expected course.

On the night of 15 February Chatham waited nervously at home, sending his carriage regularly for news from Carey, who spent the night liaising with Loftus in the lobby of the House of Commons. Strachan was terrified at the prospect of appearing before the inquiry. One of the other witnesses remembered that, 'when his name was called, his face was as white as a sheet. He was agitated, and his friends immediately sent for a glass of wine for him'.[4] The intensity of the cross-examination did little to relax him. 'Our Friend was a good deal confused at first,' Carey reported to Chatham after Strachan had been questioned for a couple of hours, and Loftus thought the Admiralty undersecretaries had begun trying to lead him.[5] Strachan certainly came across as confused and self-contradictory. He admitted he was not personally well-acquainted with the navigation of the Scheldt, confessed he had never had adequate plans of either Antwerp or Lillo and Liefkenshoek, and claimed he told Mulgrave before the expedition sailed he thought it would do no more than capture Walcheren, which put the validity of his 27 August letter into question. Upon being pressed, Strachan was forced to concede his ships would have been unable to cover the army's retreat from Antwerp without a favourable change of wind, and that any army landed on the left bank of the Scheldt would have been open to a Continental attack. He lamely explained his confusion by claiming he had 'not come prepared to answer many questions that have been put to me'.[6]

Strachan came completely unstuck when he claimed he had brought his ships through the Deurloo and obstructed communications between Flushing and Cadzand as early as 2–3 August. At this point the inquiry rose briefly to allow him to calm down.[7] While passing through the lobby, Strachan bumped into Carey. He must have known what Chatham's man was doing in the wings, but Carey nevertheless thought 'he pretended to be very civil'.[8] Once Strachan returned to the bar, having had time to collect himself, Loftus pounced with his first question. Why, he asked, did Strachan write his letter to the Admiralty of 27 August? This, at least, was a question Strachan had 'come prepared to answer', and his reply had the ring of a prepared statement:

When I wrote the letter, it was with an impression that the country would be very much dissatisfied that more was not done, and I thought it was due to myself and to the navy, to state . . . that we . . . had taken all the measures necessary to go on . . . When I saw the letter afterwards in the paper, it struck me very forcibly that it would be the means of making a breach between the two services, and then of course I expressed how very sorry I was . . . [but] I could not help regretting, and I do at this moment regret most sincerely, that, having been brought up as we were to the point of attack upon the enemy, and having worked our people up to the highest pitch of enthusiasm, we should have been under the necessity of retiring.[9]

Loftus asked Strachan if he had written any other letters to Chatham on 27 August, but Strachan had either forgotten his letter about the provision shortage, or pretended not to recall it.

Now Strachan's side of the story was on record, Chatham had no more reason to hold back his narrative. On 16 February, the day after Strachan's examination, General Loftus rose in the Commons and moved, in Chatham's name, 'That an humble Address be presented to his Majesty, that he be graciously pleased to order to be laid before the House a Copy of the Memorial presented to his Majesty by Earl Chatham, explaining the proceedings of the late Expedition to the Scheldt'.[10] The paper itself was laid before the House on the 19th.

Chatham probably thought his timing was impeccable. In fact it could not have been worse. Publishing the narrative completely altered the course of the parliamentary investigation, which had, until then, focused on blaming the ministers for the expedition's failure. Far from bringing Mulgrave's actions into question, it drew attention away from the Admiralty and provided the beleaguered Navy with a constitutional shield. 'Lord C[hatham's] paper is a firebrand for the Inquiry which . . . would not have done any body any harm,' George Canning gleefully informed his wife. 'Now it will make mischief.'[11]

* * *

There was no reason for Chatham to predict his narrative would have the seismic impact it did. Its existence, after all, was hardly a secret, although Chatham had undeniably intended its contents to remain confidential until he was ready to release them. George III had not kept his request for a report quiet: on the contrary, he had transmitted his 13 September orders through the official channel of the Commander-in-Chief. That Chatham was working on a narrative was public knowledge long before Loftus laid it before the inquiry. Even Strachan later admitted he had known about it since his return from Walcheren in September: 'I read [about] it in the newspaper; I understood that Lord Chatham had given it to the King. . . . Indeed it was in every body's mouth at that time'.[12] Perhaps Strachan's memory was playing tricks, but at least one newspaper, the *Morning Chronicle*, did comment that 'the Earl of Chatham has made his report' as early as 10 October.[13] Any supposition that the entire Cabinet had been ignorant of the narrative until Loftus's motion to produce it on 16 February would seem ludicrous.

And yet it was immediately obvious to Perceval and his colleagues that claiming ignorance was the only way out of the unexpectedly tricky situation Chatham's narrative created. The minute the narrative was laid before the Commons Lord Folkestone rose from the opposition benches and declared 'his decided opinion, that it was such a document as that House ought not to receive or allow to remain on the table'. Chatham dared champion the Army (traditionally associated with despotism and tyranny) against Britain's 'constitutional bulwark', the Navy.[14] This chance to defend the reputation of the nation's darling was a gift to the opposition, and Chatham's mode of submission compounded his crime. He had presented his narrative directly to the King, not as a privy counsellor, but as a military commander, without going through the intermediary of a Cabinet minister.[15] This was not an entirely fair representation of events, but Chatham's notorious friendship with the royal family left him open to accusations of court favouritism. 'To entertain such a document,' Folkestone thundered, was 'inconsistent with the constitution'.[16] Samuel Whitbread picked up the refrain. Chatham's narrative was '*private poison* secretly instilled' into the King's ear, and, had the ministers known of it before its submission, they deserved 'impeachment' for their collusion. He concluded with a direct challenge: 'Did the ministers know of this paper or not?'[17]

Of course ministers *had* known. Chatham had told Perceval that he was preparing a narrative in early October, and then only because Perceval himself 'expressed his expectation' that one would soon be delivered to the Cabinet; but for Perceval to admit this might well bring down his whole ministry.[18] Luckily Whitbread, by not automatically assuming

Perceval's foreknowledge of Chatham's intentions, had given him wriggle-room. Over the next four days the Cabinet discussed what line to take. The agreed strategy was to deny all knowledge of the paper until General Loftus 'moved for the production of that Narrative, [thus] . . . appriz[ing Perceval] of the existence of that document'.[19] Whitbread was sceptical: 'Were they [ministers] in the habits at all of consulting with each other? Had they any conversation with Lord Chatham, with the writer of the Narrative on the table . . .? Did they not even meet at cabinet dinners?'[20] Confident, however, that he had Perceval's ministry in the palm of his hand, he did not press the point.

Chatham was horrified, both by his narrative's reception and his colleagues' denial of it. He was more certain than ever that Perceval could not be relied on to help him, particularly now the stakes had risen so sharply. Chatham was no longer fighting merely for his military reputation: his political name, too, was at risk. The enormous fuss over the narrative combined with anticipation of his upcoming committee appearance contrived to make Chatham ill. On 20 February, the day appointed for the cross-examination, Sir Henry Halford stayed 'the Lord knows how long with Lord Chatham, making him up by draughts and nervous medicines'. It did not work, and Chatham cancelled.[21] When he managed to drag himself to Westminster two days later the Commons displayed its power by refusing to set aside the day's business to accommodate his interrogation. Chatham had to wait in the lobby from 4 in the afternoon until 9.30pm, shivering with fever, while the Commons pointedly formed itself into committee to discuss the renewal of the Distilleries Regulation Bill.[22]

In contrast to Strachan's sprawling and chaotic testimony, Chatham's was tight and mistrustful. He had probably hoped to use his testimony to elaborate the themes set out in his narrative, but the course of the questioning did not give him a chance. He was asked a few questions about the Admiralty's 19 June opinion on landing at Sandvliet, but the interrogation swiftly moved on and Chatham was unable to go into detail.[23] He did not even get a chance to talk about Strachan's 27 August letter. He knew he had very few friends in the House, even on the Treasury Bench, and frequently took refuge in convenient lapses of comprehension. 'I really do not quite understand that question', 'I do not very well know how to answer that', 'I do not perfectly understand the question' were all trotted out as responses to very simple queries.

The first half of his interrogation focused on the possibility that the campaign might have reached Antwerp at the beginning of August, had Chatham acted more quickly. Chatham tried to blame the War Office for sending him without adequate information about Antwerp, forcing him to advance cautiously (although he stopped short of accusing Castlereagh of providing him with inaccurate intelligence).[24] When asked how swiftly the army could have reached Sandvliet, Chatham replied between two and four days, but only under the most favourable circumstances (with a favourable wind and possession of Cadzand). Because his army had been divided into divisions, which sailed at different times, he argued the earliest he could have marched on Antwerp would have been 7–8 August. This was nearly two weeks before he actually began moving towards Antwerp, and historian Gordon Bond has interpreted Chatham's statement as an admission that 'the British naval forces could have forced the boom at Lillo and Liefkenshoek and approached Antwerp while the army marched along the right bank' at a time when Antwerp was still very thinly defended.[25] Chatham's testimony was nothing of the sort. As Strachan's experience had shown, Chatham could not admit undertaking a campaign he had known to be impossible without looking foolish. In fact he played down the doubts that had troubled him before accepting the command, dismissing them as 'of a general nature'. His theoretical timetable for a march on Antwerp was not a confession of what *should* have happened, but an assertion that the circumstances under which he carried out his mission made it impossible to succeed. The whole question was in any case academic, as Chatham pointed out: 'It is extremely difficult to give an opinion upon a supposed question, and under circumstances which never existed'.[26]

The second and most important part of Chatham's interrogation focused on the narrative. Although he must have been expecting it, the moment the narrative was mentioned Chatham tensed up and blundered almost immediately. When asked why he had dated the narrative 15 October when he had delivered it on 14 February, he replied, 'I thought it better to preserve the date at which it was in fact drawn up; there were after that time none but verbal or critical alterations'. This revelation that the report had gone through several editions was news to Chatham's audience. Whitbread asked the obvious follow-up: 'Is this the only Narrative or Memorial, or paper of any description, which has been delivered to His Majesty by your lordship on the subject of the

152

Expedition?' Of course it wasn't, because Chatham had sent a longer draft to the King on 15 January. As fuzzy-headed as he was, Chatham was aware of the danger of admitting he had shown the King a previous draft of a document that ought to have been delivered simultaneously to the Cabinet. He refused to answer: 'I have stated that this paper was prepared as my Report of my Proceedings in the Scheldt, and that it was delivered to His Majesty as such on the 14th of February; that is all I can state upon the subject of this paper'. This did not satisfy Whitbread, who repeated his question four times and received the same response. When Whitbread asked him whether he refused to answer because of his privilege as a privy counsellor, Chatham finally lost his temper: 'I refuse it generally. I decline answering the question.'[27]

Chatham's interrogation ended at half-past 2 in the morning.[28] 'His Lordship went thro' his examination with great good sense and clearness,' Perceval reported to the King, but towards the end of the night Chatham was 'quite done up' and suffering from the effects of his illness.[29] He was not, however, given time to rest. On the 23rd, four days before Chatham was due to complete his examination, Whitbread upped the ante in the Commons and accused him directly of abusing royal confidence. General Loftus attempted to defend his friend by reminding the House of Strachan's 27 August letter, which had rendered Chatham's narrative indispensable, but Whitbread tore him apart, playing (not for the last time) on the impact of Chatham's narrative on the Navy:

What then, Lord Chatham had so long festered his anger! . . . He nursed his wrath, and kept it warm until Sir R[ichard] Strachan had been examined at the bar of that House, until he had delivered his testimony, he would say, like a candid and gallant man; then, and not till then, came that paper from Lord Chatham, which was so heart-breaking to the navy, not because they deserved the reflections it contained, no, but because, after cooperating with all the zeal in their power, they found the colleague with whom they had acted, by whom their services had been applauded in all his public dispatches, had clandestinely put a paper into the King's hand, containing a direct depreciation of their exertions, and an attack upon their character, attempting to poison the royal mind against them.

153

Chatham's keeping back his narrative so long, which he had thought could only play in his favour, looked like a deliberate attempt to keep his attack on Strachan secret. The circumstances by which it had been made public were conveniently forgotten. Whitbread narrowly passed an address asking the King to lay 'before the House copies of all reports, memoranda, narratives or papers submitted at any time to His Majesty by the Earl of Chatham, relative to the late Expedition'.[30]

The Cabinet met several times over the next few days. Perceval was finally taking a direct interest in the Master-General of the Ordnance's looming disgrace, conscious that if he did not, Chatham might take the fledgling government down with him. Perceval's loose handling of the official response to the inquiry was criticised by backbenchers, none of whom believed for a moment in Perceval's protestations of ignorance about the narrative's existence. William Wellesley-Pole noted gloomily that 'it has been express'd to me by several Irish members, that Perceval by suffering Lord Chatham to communicate his narrative &c to the King without apprizing the Cabinet, has proved that he does not possess that control over his colleagues which a Prime Minister ought to have'.[31]

The importance of managing the situation was increased by the fatal impact of Chatham's narrative on his relations with Lord Mulgrave. The First Lord of the Admiralty had immediately seen through the narrative's verbiage to the accusations Chatham made against the over confident assurances of 19 June with which the Admiralty had sent him to Walcheren. Chatham had probably hoped his narrative would force Mulgrave out of office. His abortive attempt on 22 February to draw attention to the 19 June memorandum and its endorsement by three Lords of the Admiralty reflected his conviction that Mulgrave was trying to cover up the Admiralty Board's primary role in advising the undertaking of the expedition.[32] By the time of his examination Chatham, paranoid, hunted and desperate, was hardly a reliable witness for Mulgrave's motives. Still, it is perhaps significant that the official Admiralty Board minutes for much of the second half of 1809, as well as the correspondence with Commanders-in-Chief in the Downs for that period, are missing.[33] Nor was the Admiralty above doctoring evidence. During a debate in the House of Lords on 2 March, Lord Rosslyn pointed out that a significant passage in Sir Richard Strachan's official dispatch of 11 August had been altered in the printed version. Lord Mulgrave explained this had been done to correct a factual error, but the Admiralty had been fairly caught out.[34]

Whatever the truth, Perceval knew he would soon have to choose between Chatham and Mulgrave. For now he chose to stand by Chatham, although only because if he did not 'our conduct would be open to just criticism, as ungenerous, and directed by the policy of sacrificing him the better to escape ourselves'.[35] Privately, he was furious with Chatham for having put him in such a situation. Although Perceval had known about Chatham's narrative since October, he had not known about the January submission to the King, and this was what was causing the immediate problem in Parliament. Once Chatham had unfolded his side of the story, Perceval sought confirmation from the King in a letter warning him of Whitbread's intention to call for other Chatham papers in the royal closet. He concluded, ominously:

> Mr Perceval deeply regrets to be obliged to say that this unfortunate subject has occasioned more prejudice to the character of Your Majesty's Administration, has more encreased the opinion of a want of communication, concert and confidence amongst them, and will do more to endanger their stability than any other circumstance which has arisen out of the Walcheren expedition.[36]

The King's reply corroborated Chatham's account of his proceedings:

> The King received Lord Chatham's Report on the 15th of January, and in consequence of a wish expressed by Lord Chatham on the 7th inst. to make a few verbal alterations, his M[ajesty] returned it to him on the 10th inst. The Report, as altered, was delivered to the Secretary of State on the 14th February, and his M[ajesty] has not kept any copy or Minute of either, nor has he received at any time any other paper on the subject.[37]

While Chatham might have been suspected of lying to cover his back, the King's word could not be questioned. Perceval saw the King at Windsor on the morning of 25 February, and a Cabinet was summoned for the same evening to discuss the next step.

Chatham knew Perceval would not completely abandon him, but he still did not know how far the prime minister would go. He soon found out. Chatham did not attend the Cabinet discussion on the 25th, as he was still under the weather and preparing for his next cross-examination on the 27th. He only managed to get to Downing Street as the Cabinet was breaking up 'to learn what had passed, and what had been settled'.[38] When he arrived, Perceval was just finishing the King's proposed Answer to Whitbread's Address. He read it out for Chatham's benefit:

> The Earl of Chatham having requested His Majesty to permit him to present his Report to His Majesty, and having also requested that His Majesty would not communicate it for the present, His Majesty received it on the 15th of January last, and kept it till the 10th of this month, when, in consequence of a wish having been expressed by the Earl of Chatham, on the 7th of this month, to make verbal and critical alterations in it, His Majesty returned it to the Earl of Chatham. The Report, as altered, was again tendered to His Majesty by the Earl of Chatham on the 14th of this month, when His Majesty directed it to be delivered to His Secretary of State; and His Majesty has not kept any copy or minute of this Report as delivered at either of these times, nor has He had at any time any other Report Memorandum Narrative or Paper submitted to Him by the Earl of Chatham, relating to the late Expedition to the Scheldt.[39]

Chatham listened in rising concern, for the response glossed over several important points. First, he had not *requested* to submit his narrative to the King, but had been *ordered* to do so on 13 September. Second, he had not tendered the report to the King *again*, but submitted the final draft directly to the Secretary of State on 14 February. Third, the alterations made to the 15 January draft were not as important as 'verbal and critical' made them sound. Chatham urged a less specific response, as 'it wou'd be extremely difficult, to draw up an Answer . . . sufficiently correct . . . inasmuch as, it purported, to be a history of what had passed between us'. Perceval demurred, so instead Chatham 'desired Mr P[erceval] to give me the Paper to read myself, as it was impossible to consider it with the attention and the accuracy it required, from only hearing it cursorily read'.[40]

To Chatham's horror, Perceval refused: 'the Paper had gone thro' so many alterations and was so blotted and interlined, that he cou'd scarcely read it himself, and that I cou'd not possibly'. But from what Chatham had heard, Perceval's response 'neither contained the truth nor ye whole truth'. Unable to fight Whitbread's call for papers by either fobbing it off or producing non-existent documents, Perceval was magnifying Chatham's role in the debacle to protect the King (and the government). The Answer saddled Chatham with sole responsibility for the narrative, and made no mention of his intention to submit it to the Secretary of State as well as the King, or his wish to withhold the document until Strachan released his report.[41] Chatham was in no doubt Perceval had left these things out deliberately: 'this Answer was studiously worded, by the Minister'. The subtext was clear: Perceval was not going to force Chatham from office, but he had made it very difficult for him to remain. It was 1794 all over again, except Perceval had no intention of softening the blow of Chatham's fall.

Chatham held back from making a fuss because the Cabinet was 'clearly of opinion, that that mode was, the *best* for the King, however disadvantageous to myself'.[42] Concealing the King's responsibility for this breach of official protocol made sense, and Perceval probably knew it was the only argument that would persuade Chatham to expose himself so blatantly to parliamentary criticism. Still Chatham did not give up. 'I shou'd be happy to have a few moments' conversation with you in the course of tomorrow morning, at any hour you wou'd name most convenient to you,' Chatham wrote to Perceval the same night, but received no answer.[43] He tried calling on Perceval anyway, 'but he was gone out, or at least did not let me in'. So it was that the Answer to Whitbread's Address was delivered to the Commons on 26 February without Chatham having had more than 'twenty minutes' to review the government's planned defence of his conduct.[44]

While Whitbread planned his next move, Chatham returned to the inquiry on 27 February to complete his cross-examination. The House had had a full week to digest his narrative, and five days to consider his 22 February evidence. This had given Strachan plenty of time to arm his friends with hostile questions. The session indeed got off to a poor start, but not because of Strachan. Castlereagh had taken offence at Chatham's previous insinuations that the War Office had sent him to Walcheren with insufficient information. He caught Chatham off-guard by bringing up two memoranda he had shown him prior to the expedition's departure, and forced him to admit much of the intelligence Chatham claimed to lack – the likelihood of inundations between Lillo and Antwerp, the rapidity with which the French might reinforce the town and the possibility of bringing their fleet within the protection of the citadel walls – had been covered there. 'Did your Lordship understand that the decision upon the policy of the Expedition was formed, having those difficulties in view?' Castlereagh asked, and Chatham had no choice but to reply: 'I did.'[45]

Despite this embarrassment, Chatham cut a much better figure on the 27th than on the 22nd. Even enemies were impressed by his performance. Fox's nephew Lord Holland remarked on Chatham's ability when backed into a corner: 'The stateliness of his deportment, the firmness and compass of his voice, his self-possession, dignity, and dexterity, persuaded some who were no mean judges that the necessity of exertion would have discovered in him great parliamentary talents'.[46] This time Chatham was allowed to embroider the themes of his narrative unmolested. He again emphasised the navy's inability to advance up the West Scheldt and block the Cadzand communication, which had kept his troops before Flushing until the ships of the line forced the Deurloo on 11 August, after which the transports got stuck in the Sloe Passage. By the time everything was assembled at Bath on 25 August, further operations were out of the question. Strachan, Chatham claimed, must have agreed, or he would never have sent the private letter of 27 August drawing attention to the shortage of provisions. Aware that it largely took the sting out of the Admiral's officially published extract of the same date, Chatham had the private letter (which Strachan had previously claimed not to recall) read aloud.[47]

Chatham must have been braced for a grilling, but neither the Admiralty nor Whitbread were inclined to fight. Even the handful of questions dealing with the narrative were remarkably tame.[48] None of this was particularly comforting, and Chatham must have realised his enemies were only saving their ammunition for a grand showdown. Accordingly, Whitbread opened his assault on 2 March: 'We now know, from evidence unquestionable, that John, Earl of Chatham, in a most unconstitutional and clandestine manner, as a minion and a favourite, has abused the royal confidence, at the same time, and by the same act, that he has violated the most sacred principles of the constitution.'[49]

Whitbread moved two resolutions. The first established the 'facts' (Perceval's version, at any rate): Chatham had asked the King for permission to submit a narrative and kept it secret from the government.

The second was a direct attack on Chatham's integrity and the government of which he formed a part: 'The Earl of Chatham, by private communication with His Majesty, accompanied by a desire of secrecy, did unconstitutionally abuse the privilege of access to his Sovereign, and thereby afford an example most pernicious in its tendency to His Majesty's service, and to the general service of the State.'[50] Despite the dangerous nature of this full-frontal attack, Perceval's defence of Chatham's 'error' was limp in the extreme:

> He did not mean to say if a colleague was wrong he should, under any circumstances, be supported. But in a ballanced [*sic*] case, where a colleague was *merely in error*, he thought by deserting his cause, he should be exposed to more merited reprobation than could otherwise fall to his share, justice, decency, and propriety alike called on them to postpone coming to a decision on the resolutions that night.

Perceval proposed an adjournment until Monday 5 March.[51] This gave the government the weekend to work out its strategy, which Chatham strongly suspected would involve jettisoning him at last.

Indeed, Perceval had no choice. He had not been Prime Minister long enough to be sure of carrying the government's supporters with him on such a delicate question. 'I have heard today and yesterday of several who will keep away, and not suffer us', he told Chatham on 4 March, naming Henry Lascelles and the Master of the Rolls, 'authorities of great weight'.[52] Perceval told the King he would defend Chatham as long as he could, as 'it will be more to the credit of Your Majesty's Servants to be beat in an attempt to defend their colleague . . . than to avoid a defeat by joining in the attack against him,' but Chatham was not fooled.[53] Perceval had lied to the House by disclaiming all prior knowledge of the narrative; now he was passing it off as an 'error', and retreating as fast as he could from the disaster zone of Chatham's reputation. Perceval clearly hoped Chatham would pre-empt Whitbread's censure by resigning, but Chatham had no intention of throwing himself on his sword for the Prime Minister. He was furious at Perceval's reaction to the whole crisis, which he felt was an unfair attempt to deflect attention from the incompetence behind the planning of the expedition. Instead of investigating why the Admiralty had been so ready to promise a problem-free descent of the West Scheldt, the Commons was hung up on a tiny matter of procedure. Perceval's protestations of support meant nothing when he had proven himself unwilling to make the explanations required to take the heat off Chatham in the first place. Now Chatham could not even defend himself without implicating the King in a course of action tainted with unconstitutionality.

The 5 March debate on Whitbread's censure resolutions was long and bitter. The government stuck to the bland and unconvincing ground that Chatham ought not to be censured for a momentary 'error of judgment'. This did absolutely nothing to stall Whitbread, who thought Perceval's time had come. He particularly enjoyed the irony of accusing the son of the great Lord Chatham, the famous enemy of the Crown, of unconstitutionality and favouritism: 'Strange fatality! That in the son of that very man . . . we should find one of the agents of that occult influence which the father so long depreciated and so long resisted'.[54] Pitt was, inevitably, invoked. 'What would have been the feelings of that memorable man . . . if he had heard . . . the favourite service of the country, the British navy, the pride of the world, disgraced, and that by his own brother?' Lord Temple cried, to cries of 'No, no!' from the Treasury Bench.[55] Ponsonby went further still:

> Gentlemen would recollect, that when Lord Chatham was first lord of the admiralty, Mr Pitt, being then minister, had not hesitated to advise the King to remove him, because he did not do the duties of it in the manner which Mr Pitt thought best calculated for the public service, and so, if alive, would he now have condemned his conduct in the present instance.[56]

The government simply could not deflect the torrent of invective. Even former friends turned against Chatham. Castlereagh, who had not forgotten Chatham's attempts to indict the War Office's plans for the Walcheren campaign, felt 'it most painful to speak' on the question before the House, but had 'no hesitation' in declaring Chatham's behaviour 'to be unconstitutional, and to be such . . . as, if brought into precedent, might produce most serious mischiefs'.[57]

At last, when all seemed lost, George Canning proposed an amendment to Whitbread's second Resolution. His motives were far from pure. Rather than saving Chatham from disgrace, Canning wanted to use the occasion of Whitbread's resolutions to display his oratorical power and political skill against Perceval (who he thought had pipped him to the premiership post). Canning's suggested rewording of the second resolution certainly removed the sting of unconstitutionality, but still landed Chatham with full responsibility for the crisis:

> This House sees with regret, that any such Report should have been made to His Majesty, otherwise than through the regular official Departments, without having been previously communicated to any of the responsible Servants of the Crown, and with a request of secrecy; and is of opinion that such a practice ought to be discountenanced by this House, as pernicious in its tendency to His Majesty's Service and the general interests of the State.[58]

When Perceval's attempt to move the previous question was rejected by 221 to 188, Canning's amendment was adopted without a division.[59] Canning was jubilant. 'Huzza – Huzza – Huzza!' he wrote to his wife. His delight at having scored a point against Perceval in the lobbies prevented him feeling too sorry for Chatham, whom he believed he had saved from impeachment: 'Though Lord Chatham's friends were excessively angry with me at first, for not supporting the previous Question, I believe they left the House at last fully convinced that I had done all that could be done for him, & had saved & protected him when the Govt. *could* not'.[60]

Chatham was under no such illusion. Far from 'saving' Chatham, Canning had in fact been, in Wellesley-Pole's words, 'the mover of the question that sets his sun for ever'.[61] Canning's amended resolution, although it used the word 'regret', was still no more and no less than an official censure against Chatham's name. His resignation was only a matter of time. Still he resisted, despite heavy hints from Perceval that Whitbread would continue proposing hostile motions until Chatham was gone.[62] His clinging to office has been described by Perceval's biographer as 'incredible stupidity', but Chatham felt let down, with reason, by the Prime Minister's 'want of due explanation and cordial support': 'If the extraordinary heat on the one side, and the Management on the other, cou'd have permitted the House to have known the real merits of the case, the censure, contained, in this [second] resolution wou'd not have been agreed to'.[63] But by 7 March Chatham knew he would probably be forced out by his own colleagues if he waited any longer. 'I lose no time in apprizing you, that His Majesty has been most graciously pleased to accept of my resignation of my Office of Master General of His Majesty's Ordnance, which I tendered . . . at an audience this day after the Levee,' Chatham wrote, stiffly, to Perceval.[64] It was the end of his active political life, after twenty-two years of service with only a short intermission of thirteen months. To add insult to injury, his successor was none other than his nemesis, Lord Mulgrave, translated to the Ordnance from the Admiralty.

*   *   *

'I do most sincerely regret that any Circumstances should have occurred, which should have rendered this Step expedient either with a view to yourself or to His Majesty's Service,' Perceval wrote to Chatham in sheer relief, 'but . . . I have no difficulty in saying that in my opinion you have acted not less usefully for His Maj[esty]'s Service, than wisely & honorably for yourself, in retiring at this moment from your Office'.[65] Chatham was unimpressed: a few days before Perceval had written virtually begging him to resign. But Chatham's resignation, although it removed a load off the shoulders of the government, left him more vulnerable to his enemies at the Admiralty, who now chose to open their campaign against his narrative.

On the day of his resignation Chatham received notice that Sir Home Popham had taken advantage of the government's distraction over Whitbread's resolutions to hijack the inquiry witness box.[66] While the government was still recovering from its mauling of 5 and 6 March, Popham called Captain James Aberdour and Captain Richard Jones, who both testified that it had always been possible to land 20,000 infantry and 4,000 cavalry in 48 hours on South Beveland.[67] The next day the Admiralty released Sir Richard Strachan's official response to Chatham's narrative. Knowing he had Parliament and the Admiralty behind him, Strachan took Chatham's 'factual' statement and belligerently construed it into a personal attack: 'To impute to Me or to the Navy under the name of delay the loss of time which was passed by me in constant solicitude & by the Men in unremitting toil is not what I should have expected from Lord Chatham. . . . But I am convinced that it was not the intention of His Lordship . . . to attribute any blame to those Officers. He has closed his Report by pointing me out as the only object of his animadversion.'[68]

By claiming to be the main focus of Chatham's ire, Strachan cleverly glossed over the bigger issues affecting the Admiralty and reduced the narrative to the level of a petty personal squabble. He also took advantage of the belief, voiced by Whitbread and others, that 'Lord Chat[ham]'s perfidy to Sir R[ichard] Strachan' had been responsible for stirring up trouble between Army and Navy.[69]

But what angered Chatham most about Strachan's report was a piece of evidence he brought up for the first time, putting Aberdour and Jones's apparently off-topic evidence about landing troops on South Beveland into clearer context. Strachan fastened on Chatham's accusation 'that the Army was not brought up sooner' to Bath. Strachan referred to a meeting he had had with Chatham at Middelburg on 1 August, in which the Admiral stressed the impossibility of getting so many transports, frigates and gunboats quickly through the Sloe. He suggested an alternative: 'the only means of rapidly approaching' Antwerp was not by bringing the army to Bath by sea, but by landing them on South Beveland, marching them across the island, and re-embarking 'them in boats and schuyts and smaller vessels proper for the purpose, and land[ing] them on the opposite coast, on the spot originally designed [Sandvliet]'.[70] 'I inferred from [Lord Chatham's] Answers that he intended to modify his future Plans in consequence and to proceed by South Beveland instead of the West Scheldt,' Strachan finished. '. . . With him alone was there an option between a March of 36 hours, and a Voyage of an indefinite length'.[71]

Six days later, on 13 March, Strachan appeared a second time at the bar of the Commons, even though he had finished his cross-examination. Most of the questions revolved around the plan to march across South Beveland, as though to give him an opportunity to go into more detail about it. Strachan claimed the plan 'arose from the state of the weather and the probable difficulty that there would be of getting into the West Scheldt with the whole armament, which had then, as I conceived, been arranged to go into the East Scheldt'. When asked why he had not mentioned this in any of his official dispatches, Strachan hedged: it was merely, he said, a conversation over dinner, and not the sort of thing he would normally put in a dispatch. Still, this 'dinner conversation' had apparently been enough for Strachan to order Admiral Otway to move Lord Rosslyn's division into smaller ships to get them through the Veere Gat more easily. What had Chatham said to Strachan, specifically, to imply his acceptance of the new plan? Strachan replied evasively, 'I do not recollect any particular answer of Lord Chatham's, but he seemed to consider it as arising from necessity'.[72]

Chatham was infuriated by this new testimony. He categorically denied any proposal to march the troops across South Beveland had ever been in contemplation: 'The Adm[ira]l never alluded once to this proposal of his or to my supposed agreement to it in his own evidence first given to the House of Commons'. Had Strachan proposed such a thing, 'I must have objected to it as impracticable, but I should [also] have felt it my indispensable duty to have reported this entire departure from the Plan furnished by our Instructions to the Secretary of State, and I conceive Sir R[ichard] S[trachan] would have done the same to the Admiralty'. Chatham had no doubt who was behind this new development: 'The whole of this . . . was suggested to [Strachan] subsequent to his examination' by Sir Home Popham.[73] As Popham was the only witness of the mysterious conversation ever cited by Strachan, it is difficult to know whether Chatham was right. Circumstantial evidence suggests Strachan was at least over inflating the importance of a passing comment. Sir Edward Codrington wrote home on 20 August 1809 that Sir Home Popham told Chatham 'that all the troops not wanted for Flushing should *ascend the river* directly', something Popham surely would not have said had he thought a march across South Beveland likely to happen.[74] Sir John Hope did mention 'the Landing Troops on this Island with a view to their Re-embarking again at Batz' on 6 August, but only to dismiss it out of hand: 'they had much better be conveyed by Water'.[75] Chatham was probably wrong to accuse Strachan of making the South Beveland plan up entirely, but no military man ever seriously considered it as an option.

The only thing for it was for Chatham to recall half the high-ranking military witnesses. Brownrigg was already scheduled for 15 March, but Lord Rosslyn and Sir John Hope (among others) were brought back specifically to deny ever having heard of Strachan's South Beveland theory.[76] 'The objections to such a plan would have been numerous, and of considerable weight,' Rosslyn said, and Hope thought such a plan 'must have created very great delay and excessive labour'.[77] Brownrigg agreed it was never entertained to land the troops on South Beveland. Far from planning a march across the island, Brownrigg reminded the House he and Chatham had spent most of the first week of August pressing Strachan to get transports through the Sloe as quickly as possible. He agreed with Rosslyn and Hope that there were numerous objections to the plan. He cited only a few: the time it would have taken to disembark the troops from the transports, the bad roads on South Beveland, the lack of fresh water on the island, the difficulty of disembarking cavalry and the fact it would all have to be done again on the other side of the Bath channel.[78]

None of this made much difference to the outcome of the inquiry, which wrapped up a few days after Strachan's final appearance. Looking back, many thought (narrative aside) the evidence pointed in Chatham's favour. 'Lord Chatham at present stands clear of all blame,' Wellesley-Pole wrote. '. . . If nothing more turns up, he will appear to have done his duty and the censure will fall upon the undertaking'.[79] Unable to target Chatham or Castlereagh, both out of office, and having placed Mulgrave's Admiralty above suspicion by their censure of Chatham's narrative, the opposition had no choice but to indict the whole government. On 26 March, Lord Porchester moved eight Resolutions censuring the ministers:

> The Expedition to the Scheldt was undertaken under circumstances which afforded no rational hope of adequate success . . . The advisers of this ill-judged enterprize are, in the opinion of this House, deeply responsible for the heavy calamities with which its failure has been attended . . . Such conduct of His Majesty's advisers, calls for the severest censure of this House.[80]

Porchester's resolutions were aimed at unseating Perceval. In this the opposition over-reached itself. Chatham's humiliation over his narrative, as Perceval predicted, probably saved the ministry. Government waverers might desert on a question that affected a single Cabinet member, but when the collapse of the whole ministry was at issue they rallied 'to keep out the opposition'.[81] After having been discussed at length for 4 days, Porchester's resolutions were rejected by 272 to 232 early in the morning of 31 March. Far from calling for Perceval's resignation, the Commons went on to express approbation of the retention of Walcheren until December by 255 to 232.[82]

* * *

Chatham's political disgrace may have done more than rescue Perceval's ministry. It possibly also saved Chatham from another, potentially more serious, charge. While the government had been preparing for the approaching parliamentary session in January 1810, the 12th Report of the Commission of Military Inquiry (a board established in 1805 to investigate abuses in military expenditure) drew attention to some serious irregularities in the behaviour of the Treasurer of the Ordnance. The position of Treasurer was one of great trust, since the Treasurer controlled the release of the enormous funds at the Ordnance's disposal. Joseph Hunt had been appointed under Chatham in 1801, gone out of office with him in 1806, and returned to the same position in 1807. The Commission discovered Hunt had been withdrawing large drafts of money made out to recognised Ordnance suppliers and stealing the cash.[83] In this manner Hunt had managed to embezzle £93,296 of Ordnance funds.[84]

It appeared to be an open and shut case. Hunt resigned and promptly disappeared, having apparently been forced to make an unexpected and convenient journey to Lisbon for the benefit of his health.[85] Less than a fortnight after the end of the Walcheren inquiry, John Calcraft, who had been Lord Grenville's Clerk of the Ordnance, moved a direct censure on the Ordnance Board, accusing them of breaching protocol by failing to require a deposit of £10,000 from Hunt on his return to office in 1807.[86] The censure was rejected by 54 votes to 36, and the current Clerk of the Ordnance, Cropley Ashley-Cooper, introduced a Securities Bill on 13 April to make sure officers in positions of trust were required to give securities within a certain time.[87] Hunt was expelled from the Commons and the £93,000 deficiency made good from a surplus elsewhere.

The whole business was surprisingly tame, given the political tendency towards greater public responsibility and integrity. The opposition had, apparently, missed a sterling chance to strike a blow against Chatham, the 'spotless' Pitt's elder brother. Nobody questioned whether or not the Master-General of the Ordnance was personally implicated in Hunt's embezzlement. Calcraft ruled it out from the start: 'He did not mean to impute the slightest blame to Lord Chatham, who, he believed, knew nothing whatever of the transaction'.[88] By April 1810 Chatham had been out of office a month, and attacking him directly could not damage Perceval (whereas attacking the government's poor control over public funds when national bankruptcy was a distinct possibility might make a difference). The opposition also had little energy left for an Ordnance assault following the Walcheren inquiry. George Tierney, advising the Villiers family on the subject of similar embezzlement charges launched against former Navy Board member George Villiers, thought 'this Walcheren business fortunate', as it had made the Commons reluctant to launch inquiries into other things.[89]

But was Chatham innocent? The Ordnance's structure, with the Board and the main Ordnance officers acting in strange symbiosis under the loose presidency of the Master-General himself, may well have protected Chatham from his Treasurer's activities. Chatham, naturally, denied any involvement. 'I am extremely shocked at ye Report about Hunt,' he told Perceval when the report first became public, 'but I am not yet apprized to what extent [the defalcation] goes'.[90] Perceval accepted Chatham's protestations of innocence, but many doubted the Master-General of the Ordnance could have been entirely ignorant of his own Treasurer's activities: 'Mr Hunt declared . . . that not a shilling had ever been taken by him on *his own* acc[oun]t – from whence it is imagined that L[or]d Chatham is not free from the matter'.[91]

No evidence survives to link Chatham to Hunt's activities. The opposition's reluctance to take their investigation higher than Hunt suggests they had no evidence either, and did not believe it existed. Even so, Chatham and Hunt went back a long way. The origins of their connection are unclear, but Hunt had been Chatham's private secretary at the Admiralty, and Chatham later appointed him to the post of Commissioner of Victualling and made him a Director of Greenwich Hospital.[92] It is hard to believe Chatham could have worked with Hunt for so long, and elevated him to so many positions of responsibility, without knowing him well. Hunt's protestations that Chatham had set him up were, perhaps, to be expected, as was Chatham's denying all knowledge of Hunt's crime. But perhaps the only reason the opposition failed to carry their inquiries further up the Ordnance ladder was that Walcheren had made this a waste of political energy. Even if Chatham was innocent, it was lucky for him in the long run that Walcheren directed so much attention away from the Ordnance.

Lucky, however, was the last word Chatham would have used to describe himself in April 1810. His reputation was in tatters, his political career at an end. The extreme reaction to his narrative left him shocked, battered and bruised. In truth he had completely misjudged the direction of British politics. The man who had been so out of touch with his men on campaign, living comfortably at Middelburg while they toiled in trenches half-filled with seawater, had tried to place himself under the protection of Crown influence and discovered he had become an anachronism. Chatham's political impact relied in part on his relationship to more famous men. As such he represented the worst of 'Old Corruption': the tendency of aristocratic political families to cluster round and protect their own.[93] The lengthy war, high prices and frequent food shortages contributed to the rise of increasingly stringent calls for retrenchment, austerity and parliamentary reform. Men like Chatham had no role to play under such circumstances.

Chatham's public disgrace was the more galling because of the deliberate confusion Perceval had stirred up over the narrative. The narrative was far from being an 'error', or even an attempt to save Chatham's reputation at Strachan's expense. Chatham only composed his report because the King had *asked* for it, and he always insisted he had acted properly, viewing such a narrative as necessary to correct the impression created by Strachan's 27 August letter from Walcheren. This meant any adequate defence of his actions in writing his narrative would necessarily implicate the King in behaviour the House of Commons had publicly declared to be unconstitutional. Instead of drawing attention to the shortcomings of the Admiralty's planning of the campaign, the narrative played into Admiralty hands by directing the debate towards traditional nationalistic representations of 'libertarian' Navy versus 'despotic' Army. Mulgrave and Strachan were not slow to latch onto this, painting themselves as victims of a smear campaign:

> The Earl of Chatham has also been forced to resign, in consequence of his having secretly and unofficially presented a memorial to the king, in which he made insinuations against Sir Richard Strachan and the navy, as to their co-operation in the attack on Holland. The navy being peculiarly the favourites of the people, a great clamour arose on account of such disingenuous conduct, and to appease the storm, the Earl of Chatham resigned his place at the ordnance.[94]

But Chatham believed *he* was the victim, and with reason. After he had picked himself up and dusted himself down, his frustration settled into a cold, hard fury. Chatham knew Perceval had driven him into the political wilderness. For the King's sake he had to submit, but that did not mean he had to go quietly.

Chapter 12

Chatham in the Wilderness 1810–21

Walcheren ended Chatham's political and military career. The inquiry might have cleared him of incompetence, but it also revealed his profound lack of imagination, flexibility and experience in his first major command; nor could he serve again at Cabinet level with a parliamentary censure attached to his name. Chatham truly believed Mulgrave and Strachan had taken advantage of his poor reputation to throw their share of the blame for Walcheren on his shoulders, and that Perceval had endorsed their scheming to save himself. Betrayed as he felt himself to be, Chatham had no intention of allowing his enemies to have the last word. He and his wife, fully recovered from her long illness, made a great show of having the Royal Family's confidence, if not that of Parliament. In April 1810 Chatham was spotted at several drawing rooms, levees and court events, including a dinner for the Knights of the Garter held by the Prince of Wales at Carlton House.[1] Lady Chatham also reprised her former role as a leader of fashion. She represented her husband at various court events, including the King's birthday celebrations in June, when she wore an 'elegant dress of lilac satin, Brussels lace drapery tastefully ornamented with pearls'.[2]

As had happened after his removal from the Admiralty in 1794, Chatham channelled his fury into several memoranda explaining his reasons for composing his narrative and the process of its submission. His intention was to fight his disgrace by drawing attention to Perceval's duplicitous behaviour. He was encouraged in this by his former military secretary Thomas Carey, who acted as a link between Chatham and several influential politicians disgruntled with Perceval's government. Carey had first encountered Chatham in a professional capacity in 1804 and had been his Assistant Adjutant-General in the Eastern District since 1807. He exploited an existing connection with William Huskisson, the former Secretary of the Treasury who had resigned with Canning the previous September, and invited him to Hill Street in mid-April to hear Chatham's side of the story and advise him on 'the best mode of bringing matters to light'.[3] Having heard all Chatham's explanations and looked over all the memoranda, Huskisson admitted to Carey there was a case: 'Everything I heard from Lord C[hatham] went to confirm your Statement, and to strengthen the Impression it had left upon my Mind. He certainly has been most extremely ill used in consequence of the false Colouring given to his Conduct in all that relates to the Narrative'. But Huskisson was unwilling to espouse such an unpopular cause so openly. Chatham, he said, should not 'have allowed Himself to have been misrepresented', and should have made his explanations in February when the narrative had first become public: 'I could not have acted with the same Resignation under similar circumstances'.

Of course Chatham could not have made more of a fuss in February and March without implicating the King, and this still held true in April. Unable to find anyone influential to fight his corner, Chatham's indecision overcame his wounded pride, although Huskisson left under the impression that he still wished 'to take some Step for setting Himself right'.[4] Carey, for his part, did not want Chatham to give up. His fierce loyalty at this late stage was touching to behold. 'I shall never cease urging L[or]d C[hatham] to bring [his defence] forward,' he told Huskisson, whom he begged to bring Chatham's cause back onto the floor of debate in Parliament. Carey closed with a remarkably affectionate portrait of Chatham's character which, as a close subordinate, he was perhaps highly qualified to make:

> I know that L[or]d C[hatham] in his silence is governed by feelings the most noble, which the World however give him little credit for ... I have now lived on terms of the closest friendship with him for the last six years of my life, and the more I see of him, the more I am convinced that in understanding few equal him, & in Honor or Integrity He cannot be excelled.

But Carey knew few would agree with him. 'I fear you will laugh at me for all this & think me mad,' he concluded, sadly. 'You must however make allowances for my eagerness ... if in expressing the cause of truth & justice I am carried beyond the proper limits'.[5]

Even Carey had to admit the circumstances were not right, but within the year a more favourable opening for Chatham occurred. In October 1810 George III, distressed by the death of his daughter Princess Amelia, relapsed permanently into insanity. The government revived the 1789 Regency Bill with all its proposed restrictions on a regent's ability to distribute pensions, create peerages and manage the Royal Household. This was a brave move for a government as weak as Perceval's, and few people expected the government to last under the Prince of Wales as Regent. The Prince was just as opposed to Perceval as he had been to Pitt's much stronger ministry in 1789, which had only survived then because of the King's recovery. This seemed unlikely now the King was in his seventies, and Perceval's political weakness was soon made abundantly clear. On 4 January 1811 the House of Lords debated the proposed restrictions on the Regency Bill. The result was a shock defeat for the government of 105 to 102, although in subsequent divisions most of the Bill's restrictions were reinstated.[6]

Chatham was partly responsible for the government's defeat in the Lords. He had always modelled his political behaviour on what he thought would be most beneficial to the King, but the King was no longer in a state to care about what he said or did. Chatham therefore felt himself at liberty to revenge himself on Perceval for his previous year's disgrace. He did not attend the House of Lords on 4 January 1811, even though he was in town at the time and Perceval had been keeping him in touch all winter: nor did he deploy his proxy. Perceval's supporters were aghast, although they should not have been surprised. 'In such a moment as the present, one expected rats,' the Duke of Richmond, Lord Lieutenant of Ireland, wrote to the Home Secretary, 'but not such a man as Lord Chatham amongst them. In him, absence is as bad as opposition.'[7] Chatham's opinion mattered, as a member of the Cabinet that had framed the Bill on which the current one was modelled. Chatham, moreover, commanded the considerable parliamentary interest of the 5th Duke of Rutland, whose family and connections 'have, all through L[or]d Chatham, stood neuter upon the Regency question'.[8] As his father the 4th Duke had done in the 1780s, so the 5th Duke of Rutland laid himself entirely at Chatham's disposal in the 1800s. Despite their difference in age, he and Chatham formed a firm friendship, based on a mutual love of hunting and Chatham's long-standing connection with Rutland's family. Indeed, Chatham had probably been closer to the 4th Duke than to his own brother, and he seems

171

to have viewed the 5th Duke as the son he never had. Having Rutland in his pocket boosted Chatham's political 'consequence': as Lord Porchester (the same man who had moved for the Walcheren inquiry a year previously) wrote, 'If [Canning] and L[or]d Chatham were cordially with us it would be difficult for Percival [*sic*] to go on'.[9]

Chatham was fully aware of the significance of his actions. 'After revolving [the question] again and again in my mind, I came nearly to ye resolution of staying away,' he told Rutland. By deliberately standing aloof, and persuading his friends to do so too, he was making his disapproval of his former colleagues clear: 'the staying away, was a clearer line' than turning up and voting against.[10] Chatham did not come out into open opposition, although he flirted with it. He 'had much conversation with Lord Grenville respecting ye [Regency] Measure of 1788', much to the curiosity of the newspapers, and there were rumours the Prince of Wales was considering him as premier.[11] But if joining Grenville's opposition was a step too far, Chatham was convinced the time had come to protest publicly against Perceval's perfidy during the Walcheren inquiry. Chatham managed to procure an interview with George Canning, to whom he showed his notes on the narrative. Canning, like Huskisson, was convinced:

> I return your Paper . . . I shall have one or two questions to ask you, to enable me to understand it in all it's parts. But what you shewed me this morning clears up all the doubts of any sort of importance which I had ever entertained upon the subject of your Report. I wish I had known of the existence of that paper a twelvemonth ago, and I think I could wish that it's tenour were more distinctly set forth in your present Statement.[12]

Open support from Canning, the man responsible for amending Whitbread's censure resolution, would have been significant. But, as Huskisson had suggested in April, Chatham had waited too long to break his silence. Robert Plumer Ward reported sceptically:

> L[or]d Chatham now sets up a strange story, that Ministers used him exceedingly ill last year in regard to his narrative, which, so far from intending to keep secret from them, as was argued in the House of Commons, he laid upon the table of the Cabinet, sealed up, with a desire that it might be read at the same time with Sir

172

R[ichard] Strachan's, whenever he chose to present his, and that Mr Perceval knew this. All one can say is, that if this were so, why did he not state this in the time when it was most important to him, and when, for the want of it, he was forced out by the House of Commons for underhand dealing?[13]

Chatham's reason for waiting was clear enough. By exculpating himself, Chatham could only implicate the King more. This was less of a pressing issue now George III, whom Chatham had sacrificed himself to protect, was incapacitated. But Plumer Ward was right, and Chatham had missed his opportunity to speak out. Although he convinced everyone he spoke to, he was too much of a political pariah for men like Canning to come out and defend him a year after the fact.

For Chatham was very much a pariah. His enforced departure from public life opened the floodgates to a slew of unrestrained abuse in the press. Walcheren, the inquiry, the narrative and the public censure brought back all the old accusations of sloth, incompetence and nepotism. Even sources that might be considered friendly to Chatham were critical: the *Edinburgh Annual Register*, edited by Sir Walter Scott (whose patroness was Chatham's sister-in-law the Duchess of Buccleuch), described him as 'a man whose habits of indolence were notoriously inveterate . . . His manners were agreeable, and in conversation he displayed talents, which, as they never appeared on other occasions, seem only to have been exerted for conversational purposes, or only equal to them. Mr Pitt was known to have described him as a person of useless abilities.'[14]

Some of the attacks virtually invited Chatham to open libel proceedings. 'Thomas Brown, the Elder' published a series of biting, barely concealed portraits of public figures entitled *Bath: a satirical novel* in 1818. One of these figures was 'Lord Mediocre':

What a disadvantage it is for a little man to be the son of a great man! For a lilliputian to be begotten by a giant! . . . This misfortune, however, happened to Lord M——, whose ill fate *it is* to be the son of the *great* Lord —— and the brother of the great Mr. ——, which lays him open to observations, trite but true, of all kinds and in all languages, to his disadvantage.

'Lord Mediocre' was a mere fig-leaf, and nobody could doubt who he

173

was actually meant to be: 'He can't be *pitted* with his brother'. If that hint wasn't enough, there were plenty of allusions to his having been 'First Lord of the ——' ('a marine adrift, or a lubber afloat . . . *out of his element*'); Commander-in-Chief of a Dutch expedition ('completely out of time and place, out of his judgment, and one might almost say out of his wits'); and Master-General of the Ordnance. 'Privacy and retirement would have been the only means of averting the finger of comparison, of diverting the eye of examination, and of silencing the tongue of disappointment,' the article concluded.[15]

Chatham may never have read Brown's book – at least, one hopes he did not – but he was probably aware of it, and others like it. With these sorts of accounts cropping up so frequently in the post-Walcheren literature, Chatham reluctantly recognised his reputation was damaged beyond hope of repair. Under the circumstances, returning to office – which some believed in 1811 he was still trying to do – was impossible.[16] Into the wilderness he went to resume his duties as Commander-in-Chief of the Eastern District. From court levees and Mayfair dinners, and being a front-runner for the premiership, Chatham found himself relegated to Colchester's provincial military society.

He nevertheless made the best of it, and as the years passed Chatham relaxed more and more. His military duties were entirely ceremonial. Although promoted to full general in the January 1812 general brevet, Chatham never served abroad again. From now he lived his military experience through correspondence with his former aides-de-camp, nearly all of whom were employed in the Peninsula. Andrew Francis Barnard and Henry Hollis Bradford kept Chatham up to date with information about other acquaintances on campaign, including his niece's husband, William Henry Pringle. Chatham, for his part, sent back information about their colleagues Gardner and Carey, who remained in Colchester, and Lady Chatham sent the soldiers presents if they were wounded.[17] It was the closest Chatham got to active service; otherwise, he kept a low profile, spending half the year in his garrison and half in London.

Despite the shadow of his disgrace, these years of leisure were probably Chatham's happiest. Out of the public eye, he was not required to undertake any rigorous duties or live up to any expectations. His days were filled up with 'a thousand petit "riens"' bracketed by 'the shooting in ye morning and the Whist at night'.[18] He was able to devote himself to some of the interests he had flirted with in his youth, such as horse racing. The

5th Duke of Rutland had a sizeable stud at Cheveley and Chatham, who could not afford stables of his own, advised Rutland on breeding, training and likely purchases. In his love for the turf Chatham waxed lyrical:

> I have become enamoured of a young *Persian Princess*, the daughter of Statyra, descended from Alexander the Great. . . . I have actually entered into a sort of conditional agreement with Lord Rous, about taking to myself this fair Princess. She has every appearance of speed . . . beautiful fore Quarters and quite an Alexander head and neck. This has been my great temptation in this Speculation about which I must consult you more, when we meet.[19]

At least one horse, Virtuosa, actually ran under Chatham's name in 1813, although she is listed as Rutland's in the *General Stud Book*.[20]

Chatham left the Eastern District in 1814 and considered himself semi-retired. Now that he had even more time he decided he needed a country estate to indulge in his passion for hunting. Buying was out of the question, but after negotiations with John Mortlock, a wealthy banker with connections to the Rutlands, Chatham arranged to rent Abington Hall. Abington, 8 miles from Cambridge, was a 'small but not uncomfortable' country house of classical proportions on 40 acres of good fowling land.[21] It was an estate much celebrated for hunting, due to the flatness of the terrain and the coverage from shrubs and trees, and no doubt this was what attracted Chatham. He signed a ten-year lease with Mortlock on 15 March 1816 at a rate of £300 per year, with the exclusive right to shoot, fish and hunt on the estate. In return, Chatham pledged to carry out various repairs on the property at his own expense, including modernising the servants' quarters and repainting the exterior and interior of the building.[22] 'Having . . . at length brought my negociation [*sic*], with Mr Mortlock to a successful issue, I must take Abingdon [*sic*] in my road [to Belvoir],' Chatham wrote to George Tomline on 18 March. He and Tomline, whose residence as Bishop of Lincoln was at Buckden, became neighbours, and over the next two years Pitt's two executors grew surprisingly close. This was partly due to proximity, but it was also due to misfortune, for Chatham's tenancy of Abington was filled with misery and suffering.

In spring 1818, while the Chathams were at Abington for the hunting season, Lady Chatham suffered a severe relapse of her mental illness. This was a shock, because for nearly nine years she had been perfectly healthy. It all began with 'a severe bilious attack, attended with a good deal of fever', which left Mary 'very uncomfortably low and nervous'. At first Chatham expected she would recover quickly, and wrote to inform Tomline that he was welcome to visit whenever Lady Chatham felt better.[23] A month later, however, there was no improvement. 'I had deferred writing to you . . . in the hope from day to day, that I shou'd have been able to have sent you a more favourable account of Lady Chatham,' Chatham reported at the end of April. '. . . I am sorry to say . . . she is still in so low and reduced a state that she wou'd be quite unequal, as yet, to receiving you and Mrs Tomline'.[24]

Chatham did not know it, but he and Lady Chatham would continue living 'from day to day' until the end of her life. Far from being a refuge, Abington became a prison. Isolated in the country, they could rely on little assistance, and Chatham nursed his wife himself. Over the next few months he managed to get away from Lady Chatham's sickbed long enough to go on hunting parties with friends, but he always returned to her after a few weeks. His correspondence with Tomline initially made light of Mary's condition, but after six months he could not conceal his anxiety. Words like 'harassed' and 'distressed' appeared in his letters, and he admitted he had not managed to make much headway with the biography Tomline was writing of Pitt, which Chatham had promised to look over: 'I must confess I am not at present equal to enter upon it'.[25]

In August Chatham took his wife to the fashionable Leamington Spa. The waters did not work, and Lady Chatham's doctor, Sir Henry Halford, suggested sending her to her family at Frognal 'that she may be nearer to his advice'.[26] Chatham could have done with the rest, but Mary insisted she was well enough for their annual visit to the Rutlands at Cheveley. When Chatham finally persuaded Mary to go to Frognal in February, her state can best be gauged from the tone of the letter he wrote to Tomline:

> I have remained [at Abington] in one continual state of suspense, having fixed generally one or two days every week for removing to Frognall, and having been as constantly disappointed. We now intend going tomorrow . . . Lady Chatham, is I am sorry to say not the least better, and my situation has been most distressing.[27]

By the summer of 1819, after over a year of illness, Chatham was beginning to wonder if Mary would ever recover. By August, however, Mary was showing signs of improvement, and Chatham thought she seemed more open to having guests. He wrote to the Tomlines hesitantly suggesting that 'should it be convenient to you to give us the pleasure of your company . . . we shou'd be most happy to see you'.[28] As had happened during Lady Chatham's first illness, Chatham probably thought leading a normal life would help Mary recover faster. He was wrong, and the visit was an unmitigated disaster. Mary started out calm enough, but could not keep up the pretence of normality long. She reacted violently towards her husband before the servants had even removed the welcoming tea tray, and Mrs Tomline recorded a particularly disturbing conversation:

> She talked to me for some time about her illness in a way that affected me more than I chose to show. . . . She was told exertion was necessary, but that she could not control herself *when* – and after a sudden stop, added in a wild way, 'I must not talk of myself – but I often think it *must* end in *madness*' – looking with *eager eyes* for my opinion.

Tragically for Mary, Mrs Tomline did not recognise this as a cry for help from a desperately depressed woman. She told Lady Chatham bluntly to pull herself together: 'I placed her feelings to the account of *nerves* & urged the absolute *necessity* of *controuling* her agitation *whenever* it occurred . . . and expressed perfect confidence that she would *again* recover, provided she kept herself *calm*, for *controul* in *some way or other* was absolutely *necessary*'.

Surrounded by unsympathetic listeners, Lady Chatham's self-esteem was low and her frustration high. 'She spoke with great concern of the trouble she gave Lord C[hatham] "to whom I am sure (she said) I ought not to give a moment's pain"'. Having forbidden herself from confiding in her own husband, she found an outlet in self-harm. Her screams echoed through the house, and her maid had to prevent her 'from striking herself with a dangerous force . . . she is indeed covered with *bruises* she has given herself in various ways and with various things'. As had been the case ten years previously, she repeatedly threatened suicide: 'her threats respecting her own life are most alarming'.[29]

Chatham's own health, meanwhile, was buckling under the strain. Mrs

177

Tomline doubted he could 'much longer support such a score of suffering'. Sir Henry Halford's opinion, when sought, was not encouraging. 'The matter appears to me to be coming to a Crisis,' he wrote, 'and I can scarcely suppose that many weeks more will pass before the poor Creature is put under restraint'.[30] Chatham was horrified. He saw no reason to look forward to a 'crisis' after 18 months of nursing Lady Chatham, and feared the effect of straitjacketing her. To his credit he never referred to his wife as anything other than just that – no subhuman 'poor Creature' such as is found in Halford's and Mrs Tomline's letters – and, even when Mary's state was poor, always wrote of 'we' rather than 'I'. But things did not improve. In early 1820 a severe gastric attack nearly killed Lady Chatham, and Chatham morosely reported to Tomline that 'her state of irritation seems rather encreased'. She may have attempted suicide – Chatham's letter is ambiguous – and certainly she was even more depressed after than she had been before. The following month Lady Chatham went to Frognal again and Chatham managed to get up to Belvoir for a much-needed hunting holiday with the Duke of Rutland, 'for I stand much in need of some recruiting having passed a sad time here'.[31]

Lady Chatham's state was driven in all the more forcibly by the death of George III on 29 January 1820. Chatham had always been close to the King and was saddened by the news, but could not regret the death of an old man who had been continuously insane for so long.[32] He must have wondered if, like George III, Mary's insanity would continue unabated for the rest of her life. Another royal death, more or less at the same time, focused Chatham's mind even more on his domestic predicament. The Duke of Kent died on 23 January. He had been Governor of Gibraltar, and the day after Kent's death the Prince Regent 'spontaneously commanded' the Duke of York to offer Chatham the newly vacant post as 'a mark of His sincere Esteem and regard'.[33] The offer was also no doubt intended as a sign the royal family still considered him to have been unfairly maligned. The *Morning Post* drove in the point in a defiant, unusually effusive article:

No nomination, we are persuaded, could be more satisfactory to that garrison and the great mercantile interests connected with it – none to the army – none to the enlightened part of the nation, which has duly sympathised in the injustice to which that eminent character has been exposed, and which has too long deprived it of his great services. . . . The heir of CHATHAM and the brother of PITT takes rank with them as much as from them; that brother was the ablest counsellor, coadjutor, and friend of that consummate Minister. We do not wish to bring to minute recollection the principal circumstances under which he became the victim of *more factions than one*, during the last days of our beloved SOVEREIGN's Administration.[34]

The Governorship of Gibraltar came with a handsome salary of £2,800 a year plus £691 19*s* 7*d* from the Army Ordinaries, plus perquisites.[35] Chatham fully recognised the political significance of George IV's offer, and after many years of expensive treatment for Lady Chatham he could certainly do with the money. There was nevertheless no chance of his being able to leave his wife unless her health improved. Only when someone pointed out that the Duke of Kent had been an absentee governor himself since 1802 did Chatham decide to accept the Governorship, 'in which I believe I have acted prudently'.[36]

But British politics were in no state to tolerate expensive sinecures. In the wake of the serious post-war riots over grain shortages, opposition members found they had a much better memory of Chatham's less-than-stellar 'services to the state' than the *Morning Post*. On 20 May 1820 Colonel Thomas Davies attacked Lord Liverpool's government for appointing Chatham to the governorship: 'that noble earl, whose military achievements might be summed up in a few words as commander of the memorable expedition to Walcheren'.[37] Davies' motion for an inquiry into military expenditure was deflected by 80 votes, but when the Army Estimates were discussed the following April the radical member for Aberdeen, Joseph Hume, bluntly accused Chatham of holding a sinecure. He was answered by Lord Castlereagh, now Marquis of Londonderry. Not only had Hume insulted Chatham, Londonderry claimed, but he had also jumped the gun: 'That distinguished officer never contemplated his appointment as a sinecure, but, on the contrary, intended to make it one of effective service'.[38] Whether he wanted it or not, Chatham was now committed to taking up his governorship.

To forestall Hume's motion, Londonderry had appointed the HMS *Active* to take Chatham to Gibraltar as soon as possible.[39] The revelation that he was effectively being manhandled onto a ship horrified Chatham, who did not want to leave his sick wife. At the same time, the prospect that his salary as Governor of Gibraltar would go up by £3,500 while residing in the garrison was most welcome, for Chatham was undergoing the unfamiliar experience of being sued by one of his unpaid creditors. Some years previously he had borrowed £8,126 from Mr John Burke. At the end of 1820 Burke, perhaps encouraged by Chatham's acquiring the lucrative salary of Governor of Gibraltar, won a non-repayment suit against Chatham in the Court of King's Bench. Chatham was ordered to pay Burke's legal costs and appropriate damages, in default of which bailiffs would be sent into his house to seize his property.[40] He had no choice but to agree to pay Burke and his heirs an annuity of £691 2s 6d (later adjusted to £1,196) out of the £4,000 pension attached to the earldom.[41] Chatham also took out three life insurance policies for a total of £7,200 to be paid in case of his death to clear his debt to Burke once and for all.[42]

Just as Chatham was reeling from this humiliation, he found himself facing another legal challenge from an entirely unexpected quarter. Despite her troubled courtship, Harriot Hester Pringle and her husband remained on the best of terms with the Chathams. But, although Chatham had tried to tie off financial loose ends before leaving for Walcheren in July 1809, in 1821 Harriot Hester was still owed her dead mother's share of the Burton Pynsent proceeds. Very probably Chatham had been far too busy following his return from Walcheren to implement the terms of the bond he had signed before sailing, and neither Sir William Pringle nor Harriot Hester mentioned the subject once over the intervening 11 years – that is, until John Burke's success before the King's Bench created a precedent for securing financial damages from the beleaguered earl.

On 12 February 1821, Pringle wrote to the Bishop of Lincoln asking him to inform Chatham that Pringle would take him to court for 'culpable neglect' if provision was not made immediately to settle the missing money on Harriot Hester and her children.[43] Chatham was aghast. Again, he had no money; again, he had no choice, particularly as he did not want to alienate his niece, whose children would inherit his estate. His solution was wearingly familiar, as Pringle informed Tomline in April. Chatham proposed to secure

> the reversion of the produce of the Burton Pynsent Estate to Lady Pringle & her Children, by assigning to trustees two policies of insurance on his life made at the Equitable Insurance Office, which are valued at £11,000, & by vesting the remainder of the money

[from Burton Pynsent] in trustees, so that at his death the sum of about £16,000 would be forthcoming to those entitled to it.

This arrangement tho' certainly not so satisfactory as if the whole money had been vested, Lady Pringle & I have as far as we are concern'd, acceded to, from having been advised so to do, by our Solicitors & from being informed, & having every reason to believe, it was the best & indeed the only security Lord Chatham had to give.[44]

It is a measure of the burden Chatham inherited that his father's will was not settled until 1821, by which time all the named beneficiaries save Chatham himself had died. These financial tribulations made it even more important for Chatham to take up the active governorship of Gibraltar as soon as possible.

Before he was ready to leave, however, tragedy struck.

*   *   *

On Monday, 21 May 1821 Chatham, at home in Hill Street, received the visit of Sir William Bellingham. He and Bellingham had been in the West Indies together in the early 1780s, and since then Chatham had managed to get his old friend various appointments at the Admiralty and Ordnance.

The two men sat down to dinner at 5 o'clock. Lady Chatham did not join them. She had been unwell with a liver complaint since Saturday, and was under doctor's orders to rest. She greeted her husband's guest, then took a glass of barley water and brandy laced with laudanum and retired early to bed. Her maid remained in the room with her as she drifted peacefully off. She was so peaceful, in fact, that it was some time before the maid realised Lady Chatham was no longer sleeping.

Chatham and Bellingham were still at dinner when the maid ran into the room crying hysterically that her mistress was dead. Chatham made to go upstairs, but Bellingham had the presence of mind to stop him and went up himself. Mary had 'expired with the most perfect tranquillity'; Bellingham later told a friend he found her lying as though in a deep sleep, 'without a feature altered'.[45]

Mary Chatham's death shocked everyone. She had never been strong and had been severely ill for over three years, although few beyond close friends and family knew the real nature of her complaint. But she was only 58, and in the first half of 1821 her health seemed to have been improving. She had re-emerged socially and was preparing for a public appearance as one of the patronesses of a debutante's ball on 28 May. Only a few days before her death she told her husband she felt better than she had for five years.[46] What exactly killed her is a mystery, although the signs point to an accidental laudanum overdose. But although newspaper reports expressed their sorrow at the 'very sudden and melancholy' account of her passing, those who knew how very ill she had been could not regret it.[47] 'After a time L[ad]y Chat[ham]'s death will I am sure be a relief to all her family,' Lord Montagu, brother-in-law of Mary's sister the Duchess of Buccleuch, remarked philosophically, 'for though lately she had been better there was little probability of any real amendment & her former state was very disturbing'.[48]

Chatham may have come to agree that his wife's death was a release from the illness that had plagued her for so long, but his grief was difficult for his friends to watch. John Villiers saw him the day after Mary died. 'He was in Tears during most of the time I was with him,' Villiers told the Duke of Rutland. He added: 'I am persuaded that there are few things left him in this life, for wh[ic]h he has a greater or juster value than your friendship'.[49] Villiers was not far from the truth: Rutland was now one of Chatham's last links to the past. Chatham himself recognised it, screwing up the courage to write to the Duke five days after Mary's death: 'No one is better able to appreciate [my loss] than yourself, who knew so long, and so well, *her*, whom we are left to deplore'.[50]

Fifteen years after Pitt's death, Chatham was truly alone. His 38-year marriage had been filled with more than the usual difficulties, and he and Mary had come a long way from the youthful newly-weds clogging the road to St James's Palace with their suite during the hot summer of 1783. But Mary had been part of Chatham's life since their childhood. Losing her, even after three years of her instability, psychosis and self-harm, plunged him into a deep depression of his own.

His lowness was not helped by the uncertainty surrounding his going to Gibraltar. The *Active* frigate, appointed to carry him out, had been commandeered by King George IV's state visit to Ireland. This meant Chatham would probably not sail before the end of September at the earliest.[51] He took a trip to Leamington Spa while he was waiting, and stayed there a few weeks over the summer. But if Chatham had hoped to lift his spirits, he should not have chosen a place that held such strong memories of Mary at her worst. He felt listless and disengaged: 'Upon ye whole I have been but indifferent, indeed I cou'd not well expect otherwise'.[52] At the beginning of October he was still suffering from the bad weather and 'worried with business, and letters, ever since I came to town'.[53] He did manage a visit to Tomline (now Bishop of Winchester) at Farnham Castle in Hampshire, where he gave Mrs Tomline some trinkets that had belonged to Mary Chatham, including a bracelet made out of hair belonging to Chatham's brother William.[54] Shortly after returning to London, Chatham received word that the frigate was at Portsmouth at last and due to leave for Gibraltar on 24 October.

At noon on the 24th, as the ship's guns fired a 13-gun salute, Chatham and his suite boarded the *Active*. At 2, the frigate weighed anchor and set sail under 'light breezes and fine weather'.[55] Chatham would not see England again for four years.

Chapter 13

'Chained to Ye Rock' : Gibraltar 1821–5

The weather was clear and warm when the *Active* anchored off Ragged Staff Wharf in Gibraltar on the morning of 15 November 1821. The occasional cloud scudded across a brilliant blue sky as the frigate ran up her flags and Lord Chatham was rowed ashore under a 19-gun salute. A guard of honour accompanied him up Main Street to the Governor's residence. The Convent, as it was known, was a former friary that had been commandeered a hundred years earlier from the Franciscans. It was an unprepossessing whitewashed building, sparsely sprinkled with arched windows. Here the Lieutenant-Governor, Sir George Don, waited with the Keys of the Fortress.[1]

Chatham's second-in-command had been Gibraltar's Lieutenant-Governor and Acting Commander-in-Chief since 1814. Don's tireless improvements to military and civilian life made him extremely popular, and his efforts changed Gibraltar nearly beyond recognition.[2] He had probably hoped to succeed the Duke of Kent as Governor, but, as the offspring of a modest Edinburgh trading family, did not stand a chance.[3] Chatham knew of Don's popularity, for some of Gibraltar's most influential merchants had petitioned him earlier in the year for permission to erect Don's bust on the new Commercial Exchange building.[4] He and Don also had a history of joint military service. Don served alongside Chatham in the Helder in 1799, was Lieutenant-Governor of Jersey during Chatham's absentee governorship, and was entrusted with the task of evacuating Walcheren in 1809: Chatham must have wondered how well his second-in-command would submit to his authority. But Don was too professional to make a fuss, and remained supportive (and subordinate) for the next four years.

Chatham was not new to Gibraltar, having served as one of General

Robert Boyd's aides-de-camp in 1778–9, but more than 40 years had passed since his last residence in the garrison, and he barely recognised it. In the interim, the devastation of the 1779–82 Great Siege, Don's reforms and the huge growth of the population had wrought great changes. In 1750 Gibraltar had been a predominantly military base, with 1,810 civilians and 4,500 soldiers, a proportion that had not much changed in the 1790s. By 1813, however, due to a commercial boom during the French wars, when Gibraltar was one of the few ways in and out of Europe for British products, the number of civilians had risen to 12,423. This massive population explosion over the course of only 20 years worried Chatham. Don had tried to restrict the civilian population to 6,000–7,000 civilians, which, with a garrison of roughly 4,000 men, would bring the total population of Gibraltar to between 10,000 and 11,000, but it was a lost cause. In December 1822 Chatham ordered a census, which showed 13,565 civilians and 4,006 garrison, 17,571 in all.[5] The population under Chatham's command consisted of people of all nations and denominations. British, Genoese, Jews, Spaniards, Catholics and Protestants all crammed into Gibraltar's hot, narrow, winding streets. 'We found ourselves at once in the midst of the bustle and din of Gibraltar,' one visitor recorded in 1820. '. . . The streets were so narrow and crooked, and the crowd so great, that it was difficult to move'.[6]

Overcrowded as it was, the town under Chatham's command was nevertheless a fascinating mixture of familiarity, exoticness and rugged natural beauty. In the words of one visitor, 'The rock of Gibraltar towers stupendously in the back-ground . . . with its impregnable fortifications, its Moorish castle, its romantic town, its dizzy paths, and airy watch-towers'.[7] Clusters of coloured houses clung to the steep rock, looking out across the Bay towards the Spanish hills behind Algeciras. From the southernmost point of the peninsula were the large towns of northern Africa, and the Atlas Mountains pierced through the heat-haze of the Straits. The vast Bay was constantly filled with ships of all sizes, from majestic warships, merchant vessels and speedy packets down to smacks and fishing boats from Spain and North Africa. At the same time, no visitor could doubt they were in a military garrison: 'Whichsoever way you turn your eye, it is met by companies of soldiers marching, or by guards going the rounds. You can scarcely walk ten rods without seeing soldiers doing obeisance to their officers, who are strolling around with all the pomp and parade of military life.'[8] The town was completely enclosed by grey stone fortifications, lined with cannon and piled with ammunition. Chatham's day began with the resident regiments beating the reveille and closed with two gun salutes announcing the locking of all gates and raising of the drawbridge. The military men under his command wore uniform at all times, and he regularly presided over regimental inspections and parades, with ceremonial march-pasts and bands playing British (and Spanish) patriotic songs.[9]

Gibraltar's dual role as a military garrison and rich commercial port involved its Governor in a number of special difficulties. Disease, and the prevention of it, was a defining feature in Gibraltar's development, much to the dismay of so health-conscious a man as Chatham. Hundreds of vessels of all nationalities arrived in the Bay on a daily basis for trade, provisioning and repairs, and all had to be quarantined. Visitors were interviewed by the harbour duty health officer, who took their papers 'with a pair of tongs, immersed in water, and then spread [them], by means of the boat's tiller and some sticks' to read, and all letters were 'steeped in vinegar' before leaving quarantined vessels.[10] Chatham was acutely aware that Gibraltar's recent history increased the need for such strict precautions. In 1804, nearly 6,000 people had died during a serious yellow fever epidemic, and in 1813 a further outbreak killed nearly 1,500.[11] Memories of these disasters were still fresh, and outbreaks of disease in nearby territories made everybody jumpy. When Chatham landed in November 1821 the *Gibraltar Chronicle* was full of reports of yellow fever in Malaga and 'contagious fever' in Barcelona, Tortosa, Xerej and Las Aguilas, while North Africa was in the grips of a plague epidemic until the end of 1822.[12] Neighbouring consuls were instructed to send over any information they could on matters affecting public health in their districts, and the health of the garrison remained a constant concern for the Governor.[13]

None of this was particularly comforting to Chatham, whose spirits were remarkably low. The much-vaunted beauties of Gibraltar could not outweigh his conviction that he was 'chained to ye Rock, instead . . . of being among my friends'.[14] It was, of course, a comfortable enough exile. Old acquaintances paid him visits: his old aide-de-camp in the Southern District, Andrew Francis Barnard, spent time in Gibraltar in 1823, and the Marquis of Hastings (formerly Lord Moira) passed through on his way back from India.[15] When he was tired of his duties Chatham enjoyed the benefits of the Convent, with its extensive gardens and orange-tree-filled courtyard. When the summer heat climbed to between 25 and 30 degrees Celsius he could retreat to the Governor's cottage at Europa Point, with its cooler breezes and views of the African coast. But Chatham never forgot he was master of a godforsaken rock half-sunk into the sea, about five square miles in size. His private letters home reeked of claustrophobia and intense homesickness, coloured with the depression he had not managed to shake off since his wife's death.

Despite this, Chatham got on well with those who worked with him. He was never as active or as loved as Sir George Don, whose name was deservedly connected with Gibraltar's civil and military improvement after the end of the Napoleonic Wars, but he nevertheless made a favourable impression: 'No Governor was ever more popular than Lord Chatham, for while possessing all the high-mindedness and dignified conduct of the peer, he was a stranger to such partialities and meannesses as in former days had often been practised by those in command'.[16] He presided over a small civil staff of just over 40 people, mostly attached to the law courts and revenue collection departments.[17] In addition to his civil officers, Chatham also had a military secretary and two aides-de-camp. Lieutenant Colonel G.D. Wilson, his principal ADC, served with him throughout the four years he was in Gibraltar, but Chatham also sailed out with the son of his physician, Sir Henry Halford. When Captain Halford resigned from the army in 1822 he was replaced by Chatham's own great-nephew, William Stanhope Taylor, a captain on half pay in the 31st Foot.

Chatham's diplomatic skills were well-suited to a post requiring a complex balancing act between military and civilian interests, and which involved extensive ceremonial duties. The Governor was expected to entertain visiting military and naval officers, foreign dignitaries, and all other important persons arriving in the Mediterranean.[18] Some of Chatham's guests nicknamed him 'Nabob' because of his self-important haughtiness, but most were impressed. The British consul to Cadiz, James Robert Matthews, found Chatham 'perfectly polite & attentive'. Ever the epicure, Chatham had always dined well, and Matthews was impressed with the 'really good dinner' Chatham gave him during his visit. 'A stile one sees only in England,' he wrote approvingly. '[I] have seen no such Cook since I left England'.[19]

Chatham took a particular interest in Gibraltar's moral life. This did not go unnoticed and at least one person thought it was his greatest service to Gibraltar: 'His Christian piety has few examples; he . . . has compelled a strict observance of the Sabbath, which was before much neglected'.[20] One of his first official acts on arriving in Gibraltar was to issue a Proclamation closing all shops on the Sabbath and 'strictly prohibit[ing]' all gambling in the garrison at any time. A branch of the Society for the Propagation of Christian Knowledge was established in Gibraltar under his direct patronage and he chaired several of the meetings over the next few years.[21] Most significantly, Chatham wielded his influence on behalf of Sir George Don's project to build a Protestant cathedral. This plan had been rejected by the Treasury in 1820 as too expensive, but in July 1822 Chatham took up the banner at the request of Gibraltar's more prosperous Protestant merchants. He met the Treasury's protests about expense head-on by proposing to sell an old Barrack Office-owned storehouse known as 'White Cloister', which he was confident would produce enough money for a new church. Together with the Chief Engineer, Robert Pilkington, Chatham drew up a design that would be practical, aesthetically pleasing and cheap enough to appeal to the authorities.[22] The plan he selected was a low, square building in a 'Moorish stile' for about 1,300 people, with separate entrances at each end for civil and military worshippers and airy enough to be comfortable in the summer months. This proposal was laid before the Treasury in May of 1823, although it was not approved (after plenty of increasingly heated nudges from Chatham) until February 1825.[23] Building on what became the Cathedral of the Holy Trinity began in June 1825. It was completed in 1832, a lasting monument to Don and Chatham's period of active partnership.

Apart from this involvement in Gibraltar's spiritual life, however, Chatham remained a distant figure for those who did not come into regular contact with him. He never acquired a fondness for the town under his command and, nearly a year after his wife's death, he made minimal attempts to involve himself in its society. As Governor he was automatically patron of the Garrison Library, to which he donated 100 guineas, and he also supported various amateur theatrical and musical societies, but he did little beyond lend his name to them.[24] In a bid to distract himself he encouraged occasional horse races on a track in the Neutral Ground, on one occasion requesting that the 'Jones Arabian', a horse being carried from the Barbary Coast to the United States, be landed specifically to run against one of his own horses.[25] But nothing roused him from his apathy. An officer who stayed in Gibraltar in the 1820s later recalled Chatham 'was never seen outside his house', slept in and 'spent his nights at whist'.[26] The town was characterised by 'a stupid monotony, & complete want of life', which reflected the low mood of its Governor remarkably well.[27] 'I cannot say much for myself,' he told Tomline in February 1822.

> I am tolerably well in health, but I do not gain much ground, otherwise. I own I am not very partial, to this place, there is but little society, but what I most feel as a grievance is that the riding in Spain is so bad, and the wading to it, thro' the sand, is so tedious, that it requires great resolution, to take the exercise one ought to do here. There is a great deal of constant business, which occupies my mind, and from this, I think I have found most relief.[28]

The business to which Chatham referred was varied and complicated. Gibraltar in the early 1820s was quiet enough, but its immediate neighbours were not, and Chatham's four years on the Rock were far from easy.

*　*　*

As Commander-in-Chief of the garrison, Chatham was responsible for maintaining the fortress, defending it against attack, and the deployment and well-being of the men under his command. One of his biggest concerns was the gradual reduction of the garrison since the end of the war with France in 1815. Sir George Don had previously suggested an establishment of 3,000 rank and file, but by 1821 that had shrunk to 2,300. Chatham requested more troops in 1822, fully expecting them to be granted, but instead one of his regiments (the 27th) was transferred to the West Indies, reducing Gibraltar's effective strength to just over 2,000 men.[29] Chatham warned Lord Bathurst, Secretary of State for the Colonies, that his troops were barely adequate for everyday duties, let alone for an emergency:

> Ye Troops have certainly been upon the whole very healthy (tho' the appearance of Opthalmia [sic] at one time alarmed me much) and I have been enabled to carry on the ordinary Duties of the place, though not without some difficulty and anxiety . . . I must

therefore most earnestly submit to Your Lordship the expediency of sending out here another Regiment which would bring the strength of the Garrison to the lowest Establishment of which it ought in my judgment ever to consist.[30]

But the government was already straitened by the need for post-war retrenchment, and ignored Chatham's request.

In lieu of fresh troops, Chatham focused on improving the defences along the northern side of the garrison facing the border with Spain. In May 1821 Don had warned Bathurst the North Front was 'liable to assault by surprize' as the escarp wall was only 24ft high, but his plan to build a counterscarp was rejected by the Duke of Wellington, the Master-General of the Ordnance, whose department was responsible for carrying out alterations to Gibraltar's fortifications. Wellington suggested both lowering the ditch and raising the escarp wall to a combined height of between 34 and 36ft, but nothing was done for a year, possibly falling between the cracks after Chatham's arrival.[31] In June 1822 Chatham wrote a long letter to Lord Bathurst entreating him to reconsider the matter. His preference was to complete the work Don had begun on 'the Grand Casemated Barracks near Landport', which would concentrate a greater number of troops at Gibraltar's most vulnerable point and end the danger of a surprise attack by land. This solution would be a cheap way of securing Gibraltar from attack, Chatham pointed out temptingly, since the barracks were already underway.[32]

Whereas Chatham's request for more troops got a bland rebuff, this request was better received. The Ordnance approved £6,338 9s 6d as an advance on the supplies for 1822, 1823 and 1824 for placing Gibraltar in a better state of defence, with £3,355 to finish the Casemated Barracks and £2983 9s 6d for raising the North Front by 12ft. This last was at the express stipulation of the Duke of Wellington, who nevertheless allowed that 'those on the spot' were better placed to decide the relative importance of the two proposed works.[33] Chatham rejected Wellington's unsolicited advice and chose the casemates (now part of Grand Casemates Square in Gibraltar). These were accordingly completed in 1824, and Chatham's name was placed above the Waterport Gate in recognition of his role in securing the funds. Chatham's name was also given to a Counterguard designed to strengthen the fortifications between Orange and Montagu Bastions on the northern sea front. Chatham urged this project in a dual military and commercial light, as Gibraltar's merchants had been complaining of 'the total inadequacy of the space at present allotted for the landing and shipping Merchandize'. The prospect Chatham held out of an 'improvement of the Revenue' induced the government to hand over £12,000, although it appears the new Counterguard was mostly used for storing wine and spirits.[34]

As important as these military duties were, Chatham's role as Governor went far beyond them. Gibraltar was first and foremost an army garrison, but it was also a growing commercial centre, and Chatham's official correspondence with Lord Bathurst reflected this mixture of responsibilities. Much of his business involved issuing licences for making and for selling alcohol, receiving requests to build houses on government land and adjudicating in conflicts over property ownership. Gibraltar was a busy port, and a lot of Chatham's time was spent working with the Captain of the Port, William Sweetland, regarding import duties, vessel registration and quarantine regulations. Another large part of Chatham's attention was taken up by revenue collection, since he was responsible for allocating incoming funds, applying surpluses and justifying any deficits. On top of all this Chatham was also a Justice of the Peace and head of Gibraltar's Court of Appeals. He held quarterly civilian appeal courts and regularly heard criminal cases, presiding in person alongside the Judge Advocate to convict or acquit parties accused of stealing silver cutlery, smuggling alcohol, adulterating wheat, perjury or assault.[35]

Most importantly of all, Chatham was the King's direct representative on the Rock. In this respect his high-profile rank and status stood much in his favour. He acted as a middleman between the Colonial Office and the local envoys and consuls, passing on dispatches, keeping a watchful eye on British dignitaries' activities and expenditure, and dealing directly with (and having a say in the appointment of) the Spanish consul to Gibraltar.[36] He was careful to direct British envoys to the Foreign Office whenever he felt he was exceeding his authority, but that authority was very much open to discretion. When the Sardinian ambassador was passing through the Straits of Gibraltar on his way to treat with the Emperor of Morocco, Chatham was instructed 'to shew every disposition of personal Civility to the Gentlemen appointed . . . and you will, should your Intervention be deemed serviceable, use your good offices to promote the object entrusted to them'.[37]

This emphasis on maintaining good relations between Morocco and other European allies reflected the importance placed on Chatham's diplomatic skills in dealing with Gibraltar's immediate neighbours. Morocco was the closest African state to Gibraltar: Tangiers was only about 30 miles away. Over the course of the eighteenth century Britain had developed a close relationship with the Moroccan Empire, and had overtaken France as one of the biggest trading partners of the North African Barbary States. The most vital part of this relationship was the trade agreement by which Morocco provided cattle for Britain's armed forces in the Mediterranean. Gibraltar imported 2,000 head of cattle every year under extremely favourable terms.[38] Although there was no explicitly stated reciprocal obligation, feeding the garrison would be logistically problematic for Chatham without this agreement. It was in Britain's interest, as Bathurst delicately told him, to 'mark our sense of that peculiar Advantage as well as of the Emperor's general Conduct in his Relations with this Country . . . and to prevent the Emperor's obtaining [stores and financial assistance] through other Channels'.[39] Chatham was therefore ordered to provide the Emperor with military, financial and medical assistance whenever he requested it.

Chatham arrived in Gibraltar at a time when Morocco was in a state of political disturbance. Morocco was unlike any other country with which Chatham was familiar. Although many of Morocco's coastal towns, such as Tangiers, Fez and Tetouan, were recognisably urban and maintained strong mercantile links with the European powers, the interior was populated by nomadic tribes unable to settle long due to frequent droughts, plagues and crop failures. The Emperor was nominally the religious and political leader, but loyalty to him was not completely absolute. He held his position by virtue of a reciprocal covenant with his people, which technically allowed for legitimate challenges to his authority.[40] Morocco spent much of the eighteenth century in what one historian termed a 'chronic state of anarchy': one Emperor took the throne five times between 1729 and 1757.[41] The precedents for Morocco's political stability were not good, and when Chatham arrived in Gibraltar in November 1821 the Moroccan Emperor, Mulay Slimane, had been fighting for two years against a rebellion in the name of his nephew Mulay Said.

Chatham was committed to supporting Slimane by the importance of Gibraltar's connection with Morocco. Britain had already given Slimane a loan of $50,000 Spanish dollars, and in December 1821 and January

1822 Chatham sent artillery and several other Ordnance supplies for assaulting the important Moroccan cities of Fez and Tetouan. A few months later Bathurst gave Chatham full power to authorise any further military shipments the Emperor might request.[42] Although Slimane was forced to abandon his sieges, his unexpectedly energetic attempts to raise support in the northern reaches of Morocco were successful. Thanks to this and his holding the city of Tangiers, he was able to block supplies from reaching the insurgents.[43] Said was captured, and Chatham considered everything was over. 'The Old Emperor has been quite successful,' he wrote. 'The Nephew has been given up to him, and he has taken possession of Fez and Mequinez [Meknes]. Tetouan has also opened her Gates to him, where he has been reproclaimed Emperor.'[44] The *Gibraltar Chronicle* reported with satisfaction that the 'political disturbances' in Morocco were at an end: 'We may look upon everything as entirely concluded, to the great satisfaction of the whole Country'.[45]

This was premature. Slimane was 'more a scholar than a soldier', and he struggled to maintain his authority.[46] In the summer he suffered several further defeats at the hands of the Berber mountain tribes, and for a while Chatham worried the whole process would repeat itself. The situation was saved by Slimane's death in November 1822. His appointed successor was another nephew, Mulay Abd al Rahman, who recognised that his power rested largely on his financial, mercantile and military connections with Europe. He was also firm with the insurgents, sending out a strong message that challenges to his authority would not be tolerated. 'The new Emperor . . . had seven heads cut off a few days ago at Fez,' James Douglas, British consul to Tangiers, reported to Chatham in January 1823, adding patronisingly, 'The Moors admit that it is impossible to govern their Nation without occasional examples of this sort'.[47]

The African crisis was over, and things lapsed back into quiet routine. 'We have gone on, in one uniform round here . . . with no event to enliven us,' Chatham reported towards the end of the excitement.[48] The next crisis to face Gibraltar's Governor, however, was already brewing. This time the trouble was much closer to home, in Spain.

Spain had been politically unsettled since the 1790s when she had gone to war, first against, and then allied with, France. Her considerable economic and social problems had been exacerbated by the Continental blockade and by rebellions in her South American colonies, on which Spain depended for supplies of gold and silver. Chatham was familiar with Spain's recent history: he had been a British Cabinet minister at the time of Spain's greatest upheaval, and had also nearly commanded Britain's expeditionary force sent to take advantage of the unsettled situation in the Peninsula. Napoleon's overthrow of the Bourbon monarchy in 1808 precipitated a national uprising, which led to the formation of a series of local elected bodies known as 'juntas'. These eventually gave way to a parliament (or *cortes*) which, in 1812, proclaimed Spain's first constitution at Cadiz, partly to deflect support from Napoleonic reforms, but partly also to lay down the conditions under which the Bourbon monarchy would be re-established. Although it declared the deposed king, Fernando VII, to be the legitimate monarch, the Constitution of 1812 announced the end of the Inquisition, nationalised Church and Crown lands, introduced the concept of equality before the law and shackled the King for the first time to the constraints of annually elected parliaments. The very first thing Fernando VII did on returning to the throne in 1814 was to renounce the constitution entirely, which he was able to do with the full support of the Church and nobility.[49]

Fernando's repression of the *liberales* who had supported the 1812 Constitution scandalised his allies, and led to Spain being denied a vote at the Congress of Vienna. Fernando tried his best to turn the clock back to 1808, but, unable to correct Spain's deep-seated economic problems, he was only partially successful. Between 1814 and 1817 the *liberales* sponsored several local and military coups, or *pronunciamentos*, in Navarre, Corunna, Barcelona, Valencia, Andalucia and Madrid. In January 1820, about the time Chatham was debating whether to accept the governorship of Gibraltar, Lieutenant Colonel Rafael de Riego proclaimed the Constitution of 1812 near Cadiz and led his troops in a mutinous march inland. Riego's *pronunciamento* provoked a nationwide uprising in favour of the 1812 Constitution, and the royal army, instead of acting against the insurgents, either stood by inactive or joined them. In March the uprising spread to Madrid, and Fernando VII was forced to agree to uphold the constitution he had previously repudiated.[50] A new *cortes* was elected in July. The next three years, known retrospectively as the 'liberal triennium', were little more than a stand-off between the *liberales* of the *cortes*, the extreme Royalists who were more and more irritated by Fernando's temporising, and Fernando himself, who did all in his power to obstruct liberal measures and repeatedly called for aid against his own government from the other European powers.

Chatham had looked 'with much anxiety, to the existing state of things in Spain' for some time.[51] Civil war in the African states was worrying from a trade point of view, but Spain shared a border with Gibraltar. Britain, disapproving of any attempt to support an absolutist monarch against constitutionalists, remained neutral, but this only made Chatham's job more difficult. The delicacy of his position became clear in July 1822 when an attempt by Fernando VII at a military coup ended in disaster. Dozens of Royalist refugees, fearing liberal reprisals, rushed across the border into Gibraltar. Chatham kept Lord Bathurst updated on their number and identity, while the Spanish ambassador to London fulminated against the asylum granted to 'the miserable remnants of the anti-national faction' whose 'intrinsic nothingness and moral discredit' was just as contemptible as their intention 'to injure their country and foment the expiring agitations of the civil war'.[52]

Chatham was well aware of the need to hurry these unwelcome guests on as soon as possible, for logistical as well as political reasons. Gibraltar was dangerously overcrowded as it was, and the influx of refugees occurred at about the same time as Chatham issued the yearly Proclamation ordering those who had not yet had the 'epidemic fever' to occupy the huts in the Neutral Ground between Gibraltar and La Linea for the remainder of the year.[53] Chatham was, moreover, a *military* Commander-in-Chief of a *military* fortress, in which civilians had been allowed to settle and trade on sufferance: 'It has ever been the Policy of those in Command here, to discourage as much as possible the assemblage of Foreigners in this Garrison . . . I have accordingly drawn the extent of the Protection granted to these Persons who have sought an Asylum here, within as narrow limits as Circumstances would permit'.[54]

As Chatham must have guessed, this was merely a dress rehearsal for the real crisis. Alarmed by Greek and Neapolitan revolutionary uprisings, Russia, Austria and France proposed military intervention in Spanish affairs to restore Fernando to his throne.[55] In April 1823, Chatham learned that the French army – 'the hundred thousand sons of St Louis', as they were nicknamed by the Spanish – had crossed the Pyrenees under the Duc d'Angoulême and entered Spain with the express aim of overturning the liberal government. When Fernando VII was kidnapped by the *cortes* and taken to Cadiz, Chatham believed Spain was on the brink of political collapse. 'We must wish [the French invasion] success,' he wrote, 'for if they fail and the scourge of revolution, is once more let loose upon the world, he must be a short-sighted Politician indeed, who does not see, that the danger will be soon, at our own door'.[56] There were certainly alarming parallels with France's state in 1792 in the haste of the other absolutist European powers to nip the rebellion in the bud. Bathurst warned Chatham to expect yet more refugees, possibly even the King of Spain himself. Given recent history, Bathurst sent further secret instructions instructing Chatham not to give asylum of any sort to anyone implicated in 'a Crime of such Atrocity' in the event of Fernando's being put to death.[57]

As the French army advanced through Spain, encountering little resistance, the disturbances came alarmingly close to Gibraltar's border. *Guerrilla* skirmishing between Royalists and Constitutionalists at San Roque at the end of July provoked a cannonade from two armed brigs and a French brig of war in the Bay, a proceeding that infuriated Chatham and drew an apology from the French naval commander.[58] At about the same time, 5,000 Royalist troops arrived on the Gibraltar border and there were some military skirmishes around San Roque and La Linea. The Constitutionalists under General Ordonez were driven back into Algeciras, but to Chatham's dismay the Royalists remained encamped at Los Barrios for some weeks. In August a further 3,000 troops arrived in San Roque, bolstering the total troops in the region, Royalist and Constitutionalist, to 34,000.[59]

While all this caused Chatham headaches, the expected trickle of liberal refugees across the border began. This trickle became a flood after Cadiz fell to the Royalists on 1 October, following which the victorious Fernando VII indulged in savage reprisals against his political enemies. Members of the *cortes* and other supporters of the liberal regime flocked to Gibraltar, and over 200 refugees gathered in the Bay in the hope of asylum. Chatham did not turn them away, but firmly maintained the policy he had outlined to Bathurst of discouragement. More temporary travelling passes were granted than usual to get 'rid of numerous Refugees which had taken refuge here in Consequence of the late change of affairs in Spain'.[60] This attitude pleased virtually nobody. The Spanish government complained bitterly about any assistance granted to the *liberales*, and the refugees protested Chatham acted contrary to the dictates of common humanity in refusing them permanent residence. In England, *The Times* thought 'the conduct of the British Government [in Gibraltar] has made every one ashamed of the name of Englishmen'.[61] Several of the persecuted liberal refugees had fought alongside the British during the Peninsular War, and names such as El Empecinado and General Alava were familiar to readers of the British newspapers. Chatham's apparent indifference to their plight offered the parliamentary opposition, many of whom had financially sponsored the *liberales* through the Whig Spanish Committee, a chance to attack the government which they did not pass up.

Caught between the neutrality of his government, the outrage of the Spanish authorities, the unrealistic expectations of pro-liberal British critics and the size of the town under his command, Chatham's position was difficult. He had no sympathy with 'our Democrats at home', who saw the Spanish contest as one of liberty against despotism: 'We here . . . are surprised beyond measure, as well as shocked, at the language held in England, for the present, is indeed anything, but a Contest for liberty'.[62] He reacted pragmatically, and he treated Royalist and liberal refugees exactly the same. But when Bathurst wrote to Chatham in 1824 to recommend an ex-*cortes* member named Don José Manuel de Vadillo, who wanted to move his mercantile base from Cadiz to Gibraltar, Chatham had had enough. He granted that access to Gibraltar was essential for those fleeing for their lives, but flatly stated his opinion that Gibraltar was full up:

> I must . . . beg leave to submit to Your Lordship's consideration that [granting] . . . permission to reside in Gibraltar . . . will lead to consequences highly prejudicial to the Publick Service, and in the present state of Spain, it may be difficult to foresee to what extent it may not go. The Place is at present so much fuller than it can well bear . . . If Persons already in security, are allowed to settle here from choice or convenience, it will not only be contrary to the Policy hitherto found necessary to adopt here, but it will narrow, if not wholly exclude, the possibility of granting even a temporary refuge to those flying from pressing danger. I am therefore earnestly to entreat that Your Lordship will not require that this Gentleman should be allowed to establish himself here.[63]

There was also, necessarily, a strongly political side to Chatham's actions. Britain's obvious sympathy with the *liberales*, despite its ostensible neutrality, was an additional difficulty with which he had to contend, and no matter what he said or did the restored Spanish monarchy was always quick to suspect him of supporting its enemies. This became obvious in August 1824 when General Valdes landed in Tarifa at the head of a small liberal force and overwhelmed the Royalist garrison there. Tarifa was just down the coast from Gibraltar, and one of the men involved in the raid, Pedro Juan de Zulueta, was one of the more privileged refugees whom Chatham had been ordered by Bathurst to allow into Gibraltar following the previous year's disturbances.[64] The Spanish consul in Gibraltar, Rivas, claimed Valdes had launched his attack under Chatham's auspices, with British guns and British money. Spain's Secretary of State accordingly took up the matter with Sir William A'Court, the British ambassador in Madrid: 'Gibraltar is the focus of the revolution set on foot to overthrow the Peninsula'.[65]

Chatham was furious. 'I can confidently state to Your Excellency that no efforts on my part have been spared . . . as far as was in my power, to counteract the evil designs of those meditating anything hostile to the Peace and Tranquillity of Spain,' he wrote, haughtily, to A'Court. The accusations aimed at him by the Spanish court and consul 'are really so extravagant and vague, that it wou'd be in vain to attempt to follow them in detail, and I can only meet them with the fullest and most peremptory denial . . . I seriously hope these Outrages may now cease'.[66] Chatham's last word on the matter was his letter of 5 October 1824 to Bathurst, to which he recurred whenever the subject arose thereafter:

> There are daily, resorting to this Anchorage, on an average, not less than 300 Vessels, having on board not less than 4000 Persons.
>
> Your Lordship will therefore see that it can be no easy thing, to ascertain any Individuals, wishing to conceal themselves . . . [Even] if you succeed in discerning any one, it is scarcely possible to do anything, for I apprehend that (even if possessed of the physical means), there exists no right, to force to Sea any Vessel, in which any named Individual might be, or forcibly to take any such Person out of any Vessel in order to send him away in another. In short, the Captain of the Port possesses little or no power, or authority, in the Bay, beyond what the right of enforcing Quarantine regulations gives him.
>
> Your Lordship will therefore not be surprised, if under such circumstances an assemblage of the Brigands might easily take place in the night, in this extensive Roadstead.[67]

This was a somewhat facile argument, but it reflected the difficulties of Chatham's position as the Governor of a tiny strip of land sandwiched between Spanish, Moroccan and Ottoman sovereignty. Perhaps his reaction to the refugee crisis reflected the same lack of imagination he had betrayed at Walcheren, but his wooden response to Spain's accusations, using his supposed impotence as a shield, reflected a sensible and realistic reading of a difficult situation. Chatham was not willing to allow the Spanish to take the law into their own hands; when a Spanish armed boat attacked and captured a Gibraltar vessel suspected of helping the prime movers of the Tarifa expedition to escape, Chatham secured the vessel's release and pressed for its captors to be tried as pirates.[68] He nevertheless had no wish to commit any indiscretion that might involve Gibraltar, the Colonial Office and himself in disgrace. As one contemporary observed, 'the greatest circumspection and good management were requisite on the part of the Commander of this Fortress to steer clear of the rancour evinced by each ephemeral Government at Madrid, and keep open a friendly intercourse with the neighbourhood'.[69] This Chatham managed to do, at the cost of misunderstanding at home.

*   *   *

All the worry of this complicated diplomatic situation took its toll, and by the end of 1824 Chatham's physical health declined to match his low spirits. He had never been robust and was now in his late sixties. The summer of 1824 was an especially hot one and afterwards he was seriously unwell. In the new year of 1825 he requested a leave of absence from Lord Bathurst. 'My health, having lately considerably suffered, from the Climate of this Place,' he wrote, 'I have the honor to request, that Your Lordship wou'd have the goodness to obtain for me, His Majesty's Permission to return to England'.[70]

Bathurst's response conveying the King's agreement arrived at the beginning of March. Chatham spent the next few months wrapping up business. He was understandably keen to leave before the heat of summer set in, and the frigate appointed to carry him home, the HMS *Tribune*, had been at the New Mole preparing to carry him home since 18 May.[71] Chatham, however, had one last important duty to complete before he went. Invitations to the foundation ceremony for the Protestant church he had helped establish were issued on 30 May to the prominent merchants and citizens of the town.[72] On 1 June Chatham and Don marched out with the military and civilian authorities to the spot where the church was to be built, through a lane of troops composed of the Welch Fusiliers and the 64th Regiment of Foot. Colonel Pilkington, the Chief Engineer, presided over the lowering of the foundation stone into its resting place. Two brass plates, one with Chatham's name and one bearing Don's, were affixed to the stone, and a box containing coins and a Coronation Medal was laid beneath it. 'His Excellency went through the customary ceremony of using the trowel and mallet; and the whole concluded with prayers suited to the occasion'.[73]

Six days later troops again lined the streets as Chatham set out for the last time to Ragged Staff Wharf. The 94th Regiment provided a Guard of Honour and the saluting battery gave him a 19-gun salute as he and his aide, Colonel Wilson, stepped into the barge taking them out to the *Tribune*. The frigate 'shortly after got under weigh, and sailed into the Straits with a light breeze at East,' the *Chronicle* reported.[74] After nearly four years, Chatham was going home. Although he returned on 'leave of absence', everyone knew Gibraltar's Governor, who would be 69 in October, had left the territory he commanded for the last time.

Chapter 14

'The Venerable Earl'
1825–35

The *Tribune* anchored off Spithead on the morning of 2 July after a smooth journey.[1] Gibraltar's governor disembarked under salute and made his way to London, where he established himself at Thomas's Hotel on Berkeley Square. On 5 July he presented himself at the King's levee, and began the expected round of social visits to the friends and acquaintances he had not seen for so long.[2] His hosts were shocked at the change in him. Chatham had always appeared youthful for his age, but 'years have bent him much,' as Lord Eldon sadly remarked: 'Time has made him, who was once a very fine-looking man in face and person, no longer, as to the latter, upright and straight as an arrow, and in countenance it has left him certainly fine remains of what he was, but only remains'.[3] Nor was Eldon mistaken. Before Chatham went to Gibraltar he was weighed on the coffee scales at Berry Brothers & Rudd at a healthy 11st 13½lb. He was weighed again, a week after Eldon expressed such astonishment at his appearance, at 9st 10½lb fully dressed in boots – more than 2 stone lighter than he had been on setting out.[4]

Chatham's first concern was to recoup his shattered health. He returned to Leamington Spa in August, his second visit as a widower. He described himself as 'a good deal unwell,' but thought 'the waters agree with me, and that I gain strength'.[5] By October he was recovered enough to spend September and October shooting at Cheveley with the Duke of Rutland, and this exercise on familiar terrain helped clear the cobwebs.[6] As Chatham's health and spirits returned, rumours flew that he was considering another aspect of personal comfort. In December his first cousin, Lady Charlotte Williams Wynn, reported that the Dowager Countess of Bridgewater meditated 'a . . . *change of Situation* which the gossip of the town reported her to be induced to do by our Cousin Lord

Chatham'. Lady Bridgewater was 62 and rich, with an estate in Hertfordshire, and Charlotte Williams Wynn had no doubt what attracted Chatham to her:

> Lord Chatham will get a very good hot supper, & she a remarkably good tempered Companion to do the honors of her table. Mr Cholmondeley says of his Bride, 'we shall probably pass a couple of years tolerably comfortable together, then she will have two more years of nursing me, & then she will have her jointure'. This last cannot be Lady Bridgewater's speculation, but perhaps it may in some degree be his.[7]

But if Chatham ever did pursue Lady Bridgewater, he did not do so long. He did not spend Christmas at Ashridge, Lady Bridgewater's country house, as Lady Williams Wynn had predicted, but at Frognal with his brother-in-law Lord Sydney.[8] This choice of holiday host does not suggest Chatham was seriously considering remarriage, and Chatham never did make any attempt to marry again, either for money, love or an heir.

The unlimited funds that would have come from marriage to Lady Bridgewater would have been welcome, but, as far as money was concerned, Chatham had learned his lesson from his court case with John Burke. In February 1826 he bought a comparatively modest house in Charles Street, where he lived much more frugally than he had been accustomed to as a Cabinet minister. He also had his salary as Gibraltar's governor to rely on. His leave was nominally for six months, but when it expired, Chatham was quietly allowed to remain in England. Technically, absentee governorship of a colony was illegal under the terms of the 1782 Colonial Leave of Absence Act, but, as the Undersecretary of State for the Colonies pointed out to the Committee on Military Expenditure in 1834, there were special circumstances:

> He is upwards of 70 years of age, and has very infirm health . . . When he last came back, he said it was totally impossible for him to return to Gibraltar, the heat of the climate had disagreed with him to such an extent; and since that it has always been supposed that he would be quite unequal to the duties of his office, and it has therefore not been pressed.[9]

Chatham had nothing but bad memories of his time at Gibraltar and spent the last decade of his life with 'the fear before his eyes of being ordered off to reside upon his government'.[10]

Although from 1825 Chatham retreated almost entirely from public life, as a Pitt his opinion still mattered, and his support on big political issues was worth courting. In February 1829 Chatham was 'much grieved' to hear the Prime Minister, the Duke of Wellington, was seriously considering granting full Catholic Emancipation. Chatham had opposed emancipation since his brother Pitt had first mooted it in 1800. His disapproval had been passive at first, grounded largely on the King's dislike of it, but as the years passed Chatham's own views became firmer. He told Lord Camden:

> I have really thought of nothing else . . . One cannot, but look at the question, as it may affect the stability of the Duke of Wellington's Government, and that, I am most anxious to support to the utmost, as thinking so much depends on it. But really, as what the nature, and extent, of the measure to be proposed, exactly is, I do not at all know. I shou'd first be desirous to see it, before I cou'd venture to form an opinion as to the line, I might be able to take.[11]

Chatham's characteristic instinct was to turn the evidence over in his mind and make his decision armed with the facts, but Wellington's government did not have the luxury of time. Ireland's emancipation champion, Daniel O'Connell, had got himself elected for County Clare in 1828 by mobilising a broad base of popular support. For Wellington, O'Connell's election, and the proliferation of clubs and societies founded under his auspices, suggested Ireland teetered on the brink of a bottom-up rebellion. Where Wellington and Chatham disagreed was that Wellington believed he needed to steal O'Connell's thunder and pass Emancipation before he lost the initiative. For this he had to act fast before ultra-Protestants like Chatham could consolidate and block the measure.[12]

Chatham's relations with Wellington had never been good, and the Duke had less patience than usual with Chatham's apparently deliberate attempt at obstruction. 'It is very difficult for me to find a moment to go to Lord Chatham again who is visible only at the time that others must see me upon business,' Wellington complained to Lord Camden, with frustrated reference to Chatham's lifelong habit of sleeping in. But

Wellington knew Chatham could not be ignored. The possibility that Pitt's own brother might vote against Emancipation was alarming in itself, but, as had been the case in 1811, Chatham still had the Rutland and Manners interests with him. Wellington condescended to send Chatham a short explanation of the government's point of view, although he reminded Camden that 'there was no time to be lost'.[13] In the end Chatham's dislike of open confrontation joined with his entrenched habit of going along with whatever the King's government thought best. His objections to Emancipation had never been deeply rooted in political conviction: he did not have the imagination to be a doctrinaire. 'I cannot say that I am quite satisfied of the urgency there was of pressing forward the measure of concession,' he wrote to Camden, 'but I am clear that there is now but one course to be pursued and from my confidence in the Duke of Wellington and my anxious wish to support his government, I shall certainly vote for the bill.'[14]

Still, despite the importance of the occasion, Chatham did not come to Parliament to vote in person.[15] His absence from the House of Lords Journals from 1825 onwards suggests that, although happy to deploy his proxy when required, there was no issue important enough to persuade him to return to active politics. He preferred not to spend time thinking about it: 'It is too wide a field for me to enter upon'. Even the reform question, about which he was self-confessedly 'all anxiety', did not bring him out.[16] One newspaper observed in 1832: 'Lord Chatham has not taken his seat in Parliament during the present reign, and has long since retired from public life.'[17] It was not wrong, and Chatham's 'retirement', although at first a matter of personal choice, became necessity as his health deteriorated.

* * *

In the autumn of 1826 Chatham secured a house at 20 Marine Parade in Brighton. From 1827 he spent every winter by the sea and every summer in London. His tall, dignified figure became familiar on the Brighton scene, paying his respects to the King at the Royal Pavilion, appearing on the Parade and in various assemblies, and frequenting Molineux's Turkish steam baths on the East Cliff.[18] The movements of the 'venerable Earl' – as he was invariably known after his 70th birthday – were followed keenly, almost tenderly, by the newspapers. 'The venerable Earl of

Chatham, we are happy to hear, is well,' the *Morning Post* announced in September 1832. A year later he was described as 'quite hearty; except a little deafness he is free from all complaints'.[19] A generation on from Walcheren Chatham was viewed as a minor celebrity, and the circumstances of his fall from grace were forgotten: 'This amiable nobleman, notwithstanding the retired habits of his life, and his extreme taciturnity in general society, was held in the highest esteem by his brother, the Right Hon. William Pitt. It was always understood that Mr. Pitt took the advice of Lord Chatham on all important measures relating to finance.'[20] This must have been a novel and pleasant experience for the much-battered Chatham. After the horror of Walcheren, his wife's illnesses and death, and the homesickness and depression of Gibraltar, he needed his peace on the Brighton seafront.

As the years passed, however, and Chatham became less capable of travelling and writing, his loneliness emerged uppermost. He received occasional visits from his niece and great-nephews, but he was increasingly forced to enjoy his own company. 'It has been a cruel disappointment to me, not to have been able to come to you at Belvoir,' he wrote to the Duke of Rutland in February 1831. Such a visit 'wou'd have been everything for me, instead of the solitude I have been doomed to experience here'.[21] As he advanced into his seventies his feet and toes gave him much pain, perhaps as a result of complications from gout, or arthritis, and his letters to friends and family were filled with complaints about the effects of cold on his joints. By 1833 he had lost the ability to walk altogether without assistance, although this may have been the long-term result of a stroke. Typically, for a man who had loved riding all his life, Chatham did not let this stop him being hoisted into the saddle by his servants and led at a slow pace along the Marine Parade. When he was finally forced to abandon his daily rides, he rode out 'in an open chariot' instead.[22]

As Chatham's health began its slow deterioration, his thoughts inevitably turned to the next generation. He had long ago decided that his two eldest male relatives, John Henry Pringle and William Stanhope Taylor, would inherit his estate. The earldom, however, granted by letters patent to 'heirs male of the body' of William Pitt, 1st Earl of Chatham, could not pass to either of them. Chatham had never regretted his lack of children in any obvious way, but the imminent prospect of his title's extinction distressed him. An old friend, John Villiers, now Earl of

Clarendon, came up with an ingenious suggestion. Chatham's mother had been granted the Barony of Chatham in her own right in 1761 and, unlike the Earldom, this might theoretically pass down the female line. Clarendon convinced Chatham there was a chance Parliament might be persuaded to pass an Act allowing the Barony to pass to William Stanhope Taylor, allowing the famous Chatham title to continue. Chatham was doubtful, but allowed Villiers to help him draft a letter to the prime minister, the Duke of Wellington:

> My own infirmities lead me to contemplate the no very distant extinction of my name & family; I may perhaps be allowed to say, considering my Father's & my Brother's brilliant & important services . . . that I do so with regret. Had the fortune of my eldest sister's son, Mr Taylor, been adequate to the honor, I might perhaps have solicited your Grace to forward my respectful request to his Majesty to continue in the family the peerage which was granted to my mother; but I must not urge such a request.[23]

Unfortunately for Chatham, the political circumstances were not favourable. The Duke of Wellington's government was fighting for its life. Wellington had been given a temporary reprieve by the Catholic Relief Act of 1829, but by 1830 it was clear the next big issue – Parliamentary Reform – might finish him. Although Wellington agreed to see Major Taylor to discuss employing him, he breathed not a word on the subject of the peerage. This did not go unnoticed with Chatham, who quietly dropped any further mention of it and contented himself with finding his heir a mildly lucrative sinecure.[24]

In March 1831 Chatham possibly suffered the first of a number of strokes which chipped away at his faculties over the next few years.[25] His illness was so serious that the newspapers actually reported his death.[26] This convinced Chatham to renew his petition to continue the Barony, this time with the highest authority: the King, William IV. In contrast to the letter to Wellington, this one laid aside all reserve and all but begged for the title to pass to Taylor:

> I am the last & almost expiring bearer of a Title, associated with the glory of this country, & of a name, borne by one, whose eminence and whose services . . . it does not become me to point

out. It is with regret that I feel the honors & the memorial of such services expiring with myself; at the same time that I have, in my niece's Son, Mr Taylor, a nephew who would not discredit any mark of Your Majesty's favor, and whose children will be educated in feelings of loyalty to Your Majesty, & in principles worthy of their own descent.[27]

He never sent the letter, 'out of respect & delicacy towards his Majesty, & from the fear of seeming to abuse the personal kindness with which He often mentioned having been treated' by the royal family.[28] Possibly Chatham was afraid the answer would be no. He limited himself to trying to improve his heirs' financial prospects, drawing up several life-insurance policies in their favour.[29] He also drew up a new will, dated 6 October 1831, in which he officially recognised his two great-nephews as his heirs.

At the start of 1834 the newspapers described his strength as 'failing', and later that year Chatham suffered a severe 'paralytic stroke'. It was a temporary setback, and by January 1835 he was well enough to attend a royal dinner for military gentlemen in Brighton.[30] He returned to London for the summer, and as autumn approached made his usual preparations to return to the seaside. Orders were issued to hold his Marine Parade house ready to receive him at any moment, and he wrote to the Duke of Wellington entrusting him with his House of Lords proxy.[31] The Duke of Rutland called on Chatham in Charles Street on his way to Belvoir Castle for the shooting season. He found his old friend 'complain[ing] of being ill', but this was not unusual for Chatham, who had always been sensitive about his health. Rutland 'did not perceive any Change in him, to occasion any alarm or uneasiness to his friends', and left fully expecting to see Chatham in the spring.[32]

But Rutland never did see his friend again. Around 20 September Chatham suffered another massive stroke. This time he did not recover. He lingered a few days, without regaining consciousness, and died at 1 o'clock in the morning on 24 September, a fortnight from his 79th birthday.

Chatham's heirs, William Taylor and John Pringle, were notified and arrived in Charles Street within hours. Being left with the settlement 'of [Chatham's] just debts' must have given them pause, but to their astonishment they discovered that Chatham's quiet life as a widower had paid off. The Charles Street house, mortgaged to the Dowager Lady Suffield, brought in very little when sold, but those proceeds, along with the sale of the house's contents, did the trick. The executors kept items of family significance – locks of hair, mourning rings, dispatch boxes, a copy of the Hoare portrait of Pitt the Elder – but sold nearly everything else, from landscape paintings via the contents of Chatham's Spanish wine cellar to the silverware and the servant's bedlinen.[33] When everything was gone, enough had been produced to clear Lord Chatham's account at Coutts' Bank. The only member of his family to be taken to court for non-payment of debt, Chatham had managed to turn his private affairs around to such an extent that he was also the only member of his family to die solvent.

He was carried to the family vault in Westminster Abbey on 3 October 1835 in grand style. The arrangements for the coffin alone included a white satin lining and winding sheet, a tufted mattress and pillow, an inner coffin of elm, middle coffin of lead and outer coffin covered in crimson velvet attached with brass nails in the shape of coronets and Garter stars.[34] A man was hired to carry the gilded Earl's coronet on a velvet cushion, and the procession was led by a 'male horse' dressed in a velvet caparison with ostrich feathers. Six other horses drew the hearse, followed by ten hired men in black scarves and hatbands. The Dean, Sub-Dean and Preceptor of Westminster walked beneath a canopy, followed by the Chief Mourner, William Stanhope Taylor, two vergers and a beadle.

It was a rainy, squally day, but the procession down Whitehall attracted a large audience. The King himself sent his carriage, attended by 20 grooms and 2 men carrying wands, and several other members of the royal family also paid their respects.[35] The whole of Westminster Abbey was closed off to the public as the mourners entered the North Transept. Here Chatham was lowered into the vault beside his parents, brother, sister and wife. Pitt had died 29 years earlier, and Mary 14, but Chatham was at last reunited with his family.

Conclusion

Chatham never courted publicity, and after Walcheren he had even more reason to shun it. By the time he died public memory had softened to some degree. The newspapers merely reported on the sinecures he left vacant and the amount of public money saved by his passing. 'Lord Chatham died the day before yesterday,' Charles Greville recorded in his diary, 'which is of no other importance than that of giving some honours and emoluments . . . to distribute'.[1] Chatham's long life bridged two eras, and Greville's conclusion shows how much Chatham was a reform-era relic from a bygone age of aristocratic deference and paternalism. But Greville's catty epitaph also bristled with irony: having dismissed Chatham as a nonentity, he had nonetheless felt his death important enough to record.

Assessment of Chatham's career in 1835 seemed straightforward. He had been guaranteed a central role in national life by virtue of his title and family connections; he had had the pick of offices at the highest level of government; and he had risen effortlessly up the military ladder of promotion. Sinecures and pensions fell into his lap. Sir Nathaniel Wraxall's much-quoted description, laced with all the bitterness of jealousy, was typical of the way contemporaries viewed Chatham:

> If ever any individual drew a prize in the great lottery of human life, that man was the present Earl of Chatham . . . At scarcely three-and-twenty, he had succeeded to an earldom, to a pension of four thousand pounds a year settled on the title, and to the estate of Burton Pynsent. Lord Chatham inherited likewise his illustrious father's form and figure; but not his mind. . . . Constitutionally and habitually taciturn, cold, reserved, lofty, repulsive, his silence served as a mantle to protect him from close inspection. It did more; for it inspired respect, as though it concealed great talents under that veil. Many persons, indeed, have given him credit for judgment and capacity; but his whole life proves the contrary. . . . Of the talents attributed to him by flattery, he has exhibited no proof.[2]

The course of Chatham's public career seemed to bear out Wraxall's opinion. Thoroughly eclipsed by his father and brother until his fifties, Chatham emerged from their shadows to command one of Britain's greatest military disasters. No wonder he went down in history as an aberration in an otherwise remarkably successful family: in the words of Pitt family historian Sir Tresham Lever, 'a haughty, proud man . . . unattractive, vain, pompous . . . the most stupid and useless of the Pitts'.[3]

Wraxall and Lever's blunt-instrument assessments help explain why Chatham has fallen through the cracks of history, but they are hardly fair. Lord Eldon, who was close to Chatham, had a high opinion of him: he was 'as able a man, in point of intellect' as Pitt the Younger. 'But,' Eldon added, perceptively, 'being the first-born of their illustrious father, and the inheritor of his honours . . . as it too often happens with persons in similar circumstances, his understanding and talents had not been as assiduously cultivated'.[4] Chatham himself possibly never understood the influence coming so early to such a famous title had on his development. His character and reactions were shaped by who he was: a Pitt first, and an individual second. Far from winning Wraxall's 'great lottery of human life', Chatham's fate underlined how unfair fortune had been to him. He had enough intelligence, ambition, and respect for his family name to try and do what was expected of him, but, tragically, Pitt the Elder and Younger had set the bar far too high.

Yet Chatham's abilities were considerable, and he had the reputation of being highly sensible. Even a cursory glance over his correspondence shows a remarkably clear-headed man with a talent for crafting a crisp, well-thought out argument. He was the consummate gentleman and courtier, and his diplomatic skills – his much-lauded 'manners' – were legendary. Close associates came to like, respect and even love him. But, as his public reputation disintegrated, Chatham relied more and more on his 'manners' to cloak him from scrutiny. He was more exposed to criticism than any other politician or soldier because of the contrast of his quiet career with that of his father and brother. To measure up to one was difficult: to measure up to both, impossible, and in time Chatham may have come to believe he was as inadequate as others made him out to be. His lack of self-confidence increased over the years, fed by childhood experience, adult rivalries and the pressure of public events. By the time he received his independent command at Walcheren, he displayed all the characteristics of a man who had so long been accustomed to being viewed as incapable that he had begun to believe it himself.

This strange vulnerability cut through Chatham's entire life, and conditioned his reaction to the challenges he faced. Many of these were magnified by circumstances and extraordinarily poor luck, but Chatham's overly defensive response to them, and his refusal to admit any personal responsibility, worsened matters still further. His feud with Pitt's right-hand man, Dundas, ensured his fall from the Admiralty in 1794, and this experience poisoned his relationship with his brother and his other Cabinet colleagues. The scars manifested themselves as an almost pathological tendency to see every check and criticism as a personal challenge to his authority. It is ironic that the polite and courtier-like Chatham made enemies out of Dundas and Mulgrave so easily, but this paradox is typical. In the end, Chatham's touchiness proved his downfall, transforming military defeat at Walcheren into a crushing personal and political disaster.

John Barrow, a junior minister at the Admiralty in 1809, recalled Chatham had been 'condemned ere, indeed, he had set out' on the Walcheren expedition.[5] Barrow probably intended the line to mean Chatham was widely considered unequal to the task he had been assigned, but 'condemned ere he had set out' could well serve as a broader metaphor for Chatham's entire life. Most men who failed did so entirely on their own account, but when Chatham failed he carried the weight of his father and brother down with him. He was one of the best-connected politicians of the period, closely related to three prime ministers and on friendly terms with all three late Georgian monarchs. He held some of the highest offices of state during the French Revolutionary and Napoleonic wars, and fought in them personally. As such, he has much to tell us about the milieu in which he lived. Even on his own merits, however, 'the late Lord Chatham' is owed a reassessment.

Notes

Chapter One: Lord Pitt, 1756–78

1. *Public Advertiser*, 14 October 1756.
2. The precise date of John Pitt's birth is disputed. His baptismal record, reproduced in Canon Thompson, *The History of Hayes in the County of Kent* (London, 1935), notes his date of birth as 10 October 1756. This accords with the several letters written by Pitt to announce the birth, all of which state John to have been born in the morning on the 10th. It appears, however, that the family celebrated John's birthday on the 9th, from a letter written by Pitt to his son William on 9 October 1773, 'the happy day that gave us your brother' (William Stanhope Taylor and John Henry Pringle (eds), *The Correspondence of William Pitt, 1st Earl of Chatham*, 4 vols (London, 1839) (hereafter *CC*), Vol. III, p. 290). John himself provided the date of 9 October 1756 for his pedigree, delivered to the House of Lords in August 1791 (Parliamentary Archives, HL/PO/JO/22/1/3, f. 42).
3 Pitt to George Grenville, 10 October 1756, William J. Smith, *The Grenville Papers*, 4 vols (London, 1843), Vol. I, pp. 173–4.
4. Horace Walpole to George Montagu, 21 October 1759, *Private Correspondence of Horace Walpole, Earl of Orford*, 4 vols (London, 1820), Vol. II, p. 119.
5. Marie Peters, *The Elder Pitt* (London, 1998), pp. 172–3.
6. Lady Hester Pitt to Pitt, 18 July 1766, TNA, PRO 30/8/9, f. 23.
7. Edward Wilson to Lady Chatham, 26 July 1766, TNA, PRO 30/8/67, f. 3.
8. Lady Chatham to Temple, 25 September 1769, *Grenville Papers*, Vol. IV, p. 463.
9. Pitt to Lady Chatham, undated but August 1769, TNA, PRO 30/70/5, f. 329h.
10. Lady Chatham to Chatham, 11 April 1772, TNA, PRO 30/8/9, f. 106.
11. Lady Chatham to Chatham, undated, TNA, PRO 30/8/9, f. 29.
12. Pitt to Lady Hester Pitt, undated but spring 1758, TNA, Hoare MSS PRO 30/70/5, f. 310.
13. Chatham to Lady Chatham, 15 August 1770, TNA, PRO 30/8/5, f. 257; Lady Chatham to Chatham, undated, TNA, PRO 30/8/9, f. 46. The *Middlesex Journal* for 23 April 1774 recorded 'a beautiful Aurora Borealis . . . in the North East part of the horizon, which . . . continued till near day light'.
14. Chatham to Dr Addington, 23 November 1771, *CC*, Vol. IV, pp. 184–6.
15. Lord Pitt to Wilson, 3 February 1772, Pitt Papers, David M. Rubenstein Rare Book and Manuscript Library, Duke University.
16. Lady Chatham to Mrs Pitt, 25 October 1777, British Library (hereafter BL), Add MSS 59490, f. 61.
17. William Pitt to Lord Pitt, 31 July 1770, quoted in J.H. Rose, *William Pitt and National Revival* (London, 1909), p. 45.
18. Elizabeth Grenville to Lady Chatham, undated, quoted in Vere Birdwood, *So Dearly Loved, So Much Admired* (London, 1994), p. 145.
19. Lady Chatham to Chatham, 11 August 1770, TNA, PRO 30/8/9, f. 70.

NOTES

20. Quoted in *CC*, Vol. IV, p. 240 n. 1. Another version of the same story was given by Henry Addington, in 1839: 'Old Lord Chatham made his five children . . . act a play. I [Addington] was present. After the play, Lord Chatham said to my father with some disappointment, "Did you observe how superior Pitt [Lord Pitt] was to William; how much better he felt and spoke the speeches," and seemed mortified at thinking that his little favourite did not promise to be an orator.' Louis J. Jennings (ed.), *The correspondence and diaries of John Wilson Croker*, 2 vols (London, 1884), Vol. II, pp. 339–40.

21. Brian Tunstall, *William Pitt, Earl of Chatham* (London, 1938), p. 432.

22. For example, William Hayley's verdict in 1773: 'The youngest, afterwards the great William Pitt, was now a wonderful boy of fourteen, who eclipsed his brother in conversation'. William Hayley, *Memoirs of the Life and Writings of William Hayley*, 2 vols (London, 1823), Vol. I, p. 123.

23. Chatham to Hollis, 13 April 1773; Chatham to Hollis, 18 April 1773, quoted in J.H. Jesse, *Memoirs of the life and reign of King George III*, 3 vols (London, 1867), Vol. II, pp. 554–5, 556.

24. A.L. Humphreys, *Lyme Regis: a retrospect* (London, 1922), p. 219.

25. Chatham to Lady Chatham, 20 June 1773, TNA, PRO 30/8/5, f. 300.

26. Chatham to Lady Chatham, undated, TNA, PRO 30/8/5, f. 288.

27. Tony Hayter (ed.), *An eighteenth-century Secretary-at-War: The papers of William, Viscount Barrington* (London, 1988), pp. 306–9.

28. *Middlesex Journal*, 7 July 1774.

29. Paul David Nelson, *General Sir Guy Carleton, Lord Dorchester* (Madison, NJ, 2000), pp. 16–17.

30. For the situation in Canada see Nelson, *Sir Guy Carleton*; Paul R. Reynolds, *Guy Carleton: A Biography* (Toronto, 1980); Gustave Lanctot, *Canada and the American Revolution* (London, 1967); R. Coupland, *The Quebec Act* (Oxford, 1925).

31. John Wood to Lord and Lady Chatham, 13 November 1774, TNA, PRO 30/70/5, f. 345.

32. *London Evening Post*, 1 February 1776; *London Chronicle*, 1 February 1776, quoted in James M. Hadden, *Hadden's Journal and Orderly Book* (Albany, NY, 1884), p. 216 n.; General Arnold's Instructions, 14 September 1775, in W.C. Ford, *The writings of George Washington*, 14 vols (New York, NY, 1889), Vol. III, 123.

33. Isaac Barré's words, *CC*, Vol. IV, p. 410 n. 1.

34. Lady Chatham to Lord Pitt, TNA, PRO 30/8/10, f. 18.

35. Lady Chatham to Pitt, 18 July 1775, TNA, PRO 30/8/10, f. 25; Lady Chatham to Caldwell, July 1775, *CC*, Vol. IV, pp. 410–13.

36. Hadden, *Hadden's Journal and Orderly Book*, p. 216 n.; Carleton to Chatham, 21 September 1775, *CC*, Vol. IV, pp. 413–14; *St James's Chronicle*, 5 November 1775.

37. Lady Chatham to Thomas Pitt, 7, 8 February 1776, BL, Add MSS 59490, ff. 28, 29.

38. *Morning Post*, 2 October 1776.

39. Molly Hood to Lady Chatham, Birdwood, *So Dearly Loved*, p. 120.

40. Lady Harriot Pitt to Lady Chatham, 11 May [1776], 29 November [1777], John Rylands Library (hereafter JRL), Papers of Lady Harriot Eliot, Eng MS 1272, ff. 12, 13.

41. Acting as scribe: Chatham to Richmond, 6 April 1778, *CC*, Vol. IV, p. 518. Keeping

family informed: Lord Pitt to Thomas Pitt, April 1777, BL, Add MSS 59490, f. 47. Attending court: Lord Pitt to Lady Chatham, 30 March 1778, TNA, PRO 30/70/5, f. 354.

42. *New Morning Post*, 11 December 1776.

43. Peters, *The Elder Pitt*, p. 222; Basil Williams, *The life of William Pitt, Earl of Chatham*, 2 vols (London, 1915), Vol. II, p. 323.

44. *London Evening Post*, 25 April 1778; *London Gazette*, 20 June 1778; *General Advertiser and Morning Intelligencer*, 7 May 1778.

45. *Parliamentary History to 1803*, XIX, 1023.

46. *CC,* Vol. IV, p. 526 n.

47. *London Chronicle*, 16 May 1778.

48. Chatham to Granby, 15 May 1778, HMC, *Manuscripts of the Duke of Rutland*, 4 vols (London, 1894) (hereafter *Rutland*), Vol. IV, p. 238.

Chapter 2: 'The Child of the Publick', 1778–88

1. *Public Advertiser*, 15 May 1778.

2. Grantham to Frederick Robinson, 27 March 1779, Bedfordshire Archives, L30/15/54/127; Frederick Robinson to Grantham, 27 April 1779, Bedfordshire Archives, L30/14/333/198.

3. Frederick Robinson to Grantham, 11 May 1779, Bedfordshire Archives, L30/14/333/ 207; J.H. Burton (ed.), *Benthamiana, or select extracts from the works of Jeremy Bentham* (London, 1843), p. 333.

4. Grantham to Frederick Robinson, 25 and 27 March, 5 and 6 April 1779, Bedfordshire Archives, L30/15/54/126, 127, 131, 132; Grantham to Anne Robinson, 2 April 1779, Bedfordshire Archives, L30/17/4/245a; Sir Nathaniel Wraxall, *Posthumous Memoirs of my Own Time*, 3 vols (London, 1836), Vol. III, p. 129.

5. Burton (ed.), *Benthamiana*, p. 333; *London Evening Post*, 18 June 1779.

6. 1 March 1779, Governor's Diary, 1778–82, Gibraltar National Archives (hereafter GNA).

7. *London Evening Post*, 18 June 1779; House of Lords Journal (hereafter HLJ), 35, 800.

8. HLJ, 36, 711–12.

9. Rutland to Chatham, 30 January 1780, TNA, PRO 30/70/5, f. 356; Rutland to Chatham, 14 February 1785, TNA, PRO 30/70/3, f. 145; Belvoir Castle Manuscripts. I am grateful to Emma Ellis for her help with this.

10. Pitt to Lady Chatham, 26 February 1780, TNA, PRO 30/8/12, f. 141; Pitt to Lady Chatham, TNA, PRO 30/8/12, f. 167; *St James's Chronicle*, 14 September 1780.

11. Pitt to Lady Chatham, 24 January 1780, TNA, PRO 30/8/12, f. 137.

12. TNA, WO 65/33; Chatham to Wilson, 17 December 1782, Pitt Papers, David M. Rubenstein Rare Book and Manuscript Library, Duke University.

13. Philip Henry Stanhope, *Life of the Right Honourable William Pitt*, 4 vols (London, 1861–2), Vol. I, p. 24.

14. William Douglas Home (ed.), *The Prime Ministers* (London, 1987), p. 55.

15. Abstract of Title for Burton Pynsent, Somerset Record Office, DD/LC/54/9, ff. 61–5.

16. Williams, *The life of William Pitt*, Vol. II, p. 285.

17. Chatham's will, TNA, PROB/11/1044; indenture of 23 February 1782, Somerset Record Office, DD/GL/188.

18. The breakdown (TNA, PRO 30/8/10, f. 6) was:

£4,396 8*s* 4*d* to Pitt

£2500 0*s* 0*d* to Edward James Eliot, widower of Chatham's sister Harriot

£958 7*s* 5*d* to Chatham

£244 2*s* 8*d* to the heirs of Chatham's dead sister Hester, Lady Mahon

£718 15*s* 0*d* further yet to be paid to Eliot

£911 6*s* 1*d* further to be paid to Pitt

£100 0*s* 0*d* to Christian Wulbier, an old associate of the first Earl

£200 1*s* 5*s* to Augustine Greenland, Chatham's agent

Total: £8540 0*s* 0.

19. John Ehrman *The Younger Pitt: The Years of Acclaim* (London, 1969), p. 20; bond, 1 December 1780, Suffolk Record Office, HA 119/4/4/9/3/2.

20. Sir Tresham Lever, *The House of Pitt* (London, 1947), p. 359.

21. E.T. Gould to the Duke of Portland, 27 November 1780, University of Nottingham Manuscripts and Special Collections, PwF 4.284. He had a horse running in 1781 (Mistley): *Sporting Magazine*, 22 (1828), 439. He subscribed to the *Racing Calendar* from at least 1785 until his death.

22. Paul Kelly, 'Strategy and counter-revolution: the Journal of Sir Gilbert Elliot, 1–22 September 1793', *EHR* 98 (387) April 1974, 328–48, 342; Burton (ed.), *Benthamiana*, p. 333.

23. Egerton Castle (ed.), *The Jerningham Letters, 1780–1843*, 2 vols (London, 1896), Vol. I, p. 322.

24. Grantham to Frederick Robinson, 2 May 1779, Bedfordshire Archives, L30/15/54/139.

25. Frederick Robinson to Grantham, 25 May 1779, Bedford Archives, L30/14/333/211.

26. Stanhope, *Life of the Right Honourable William Pitt*, Vol. I, p. 81.

27. Elizabeth Townshend to Lady Chatham, 14 August 1782, TNA, PRO 30/8/60, f. 232.

28. Lady Harriot Pitt to Lady Chatham, [1 May 1783], JRL, Eng MS 1272, f. 32.

29. Lady Harriot Pitt to Lady Chatham, [3 May 1783], JRL, Eng MS 1272, f. 33; Lady Harriot Pitt to Lady Chatham, [5 May 1783], JRL, Eng MS 1272, f. 34.

30. Lady Harriot Pitt to Lady Chatham, [19 May 1783], JRL, Eng MS 1272, f. 38.

31. Bromley Local Studies and Archives, 1080/3/1/1/26.

32. The rumour of the mistress appears in Charles Meryon, *Memoirs of the Lady Hester Stanhope*, 3 vols (London, 1845), Vol. II, pp. 76–7. Although Lady Hester was Chatham's niece, the 'mistress' he never travelled without is entirely invisible in the historical record.

33. *Morning Post*, 1 August 1783. I am grateful to Therese Holmes for providing me with this reference.

34. *London Chronicle*, 31 July 1783; *Morning Chronicle*, 1 August 1783.

35. HLJ, 37, 19–29.

36. Chatham to Dowager Lady Chatham, December 1783, TNA, PRO 30/8/13.

37. Memorandum, February 1821, Suffolk Record Office, HA119/562/688.

38. Lady Harriot Pitt to Dowager Lady Chatham, 19 May 1783, JRL, Eng MS 1272, f. 38.

39. *Morning Chronicle*, 20 January 1784; *Public Advertiser*, 1 March 1784; *Gazetteer and New Daily Advertiser*, 30 December 1784.

40. Georgiana Townshend to Dowager Lady Chatham, 20 April 1784, TNA, PRO 30/8/64, f. 167.

41. Anne Robinson to Grantham, 5 November 1784, Bedfordshire Archives, L30/15/50/56; Dowager Lady Chatham to Pitt, 14 October 1795, TNA, PRO 30/8/10, f. 31.

42. Grantham to Frederick Robinson, 3 January 1785, Bedfordshire Archives, L30/15/54/ 238; Grantham to Frederick Robinson, 14 January 1785, Bedfordshire Archives, L30/15 /54/246; Grantham to Frederick Robinson, 17 January 1785, Bedfordshire Archives, L30/ 15/54/249.

43. Wilson to Dowager Lady Chatham, 7 October 1785, TNA, PRO 30/8/67, f. 113.

44. Army Lists, 1784–7, TNA, WO 65/34-7.

45. Pitt to Chatham, 29 September 1786, TNA PRO 30/8/101, ff. 109, 111.

46. Wilson to Dowager Lady Chatham, 5 November 1786, TNA, PRO 30/8/67, f. 134.

47. James Greig (ed.), *The Farington Diary*, 8 vols (London, 1922), Vol. I, p. 64.

48. *London Chronicle*, 14 June 1788.

49. *World*, 19 June 1788.

50. Westmorland to Chatham, 15 August 1791, TNA, PRO 30/8/369, f. 221; Wilson to Dowager Lady Chatham, 18 November 1791, TNA, PRO 30/8/67, f. 53; *Geneve Post*, 28 July 1791; *London Chronicle*, 2 July; *Star*, 5 July, 14 July, 23 July; *Morning Herald*, 21 July; *Evening Mail*, 12 August 1791.

51. *Gazetteer and New Daily Advertiser*, 9 October 1784 (for the quotation); *London Chronicle*, 28 September 1784; *General Advertiser*, 26 October 1784; *Morning Chronicle*, 10 November 1779.

52. *Morning Herald*, 31 January 1785. The rebuttal is in the *General Advertiser*, 4 February 1785.

53. Pitt to Bishop of Lincoln, 4 November 1787, Suffolk Record Office, HA 119/T108/42; Wraxall, *Posthumous Memoirs*, Vol. III, pp. 130–1.

54. Pulteney to Rutland, 26 June, 6 July 1784, HMC, *Rutland*, Vol. IV, pp. 115, 122.

Chapter 3: First Lord of the Admiralty, 1788–93

1. Grenville to Buckingham, 1 April 1788, Duke of Buckingham and Chandos (ed.), *Memoirs of the Court and Cabinets of George III*, 4 vols (London, 1853–5), Vol. I, p. 369.

2. *Parliamentary History to 1803*, XXV, 389.

3. Pitt to Dowager Lady Chatham, 19 June 1788, Stanhope, *Life of the Right Honourable William Pitt*, Vol. I, p. 376.

4. Grenville to Buckingham, 16 May 1788, Buckingham and Chandos (ed.), *Memoirs*, Vol. I, p. 385. See also John E. Talbott, *The Pen & Ink Sailor: Charles Middleton and the King's Navy, 1778–1813* (London, 1998), p. 129, and P.K. Crimmin, 'Admiralty Administration, 1783–1806' (MA, University of London, 1965), p. 19.

5. N.A.M. Rodger, *The Command of the Ocean: A Naval History of Britain, 1649–1815* (London, 2004), pp. 363, 376.

6. Chatham to [Dundas], 7 March 1794, William L. Clements Library (University of Michigan), Pitt Papers.

7. Brian Lavery, *Nelson's navy: the ships, men and organisation* (London, 2012), pp. 21–2.

8. Clive Wilkinson, *The British navy and the state in the 18th century* (Woodbridge, 2004),

pp. 12–13, 16, 18–19, 21–3; Rodger, *Command of the Ocean*, pp. 388–9; N.A.M. Rodger, *The Admiralty* (Lavenham, 1979), p. 75; Lavery, *Nelson's navy*, pp. 23, 25.

9. Rodger, *Command of the Ocean*, p. 373.

10. Dundas to Spencer, 14 December 1794, Julian S. Corbett (ed.), *Private Papers of George, Second Earl Spencer*, 2 vols (London, 1914), Vol. I, p. 6.

11. Middleton to Chatham, 23 May [1794], TNA, PRO 30/8/365, f. 40.

12. John R. Breihan, 'William Pitt and the Commission on Fees, 1785–1801', *Historical Journal* 27 (1) (1984), 66–7; Rodger, *Command of the Ocean*, pp. 376–7.

13. Rodger, *Admiralty*, p. 81; Leslie Gardiner, *The British Admiralty* (London, 1968), p. 181; Sir Oswyn A.R. Murray, 'The Admiralty VI', *Mariner's Mirror*, 24 (3) 1938, 338; Patricia K. Crimmin, 'Admiralty relations with the Teasury, 1783–1806: the preparation of naval estimates and the beginnings of Treasury control', *Mariner's Mirror*, 53 (1) (1967), 66–7; Breihan, 'William Pitt and the Commission on Fees', 59, 66.

14. Georgiana Townshend to Dowager Lady Chatham, [July 1788], TNA, PRO 30/8/64, f. 190; Pitt to Dowager Lady Chatham, 29 August 1788, Stanhope, *Life of the Right Honourable William Pitt*, Vol. I, p. 382; *World*, 12 August 1788.

15. Chatham to Alexander Hood, 1 October 1788, BL, Add MSS 35194, f. 8; *Morning Herald*, 2 October 1788.

16. For his attendance record see Admiralty Board Minutes, TNA, ADM 3/104–105: by the end of December 1788 Chatham had missed only 31 meetings out of a potential 124 (a 76 per cent attendance record). For Chatham's leg flare-ups, see Dowager Lady Chatham to Eliot, 31 December 1788, 11 March 1789, 6 April 1789, Suffolk Record Office, HA 119/T108/40.

17. *World*, 6 April 1789.

18. Chatham to Middleton, 7 March 1789, National Maritime Museum (hereafter NMM), MID/1/147.

19. Chatham to Middleton, 11 December 1789, NMM, MID/1/147.

20. Rodger, *Command of the Ocean*, p. 377; Rodger, *Admiralty*, p. 81; Gardiner, *British Admiralty*, pp. 181–2; Murray, 'The Admiralty VI', 338–9; Sir John Knox Laughton (ed.), *Letters and Papers of Charles, Lord Barham*, 3 vols (London, 1907), Vol. II, pp. 347–50.

21. HLJ, 36, 711–12.

22. Rodger, *Command of the Ocean*, pp. 363–4, 473; Talbott, *The Pen & Ink Sailor*, p. 132; Paul Webb, 'The rebuilding and repair of the fleet, 1783–1793', *Bulletin of the Institute of Historical Research*, 50 (122) (1977), 200, 206–8.

23. Ehrman, *Years of Acclaim*, p. 317.

24. Breihan, 'William Pitt and the Commission on Fees', 70–2, 77–9, 81.

25. Rodger, *Command of the Ocean*, pp. 431–3, 473, 476; Gardiner, *British Admiralty*, pp. 188–9; Roger Knight, *Britain against Napoleon: the organization of victory, 1793–1815* (London, 2013).

26. Rodger, *Command of the Ocean*, pp. 474–5. Impress Service: Lavery, *Nelson's navy*, pp. 120–1; J.R. Hill (ed.), *The Oxford Illustrated History of the Royal Navy* (Oxford, 1995), p. 135. Transport Board: Lavery, *Nelson's navy*, p. 25, M.E. Condon, 'The establishment of the Transport Board: a sub-division of the Admiralty, 4 July 1794', *Mariner's Mirror*, 58 (1) (1972), 78–9, 81–2, and correspondence between Chatham

and Middleton in January 1794, NMM, MID/1/147. Also Crimmin, 'Admiralty relations with the Treasury', 69–71; Breihan, 'William Pitt and the Commission on Fees', 79.

27. Rodger, *Command of the Ocean*, pp. 362, 376–7; Webb, 'The rebuilding and repair of the fleet', 194–5; Paul Webb, 'The naval aspects of the Nootka Sound crisis', *Mariner's Mirror*, 61 (2) (1975), 135–6.

28. Chatham to Alexander Hood, 11 November 1790, BL, Add MSS 35194, f. 140.

29. Lavery, *Nelson's navy*, pp. 97–8; Rodger, *Command of the Ocean*, pp. 388–90; Hill (ed.), *Oxford Illustrated History of the Royal Navy*, pp. 153–4; Charles Consolvo, 'The prospects and promotion of British Naval Officers, 1793–1815', *Mariner's Mirror*, 91 (2) 2005, 149, 151–2, 156.

30. Lord Hood to Alexander Hood, 11 December 1790, BL, Add MSS 35194, f. 150.

31. Chatham to Alexander Hood, 10 August 1790, BL, Add MSS 35194, f. 63.

32. *Morning Star*, 4 September 1789.

33. Collier to Portland, 13 August 1794, 24 October 1794, University of Nottingham Manuscripts and Special Collections, PwF 3.003, PwF 3.007.

34. William Smith to R. Gray, 8 May 1793, A. Aspinall (ed.), *Correspondence of George, Prince of Wales, 1770–1812*, 7 vols (London, 1963–70), Vol. II, p. 356.

35. Portland to Collier, 20 October 1794, University of Nottingham Manuscripts and Special Collections, PwV 108, f. 123.

36. Rodger, *Command of the Ocean*, p. 518; Consolvo, 'The prospects and promotion of British Naval Officers', 144.

37. Burke to Chatham, 20 December 1794, TNA PRO 30/70/3, f. 190.

38. Sydney to Lord Ailesbury, 4 February 1793, Wiltshire and Swindon Record Office, 9/35/254.

39. *World*, 12 August 1789; Grenville to Buckingham, 16 May 1788, Buckingham and Chandos (ed.), *Memoirs*, Vol. I, p. 385.

40. King to Chatham, 25 July 1788, TNA, PRO 30/70/3, f. 150.

41. Ghita Stanhope, *The life of Charles, 3rd Earl Stanhope* (London, 1914), p. 19; *Whitehall Evening Post*, 4 June 1789; *The Times*, 19 January 1793.

42. Lord Stavordale (ed.), *Further memoirs of the Whig Party, 1807–21 . . . by Lord Holland* (London, 1905), pp. 31–3.

43. TNA, ADM 3/104–114.

44. *Star*, 23 July 1791.

45. Middleton to Spencer, 19 December 1794, Corbett (ed.), *Private Papers*, Vol. I, pp. 8–12.

46. Greig (ed.), *Farington*, Vol. I, p. 64.

47. Wilson to Dowager Lady Chatham, 7 June 1791, TNA, PRO 30/8/67, f. 193.

48. Greig (ed.), *Farington*, Vol. I, p. 53.

49. Chatham to Alexander Hood, 10 August 1790, BL, Add MSS 35194, f. 63.

50. *Ibid.*

51. Rodger, *Command of the Ocean*, p. 365; Webb, 'The naval aspects of the Nootka Sound crisis', 134–5, 151.

52. Hill (ed.), *Oxford Illustrated History of the Royal Navy*, p. 108; Paul Webb, 'Sea power in the Ochakov affair of 1791', *International History Review*, 2 (1) (January 1980), 22.

53. King to Pitt, 12 December 1790, Stanhope, *Life of the Right Honourable William Pitt*, Vol. II, Appendix xii.

54. King to Pitt, 14 December 1790, Stanhope, *Life of the Right Honourable William Pitt*, Vol. II, Appendix xiii.

55. Lady Hester Stanhope to Lord Haddington, 15 November 1803, National Records of Scotland (hereafter NRS), GD249/2/5, f. 25.

56. Jeremy Black, *British Foreign Policy in an Age of Revolutions, 1783–93* (Cambridge, 1994), pp. 309–13; Webb, 'Ochakov', 14–7, 22, 26–8, 31; Hill (ed.), *Oxford Illustrated History of the Royal Navy*, p. 108.

57. Quoted in Black, *British Foreign Policy*, pp. 318–19.

58. *London Recorder*, 14 October 1792.

59. Memorandum by Chatham, TNA, PRO 30/8/364, f. 1; Murray, 'The Admiralty VI', 340; Webb, 'Ochakov', 13.

60. Rodger, *Admiralty*, pp. 75–6, 81; Gardiner, *British Admiralty*, pp. 180–2; Condon, 'The establishment of the Transport Board', 71–2; Breihan, 'William Pitt and the Commission on Fees', 65; Webb, 'The rebuilding and repair of the fleet', 200, 207–8; Michael Duffy and Roger Morriss (eds), *The Glorious First of June 1794: a naval battle and its aftermath* (Exeter, 2001), p. 32.

61. John Ehrman, *The Younger Pitt: The Reluctant Transition* (Stanford, CA, 1983), pp. 379, 499.

Chapter 4: 'A Fatality of Temper', 1793–4

1. Ehrman, *Reluctant Transition*, pp. 263–6, 283–7; Alfred H. Burne, *The Noble Duke of York: the military life of Frederick Duke of York and Albany* (London, 1949), p. 46.

2. Michael Duffy, '"A particular service": the British government and the Dunkirk expedition of 1793', *English Historical Review*, 91 (360) July 1976, 540–1, 544, 547–8; Ehrman, *Reluctant Transition*, p. 289; Burne, *The Noble Duke of York*, p. 72; Robert Harvey, *The War of Wars: the epic struggle between Britain and France, 1789–1815* (London, 2007), p. 129.

3. *Morning Chronicle*, 11 September 1793; *The Times*, 14 September 1793.

4. Kelly, 'Strategy and counter-revolution', 342; Alison Gilbert Olson, *The Radical Duke: the career and correspondence of Charles Lennox, 3rd Duke of Richmond* (Oxford, 1961), pp. 97–8; Lord Rosebery (ed.), *The Windham Papers*, 2 vols (London, 1913), Vol. I, p. 153; Duffy, 'A particular service', 552–4.

5. Buckingham to Grenville, 26 August 1793, HMC, *Manuscripts of J B Fortescue, Esq. Preserved at Dropmore* (hereafter *Dropmore*), 9 vols (London, 1905–10), Vol. II, p. 418.

6. Memorandum by Chatham, TNA, PRO 30/8/364, f. 221.

7. Ehrman, *Reluctant Transition*, p. 298; Malcolm Crook, *Toulon in war and revolution: from the ancien regime to the Restoration, 1750–1820* (Manchester, 1991), pp. 138–9.

8. Michael Duffy, *Soldiers, sugar, and seapower: the British expeditions to the West Indies and the war against Revolutionary France* (Oxford, 1987), pp. 15–16, 25, 52, 54, 56; Ehrman, *Reluctant Transition*, p. 352.

9. Bernard Ireland, *The fall of Toulon: the last opportunity to defeat the French Revolution* (London, 2006), pp. 210–11, 213, 219, 261; Ehrman, *Reluctant Transition*, pp. 314, 317.

10. Ireland, *Fall of Toulon*, p. 284; Crook, *Toulon in war and revolution*, pp. 145–8; Ehrman, *Reluctant Transition*, pp. 316–17.
11. Chatham to Lord Hood, 28 January 1794, TNA, PRO 30/8/364, f. 18.
12. Memorandum by Chatham, January 1795, TNA, PRO 30/8/364, f. 171.
13. Chatham to Pitt, 1 December 1794, Cambridge University Library (hereafter CUL), Pitt Papers, Add MS 6958, f. 1558.
14. Kelly, 'Strategy and counter-revolution', 344, 346; HMC, *Dropmore*, Vol. II, Dundas to Grenville, [July 1793], 28 July 1793, 18 August 1793, 7 October 1793, pp. 407–8, 416, 440.
15. Dundas to Pitt, [1793], TNA, PRO 30/8/157, f. 168.
16. Crimmin, 'Admiralty Administration', p. 22.
17. Duffy, *Soldiers, sugar, and seapower*, p. 51.
18. Chatham to [Dundas], 7 March 1794, William L. Clements Library, Pitt Papers.
19. David Wilkinson, *The Duke of Portland: politics and party in the age of George III* (London, 2003), p. 106.
20. Pitt to Chatham, 12 July 1794, TNA, PRO 30/8/101, f. 121.
21. Pitt to Grenville, 5 July 1794, HMC, *Dropmore*, Vol. II, p. 595.
22. Duffy and Morriss (eds), *The Glorious First of June 1794*, pp. 2, 30–2, 37–8; Sam Willis, *The Glorious First of June: fleet battle in the reign of terror* (London, 2011), pp. 233–4, 276–7.
23. Willis, *Glorious First of June*, pp. 237–8, 261–6; Quintin Colville and James Davey (eds), *Nelson, Navy and Nation: the Royal Navy and the British people 1688–1815* (London, 2013), pp. 9–11; Rodger, *Command of the Ocean*, p. 430; Duffy and Morriss (eds), *The Glorious First of June 1794*, pp. 68–9.
24. Chatham to Montagu, 25 July 1794, TNA, PRO 30/8/364, f. 37.
25. I am obliged to Sam Willis for helping me track down these references, which first came to my notice in his book on the Glorious First of June. Willis, *Glorious First of June*, p. 277; St Vincent to Chatham, 31 May 1801, and to Montagu, 17 September 1802, and Addington, 17 May 1803, David Bonner Smith (ed.), *Letters of Admiral of the Fleet the Earl of St Vincent whilst First Lord of the Admiralty, 1801–4*, 2 vols (London, 1922), Vol. I, p. 99, Vol. II, pp. 261, 290.
26. Chatham to [Sir John Jervis], [September 1794], TNA, PRO 30/8/364, f. 169; Pitt to Dowager Lady Chatham, 17 September 1794, TNA, PRO 30/8/12, f. 462.
27. Pitt to Chatham, 22 September 1794, TNA, PRO 30/8/101, f. 123.
28. Duffy, *Soldiers, Sugar, and Seapower*, pp. 125–8.
29. Dundas to Chatham, 13 September 1794, TNA, PRO 30/8/368, f. 26.
30. Lord Hood's statement, 18 March 1795, Sir John Knox (ed.), *The Naval Miscellany*, 2 vols (London, 1902), Vol. I, pp. 244–5.
31. Memorandum by Chatham, after September 1794, TNA, PRO 30/8/364, f. 1; memorandum by Chatham, January 1795, TNA, PRO 30/8/364, f. 171.
32. Dundas to Chatham, 14 September 1794, TNA, PRO 30/8/368, f. 28.
33. Chatham to [Sir John Jervis], draft, undated but September 1794, TNA, PRO 30/8/364, f. 169.
34. Memorandum by Chatham, [1795], TNA, PRO 30/8/364, f. 208.
35. Memorandum by Chatham, [January 1795], TNA, PRO 30/8/364, f. 171.

36. Chatham to [Dundas], 9 November 1794, William L. Clements Library, Pitt Papers.
37. Pitt to Spencer, 28 November [1794], Corbett (ed.), *Private Papers*, Vol. I, p. 5.
38. Pitt to Chatham, [1 December] 1794, CUL, Pitt Papers, Add MS 6958, f. 1557.
39. Chatham to Pitt, 1 December 1794, CUL, Pitt Papers, Add MS 6958, f. 1558.
40. Pitt to Chatham, 2 December 1794, CUL, Pitt Papers, Add MS 6958, f. 1561.
41. Chatham to Pitt, 2 December 1794, CUL, Pitt Papers, Add MS 6958, f. 1560.
42. Chatham to Pitt, 5 December 1794, CUL, Pitt Papers, Add MS 6958, f. 1565.
43. Chatham to Pitt, 4 December 1794, CUL, Pitt Papers, Add MS 6958, f. 1564.
44. Pitt to the King, 8 December 1794, A. Aspinall (ed.), *The Later Correspondence of George III*, 5 vols (Cambridge, 1963–70), Vol. I, pp. 278–9.
45. *Morning Chronicle*, 16 December 1794.

Chapter 5: 'He Can Never Set It Right', 1795–1801
1. Chatham to Camden, 13 December 1794, Kent Archives, U840 C254/1.
2. *Morning Chronicle*, 8 January 1795.
3. *Ibid.*
4. J.J. Angerstein to Chatham, 10–13 January 1795, TNA, PRO 30/8/365, ff. 9, 11, 14.
5. TNA, PRO 30/8/364, ff. 206, 221.
6. TNA, PRO 30/8/364, f. 208.
7. TNA, PRO 30/8/364, f. 171.
8. Peter Jupp (ed.), *The Letter-Journal of George Canning, 1793–5* (Cambridge, 1991), p. 182.
9. J.C. Villiers to Camden, 20 April 1796, Kent Archives, U840/C132/1.
10. Chatham to Camden, 7 August 1796, Kent Archives U840/C254/4.
11. Chatham to Wilson, 26 September 1796, Pitt Papers, David M. Rubenstein Rare Book and Manuscript Library, Duke University.
12. Mornington to Camden, 24 November 1796, Kent Archives, U840/C121/3.
13. Bathurst to Camden, undated, Kent Archives, U840/C/226/3.
14. Chatham to Camden, 23 December 1796, Kent Archives, U840/C254/6.
15. Chatham to Addington, 26 September 1797, Devon Record Office, 152M/C1797/F10.
16. Chatham to Camden, 8 June 1797, Kent Archives, U840/C102/3.
17. Melville to the Duke of Buccleuch, 27 February 1810, NRS, GD224/30/10, f. 19.
18. TNA, PRO 30/70/5–6.
19. King to Addington, 7 February, 12 February 1801, George Pellew, *Life of Henry Addington, 1st Viscount Sidmouth*, 3 vols (London, 1847), Vol. I, pp. 299, 304.
20. Chatham to the King, 25 March 1805, King to Chatham, 26 March 1805, Aspinall (ed.), *Later Correspondence*, Vol. IV, pp. 303–4.
21. Bathurst to Camden, undated, Kent Archives, U840/C224/3.
22. Bathurst to Camden, 29 March 1797, Kent Archives, U840/C226/4.
23. Memorandum by Chatham, undated, TNA, PRO 30/8/364, f. 199.
24. Chatham to Camden, 8 June 1797, Kent Archives, U840/C102/3.
25. *Ibid.*
26. *The Times*, 24 September 1798.
27. Grenville to Thomas Grenville, 7 August 1798, BL, Add MSS 41852, f. 31; Patrick M. Geoghegan, *The Irish Act of Union* (Dublin, 1999), p. 2.

28. *Aberdeen Journal*, 25 February 1799.

29. Camden to Castlereagh, 30 June 1800, PRONI, D3030/1385; Camden to Pitt, 1 August 1800, Kent Archives, U840/C30/6.

30. Dundas to the King, 3 March 1800, King to Dundas, 4 March 1800, Aspinall (ed.), *Later Correspondence*, Vol. III, p. 325.

31. John Ehrman, *The Younger Pitt: The Consuming Struggle* (Stanford, CA, 1996), pp. 214–18, 237–41, 244–8; Peter Jupp, *Lord Grenville* (Oxford, 1985), pp. 222–9; Piers Mackesy, *Statesmen at war: the strategy of overthrow, 1798–9* (London, 1974), p. 153; A.B. Rodger, *The war of the Second Coalition, 1798 to 1801* (Oxford, 1964), pp. 176–7.

32. Subaltern, *The campaign in Holland, 1799* (London, 1861), p. 77; *United Service Journal*, 1830 (Part II), 560; L. Cowper, *The King's Own: the story of a regiment*, 3 vols (Oxford, 1939), Vol. I, p. 302. Mackesy gives slightly different numbers: *Statesmen at war*, p. 239.

33. Edward Walsh, *A narrative of the expedition to Holland in the autumn of the year 1799* (London, 1800), p. 45; Aspinall (ed.), *Later Correspondence*, Vol. III, pp. 262, 264.

34. Walsh, *A narrative of the expedition to Holland*, pp. 47–8.

35. J.W. Fortescue, *A History of the British Army*, 13 vols (London, 1899–1930), Vol. IV(2), p. 673; A.M. Piechowiak, 'The Anglo-Russian Expedition to Holland in 1799', *The Slavonic and East European Review*, 41 (96) December 1962, 190–2; Subaltern, *Campaign in Holland*, pp. 31–5.

36. Sir Henry Bunbury, *A narrative of the campaign in North Holland, 1799* (London, 1849), pp. 12–13; Fortescue, *History of the British Army*, Vol. IV(2), pp. 671–8; Walsh, *A narrative of the expedition to Holland*, pp. 111–15.

37. Chatham to Pitt, 29 September [1799], BL, Add MSS 89036/1/5, f. 65.

38. *Ibid*. Subaltern, *Campaign in Holland*, p. 41.

39. James, Lord Dunfermline, *Sir Ralph Abercromby, KB, 1793–1801: a memoir by his son* (London, 1861), p. 184; Fortescue, *History of the British Army*, Vol. IV(2), p. 666 and n. 1; Mackesy, *Statesmen at war*, pp. 243–4.

40. Abercromby to Dundas, 26 October 1799, Mackesy, *Statesmen at war*, p. 313.

41. Walsh, *A narrative of the expedition to Holland*, p. 123; Subaltern, *Campaign in Holland*, p. 45.

42. Fortescue, *History of the British Army*, Vol. IV(2), pp. 688–91.

43. Coote to General Grey, 4 October 1799, HMC, *Dropmore*, Vol. V, p. 451.

44. Walsh, *A narrative of the expedition to Holland*, p. 125; *Sun*, 8 October 1799; York to the King, 4 October 1799, Aspinall (ed.), *Later Correspondence*,Vol. III, p. 274.

45. Subaltern, *Campaign in Holland*, pp. 46–8; Walsh, *A narrative of the expedition to Holland*, pp. 125–6; Mackesy, *Statesmen at war*, p. 288; Cowper, *The King's Own*, Vol. I, pp. 308–9.

46. Major Francis Maule, *Memoirs of the principal events in the campaigns of North Holland and Egypt . . .* (London, 1816), pp. 10–11; Mackesy, *Statesmen at war*, pp. 207–8; Rodger, *War of the Second Coalition*, p. 178; Simon Schama, *Patriots and Liberators: revolution in the Netherlands, 1780–1813* (London, 1992), p. 391; Subaltern, *Campaign in Holland*, p. 57; Fortescue, *History of the British Army*,Vol. IV(2), pp. 683, 698.

47. Chatham to Dowager Lady Chatham, 4 October 1799, Lord Ashbourne, *Pitt: some chapters of his life and times* (London, 1898), pp. 168–9.

48. Bunbury, *A narrative of the campaign in North Holland*, p. 26; Fortescue, *History of the British Army*, Vol. IV(2), pp. 694–5; Subaltern, *Campaign in Holland*, pp. 57–8; Mackesy, *Statesmen at war*, p. 296.

49. Walsh, *A narrative of the expedition to Holland*, p. 75.

50. Bunbury, *A narrative of the campaign in North Holland*, pp. 26–7.

51. Christopher Hely-Hutchinson to Lord Donoughmore, 7 October 1799, PRONI, T3459/D/43/3.

52. Cowper, *The King's Own*, Vol. I, p. 311; Fortescue, *History of the British Army*, Vol. IV(2), p. 697; Bunbury, *A narrative of the campaign in North Holland*, p. 27; Walsh, *A narrative of the expedition to Holland*, pp. 135–6; Subaltern, *Campaign in Holland*, pp. 87–9.

53. *Sun*, 16 October 1799; Walsh, *A narrative of the expedition to Holland*, pp. 60–1; Sir J.F. Maurice (ed.), *The diary of Sir John Moore*, 2 vols (London, 1904), Vol. I, p. 358; Pitt to Lady Chatham, 14 October 1799, TNA, PRO 30/8/101, f. 151.

54. *Account, presented to the House of Commons, of the distribution of the sum of £2,500,000 granted to His Majesty to defray the Extraordinary Services of the Army for the year 1800 . . .* (London, 1801), p. 18; TNA, WO 65/49; Richard Cannon, *Historical record of the 4th or King's Own Regiment of Foot* (London, 1839), p. 78.

55. Miss Berry to Miss Cholmondeley, 12 November 1799, Lady Theresa Lewis (ed.), *Extracts of the Journals and Correspondence of Miss Berry*, 3 vols (London, 1865), Vol. II, p. 104; *Sun*, 15 October 1799; Colonel MacDonald to Dundas, 7 October 1799, NRS, GD51/1/710.

56. Fortescue, *History of the British Army*, Vol. IV(2), pp. 698–9; Bunbury, *A narrative of the campaign in North Holland*, pp. 29–30; Jupp, *Grenville*, p. 237; Subaltern, *Campaign in Holland*, p. 63.

57. Subaltern, *Campaign in Holland*, pp. 64–5.

58. Chatham to Pitt, 14 October 1799, TNA, PRO 30/8/122, f. 143.

59. Fortescue, *History of the British Army*, Vol. IV(2), pp. 700–1.

60. Dunfermline, *Sir Ralph Abercromby*, p. 201.

61. Chatham to Pitt, 19 October 1799, TNA, PRO 30/8/122, f. 145.

62. *Evening Mail*, 30 October 1799.

63. Jupp, *Grenville*, pp. 243–4, 260–1; Ehrman, *Consuming Struggle*, pp. 349–50, 397.

64. Dundas to Pitt, 3 November 1799, BL, Add MSS 40102.

65. *Ibid*.

66. Pitt to Dundas, 4 November 1799, William L. Clements Library, Pitt Papers. I am grateful to Diana Mankowski for locating this letter for me.

67. Dundas to Pitt, 4 November [1799], TNA, PRO 30/8/157, f. 270.

68. Francis Bickley (ed.), *The Diaries of Sylvester Douglas, Lord Glenbervie*, 2 vols (London, 1928), Vol. I, p. 278; Jupp, *Grenville*, pp. 209–10, 214, 248–9; Piers Mackesy, *War Without Victory: The Downfall of Pitt, 1799–1802* (Oxford, 1984), pp. 38–9, 93; Cyril Matheson, *Henry Dundas, Viscount Melville* (London, 1933), p. 274.

69. Mrs Henry Baring (ed.), *The diary of the Rt. Hon. William Windham, 1784 to 1810* (London, 1866), p. 422; HMC *Dropmore*, Vol. VI, pp. 170–1; Mackesy, *War Without*

Victory, pp. 62, 78–9; York to Dundas, 28 February 1800, Aspinall (ed.), *Later Correspondence*, Vol. III, pp. 318–23.

70. Mackesy, *War Without Victory*, pp. 84–6; Dundas to Chatham, 22 March 1800, BL, Add MSS 40102, f. 40.

71. Chatham to Dundas, 17 April 1800, William L. Clements Library, Pitt Papers.

72. Chatham to Dundas, 23 July 1800, William L. Clements Library, Pitt Papers.

73. Castlereagh to Cornwallis, 9 February 1801, CUL, Pitt Papers, Add MS 6958, f. 2847; Richard Willis, 'William Pitt's resignation in 1801: re-examination and document', *Bulletin of the Institute of Historical Research*, 44 (1971), 250.

74. Princess Elizabeth to Lady Chatham, 22 June 1800, TNA, PRO 30/70/6/13/58; *Morning Herald*, 24 June 1800; *Whitehall Evening Post*, 15 July 1800.

75. Revd L.V. Harcourt (ed.), *The Diaries and Correspondence of the Rt. Hon. George Rose*, 2 vols (London, 1860), Vol. I, p. 328.

76. Chatham to Camden, 2 February 1801, Kent Archives, U840/C102/6.

77. Willis, 'Pitt's resignation', 251–2.

78. Ehrman, *Consuming Struggle*, p. 503.

79. Pitt to the King, 31 January 1801, Stanhope, *Life of the Right Honourable William Pitt*, Vol. IV, Appendix xxvii.

80. Philip Ziegler, *Addington: A Life of Henry Addington, First Viscount Sidmouth* (New York, NY, 1965), pp. 94–6, 103; Charles John Fedorak, *Henry Addington, Prime Minister, 1801–4: Peace, War and Parliamentary Politics* (Akron, OH, 2002), pp. 23–5, 31–2.

81. Pitt to Chatham, 5 February 1801, Ashbourne, *Pitt*, pp. 309–11.

82. Chatham to Pitt, 6 February 1801, TNA, PRO 30/8/122.

83. Chatham to Addington, 8 February 1801, Pellew, *Life of Henry Addington*, Vol. I, p. 301 n.

84. Harcourt (ed.), *Diaries and Correspondence*, Vol. I, pp. 296–7.

85. *Ibid.*, p. 295.

86. Fox to Richard Fitzpatrick, 10 February 1801, BL, Add MSS 47581, f. 89.

87. Charles Abbot, Lord Colchester (ed.), *The Diary and Correspondence of Charles Abbot, Lord Colchester*, 3 vols (London, 1861) (hereafter *Colchester*), Vol. I, p. 224.

88. King to Addington, 11 February 1801, Pellew, *Life of Henry Addington*, Vol. I, p. 303.

89. King to Chatham, 18 February 1801, TNA, PRO 30/8/364, f. 149.

90. Chatham to the King, 18 February 1801, Aspinall (ed.), *Later Correspondence*,Vol. III, p. 504.

91. King to Pitt, 18 February 1801, Stanhope, *Life of the Right Honourable William Pitt*, Vol. III, Appendix xxxii.

Chapter 6: Master-General of the Ordnance, 1801–6

1. Cornwallis to General Ross, 8 December 1803, Charles Ross (ed.), *Correspondence of Charles, First Marquis Cornwallis*, 3 vols (London, 1859), Vol. III, p. 507.

2. Richard Glover, *Peninsular Preparation: The Reform of the British Army, 1795–1809* (Cambridge, 1963), pp. 37–9; Richard Glover, *Britain at Bay: Defence against Bonaparte, 1803–14* (London, 1973), p. 35; S.G.P. Ward, 'Defence works in Britain, 1803–5', *Journal of the Society for Army Historical Research*, 27 (1949), 20–1; Ehrman,

NOTES

Reluctant Transition, p. 492; Mark S. Thompson, 'The rise of the scientific soldier as seen through the performance of the corps of Royal Engineers during the early 19th century' (PhD, University of Sunderland, 2009), p. 34; Rory Muir, *Wellington: Waterloo and the fortunes of peace, 1814–1852* (New Haven, CT, 2015), pp. 246–7.

3. Gareth Cole, *Arming the Royal Navy, 1793–1815* (London, 2012) [ebook].
4. *Ibid.*; Norman Skentelbery, *Arrows to Atom Bombs: a history of the Ordnance Board* (London, 1975), p. 14; Maj. D.M.O. Miller, *The Master-General of the Ordnance: a short history of the office* ([n.p.], [1973/4]), p. 16; Charles M. Clode, *The military forces of the crown: their administration and government*, 2 vols (London, 1869), Vol. I, p. 204.
5. Cole, *Arming the Royal Navy* [ebook]. Jenny West, *Gunpowder, Government and War in the mid-18th Century* (Woodbridge, 1991), p. 10; H.C. Tomlinson, *Guns and Government: the Ordnance Office under the later Stuarts* (London, 1979), p. 51; Skentelbery, *Arrows to Atom Bombs*, p. 13.
6. Commissioners of Military Enquiry, *Twelfth Report of the Commissioners of Military Enquiry: Office of Ordnance: Treasurer* (London, 1810), p. 234.
7. Select Committee on the Public Income and Expenditure of the United Kingdom, *Second Report from the Select Committee of the Public Income and Expenditure of the United Kingdom: Ordnance Estimates* (London, 1828), p. 84.
8. Tomlinson, *Guns and Government*, p. 50; Olson, *The Radical Duke*, pp. 94–5; Francis Duncan, *History of the Royal Regiment of Artillery*, 2 vols (London, 1879), Vol. I, p. 19; General A. Forbes, *A history of the Army Ordnance Services*, 3 vols (London, 1929), Vol. I, p. 184.
9. O.F.G. Hogg, *The Royal Arsenal: its background, origin, and subsequent history*, 2 vols (London, 1963), Vol. II, p. 1053; Miller, *The Master-General of the Ordnance*, pp. 16–17.
10. Commissioners of Military Enquiry, *Twelfth Report of the Commissioners of Military Enquiry*, p. 235.
11. Glover, *Peninsular Preparation*, p. 37.
12. Wendy Hinde, *Castlereagh* (London, 1981), p. 119.
13. Sir John Macpherson to Sir James Pulteney, 7 November 1807, Department of Literary and Historical Manuscripts, The Morgan Library and Museum, New York, MA 1268, f. 49.
14. Lady Chatham to Mrs Stapleton, undated, National Army Museum (hereafter NAM), 8408-114.
15. Chatham was one of the more warlike members of the Cabinet. On 7 April 1803, when the possibility of a new war was still in doubt, the *Morning Post* included the following paragraph on the division of Cabinet opinion: 'The cause of the fluctuation and uncertainty in the Councils of our Ministers has at last been discovered. It is occasioned by the moving about of the Cabinet Councils. When the Council sits at Lord Chatham's, there being *good wine* in his Lordship's cellar, Ministers are all *for War*: when it sits at Lord Hawkesbury's, *water* alone is drank, then they are all *for Peace*; and when they sit at Mr Addington's, he allowing only *wine and water*, Ministers take *half measures*, and it becomes quite doubtful whether we shall have *War* or *Peace*!'.
16. Statistics: list of muskets etc. in store, 11 August 1803, TNA, WO 46/25; regulars and

militia: Devon Record Office, 152M/C1808/OM, PRONI, D3030/1837; 1790s manufacturing: Keith J. Bartlett, 'The development of the British Army during the wars with France, 1793–1815' (PhD, Durham University, 1998), pp. 214–17, D.W. Bailey, *British Board of Ordnance Small Arms Contractors 1689–1840* (Rhyl, 1999), pp. 19–20.

17. Austin Gee, *The British Volunteer Movement, 1794–1814* (Oxford, 2003), p. 45; J.E. Cookson, *The British Armed Nation, 1793–1815* (Oxford, 1997), p. 80.

18. H.F.B. Wheeler and A.M. Broadley, *Napoleon and the invasion of England: the story of the Great Terror*, 2 vols (London, 1908), Vol. II, p. 149 n. 1.

19. List of counties in England and Wales where the volunteers were completely armed, 9 March 1804, TNA, HO 51/137; statement of arms received at the Tower 1803–8, JRL, Eng MS 1271, ff. 81/11, 81/13; Bailey, *British Board of Ordnance Small Arms Contractors*, p. 21; Forbes, *A history of the Army Ordnance Services*, Vol. I, p. 191.

20. Chatham to Canning, 10 April 1809, BL, WYL 250/8/31/6.

21. Statement of Small Arms Issues from the Tower, 1803-8, JRL, Eng MS 1271, f. 81/8; Statement of Small Arms in store 26 May 1808, JRL, Eng MS1271, f. 71; Select Committee on Finance, *Third Report from the Select Committee on Finance: Ordnance* (London, 1817), pp. 65, 67–8.

22. Peter Bloomfield, *Kent and the Napoleonic Wars* (London, 1987), pp. 34–5; Twiss to Chatham, 3 December 1804, TNA, WO 1/783.

23. Bloomfield, *Kent and the Napoleonic Wars*, pp. 30–2.

24. Chatham to York, 7 July 1803, JRL, Eng MS 1271, f. 13.

25. Ehrman, *Reluctant Transition*, pp. 493–4; Glover, *Peninsular Preparation*, p. 37; Ward, 'Defence works', 20; Glover, *Britain at Bay*, pp. 35, 107–8; Knight, *Britain against Napoleon*, p. 275.

26. Chatham to Camden, 30 December 1804, TNA, WO 1/783.

27. Commissioners of Military Enquiry, *Fourteenth Report of the Commissioners of Military Enquiry: Ordnance Estimates* (London, 1811), pp. 255–6, 259.

28. Glover, *Peninsular Preparation*, p. 37; Glover, *Britain at Bay*, pp. 109–10, 115, 124; Ward, 'Defence Works', pp. 25, 27, 29–30.

29. Chatham to Hobart, 9 February 1804, TNA, WO 1/783.

30. Ward, 'Defence Works', 30–1.

31. Chatham to Morse, 16 September 1804, JRL, Eng MS 1271, f. 35.

32. W.H. Clements, *Towers of strength: Martello towers worldwide* (Barnsley, 1999) [ebook].

33. Chatham to Castlereagh, 21 September 1805, TNA, WO 1/783.

34. Lt Col. K.W. Maurice-Jones, *The history of Coast Artillery in the British Army* (Uckfield, 2012), p. 107.

35. Chatham to Morse, 16 September 1804, JRL, Eng MS 1271, f. 35.

36. York to Chatham, 5 July 1803, JRL, Eng MS 1271, f. 11.

37. Chatham to Hobart, 9 February 1804, TNA, WO 1/783.

38. Memorandum by Chatham, July 1808, JRL, Eng MS 1271, f. 76.

39. Richmond to Chatham, 5 February 1804, JRL, Eng MS 1271, f. 26.

40. Select Committee on Finance, *Third Report from the Select Committee on Finance*, pp. 67–8.

41. *Ibid.*, p. 86.

NOTES

42. Commissioners of Military Enquiry, *Twelfth Report of the Commissioners of Military Enquiry*, p. 235.

43. Knight, *Britain against Napoleon*, pp. 375–6.

44. Hadden to Lord Sheffield, 18 February 1806, East Sussex Record Office, Sheffield Papers, Box A.

45. Horace Twiss, *The Life of Lord Eldon*, 3 vols (London, 1844), Vol. II, p. 326.

46. *Colchester*, Vol. II, p. 181.

Chapter 7: 'The Misfortunes of Late Years', 1801–7

1. *Morning Post*, 13 July 1801; George Rose to Bishop of Lincoln, 1 August 1801, Suffolk Record Office, HA 119/T108/45.

2. Bickley (ed.), *The Diaries of Sylvester Douglas*, Vol. I, p. 253; *Morning Post*, 2 October 1801, 16 October 1801.

3. *Morning Post*, 8 June 1801.

4. Fedorak, *Henry Addington*, pp. 95–7, 183.

5. George Canning's Diary, 24, 28 May 1802, BL, WYL 250/8/29di/11; George Rose to Bishop of Lincoln, 29 May 1802, Suffolk Record Office, HA119/T108/44, Part 2; Bishop of Lincoln to George Rose Jr., 19 November 1801, Suffolk Record Office, HA 119/T108/45.

6. Notes by George Rose, November 1802, Suffolk Record Office, HA119/T108/44.

7. Pitt to Chatham, 28 March 1803, TNA, PRO 30/8/101, f. 180; Harcourt (ed.), *Diaries and Correspondence*, Vol. I, p. 31; Ehrman, *Consuming Struggle*, pp. 584–5; Fedorak, *Henry Addington*, pp. 131–2; Ziegler, *Addington*, pp. 176–7.

8. *Colchester*, Vol. I, p. 416.

9. *Morning Post*, 5 October 1803; *Derby Mercury*, 20 October 1803; *Morning Chronicle*, 2 November 1803; *Morning Post*, 26 September, 5 October, 28 December 1804; Lady Chatham to Lady Sydney [her sister-in-law], [September 1803], Huntington Library, Townshend Family Papers.

10. Ziegler, *Addington*, p. 215.

11. Fedorak, *Henry Addington*, pp. 209–10.

12. Ehrman, *Consuming Struggle*, p. 807; Stanhope, *Life of the Right Honourable William Pitt*, Vol. IV, pp. 339, 361–2, Appendices xxvii–xxviii.

13. Chatham to Colonel Gordon, 5 October 1805, BL, Add MSS 49500, f. 113.

14. Marriage settlement of H.H. Eliot and W.H. Pringle, 16 May 1806, Cornwall Record Office, EL/647. I am grateful to Stephenie Woolterton for putting this my way. See also Chatham to Tomline, 14 March 1806, Suffolk Record Office, HA 119/T99/123/11; Tomline to Mrs Tomline, 22 January 1806, Suffolk Record Office, HA 119/T99/26.

15. Canning to his wife, 14 January 1806, BL, WYL 250/8/21.

16. Tomline to Mrs Tomline, 15 January 1806, Suffolk Record Office, HA 119/T99/26.

17. Tomline to Mrs Tomline, 21 January 1806, Suffolk Record Office, HA 119/T99/26.

18. *Morning Post*, 23 January 1806; *Hampshire Telegraph*, 27 January 1806; Lord Essex to Lord Lonsdale, 23 January 1806, HMC, *Manuscripts of the Earl of Lonsdale. HMC 13th Report Part 7* (London, 1893), pp. 158–9.

19. Tomline to Mrs Tomline, 24 January 1806, Suffolk Record Office, HA 119/T99/26.

20. Norman Gash, *Lord Liverpool* (London, 1984), pp. 65–6.

21. *Bury and Norwich Post*, 15 January 1806; Tomline to Mrs Tomline, 31 January 1806, Suffolk Record Office, HA 119/T99/26; Canning to his wife, 28 January 1806, BL, WYL 250/8/21.
22. Chatham to General MacLeod, 9 February 1806, NAM, 1977-01-13.
23. Thomas Carey to William Huskisson, 3 May 1810, BL, Add MSS 38739, f. 26.
24. Tomline to Mrs Tomline, 31 January 1806, Suffolk Record Office, HA 119/T108/45; Tomline to Mrs Tomline, 31 January 1806, Suffolk Record Office, HA 119/T99/26; Chatham to Lord Dartmouth, 6 February 1806, HMC, *Manuscripts of the Earl of Dartmouth* (London, 1895), Vol. III, p. 290.
25. Chatham to Tomline, 14 March 1806, Suffolk Record Office, HA 119 T99/123/11.
26. Stanhope, *Life of the Right Honourable William Pitt*, Vol. IV, pp. 384–5; Ehrman, *Consuming Struggle*, p. 834 n. 3.
27. Tomline to Mrs Tomline, 30 January [1806], Suffolk Record Office, HA 119 T99/123/10.
28. Tomline to Mrs Tomline, 24 January 1806, Suffolk Record Office, HA 119 T99/27.
29. Coutts to Tomline, 2 February 1806; Coutts to Joseph Smith, 18 March 1806, Kent Archives, U1590/S5/C42. I am grateful to Stephenie Woolterton for bringing this to my attention.
30. Chatham to Tomline, 25 July 1821, Suffolk Record Office, HA 119/562/688; Ehrman, *Years of Acclaim*, pp. 601–2, 602 n. 1.
31. Perceval to Chatham, undated, Kent Archives, U1590/S5/C42.
32. Chatham to Tomline, 11 December 1808, Kent Archives, U1590/S5/C42.
33. Tomline to Chatham, 13 December 1808, Kent Archives, U1590/S5/C42; Ehrman, *Consuming Struggle*, p. 835; Chatham to Tomline, 15 August 1821, 2 May 1822, Suffolk Record Office, HA 119/562/688.
34. Chatham to Tomline, 25 April 1818, Suffolk Record Office, HA 119/562/688.
35. Minutes by Lord Camden, 21 June 1834, Leicestershire and Rutland Record Office, DG24/1000; Camden to Sir Henry Halford, 22 June 1834, Leicestershire and Rutland Record Office, DG24/825/33.
36. Chatham to Tomline, 14 March 1806, Suffolk Record Office, HA 119 T99/123/11.
37. Lady Hester Stanhope to W.D. Adams, 26 January 1806, BL, Add MSS 89036/2/1, f. 10.
38. Lady Hester Stanhope to T.J. Jackson, 13 February 1802, Duchess of Cleveland (ed.), *The life and letters of Lady Hester Stanhope* (London, 1914), p. 32.
39. James Stanhope to W.D. Adams, undated, BL, Add MSS 89036/2/4, f. 101.
40. *Debrett's Parliamentary Register*, Vol. VII, pp. 213–14; *Estimates, presented to the House of Commons on the 14th and 15th January 1806, of the army services, for the year 1807* (London, 1807), p. 15; Commissioners of Military Enquiry, *Thirteenth Report of the Commissioners of Military Enquiry: The Master General and Board of Ordnance* (London, 1811), p. 9.
41. Bonds between Chatham and Camden, 3 October 1797 and 24 June 1806, Kent Archives, U840/E20, E21.
42. H.H. Eliot to E.J. Eliot, 9 February 1794, Suffolk Record Office, HA 119/678/1; Debois Landscape Survey Group, 'Burton Pynsent, a history of the landscape' (February 2002), p. 3.
43. *Bury and Norwich Post*, 24 October 1804; sales particulars, Burton Pynsent, 16

October 1804, Somerset Record Office, DD/MK 101/1; Chatham v Louch, TNA, Chancery Rolls, C13/76/18.

44. Note by Lancelot Shadwell on behalf of Robert Uttermore, a purchaser of Burton Pynsent estate, on an Abstract of Title for Burton Pynsent, 16 November 1806, Somerset Record Office, A/BQV; Chatham v Louch, TNA, Chancery Rolls, C13/76/18; Chatham v Pinney, TNA, Chancery Rolls, C13/1596/25.

45. Indenture between Lord Temple and Alexander Hood, 25 and 26 February 1778, Somerset Record Office, DD/LC 54/9, f. 65; Indenture, 28 July 1807, Somerset Record Office, DD/GL/188; Indenture, 3 September 1808, Somerset Record Office, DD/GL/188.

46. Marriage settlement of H.H. Eliot and W.H. Pringle, 16 May 1806, Cornwall Record Office, EL/647.

47. Chatham to Mrs Stapleton, 13 December 1807, NAM, 8408-114.

48. Chatham to Mrs Stapleton, 11 May 1808, NAM 9506-61.

49. *Morning Post*, 10 April, 21 April, 24 April 1807, 13 June 1807, 22 September 1807.

50. [Georgiana Townshend] to Vaughan, 14 April 1807, Leicestershire Record Office, DG 24/819/1.

51. Mary Townshend to Lord Sydney, [10 October 1807], William L. Clements Library, Townshend Papers, Box 16.

52. [Georgiana Townshend] to Vaughan, 14 April [1807], Leicestershire Record Office, DG 24/819/2.

53. Lady Dalkeith to Lord Sydney, 29 November 1807, Huntington Library, Townshend Family Papers.

54. *Morning Post*, 5 October 1803.

55. [Georgiana Townshend] to Vaughan, 14 April 1807, Leicestershire Record Office, DG 24/819/1.

56. Chatham to Sydney, 27 October 1807, William L. Clements Library, Townshend Papers, Box 16.

57. Chatham to Mrs Stapleton, 11 May 1808, NAM, 9506-61-3.

58. Chatham to Coutts, 23 November 1808, Kent Archives, U1590/S5/C42.

59. Chatham to Mrs Stapleton, 2 December 1810, NAM, 8408-114.

Chapter 8: The 'Mischievous Intriguer', 1807–9

1. Aspinall (ed.), *Later Correspondence*, Vol. IV, pp. 529, 533–4 n. 5.

2. Chatham to King, 23 March 1807, Aspinall (ed.), *Later Correspondence*, Vol. IV, pp. 533–4.

3. Sir John Macpherson to Sir James Pulteney, 7 November 1807, Department of Literary and Historical Manuscripts, The Morgan Library and Museum, NY, MA 1268, f. 49.

4. Canning's memorandum of an audience with the King, 13 September 1809, Aspinall (ed.), *Later Correspondence*, Vol. V, p. 345.

5. Wendy Hinde, *George Canning* (New York, NY, 1974), p. 155.

6. Lord Temple to Auckland, 2 October 1807, BL, Add MSS 34457, f. 369.

7. Bathurst to Richmond, 4 January 1808, Aspinall (ed.), *Later Correspondence*, Vol. IV, p. 657 n. 4.

8. Hawkesbury to Portland, 2 March 1808, University of Nottingham Manuscripts and Special Collections, PwF 5.849.

9. Hawkesbury to Sir Arthur Wellesley, 22 October 1807, University of Southampton, Wellington Papers, 1/175/58.
10. Canning to his wife, 10 March 1806, BL, WYL 250/8/21.
11. Canning to his wife, 27 February 1807, BL, WYL 250/8/22.
12. Canning to Robert Dundas, 3 October 1809, BL, WYL 250/8/34/5.
13. A.D. Harvey, 'The Ministry of All the Talents: The Whigs in Office, February 1806 to March 1807', *Historical Journal*, 15, 4 (1972), 634–6; A.D. Harvey, *Britain in the Early Nineteenth Century* (New York, NY, 1978), pp. 177–80; Thomas Munch Petersen, *Defying Napoleon: how Britain bombaded Copenhagen and seized the Danish fleet in 1807* (Stroud, 2007), pp. 16–17, 20–4, 244–5.
14. Canning to Chatham, 23 June 1809, BL, WYL 250/8/31/6.
15. Cole, *Arming the Royal Navy*, p. 53.
16. Charles Neville to Colonel Bunbury, 30 January 1810, TNA, WO 1/786.
17. Chatham to Liverpool, 22 December, 31 December 1809, 2 January 1810, TNA, PRO 30/8/364, ff. 30, 32, 34.
18. R.W. Horton to Chatham, 29 September 1823, GNA, Dispatches to Gibraltar 1823; Chatham to R.W. Horton, 17 November 1823, TNA, CO 91/80; R.W. Horton to Chatham, 31 December 1823, TNA, CO 92/6.
19. Quoted in Denis Gray, *Spencer Perceval: The Evangelical Prime Minister* (Manchester, 1963), p. 300.
20. Desmond Gregory, *Sicily: the insecure base* (London, 1988), pp. 61–5.
21. Chatham to Canning, 15 November 1807, BL, WYL 250/8/31/6; Canning to Chatham, 14 November 1807, BL, WYL 250/8/31/6.
22. *Caledonian Mercury*, 11 July 1808; *Hull Packet*, 12 July 1808; *Morning Post*, 18 July 1808; *Aberdeen Journal*, 13, 20 July 1808.
23. Chatham to Canning, 18 September 1808, BL, WYL 250/8/31/6.
24. *Morning Post*, 15 December 1808; *Morning Post*, 17 December 1808.
25. D.W. Davies, *Sir John Moore's Peninsular Campaign, 1808–9* (The Hague, 1974) [ebook]. See also Rory Muir, *Wellington: the path to victory, 1769–1814* (New Haven, CT, 2013), pp. 232–3, 237; Rory Muir, *Britain and the Defeat of Napoleon, 1807–15* (London, 1996), pp. 44–6; *Aberdeen Journal*, 13 July 1808.
26. Thomas Grenville to Grenville, 9 January 1808, HMC, Dropmore , Vol. IX, p. 171.
27. Fortescue, *History of the British Army,* Vol. VII, pp. 36–7, 40–4; Gordon Bond, *The Grand Expedition* (Athens, GA, 1971), pp. 6–7; Carl A. Christie, 'The Walcheren Expedition of 1809' (PhD, University of Dundee, 1975), pp. 38–9, 54, 56.
28. Prince of Orange to King of Prussia, 15 August 1809, H.T. Colenbrander, *Gedenkstukken der Algemeene Geschiedenis van Nederland van 1795 tot 1840 . . .* (The Hague, 1905–22), Vol. V, p. 588; Bond, *Grand Expedition,* p. 12; Christie, pp. 9–10, 56–7, 67–8.
29. Christie, 'The Walcheren Expedition', p. 188 n. 1; Bond, *Grand Expedition*, p. 146; list of ships under Strachan's command, 17 July 1809, *A Collection of papers relating to the expedition to the Scheldt, presented to Parliament in 1810* (London, 1811), pp. 349–51; Parliamentary Debates (hereafter *PD*), XV, Sir Thomas Trigge's testimony, 8 February 1810, Appendix cxxxviii; Cathcart to Thomas Graham, 8 July 1809, NLS, MS 3605, f. 171.
30. Fortescue, *History of the British Army*, Vol. VII, p. 56.

NOTES

Chapter 9: Walcheren, 1809

1. Canning to Chatham, 24 December 1808, TNA, PRO 30/70/4, f. 274; Chatham to Colonel Gordon, 2 January 1809, BL, Add MS 49504, f. 48; Chatham to Dowager Duchess of Rutland, 9 January 1809, Belvoir Castle Manuscripts.

2. Castlereagh to Chatham, 18 May 1809, TNA, PRO 30/8/366, ff. 58–9.

3. Chatham to Castlereagh, 18 May 1809, PRONI, D3030/3087.

4. Memorandum from Castlereagh to Chatham, PRONI, D3030/3185; *PD*, XV, Appendices ccccxxiv–xxvii.

5. *PD*, XV, Sir David Dundas's testimony, 5 February 1810, Appendices xcviii, xcix.

6. Martin R. Howard, *Walcheren 1809: the scandalous destruction of a British army* (Barnsley, 2012), p. 27; Palmerston to John Sulivan, 15 September 1809, Kenneth Bourne (ed.), *Letters of the 3rd Viscount Palmerston to Laurence and Elizabeth Sulivan, 1804–63* (London, 1979), pp. 110–12.

7. *Examiner*, 10 July 1808. Chatham was the 26th most senior lieutenant general. Cathcart was 11th and Moira was a full general: TNA, WO 65/59.

8. Bond, *Grand Expedition*, p. 178 n. 15.

9. 'Pay of the Staff', 25 December 1808, NRS, GD 164/1357, f. 5.

10. See Chapter 8 in this volume.

11. Canning to Robert Dundas, 3 October 1809, BL, WYL 250/8/34/5.

12. Fortescue, *History of the British Army*, Vol. VII, p. 54; Christie, 'The Walcheren Expedition', pp. 74–5; Bond, *Grand Expedition*, p. 18; Howard, *Walcheren 1809*, p. 27.

13. Charles Stewart to Castlereagh, 20 October 1809, PRONI, D3030/P/231.

14. Christie, 'The Walcheren Expedition', pp. 74–5.

15. Sir John Hope's testimony, 21 February 1810, *PD*, XV, Appendix cccxxx; Huntly's testimony, 20 February 1810, *PD*, XV, Appendix ccxcii; Erskine's testimony, 20 February 1810, *PD*, XV, Appendix cccv; Rosslyn's testimony, 21 February 1810, *PD*, XV, Appendices xxxxlvi–vii, Coote's testimony, 27 February 1810, *PD*, XV, Appendices ccccxvi–vii. Coote, upon being asked if *anyone* had thought the Expedition a good idea before it sailed, replied evasively: 'I had so little communication upon the subject that I really did not hear opinions.' Brigadier General Sontag was one of the few willing to admit 'the most sanguine hopes and confidence that the attempt might succeed': Sontag's testimony, 6 March 1810, *PD*, XV, Appendix ccccxlii.

16. Chatham's Instructions, 16 July 1809, *A Collection of papers relating to the expedition to the Scheldt*, pp. 21–2.

17. Hugh Popham, *A damned cunning fellow: the eventful life of rear-admiral Sir Home Popham 1762–1820* (Tywardreath, 1991), pp. 32–3, 44, 46, 52, 61, 74–6, 103–4, 146, 166–7, 184; Lowther to Lord Lonsdale, [20 July] 1809, Cumbria Record Office, DLONS L1/2/70, f. 4.

18. 'Proposed Disposition for the Attack of the Island of Walcheren', NRS, MSS GD364/1/1189/20.

19. Chatham to Castlereagh, 13 June 1809, PRONI, D3030/3135.

20. Memorandum by Chatham, TNA, PRO 30/8/260, f. 100.

21. Castlereagh to King, 14 June 1809, PRONI, D3030/3137.

22. Memorandum by Chatham, TNA, PRO 30/8/260, f. 100.

23. Parliamentary Papers 1810 (89), 'Respecting the Practicability of effecting a Landing between Sandfleet and Fort Lillo'.

24. Memorandum by Chatham, TNA, PRO 30/8/260, f. 100; Chatham's testimony, 22 February 1810, *PD*, XV, Appendix ccclv.

25. Thomas A. Wise, 'The Life and Naval Career of Admiral Sir Richard John Strachan', *Transactions of the Royal Historical Society*, 2 (1873), 39–40.

26. Bond, *Grand Expedition*, pp. 21, 179 n. 26.

27. John Bew, *Castlereagh* (London, 2011), pp. 258–9.

28. Cooke to Charles Stewart, 21 September 1809, PRONI, D3030/Q/3, f. 5.

29. Lowther to Lord Lonsdale, [20 July 1809], [24 July 1809], Cumbria Record Office, DLONS L1/2/70, ff. 4, 6; Lowther to Lord Lonsdale, 2 August [1809], Cumbria Record Office, DLONS L1/2/70, f. 7.

30. *Morning Post*, 28 June 1809.

31. *Morning Chronicle*, 19 July 1809.

32. Palmerston to John Sulivan, 15 September 1809, Bourne (ed.), *Letters of the 3rd Viscount Palmerston*, pp. 110–12; Bond, *Grand Expedition*, pp. 31–2, 34; Théo Fleischman, *L'expédition Anglaise sur le continent en 1809* (Mouscron, 1973), p. 23.

33. Bond, 17 July 1809, between Chatham, W.H. Pringle, H.H. Pringle, Bishop of Lincoln and William Eliot, Somerset Record Office, DD/GL/188.

34. *Morning Chronicle*, 28 July 1809; Liverpool to Chatham, 14 August [1809], TNA, PRO 30/70/6, f. 417.

35. *The Times*, 20 July 1809.

36. Bond, *Grand Expedition*, p. 160.

37. Lady Downshire to Mr Handley, 28 July 1809, PRONI, D607/I/155.

38. Sir John Hope to Alexander Hope, 25 July 1809, NRS, MSS GD364/1/1188/20.

39. C.G. Gardyne, *The life of a regiment: the history of the Gordon Highlanders from its formation in 1794 to 1826* (Edinburgh, 1901), p. 207.

40. Lowther to Lord Lonsdale, Tuesday, [25 July 1809], Cumbria Record Office, DLONS/L1/1/70, f. 5.

41. Hendrik Fagel to W.D. Adams, 30 July 1809, BL, Add MSS 89036/6/6, f. 122.

42. Bond, *Grand Expedition*, pp. 42–3; Christie, 'The Royal Navy and the Walcheren Expedition', pp. 193–4.

43. Chatham to Camden, 27 July 1809, Kent Archives, U840 C86/5/1.

44. Castlereagh to Chatham, 16 July 1809, PRONI, D3030/3175.

45. Chatham to Camden, 27 July 1809, Kent Archives, U840 C86/5/1.

46. Ship's Log of *Venerable*, 28 July 1809, TNA, ADM 51/2957.

47. Journal, 29, 30 July 1809, William L. Clements Library, Coote MSS, Box 29/3.

48. Chatham to Castlereagh, 2 August 1809, *A Collection of papers relating to the expedition to the Scheldt*, pp. 69–73.

49. Brownrigg's testimony, 15 March 1810, *PD*, XV, Appendix 5xc.

50. Proceedings, 30 July 1809, TNA, WO 190; Journal, 30 July 1809, William L. Clements Library, Coote MSS, Box 29/3. The aide is identified as Captain Henry Worsley in the William L. Clements Library's catalogue, but it cannot have been written by Worsley as he is mentioned (for example, in the entry for 20 September 1809: 'Capn. Worsley was to have gone off yesterday with the dispatches').

51. *Morning Post*, 8 August 1809.
52. Ship's Log of *Venerable*, 30 July 1809, TNA, ADM 51/2957; Proceedings, 30 July 1809, TNA, WO 190.
53. At the inquiry Chatham claimed he had three aides, but the official list in the *Scots Magazine* (71), 623 and the *Tradesman* (3) 1809, 168 is longer: Major Henry Hollis Bradford, Captain W.A. Gardner, Captain W.F. Hadden, Captain Daniel Falla, Major Linsingen and Lords Robert and Charles Manners. Colonel Thomas Carey, the last name on the list, was military secretary. Chatham's testimony, 27 February 1810, *PD*, XV, Appendix ccclxxxii.
54. Journal, 30 July 1809, William L. Clements Library, Coote MSS, Box 29/3.
55. Lowther's diary, 30 July 1809, Cumbria Record Office, DLONS/L2/12.
56. Proceedings, 31 July 1809, TNA, WO 190.
57. Proceedings, 31 July, 1 August 1809, TNA, WO 190.
58. Memorandum by Chatham, TNA, Chatham MSS, PRO 30/8/260, f. 100.
59. Coote to Chatham, 8 August 1809, Christie, 'The Walcheren Expedition', p. 325; Bond, *Grand Expedition*, pp. 82–3.
60. Owen's testimony, 9 February 1810, *PD*, XV, Appendix cciii, 8 March 1810, *PD*, XV, Appendix ccccvcvii; Brownrigg's testimony, 15 March 1810, *PD*, XV, Appendix 5xciii; Gardner's testimony, 15 February 1810, *PD*, XV, Appendix cclxix; Huntly's testimony, 20 February 1810, *PD*, XV, Appendix ccxc.
61. Strachan to Gardner, 2 August 1809, Christie, 'The Walcheren Expedition', p. 230.
62. Chatham's annotated copy of Strachan's narrative, 5 March 1810, TNA, PRO 30/8/260, f. 52; depositions of deserters from Flushing, 6 and 7 August 1809, PRONI, D3030/3211–12, 3215; Proceedings, 2 August, 4–5 August 1809, TNA, WO 190.
63. Strachan to Chatham, 8 August 1809, TNA, PRO 30/8/369, f. 102.
64. Proceedings, 6 August 1809, TNA, WO 190.
65. Brownrigg to Colonel Gordon, 8 August 1809, BL, Add MSS 49505, f. 9; Brownrigg to Alexander Hope, 10 August 1809, NRS, GD364/1/1189/8/1II.
66. Journal, 31 July, 1 August 1809, William L. Clements Library, Coote MSS, Box 29/3.
67. Notes on conversation between Coote and Chatham, 18 August 1809, William L. Clements Library, Coote MSS, Box 14/16.
68. Chatham to Coote, 12 August 1809, William L. Clements Library, Coote MSS, Box 13/38.
69. Journal, 11 August 1809, William L. Clements Library, Coote MSS, Box 29/3.
70. Brownrigg to Alexander Hope, 10 August 1809, NRS, GD364/1/1189/8/1II.
71. Chatham to Castlereagh, 8 August 1809, *A Collection of papers relating to the expedition to the Scheldt*, pp. 86–7.
72. Chatham to Castlereagh, 7 August 1809, *A Collection of papers relating to the expedition to the Scheldt*, pp. 82–4; Chatham to Castlereagh, 11 August 1809, PRONI, D3030/3220.
73. Brownrigg to Alexander Hope, 11/12 August 1809, NRS, GD364/1/1189/12II.
74. Greig (ed.), *Farington*, Vol. V, p. 224; Journal, 12 August, William L. Clements Library, Coote MSS, Box 29/3.
75. Captain Boys to his brother, 25 August 1809, Laughton (ed.), *Naval Miscellany*, Vol. II, pp. 390–1.

76. Temple to Buckingham, 3 September 1809, Buckingham and Chandos (ed.), *Memoirs*, Vol. IV, p. 356.
77. *The Times*, 29 December 1809.
78. Fleischman, *L'éxpedition Anglaise sur le continent en 1809*, p. 70 n. 7; *Journal de Paris*, 6 September 1809.
79. *Letters from Flushing: containing an account of the expedition to Walcheren . . . under the command of the Earl of Chatham . . . by an Officer of the Eighty-First Regiment* (London, 1809), p. 126.
80. Charles Kinloch to his mother, 17 August 1809, NRS, GD453/30/1.
81. Chatham to Castlereagh, 11 August 1809, PRONI, D3030/3220.
82. Chatham to Castlereagh, 11 August 1809, *A Collection of papers relating to the expedition to the Scheldt*, pp. 92–3.
83. Christie, 'The Walcheren Expedition', pp. 332–4; Brownrigg's testimony, 15 March 1810, *PD*, XV, 5xcv; Brownrigg to Colonel Gordon, 8 August 1809, BL, Add MSS 49505, f. 9.
84. Brownrigg to Colonel Gordon, 12 August 1809, BL, Add MSS 49505, f. 19.
85. The sixth, the Seamen's Battery, was not completed until the following morning.
86. Proceedings, 13 August 1809, TNA, WO 190.
87. *Letters from Flushing*, p. 159.
88. Brownrigg to Colonel Gordon, 16 August 1809, BL, Add MSS 49505, f. 25.
89. *Letters from Flushing*, p. 148.
90. Lowther's diary, 14 August 1809, Cumbria Record Office, DLONS/L2/12.
91. Diary of Adjutant General Long, 14 August 1809, Christie, 'The Walcheren Expedition', p. 369 n. 91.
92. Journal, 14 August 1809, William L. Clements Library, Coote MSS, Box 29/3; Proceedings, 14 August 1809, TNA, WO 190.
93. Journal, 14 August 1809, William L. Clements Library, Coote MSS, Box 29/3.
94. *Morning Chronicle*, 18 August 1809.
95. Castlereagh to Chatham, 21 August 1809, *A Collection of papers relating to the expedition to the Scheldt*, pp. 30–1.
96. Castlereagh to Chatham, 21 August 1809, TNA, PRO 30/8/366, f. 86.
97. Intelligence reports, 3 February 1809, 1 July 1809, *A Collection of papers relating to the expedition to the Scheldt*, pp. 235–6, 292–5; Brownrigg to Alexander Hope, 11/12 August 1809, NRS, GD364/1/1189/12II.
98. Journal, 18 August 1809, William L. Clements Library, Coote MSS, Box 29/3; Lowther's diary, 18 August 1809, Cumbria Record Office, DLONS/L2/12.
99. Ian Fletcher (ed.), *In the service of the King: the letters of William Thornton Keep . . . 1808–14* (Staplehurst, 1997), p. 55.
100. Chatham to Castlereagh, 19 August 1809, *A Collection of papers relating to the expedition to the Scheldt*, p. 118.
101. Extract from Graham to Cathcart, 21 August 1809, NRS, GD364/1/1189/30; Proceedings, 17 August 1809, TNA, WO 190.
102. Sir John Hope to Alexander Hope, 23 August 1809, NRS, GD364/1/1190/3/3/1.
103. Sir John Hope's testimony, 21 February 1810, *PD*, XV, Appendices cccxxviii–ix.
104. Rosslyn's testimony, 21 February 1810, *PD*, XV, Appendix cccxlvi.

NOTES

105. Brownrigg to Gordon, 20 August 1809, BL, Add MSS 49505, f. 30.

106. Brownrigg to Alexander Hope, 21 August 1809, NRS, GD364/1/1189/18I.

107. Sir John Hope to Alexander Hope, 19 August 1809, NRS, GD364/1/1189/27; Sir John Hope to Alexander Hope, 23 August 1809, NRS, GD364/1/1190/3/3/1.

108. Sir John Hope to Brownrigg, 18 August 1809, NRS, GD364/1/1189/25.

109. Strachan's testimony, 15 February 1810, *PD*, XV, Appendices cclv–vi; Proceedings, 25 August 1809, TNA, WO 190.

110. David Yarrow, 'A journal of the Walcheren expedition 1809', *Mariner's Mirror*, 61 (2) 1975, 186.

111. Proceedings, 25 August 1809, TNA, WO 190.

112. *Letters from Flushing*, p. 120; Brownrigg to Colonel Gordon, 8 August 1809, BL, Add MSS 49505, ff. 9; Chatham to Castlereagh, 11 August 1809, PRONI, D3030/3220.

113. John Webb to Surgeon General, 27 August 1809, *A Collection of papers relating to the expedition to the Scheldt*, pp. 588–90.

114. Proceedings, 22–8 August 1809, TNA, WO 190. Rosslyn, Grosvenor, Graham and Picton were among the general officers who fell ill: Journal, 26 August, 5 September 1809, William L. Clements Library, Coote MSS, Box 29/3.

115. Journal, 1 September 1809, William L. Clements Library, Coote MSS, Box 29/3.

116. Bond, *Grand Expedition*, pp. 134–5; Howard, *Walcheren 1809*, p. 161; D'Arcy to Chatham, 8 September 1809, TNA, PRO 30/8/366, f. 165.

117. Brownrigg to Colonel Gordon, 12 August 1809, BL, Add MSS 49505, f. 19.

118. Howard, *Walcheren 1809*, pp. 164–6; Bond, *Grand Expedition*, pp. 133, 205 n. 38.

119. Strachan's testimony, 13 March 1810, *PD*, XV, Appendix 5xlvi.

120. Proceedings, 26 August 1809, TNA, WO 190.

121. *Morning Chronicle*, 6 September 1809.

122. Brownrigg's memorandum, 26 August 1809, BL, Add MSS 49505, f. 45.

123. Opinion of the lieutenants general, 27 August 1809, *PD*, XV, Appendix cccxix.

124. Chatham to Castlereagh, 29 August 1809, *A Collection of papers relating to the expedition to the Scheldt*, pp. 119–20.

125. Chatham to Castlereagh, 6 September 1809, *A Collection of papers relating to the expedition to the Scheldt*, pp. 122–3.

126. Brownrigg to Colonel Gordon, 8 September 1809, BL, Add MSS 49505, f. 69.

127. *Caledonian Mercury*, 14 September 1809.

128. Notes of a conversation between Coote and Chatham, 8, 9 September 1809, William L. Clements Library, Coote MSS, Box 14/16.

129. Notes of a conversation between Coote and Chatham, 3 September 1809, William L. Clements Library, Coote MSS, Box 14/16.

130. Chatham's testimony, 27 February 1810, *PD*, XV, Appendix cccxcviii; Sir Richard Keats' testimony, 19 February 1810, *PD*, XV, Appendix clxxxv.

131. Bathurst to Camden, [1809], Kent Archives, U840/C86/5/2.

132. *A Collection of papers relating to the expedition to the Scheldt*, pp. 31–2.

133. Coote to Chatham, 29 September 1809, TNA, PRO 30/8/366, f. 141.

134. Brownrigg to Colonel Gordon, 8 September 1809, BL, Add MSS 49505, f. 69.

Chapter 10: 'The Clamour Raised Against Me', 1809–10

1. *Morning Chronicle*, 7 September, 21 September 1809.
2. C. Bentinck to W.D. Adams, 11 August 1809, BL, Add MSS 89036/3/3, f. 126.
3. Notes of a conversation between Coote and Chatham, 8 September 1809, William L. Clements Library, Coote MSS, Box 14/16.
4. Perceval's notes on a conversation with the King, September 1809, Aspinall (ed.), *Later Correspondence*, Vol. V, p. 363 n. 2.
5. Chatham to Perceval, 17 September 1809, CUL, Perceval Papers, Add.8713/VII/B/1.
6. Camden to Chatham, 8 September 1809, TNA, PRO 30/8/366, f. 16.
7. Strachan to Chatham, 27 August 1809, *PD*, XV, Appendix cccc.
8. Chatham's testimony, 27 February 1810, *PD*, XV, Appendix cccciii.
9. *London Gazette*, 29 August–2 September 1809.
10. *Morning Chronicle*, 4 September 1809.
11. Brownrigg to Colonel Gordon, 8 September 1809, BL, Add MSS 49505, f. 69.
12. Memorandum by Chatham, TNA, PRO 30/8/260, f. 126; Chatham to Perceval, 23 January 1810, CUL, Perceval Papers, Add.8713/VII/B/9.
13. Strachan to Wellesley-Pole, 27 August 1809, *A Collection of papers relating to the expedition to the Scheldt*, p. 464; precis in TNA, ADM 1/3987.
14. Journal, 7 September 1809, William L. Clements Library, Coote MSS, Box 29/3.
15. King to Chatham, 19 September 1809, TNA, PRO 30/8/364, f. 165.
16. *Morning Post*, 21 September 1809.
17. Perceval's notes on a conversation with the King, September 1809, Aspinall (ed.), *Later Correspondence*, Vol. V, p. 363 n. 2.
18. Camden to Chatham, 8 September 1809, TNA, PRO 30/8/366, f. 16.
19. Sir David Dundas to Brownrigg, 13 September 1809, TNA, PRO 30/8/366, f. 182; copy in Chatham's handwriting, TNA, PRO 30/8/260, f. 98.
20. 20 September 1809, Supplementary Minutes 1809–10, TNA, ADM 3/258.
21. Chatham's testimony, 22 February 1810, *PD*, XV, Appendices ccclxx–xxi.
22. Strachan to Gardner, 5 October 1809, TNA, PRO 30/8/369, f. 168.
23. Notes by Chatham on a conversation with Perceval, TNA, PRO 30/8/260, f. 126; memorandum by Chatham, TNA, PRO 30/8/260, f. 112.
24. Chatham to Sir Andrew Snape Hamond, 28 January 1810, TNA, PRO 30/8/364, f. 16.
25. Chatham's notes on Strachan's narrative, TNA, PRO 30/8/260, f. 146.
26. Chatham's Narrative, 15 October 1809, TNA, PRO 30/8/260, f. 20.
27. *PD*, XV, 581.
28. My italics: Instructions, TNA, PRO 30/8/260, f. 12.
29. Chatham's testimony, 22 February 1810, *PD* XV, Appendix ccclxix.
30. Memorandum by Chatham, TNA, PRO 30/8/260, f. 112.
31. Notes by Chatham on a conversation with Perceval, TNA, PRO 30/8/260, f. 126.
32. Memorandum by Chatham, TNA, PRO 30/8/260, f. 112.
33. Memorandum by Chatham, TNA, PRO 30/8/260, f. 112.
34. Notes by Chatham on Strachan's evidence, TNA, PRO 30/8/260, f. 146.
35. *Morning Chronicle*, 25 September 1809.
36. Chatham to Charles Yorke, 27 October 1809, BL, Add MSS 45052, f. 90.
37. Coote to Castlereagh, 23 October 1809, *A Collection of papers relating to the*

expedition to the Scheldt, pp. 177–8; Lt Col. Monsheim to Colonel Walsh, 24 October 1809, *A Collection of papers relating to the expedition to the Scheldt*, pp. 488–9.

38. *Morning Chronicle*, 19 October 1809; *Morning Post*, 26 October, 31 October, 9 November 1809.
39. Chatham to Rutland, 7 October 1809, Belvoir Castle Manuscripts.
40. Notes by Chatham, TNA, PRO 30/8/260, f. 112.
41. *Morning Chronicle*, 6 December 1809.
42. *Annual Register 1809*, LI, 591; Chatham to Liverpool, 31 December 1809, TNA, PRO 30/8/364, f. 31.
43. *A Collection of papers relating to the expedition to the Scheldt*, pp. 126–7; draft, TNA, PRO 30/8/364, f. 30.
44. *A Collection of papers relating to the expedition to the Scheldt*, p. 4; Chatham to Perceval, 16 January 1810, CUL, Perceval Papers, Add.8713/VII/B/7; Perceval to Chatham, 16 January 1810, TNA, PRO 30/8/368, f. 141.
45. Notes by Chatham, TNA, PRO 30/8/260, ff. 112, 120.
46. Notes by Chatham, TNA, PRO 30/8/260, f. 112.
47. *PD*, XV, 162.
48. *PD*, XV, 73, 200–1.
49. Grenville to Auckland, 8 March 1810, BL, Add MSS 34458, f. 51.

Chapter 11: 'Unconstitutional and Clandestine', 1810

1. Owen's testimony, 9 February 1810, *PD*, XV, Appendices ccii–xii.
2. Alexander Hope to Brownrigg, 14 February 1810, TNA, PRO 30/8/367, f. 157.
3. *Ibid.*; Carey to Chatham, [15 February 1810], TNA, PRO 30/8/366, f. 38.
4. Sir James McGrigor, *The autobiography and services of Sir James McGrigor, Bart.* (London, 1861), p. 248.
5. Carey to Chatham, [15 February 1810], TNA, PRO 30/8/366, f. 38.
6. Strachan's testimony, 15 February 1810, *PD*, XV, Appendices cclii–cclxv.
7. Strachan's testimony, 15 February 1810, *PD*, XV, Appendices ccxxxix–ccl.
8. Carey to Chatham, [15 February 1810], TNA, PRO 30/8/366, f. 38.
9. Strachan's testimony, 15 February 1810, *PD*, XV, Appendices ccliii–iv.
10. *Morning Post*, 17 February 1810; 16 February 1810, House of Commons Journal (hereafter HCJ), LXV, 100.
11. Canning to his wife, 20 February 1810, BL, WYL 250/8/24/44.
12. Strachan's testimony, 13 March 1810, *PD*, XV, Appendices 5xxxix–xl.
13. *Morning Chronicle*, 10 October 1809.
14. Colville and Davey, *Nelson, Navy and Nation*, pp. 10–13; Muir, *Wellington: the path to victory*, p. 228.
15. *PD*, XV, 482.
16. *PD*, XV, 485.
17. *PD*, XV, 490.
18. Notes by Chatham on a conversation with Perceval, TNA, PRO 30/8/260, f. 126; memorandum by Chatham, TNA, PRO 30/8/260, f. 112.
19. *PD*, XV, 569–70.
20. *PD*, XV, 587.

21. Sir Herbert Maxwell (ed.), *The Creevey Papers: a selection from the correspondence and diaries of the late Thomas Creevey, MP* (New York, NY, 1904), p. 130.
22. HCJ, LXV, 115; *PD*, XV, 537–40; Perceval to King, 23 February 1810, Aspinall (ed.), *Later Correspondence*, Vol. V, p. 52.
23. Chatham's testimony, 22 February 1810, *PD*, XV, ccclv.
24. *Ibid.*, XV, ccclix.
25. Bond, *Grand Expedition*, pp. 146–7, 162.
26. Chatham's testimony, 22 February 1810, *PD*, XV, ccclviii, ccclxi.
27. *Ibid.*, XV, ccclxvii, ccclxx–ccclxxiii.
28. Perceval to King, 23 February 1810, Aspinall (ed.), *Later Correspondence*, Vol. V, p. 52.
29. *Ibid.*, Vol. V, p. 521; *PD*, XVI, 12*.
30. *PD*, XV, 559, 564, 572, 574–5, 584, 587.
31. Wellesley-Pole to Richmond, 24 February 1810, Aspinall (ed.), *Later Correspondence*, Vol. V, p. 523 n. 3.
32. Memorandum by Chatham, TNA, PRO 30/8/260, f. 100.
33. Correspondence with Downs commanders (TNA, ADM 1/681) goes up to the beginning of August; the Admiralty Board minutes are patchy from June to December 1809, and missing for January to June 1809. ADM 3/257 (Special Minutes 1808–12) contains nothing for 1808–10. The Supplementary Minutes in ADM 3/258 contain some material from August 1809 onwards, but little on Walcheren. The Admiralty Board did compile precis of all intelligence and correspondence collected for publication, and these can be found at ADM 1/3987 and ADM 1/6040.
34. *PD*, XVI, 8.
35. Perceval to Richmond, 8 March 1810, Aspinall (ed.), *Later Correspondence*, Vol. V, p. 535 n. 2.
36. Perceval to King, 24 February 1810, Aspinall (ed.), *Later Correspondence*, Vol. V, pp. 523–4.
37. King to Perceval, 25 February 1810, Aspinall (ed.), *Later Correspondence*, Vol. V, p. 524
38. Notes by Chatham, TNA, PRO 30/8/260, f. 92.
39. 26 February 1810, HCJ, LXV, 128; Perceval to King, 27 February 1810, Aspinall (ed.), *Later Correspondence*, Vol. V, pp. 526–7.
40. Notes by Chatham, NA PRO 30/8/260, f. 92.
41. *Ibid.*
42. *Ibid.*
43. Chatham to Perceval, 'Sunday Night' [25 February 1810], CUL, Perceval Papers, Add.8713/VII/B/2.
44. Notes by Chatham, TNA, PRO 30/8/260, f. 92.
45. Chatham's testimony, 27 February 1810, *PD*, XV, Appendices ccclxxxvi–vii.
46. Holland, *Further memoirs of the Whig Party*, p. 33.
47. Chatham's testimony, 27 February 1810, *PD*, XV, Appendices cccc, cccvcvii, cccxcix.
48. Chatham did have to endure one embarrassment, although this had nothing to do with Walcheren. Sir John Fuller, MP for Sussex, whom Perceval considered to have been 'drunk', was annoyed when several off-topic questions of his were ignored and complained: 'God d—n me, Sir, I have as much right to be heard as any man who is

paid for filling the place he holds'. The session was interrupted to bring back the Speaker, and Fuller's intemperate words were entered into the House of Commons Journal. The Speaker rose to name the member who had used such unparliamentary language – effectively the first warning before disciplinary action – but Fuller replied, 'You need not be diffident, it's I, Jack Fuller.' Fuller was dragged out of the House, whereupon a vote was carried to commit him to the custody of the Serjeant at Arms. Fuller, when informed, rushed back shouting that the Speaker ('the insignificant little fellow in the wig') had no power to imprison him. A full-on fight ensued, during which Fuller kicked over Chatham's chair, and was at length removed 'with difficulty' by the Serjeant at Arms and no fewer than four House Messengers. Aspinall (ed.), *Later Correspondence*, Vol. V, p. 528 n. 3; *The Times*, 28 February 1810.

49. *PD*, XVI, 4*.
50. *PD*, XVI, 5*–7*.
51. *PD*, XVI, 1**.
52. Perceval to Chatham, 4 March 1810, TNA, PRO 30/8/368, f. 145.
53. Perceval to King, 2 March 1810, Aspinall (ed.), *Later Correspondence*, Vol. V, pp. 530–1.
54. *PD*, XVI, 5*.
55. *Ibid.*, XVI, 3***.
56. *Ibid.*, XVI, 13.
57. *Ibid.*, XVI, 16–9*.
58. HCJ, LXV, 147.
59. Perceval to King, 6 March 1810, Aspinall (ed.), *Later Correspondence*, Vol. V, p. 533; Perceval to Chatham, 6 March 1810, TNA, PRO 30/8/368, f. 159.
60. George Canning to his wife, 6 March 1810, BL, WYL 250/8/24/58.
61. Wellesley-Pole to Richmond, 7 March 1810, Aspinall (ed.), *Later Correspondence*, Vol. V, pp. 534–5 n. 2.
62. Perceval to Chatham, [6 March 1810], TNA, PRO 30/8/368, f. 135.
63. Memorandum by Chatham, TNA, PRO 30/8/260, f. 110; Rosslyn to Chatham, 7 March 1810, TNA, PRO 30/8/368, f. 229; Gray, *Spencer Perceval*, p. 302.
64. Chatham to Perceval, 7 March 1810, CUL, Perceval Papers, Add.8713/VII/B/12.
65. Perceval to Chatham, 7 March 1810, TNA, PRO 30/70/4, f. 283.
66. Perceval to Chatham, 7 March 1810, TNA, PRO 30/8/368, f. 152.
67. Testimonies of James Aberdour and Richard Jones, 6 March 1810, *PD*, XV, Appendices ccccxxxvii–ix.
68. Strachan's narrative, 5 March 1810, TNA, PRO 30/8/260, f. 52.
69. Canning to his wife, 12 March 1810, BL, WYL 250/8/24/67.
70. Strachan's testimony, 13 March 1810, *PD*, XV, 5xxxvi–vii.
71. Strachan's narrative, 5 March 1810, TNA, PRO 30/8/260, f. 52.
72. Strachan's testimony, 13 March 1810, *PD*, XV, 5xxx–xxxiv.
73. Chatham's notes on Strachan's narrative, 5 March 1810, TNA, PRO 30/8/260, f. 52.
74. Codrington to his wife, 20 August 1809, Lady Bourchier, *Memoir of the Life of Admiral Sir Edward Codrington*, 2 vols (London, 1873), Vol. I, p. 143.
75. Sir John Hope to Brownrigg, 6 August 1809, NRS, GD364/1/1189/17ii).

76. Perceval to Chatham, 7 March 1810, TNA, PRO 30/8/368, f. 152.
77. Testimonies of Rosslyn and Sir John Hope, 15 March 1810, *PD*, XV, Appendices 5lxxviii–ix, 5lxxxiii.
78. Brownrigg's testimony, 15 March 1810, *PD*, XV, Appendices 5xcvi–viii.
79. Wellesley-Pole to Richmond, 7 March 1810, Aspinall (ed.), *Later Correspondence*, Vol. V, p. 535 n. 2.
80. *PD*, XVI, 78–80.
81. Canning to his wife, 24 March 1810, BL, WYL 250/8/24/88; Michael Roberts, *The Whig Party, 1807–12* (London, 1962), pp. 145–7.
82. *PD*, XVI, 421–2.
83. Cole, *Arming the Royal Navy*, p. 28.
84. *PD*, XVI, 637–8.
85. *Ibid.*, XVI, 733–4.
86. *Ibid.*, XVI, 639.
87. *Ibid.*, XVI, 657.
88. *Ibid.*, XVI, 637–8.
89. Lord Boringdon to Lady Morley, 7 February 1810, BL, Add MSS 48227, f. 200.
90. Chatham to Perceval, 23 January 1810, CUL, Perceval Papers, Add.8713/VII/B/9.
91. Lord Boringdon to Lady Morley, 27 January [1810], BL, Add MSS 48227, f. 175.
92. *Morning Chronicle*, 30 January 1810; *St James's Chronicle*, 3 April 1790.
93. Philip Harling, *The waning of 'Old Corruption'* (Oxford, 1996), p. 1; Philip Harling, 'Parliament, the state, and "Old Corruption": conceptualizing reform, c 1790–1832', in Arthur Burnes and Joanna Innes (eds), *Rethinking the Age of Reform* (Cambridge, 2003), p. 98.
94. *Belfast Monthly Magazine*, XIV (January–June 1810), 223.

Chapter 12: Chatham in the Wilderness, 1810–21

1. *Morning Post*, 24 April 1810; St George's Chapel Archives, Registers of the Order of the Garter, 1805–1861 (G.6), f. 11.
2. *Morning Post*, 5 June 1810.
3. Carey to Huskisson, 14 April 1810, BL, Add MSS 38738, f. 16.
4. Huskisson to Carey, 29 April 1810, TNA, PRO 30/70/4, f. 284.
5. Carey to Huskisson, 3 May 1810, BL, Add MSS 38738, f. 26. For Carey, see Jonathan Duncan, *The history of Guernsey, with occasional notices of Jersey, Alderney, and Sark . . .* (London, 1841), pp. 613–15.
6. *PD*, XVIII, 747–9.
7. Duke of Richmond to Richard Ryder, 10 January 1811, PRONI, T3228/4/9.
8. Hon. Edmund Phipps (ed.), *Memoirs of the political and literary life of Robert Plumer Ward, esq.*, 2 vols (London, 1850), Vol. I, p. 369.
9. Lord Porchester to Lady Porchester, 11 January 1811, Hampshire Record Office, 75M91/C5/27.
10. Chatham to Rutland, 5 January 1811, Belvoir Castle Manuscripts.
11. *Morning Post*, 12 January 1811; Phipps (ed.), *Memoirs*, Vol. I, pp. 325, 327, 332; Chatham to Rutland, 5 January 1811, Belvoir Castle Manuscripts.
12. Canning to Chatham, 25 January 1811, TNA, PRO 30/70/4, f. 287.
13. Phipps (ed.), *Memoirs*, Vol. I, pp. 369–70.

14. *Edinburgh Annual Register 1808–26*, Vol. II (1), p. 660.
15. 'Lord Mediocre', in 'Thomas Brown the Elder', *Bath: a satirical novel*, 3 vols (London, 1818),Vol. III, pp. 51–5.
16. Phipps (ed.), *Memoirs*, Vol. I, pp. 342–3; *Morning Post*, 12 January 1811; Chatham to Tomline, 13 March 1811, Suffolk Record Office, HA119/T108/45/22.
17. See, for example, A.F. Barnard to Chatham, 1812–13, TNA, Chatham MSS PRO 30/8/365, ff. 174, 178, 180; H.H. Bradford to Chatham, 1812–13, TNA, Chatham MSS PRO 30/8/365, ff. 227, 232, 236, 238.
18. Chatham to Rutland, 12 December 1811, Belvoir Castle Manuscripts.
19. *Ibid.*
20. *Racing Calendar*, 1813, p. 233; *General Stud Book*, 4 vols (Brussels, 1839), Vol. II, p. 293.
21. Chatham to Tomline, 17 March 1818, Suffolk Record Office, HA119/T108/24/7.
22. Lease between Chatham and Mortlock, 15 March 1816, Cambridgeshire Record Office, 509/T158.
23. Chatham to Tomline, 17 March 1818, Suffolk Record Office, HA119/T108/24/7.
24. Chatham to Tomline, 24 April 1818, Suffolk Record Office, HA119/562/688.
25. Chatham to Tomline, 14 October 1818, Suffolk Record Office, HA 119/562/688.
26. *Ibid.*
27. Chatham to Tomline, 1 February 1819, Suffolk Record Office, HA 119/562/688.
28. Chatham to Tomline, 17 August 1819, Suffolk Record Office, HA 119/562/688.
29. Mrs Tomline to Sir Henry Halford, Suffolk Record Office, HA 119/562/716.
30. Sir Henry Halford to Mrs Tomline, 10 September 1819, Suffolk Record Office, HA 119/562/716.
31. Chatham to Tomline, 19 January 1820, 5 February 1820, Suffolk Record Office, HA 119/562/688.
32. Chatham to Tomline, 5 February 1820, Suffolk Record Office, HA 119/562/688.
33. Duke of York to Chatham, 24 January 1820, TNA, PRO 30/8/70, f. 289.
34. *Morning Post*, 29 January 1820.
35. Select Committee on the Colonial Military Expenditure, *Report from Select Committee on the Colonial Military Expenditure, with the minutes of evidence* (London, 1834), Appendix No. 1: Mediterranean: Gibraltar, p. 7.
36. Chatham to Tomline, 19 January 1820, 5 February 1820, Suffolk Record Office, HA 119/562/688.
37. *PD*, I (New Series), 433–4.
38. *PD*, V (New Series), 475.
39. *The Times*, 1 May 1821.
40. Bond between Chatham, John Burke and Joseph Ward, 11 January 1821, TNA, PRO 30/8/370, f. 183.
41. *Ibid.*; Bond between Francis Robertson and Louisa Angelo Burke, 17 June 1828, TNA, PRO 30/8/370, f. 238.
42. Bond between Francis Robertson and Louisa Angelo Burke, 17 June 1828, TNA, PRO 30/8/370, f. 238. Burke died in December 1824. His widow received about £13,000 from Chatham: TNA, Chatham MSS PRO 30/8/370, f. 152.
43. W.H. Pringle to the Tomline, 12 February 1821; William Eliot to Tomline, 5 March 1821, Suffolk Record Office, HA 119/562/688.

44. W.H. Pringle to Tomline, 27 April 1821, Suffolk Record Office, HA 119/562/688.
45. J.C. Villiers to Rutland, 22 May 1821; William Sloane to Rutland (reporting a conversation with Bellingham), 22 May 1821, Belvoir Castle Manuscripts.
46. J.C. Villiers to Rutland, 22 May 1821, Belvoir Castle Manuscripts; *Morning Post*, 12 May 1821.
47. *Morning Post*, 23 May 1821.
48. Montagu to Sir Walter Scott, 30 May 1821, NLS, MS 3892, f. 142.
49. J.C. Villiers to Rutland, 22 May 1821, Belvoir Castle Manuscripts.
50. Chatham to Rutland, [26 May 1821], Belvoir Castle Manuscripts.
51. Chatham to Tomline, 15 August 1821, Suffolk Record Office, HA 119/562/688.
52. Chatham to Tomline, 6 September 1821, Suffolk Record Office, HA 119/562/688.
53. Chatham to Tomline, 6 October 1821, Suffolk Record Office, HA 119/562/688.
54. Suffolk Record Office, HA119/6387/2. It's unclear whether the 'Lady Chatham' referred to on the wrapper was Chatham's mother or wife, but the fact Chatham gave it to the Tomlines shortly after Mary's death points towards the bracelet being hers.
55. 24 October 1821, HMS *Active* Ship's Log, TNA, ADM 52/4036.

Chapter 13: 'Chained to Ye Rock', Gibraltar, 1821–5

1. *Gibraltar Chronicle*, 15 and 16 November 1821; ship's log of the HMS *Active*, TNA, ADM 52/4036; Tito Benady, *Essays on the history of Gibraltar* (Gibraltar, 2014), pp. 99, 103, 107–8; Pepe Rosado, *The Convent: an illustrated guide-book* (Gibraltar, 2012), pp. 2–3, 5.
2. Benady, *Essays*, p. 124; T.J. Finlayson, *Gibraltar: military fortress or commercial colony?* (Gibraltar, 2011), pp. 84, 88–9; William G.F. Jackson, *The Rock of the Gibraltarians: a history of Gibraltar* (Gibraltar, 1990), pp. 227–8; Marc Alexander, *Gibraltar: conquered by no enemy* (Stroud, 2008) [ebook]; John Hennen, *Sketches of the medical topography of the Mediterranean . . .* (London, 1830), pp. 65, 81–2, 88–9.
3. Sam G. Benady, *Sir George Don and the dawn of Gibraltarian identity* (Gibraltar, 2006), pp. 5, 50.
4. John Duguid to Don, 6 February 1821; Don to Chatham, 15 February 1821; Chatham to Bathurst, 14 March 1821, TNA, CO 91/78.
5. Census return, 17 December 1822, in Chatham to Bathurst, 27 June 1823, TNA, CO 91/80; George Hills, *Rock of contention: a history of Gibraltar* (London, 1974), pp. 372–3; Jackson, *The Rock of the Gibraltarians*, pp. 225–6; Alexander, *Gibraltar* [ebook]; Hennen, *Sketches*, p. 66; Government of Gibraltar, *Census of Gibraltar, 2012* (Gibraltar, 2012), p. 3; Finlayson, *Gibraltar*, pp. 86–7.
6. Theodore Dwight, *A journal of a tour in Italy, in the year 1821 . . .* (New York, 1824), pp. 13–14.
7. Thomas Steele, *Notes of the war in Spain . . .* (London, 1824), pp. 190–1.
8. *Quarterly Christian Spectator*, IV (1822), p. 74.
9. Dwight, *A journal of a tour in Italy*, pp. 16–17, 26; *General Regulations and Standing Orders for the Garrison of Gibraltar, by General the Earl of Chatham, KG, Governor* (Gibraltar, 1825), pp. 6, 13, 16–17, 19; Rivas to Secretary of State, 5 August 1824, TNA, CO 91/82.
10. Steele, *Notes of the war in Spain*, p. 199; Dwight, *A journal of a tour in Italy*, p. 10.

NOTES

11. Hennen, *Sketches*, pp. 66, 92, 98, 113. There was a further outbreak of yellow fever in 1828, when nearly 1,700 people died: R. Montgomery Martin, *History of the British Colonies*, 5 vols (London, 1835), Vol. V, p. 79.

12. *Gibraltar Chronicle*, 15, 16, 21 November 1821; Mohamed El Mansour, *Morocco in the reign of Mawlay Sulayman* (Wisbech, 1990), pp. 186–8; Chatham to Bathurst, 29 May 1822; Chatham to William Sweetland, 29 May 1822, 30 May 1822; S.R. Chapman to Consul in Cadiz, 7 June 1822; Francis Stokes to William Sweetland, 14 November 1822, GNA, Dispatches from Gibraltar, 1820–5, Military Secretary's Correspondence, 1821–5, Local Correspondence, 1818–29.

13. Consuls: S.R. Chapman to consul at Marseilles, 19 November 1821; circular letter from Chatham to 'the different Consuls in the Neighbourhood', 19 November 1821, GNA, Military Secretary's Correspondence, 1820–5. Health of troops: Chatham to Bathurst, 15 November 1823, GNA, Dispatches from Gibraltar, 1820–5; Chatham to Bathurst, 19 July 1823, TNA, CO 91/80.

14. Chatham to Rutland, 10 July 1823, Belvoir Castle Manuscripts.

15. Anthony Powell (ed.), *Barnard Letters, 1778 – 1824* (London, 1928), pp. 305–6; *Morning Post*, 15 May 1823; Edward Townsend's diary, 29 April 1823, BL, Add MSS 64818.

16. James Bell, *The history of Gibraltar, from the earliest period . . .* (London, 1845), p. 194. For Chatham's popularity see also Lord Porchester, *The Moor* (London, 1825), p. 296.

17. Stephen Constantine, *Community and identity: the making of modern Gibraltar since 1704* (Manchester, 2009), pp. 82–3; Abstract of Revenue and Expenditure, 1822, in Chatham to Bathurst, 1 March 1823, TNA, CO 91/80.

18. Select Committee on the Colonial Military Expenditure, *Report from Select Committee*, p. 3.

19. Diary of James Robert Matthews, 2 April 1822, Pitt Papers, David M. Rubenstein Rare Book and Manuscript Library, Duke University. I am grateful to Stephenie Woolterton for bringing Matthews' diary to my attention.

20. *Morning Post*, 2 July 1825.

21. *Gibraltar Chronicle*, 26 January, 17 July, 23 July 1822, 8 July 1823.

22. Chatham to Bathurst, 26 July 1822, GNA, Military Secretary's Office 1819–27.

23. Pilkington to Chatham, 8 February 1823, TNA, CO 91/80; George Harrison to Chatham, 22 February 1825, GNA, Dispatches to Gibraltar 1825.

24. *Gibraltar Chronicle*, 5 December 1821, 3 March 1824.

25. Lucretia Ramsey Bishko, 'A Spanish stallion for Albemarle', *The Virginia Magazine of History and Bibliography*, 76(2) April 1968, 179.

26. *Colburn's United Service Magazine*, 1863(1), 345–6.

27. Edward Townsend to his mother, 10 September 1823, BL, Add MSS 64818.

28. Chatham to Tomline, 27 February 1822, Suffolk Record Office, HA 119/562/688.

29. Chatham to Bathurst, 16 June 1822, TNA, CO 91/79; Sir Herbert Taylor to R.W. Horton, 1 July 1823, TNA, CO 91/80; Bathurst to Chatham, 5 November 1823, TNA, CO 92/6.

30. Chatham to Bathurst, 15 November 1823, GNA, Dispatches from Gibraltar, 1820–5.

31. Bathurst to Don, 30 August 1821, TNA, CO 92/6.

32. Chatham to Bathurst, 16 June 1822, TNA, CO 91/79.

33. Fitzroy Somerset to Wilmot Horton, 22 August 1822, TNA, CO 91/79.

34. Chatham to Bathurst, 19 March 1824, TNA, CO 91/81; Bathurst to Chatham, 31 August 1824, GNA, Dispatches to Gibraltar, 1824; Chatham to Francis Stokes, 23 May 1825, GNA, Military Secretary's Office, 1820–5.

35. Chatham's General Sessions and Appeals Courts were held on 18 December 1821, 10 July 1822, 29 November 1822, 21 and 22 January 1823, 6 April 1824, 4 January 1825 and 12 April 1825 (there were probably more which were not reported in the *Gibraltar Chronicle*).

36. Ambassadors: Chatham to the Ambassadors of Madrid and Naples and the Governor of Malta, 21 November 1821, GNA, Military Secretary's Correspondence, 1820–5. Chatham as intermediary: R.W. Horton to Chatham, 4 February 1824, GNA, Dispatches to Gibraltar, 1824; and Chatham's reply, 19 March 1824, GNA, Military Secretary's Office, 1819–27. Spanish consul: Bathurst to Chatham, 1 July 1823, TNA, CO MSS CO 92/6; Chatham's reply, 19 July 1823, GNA, Military Secretary's Office, 1819–27.

37. Bathurst to Chatham, 31 May 1822, TNA, CO 92/6.

38. 'Relations of Morocco with the Powers of Europe and the Upper Barbary States', TNA, CO 91/79; Mansour, *Morocco in the reign of Mawlay Sulayman*, pp. 61–4, 113–14.

39. Bathurst to Chatham, 6 March 1822, TNA, CO 92/6.

40. Barnaby Rogerson, *North Africa: a history from the Mediterranean shore to the Sahara* (London, 2012), p. 254; C.R. Pennell, *Morocco since 1830* (London, 2000), pp. 4–8, 11, 14–16, 18; Mansour, *Morocco in the reign of Mawlay Sulayman*, pp. 17–18; Lucette Valensi, *On the eve of colonialism: North Africa before the French conquest* (London, 1977), pp. 35–6, 72–4; Charles-André Julien, trans. John Petrie, *History of North Africa* (London, 1970), p. 270.

41. Julien, *History of North Africa*, p. 262; Pennell, *Morocco since 1830*, pp. 12–13.

42. Mansour, *Morocco in the reign of Mawlay Sulayman*, pp. 201–2; S.R. Chapman to J.S. Douglas, 2 December 1821, 8 January 1822, GNA, Military Secretary's Correspondence, 1820–5; Bathurst to Chatham, 5 July 1822, TNA, CO 92/6.

43. Mansour, *Morocco in the reign of Mawlay Sulayman*, pp. 200–1.

44. Chatham to Porchester, 7 May 1822, Hampshire Record Office, 75M91/E43/29A.

45. *Gibraltar Chronicle*, 6 May 1822.

46. Valensi, *On the eve of colonialism*, pp. 73–4; Mansour, *Morocco in the reign of Mawlay Sulayman*, pp. 18–19, 218.

47. J.S. Douglas to Chatham, 8 January 1823, TNA, CO 91/80.

48. Chatham to Henry Halford, 2 September 1822, Leicestershire and Rutland Record Office, DG24/1058/1.

49. Charles J. Esdaile, *Spain in the liberal age: from constitution to civil war, 1808–1939* (Oxford, 2000), pp. 4–8, 26–7, 33, 40; David Howarth, *The invention of Spain: cultural relations between Britain and Spain, 1770–1870* (Manchester, 2007), p. 29; Butler Clarke, *Modern Spain, 1815–98* (Cambridge, 1906), pp. 22–5, 28, 33–5; Raymond Carr, *Spain, 1808–1939* (Oxford, 1966), pp. 118–19.

50. Clarke, *Modern Spain*, pp. 37, 44–6; Esdaile, *Spain in the liberal age*, pp. 45–52.

51. Chatham to Bathurst, 16 June 1822, TNA, CO 91/79.

NOTES

52. Spanish ambassador to Canning, 27 November 1822, Chatham to Bathurst, 20 December 1822, TNA, CO 91/79.
53. *Gibraltar Chronicle*, 8 July 1822, TNA, CO 91/80.
54. Chatham to A'Court, 16 November 1822, TNA, CO 91/79.
55. Howarth, *The invention of Spain*, pp. 42–3; Clarke, *Modern Spain*, pp. 57, 65; Esdaile, *Spain in the liberal age*, pp. 60–1.
56. Chatham to Rutland, 10 July 1823, Belvoir Castle Manuscripts.
57. Bathurst to Chatham, 25 June 1823, 26 June 1823, TNA, CO 92/6.
58. *The Times*, 23 August 1823.
59. *Gibraltar Chronicle*, 22 July, 24 July, 26 July, 28 July, 31 July, 11 August 1823.
60. S.R. Chapman to British consul in Cadiz, 10 March 1824, GNA, Military Secretary's Correspondence, 1820–5.
61. *The Times*, 8 December 1823.
62. Chatham to Rutland, 10 July 1823, Belvoir Castle Manuscripts.
63. Chatham to Bathurst, 28 May 1824, GNA, Dispatches to Gibraltar, 1824.
64. Bathurst to Chatham, 23 April 1824, Chatham to Bathurst, 29 May 1824, GNA, Dispatches to Gibraltar, 1824; Jose M. de Castillo to Canning, 26 August 1824, TNA, CO 91/82.
65. Rivas to Secretary of State, 5, 7 August 1824, TNA, CO 91/82; Secretary of State to A'Court, 12 August 1824, TNA, CO 91/82.
66. Chatham to A'Court, 24 August 1824; Chatham to Bathurst, 5 October 1824, TNA, CO 91/81.
67. Chatham to Bathurst, 5 October 1824, TNA, CO 91/81.
68. *Morning Herald*, 24 May 1825.
69. Bell, *The history of Gibraltar*, p. 195.
70. Chatham to Bathurst, 2 January 1825, TNA, CO 91/83.
71. Ship's log of the HMS *Tribune*, TNA, ADM 53/1418.
72. GNA, Local Correspondence, 1818–29.
73. *Gibraltar Chronicle*, 1 June 1825.
74. *Gibraltar Chronicle*, 8 June 1825.

Chapter 14: 'The Venerable Earl', 1825–35

1. 2 July 1825, ship's log of the HMS *Tribune*, TNA, ADM 53/1418.
2. *Morning Chronicle*, 6 July 1825.
3. Eldon to his son, 24 July 1825, Twiss, *The Life of Lord Eldon*, Vol. II, pp. 559–60.
4. Ledgers at Berry Brothers & Rudd.
5. Chatham to Tomline, 17 August 1825, Suffolk Record Office, HA 119/562/688.
6. *Morning Post*, 15 October, 19 November 1825.
7. Charlotte Williams Wynn to Fanny Williams Wynn, 20, 27 December 1825, Rachel Leighton (ed.), *Correspondence of Charlotte Grenville, Lady Williams Wynn, and her three sons . . . 1795–1832* (London, 1920), pp. 333–4.
8. *Morning Post*, 28 December 1825.
9. Select Committee on the Colonial Military Expenditure, *Report from Select Committee*, p. 1.
10. Buckingham to Wellington, 27 September 1831, University of Southampton, Wellington Papers, 1/1196/18.

11. Chatham to Camden, 12 February 1829, Kent Archives, U840/C102/7.

12. R.F. Foster, *Modern Ireland, 1600–1972* (London, 1990), pp. 298–301.

13. Wellington to Camden, 31 March 1829, University of Southampton, Wellington Papers, 1/1007/46.

14. Chatham to Camden, 1 April 1829, University of Southampton, Wellington Papers, 1/1008/8; Westmorland to Wellington, 8 February 1829, University of Southampton, Wellington Papers, 1/995/11.

15. Camden voted for Chatham: Parliamentary Archives, HL/PO/JO/13/106 (Proxy Book, 1829), 2 April.

16. Chatham to Rutland, 19 February 1831, Belvoir Castle Manuscripts.

17. *Belfast News-Letter*, 19 October 1832.

18. *Morning Post*, 7 October 1826, 11 September 1827, 28 October 1833.

19. *Morning Post*, 30 September 1833.

20. *Standard*, 8 November 1833.

21. Chatham to Rutland, 19 February 1831, Belvoir Castle Manuscripts.

22. *Morning Post*, 12 January, 11 February, 28 October 1833, 23 October 1834.

23. Chatham to Wellington, in Clarendon's handwriting, August 1830, TNA, PRO 30/70/4/ 292.

24. Wellington to Chatham, 5 August 1830, TNA, PRO 30/70/4/293; Chatham to Wellington, 6 August 1830, University of Southampton, Wellington Papers, 1/1133/3.

25. The stroke affected his right hand, for his handwriting deteriorated markedly: see Chatham to Lady Pringle, 1 January 1832; to Lord Sydney, 8 July 1832, Huntington Library, Townshend Family Papers.

26. *Lancaster Gazette*, 26 March 1831 and *Leicester Chronicle*, 26 March 1831; *Standard*, 25, 28 March 1831.

27. Chatham to William IV, undated, TNA, PRO 30/70/295d.

28. Clarendon to W.S. Taylor, 20 March 1836, TNA, PRO 30/70/4 295e.

29. For example, 17 August 1833 (in favour of W.S. Taylor), TNA, PRO 30/8/370, f. 89.

30. *Morning Post*, 10 February, 5 August 1834; *The Times*, 14 January 1835.

31. Wellington to Chatham, 12 July 1835, TNA, PRO 30/70/6/427.

32. Rutland to W.S. Taylor, 2 October 1835, TNA, PRO 30/70/6/429.

33. Sale of the late Earl of Chatham's belongings at Christie's, 16 May 1836, TNA, PRO 30/8/370, f. 147.

34. TNA, PRO 30/8/370, f. 152. It cost 15s just to carry the coffin downstairs.

35. George Bentinck to his mother, 3 October 1835, University of Nottingham Manuscripts and Special Collections, PwM 205; TNA, PRO 30/8/370, ff. 152, 156.

Conclusion

1. Henry Reeve (ed.), *The Greville Memoirs: a journal of the reigns of King George IV and King William IV by the late Charles C.F. Greville, Esq.*, 3 vols (London, 1875), Vol. III, p. 323.

2. Wraxall, *Posthumous Memoirs*, Vol. III, pp. 128–31.

3. Lever, *House of Pitt*, pp. 360–2.

4. Eldon to his son, 24 July 1825, Twiss, *The Life of Lord Eldon*, Vol. II, pp. 559–60.

5. Sir John Barrow, *An autobiographical memoir of Sir John Barrow, Bart.* (London, 1847), pp. 304, 307.

Bibliography

Manuscript Sources
Bedfordshire Archives
Wrest Park (Lucas) Papers (L30)

Belvoir Castle
Belvoir Castle Manuscripts

The British Library
Auckland Papers (Add MSS 34412–34471, 37689–37718, 45728–30, 46490–1, 46519, 54238, 59704)
Bridport Papers (Add MSS 35191–35202)
Canning Papers (formerly Harewood MSS, Leeds Record Office) (WYL 250/8)
Dacre Adams Papers (Add MSS 89036)
Diary of Edward Townsend (Add MSS 64818)
Dropmore Papers (Add MSS 58855–59494, 69038–69411)
Fox/Holland Papers (Add MSS 47559–47597)
Gordon Papers (Add MSS 49500–49505)
Hardwicke Papers (Add MSS 35349–36278, 45030–45047)
Huskisson Papers (Add MSS 38734–70, 39948–9)
Liverpool Papers (Add MSS 38190–38489, 38564–38581, 59772, 61818)
Melville Papers (Add MSS 41079–41085)
Perceval Papers (Add MSS 49173–49195)

Bromley Local Studies and Archives
Marsham-Townshend Papers (1080)

Cambridge University Library
Pitt Papers (MS Add 6958)
Spencer Perceval Papers (MS Add 8713)

Cambridgeshire Record Office
Mortlock Papers (509)

William L. Clements Library, University of Michigan, USA
Coote Papers
Pitt Papers
Townshend Papers

Cornwall Record Office
Eliot Papers (EL)

Cumbria Record Office
Lonsdale Papers (DLONS)

Devon Record Office
Sidmouth Papers (152M)

East Sussex Record Office
Sheffield Papers (SPK)

Gibraltar National Archives
Civil Secretary's Correspondence, 1821–5
Dispatches to Gibraltar, 1821–5 (from the Colonial Office)
Dispatches from Gibraltar, 1821–5 (from the Governor)
Local Correspondence, 1818–29
Military Secretary's Correspondence, 1820–5
Military Secretary's Office, 1819–27
Miscellaneous Correspondence, 1821–5
Miscellaneous Papers, 1821–5

Hampshire Record Office
Carnarvon Papers (75M91)

Huntington Library, California
Townshend Family Papers

John Rylands Library, University of Manchester
Papers of the 2nd Earl of Chatham (Eng MS 1271)
Papers of Lady Harriot Eliot (Eng MS 1272)

Kent Archives
Camden Papers (U840)
Stanhope (Pitt) Papers (U1590)

Leicestershire and Rutland Record Office
Halford Papers (DG24)

Morgan Library and Museum Department of Literary and Historical Manuscripts, New York, USA
Pulteney Manuscripts (MA 1268)

The National Archives
Admiralty Papers (ADM)
Army Lists (WO 65)
Chancery Rolls (C)
Chatham Papers (PRO 30/8)

BIBLIOGRAPHY

Colonial Office Papers (CO)
Hoare Papers (PRO 30/70)
Home Office Papers (HO)
War Office Papers (WO)

National Army Museum
Combermere Papers (8408, 9506)
MacLeod Papers (1977)

National Library of Scotland
Lynedoch Papers (MS 3605)
Sir Walter Scott Papers (MS 3892)

National Records of Scotland
Hope of Luffness Papers (GD364)
Melville Castle Muniments (GD51)

National Maritime Museum
Middleton Papers (MID)

Parliamentary Archives
House of Lords Pedigrees (HL/PO/JO/22/1/3)
House of Lords Proxy Books, 1778–1835 (HL/PO/JO/13)

Public Record Office of Northern Ireland
Castlereagh Papers (D3030)

David M. Rubenstein Rare Book and Manuscript Library, Duke University, USA
James Robert Matthews Papers
Pitt Papers

St George's Chapel Archives, Windsor
Registers of the Order of the Garter, 1688–1861, SGC G.5 and G.6

Somerset Record Office
Papers and Deeds Relating to Burton Pynsent (DD)

Suffolk Record Office, Ipswich
Pretyman-Tomline Papers (HA 119)

University of Nottingham Manuscripts and Special Collections
Portland (Welbeck) Collection (Pw)

University of Southampton
Wellington Papers (WP1)

Wiltshire and Swindon Record Office
Ailesbury Papers (9/35)

Newspapers, Magazines and Periodicals
Aberdeen Journal
Belfast Monthly Magazine
Belfast News-Letter
Bury and Norwich Post
Caledonian Mercury
Colburn's United Service Magazine
Edinburgh Annual Register
Evening Mail
Examiner
Gazetteer and New Daily Advertiser
General Advertiser
Geneve Post
Gibraltar Chronicle
Hampshire Telegraph
Hull Packet
Journal de Paris
Lancaster Gazette
Leicester Chronicle
London Chronicle
London Evening Post
London Gazette
London Recorder
Middlesex Journal
Morning Chronicle
Morning Herald
Morning Post
Morning Star
New Morning Post
Public Advertiser
Quarterly Christian Spectator
Racing Calendar
St James's Chronicle
Scots Magazine
Sporting Magazine
Standard
Star
Sun
The Times
Tradesman or Commercial Magazine
United Service Journal
Whitehall Evening Post
World

BIBLIOGRAPHY

Primary Sources

Abbot, Charles, Lord Colchester (ed.), *The diary and correspondence of Charles Abbot, Lord Colchester*, 3 vols (London, 1861)

Account, presented to the House of Commons, of the distribution of the sum of £2,500,000 granted to His Majesty to defray the Extraordinary Services of the Army for the year 1800 . . . (London, 1801)

Aspinall, A. (ed.), *Later correspondence of George III*, 5 vols (Cambridge, 1963–70)

Aspinall, A. (ed.), *Correspondence of George, Prince of Wales, 1770–1812*, 7 vols (London, 1963–70)

Barrow, Sir John, *An autobiographical memoir of Sir John Barrow, Bart.* (London, 1847)

Bickley, Francis (ed.), *The diaries of Sylvester Douglas, Lord Glenbervie*, 2 vols (London, 1928)

Bourchier, Lady, *Memoir of the life of Admiral Sir Edward Codrington*, 2 vols (London, 1873)

Bourne, Kenneth (ed.), *Letters of the 3rd Viscount Palmerston to Laurence and Elizabeth Sulivan, 1804–63* (London, 1979)

'Brown the Elder, Thomas', *Bath: a satirical novel*, 3 vols (London, 1818)

Buckingham and Chandos, Duke of (ed.), *Memoirs of the court and cabinets of George III*, 4 vols (London, 1853–5)

Bunbury, Sir Henry, *A narrative of the campaign in North Holland, 1799* (London, 1849)

Burton, J.H. (ed.), *Benthamiana, or select extracts from the works of Jeremy Bentham* (London, 1843)

Castle, Egerton (ed.), *The Jerningham letters, 1780–1843*, 2 vols (London, 1896)

A Collection of papers relating to the expedition to the Scheldt, presented to Parliament in 1810 (London, 1811)

Commissioners of Military Enquiry, *Twelfth Report of the Commissioners of Military Enquiry: Office of Ordnance: Treasurer* (London, 1810)

Commissioners of Military Enquiry, *Thirteenth Report of the Commissioners of Military Enquiry: The Master General and Board of Ordnance* (London, 1811)

Commissioners of Military Enquiry, *Fourteenth Report of the Commissioners of Military Enquiry: Ordnance Estimates* (London, 1811)

Corbett, Julian S., *Private papers of George, Second Earl Spencer*, 2 vols (London, 1914)

Debrett's Parliamentary Register

Dwight, Theodore, *A journal of a tour in Italy, in the year 1821 . . .* (New York, NY, 1824)

Estimates, presented to the House of Commons on the 14th and 15th January 1806, of the army services, for the year 1807 (London, 1807)

Fletcher, Ian (ed.), *In the service of the King: the letters of William Thornton Keep . . . 1808–14* (Staplehurst, 1997)

Ford, W.C., *The writings of George Washington*, 14 vols (New York, NY, 1889)

Garlick, Kenneth and Angus Macintyre (eds), *The diary of Joseph Farington*, 16 vols (New Haven, CT, 1978)

General Regulations and Standing Orders for the Garrison of Gibraltar, by General the Earl of Chatham, KG, Governor (Gibraltar, 1825)

General Stud Book, 4 vols (Brussels, 1839)

Greig, James (ed.), *The Farington diary*, 8 vols (London, 1922)

Hadden, James M., *Hadden's journal and orderly book* (Albany, NY, 1884)

Harcourt, Revd L.V. (ed.), *The diaries and correspondence of the Rt. Hon. George Rose*, 2 vols (London, 1860)
Hayley, William, *Memoirs of the life and writings of William Hayley*, 2 vols (London, 1823)
Hennen, John, *Sketches of the medical topography of the Mediterranean . . .* (London, 1830)
HMC, *Manuscripts of the Earl of Lonsdale. HMC 13th Report Part 7* (London, 1893)
HMC, *Manuscripts of the Duke of Rutland*, 4 vols (London, 1894)
HMC, *Manuscripts of the Earl of Dartmouth* (London, 1895)
HMC, *Manuscripts of J B Fortescue, Esq. preserved at Dropmore*, 9 vols (London, 1905–10)
House of Commons Journal
House of Commons Parliamentary Papers (Walcheren Enquiry) 1810
House of Lords Journal
Jesse, J.H., *Memoirs of the life and reign of King George III*, 3 vols (London, 1867)
Jupp, Peter (ed.), *The letter-journal of George Canning, 1793–5* (Cambridge, 1991)
Leighton, Rachel (ed.), *Correspondence of Charlotte Grenville, Lady Williams Wynn, and her three sons . . . 1795–1832* (London, 1920)
Letters from Flushing: containing an account of the expedition to Walcheren . . . under the command of the Earl of Chatham . . . by an Officer of the Eighty-First Regiment (London, 1809)
Lewis, Lady Theresa (ed.), *Extracts of the journals and correspondence of Miss Berry*, 3 vols (London, 1865)
McGrigor, Sir James, *The autobiography and services of Sir James McGrigor, Bart.* (London, 1861)
Maule, Major Francis, *Memoirs of the principal events in the campaigns of North Holland and Egypt . . .* (London, 1816)
Maurice, Sir J.F. (ed.), *The diary of Sir John Moore*, 2 vols (London, 1904)
Maxwell, Sir Herbert (ed.), *The Creevey Papers: a selection from the correspondence and diaries of the late Thomas Creevey, MP* (New York, NY, 1904)
Meryon, Charles, *Memoirs of the Lady Hester Stanhope*, 3 vols (London, 1845)
Ordnance Estimates, 1806–10
Parliamentary Debates from the year 1803 to the Present Time
Parliamentary History to 1803
Phipps, Hon. Edmund (ed.), *Memoirs of the political and literary life of Robert Plumer Ward, esq.*, 2 vols (London, 1850)
Porchester, Lord, *The Moor* (London, 1825)
Powell, Anthony (ed.), *Barnard Letters, 1778–1824* (London, 1928)
Private correspondence of Horace Walpole, Earl of Orford, 4 vols (London, 1820)
Reeve, Henry (ed.), *The Greville Memoirs: a journal of the reigns of King George IV and King William IV by the late Charles C.F. Greville, Esq.*, 3 vols (London, 1875)
Rosebery, Lord (ed.), *The Windham Papers*, 2 vols (London, 1913)
Ross, Charles (ed.), *Correspondence of Charles, First Marquis Cornwallis*, 3 vols (London, 1859)
Select Committee on the Colonial Military Expenditure, *Report from Select Committee on the Colonial Military Expenditure, with the minutes of evidence* (London, 1834)
Select Committee on Finance, *Third Report from the Select Committee on Finance: Ordnance* (London, 1817)

BIBLIOGRAPHY

Select Committee on the Public Income and Expenditure of the United Kingdom, *Second Report from the Select Committee of the Public Income and Expenditure of the United Kingdom: Ordnance Estimates* (London, 1828)

Smith, David Bonner (ed.), *Letters of Admiral of the Fleet the Earl of St Vincent whilst First Lord of the Admiralty, 1801–4*, 2 vols (London, 1922)

Smith, William J., *The Grenville Papers*, 4 vols (London, 1843)

Stavordale, Lord (ed.), *Further memoirs of the Whig Party, 1807–21 . . . by Lord Holland* (London, 1905)

Steele, Thomas, *Notes of the war in Spain . . .* (London, 1824)

Subaltern, *The campaign in Holland, 1799* (London, 1861)

Taylor, William Stanhope and John Henry Pringle (eds), *The correspondence of William Pitt, 1st Earl of Chatham*, 4 vols (London, 1839)

Walsh, Edward, *A narrative of the expedition to Holland in the autumn of the year 1799* (London, 1800)

Wraxall, Sir Nathaniel, *Posthumous memoirs of my own time*, 3 vols (London, 1836)

Articles and Chapters

Bishko, Lucretia Ramsey, 'A Spanish stallion for Albemarle', *The Virginia Magazine of History and Bibliography*, 76 (2) April 1968, 146–80

Breihan, John R., 'William Pitt and the Commission on Fees, 1785–1801', *Historical Journal*, 27 (1) (1984), 59–81

Christie, Carl A., 'The Royal Navy and the Walcheren Expedition of 1809', in Craig L. Symonds (ed.), *New aspects of naval history* (Annapolis, MD, 1979), pp. 190–200

Condon, M.E., 'The establishment of the Transport Board: a sub-division of the Admiralty, 4 July 1794', *Mariner's Mirror*, 58 (1) (1972), 69–84

Consolvo, Charles, 'The prospects and promotion of British Naval Officers, 1793–1815', *Mariner's Mirror*, 91 (2) 2005, 137–59

Crimmin, Patricia K., 'Admiralty relations with the Teasury, 1783–1806: the preparation of naval estimates and the beginnings of Treasury control', *Mariner's Mirror*, 53 (1) (1967), 63–72

Duffy, Michael, '"A particular service": the British government and the Dunkirk expedition of 1793', *English Historical Review*, 91 (360) July 1976, 529–54

Harling, Philip, 'Parliament, the state, and "Old Corruption": conceptualizing reform, c 1790–1832', in Arthur Burnes and Joanna Innes (eds), *Rethinking the Age of Reform* (Cambridge, 2003), pp. 98–113

Harvey, A.D., 'The Ministry of All the Talents: The Whigs in office, February 1806 to March 1807', *Historical Journal*, 15, 4 (1972), 619–48

Kelly, Paul, 'Strategy and counter-revolution: the journal of Sir Gilbert Elliot, 1–22 September 1793', *EHR*, 98 (387) April 1974, 328–48

Murray, Sir Oswyn A.R., 'The Admiralty VI', *Mariner's Mirror*, 24(3) 1938, 329–52

Piechowiak, A.M., 'The Anglo-Russian Expedition to Holland in 1799', *The Slavonic and East European Review*, 41 (96) December 1962, 182–95

Ward, S.G.P., 'Defence works in Britain, 1803–5', *Journal of the Society for Army Historical Research*, 27 (1949), 18–37

Webb, Paul, 'The naval aspects of the Nootka Sound crisis', *Mariner's Mirror*, 61 (2) (1975), 133–54

Webb, Paul, 'The rebuilding and repair of the fleet, 1783–1793', *Bulletin of the Institute of Historical Research*, 50 (122) (1977), 194–209

Webb, Paul, 'Sea power in the Ochakov affair of 1791', *International History Review*, 2 (1) (January 1980), 13–33

Willis, Richard, 'William Pitt's resignation in 1801: re-examination and document', *Bulletin of the Institute of Historical Research*, 44 (1971), 239–57

Wise, Thomas A., 'The life and naval career of Admiral Sir Richard John Strachan', *Transactions of the Royal Historical Society*, 2 (1873), 32–53

Yarrow, David, 'A journal of the Walcheren expedition 1809', *Mariner's Mirror*, 61 (2) (1975), 183–9

Unpublished Books and Theses

Bartlett, Keith J., 'The development of the British Army during the wars with France, 1793–1815' (PhD, Durham University, 1998)

Christie, Carl A., 'The Walcheren Expedition of 1809' (PhD, University of Dundee, 1975)

Crimmin, P.K., 'Admiralty administration, 1783–1806' (MA, University of London, 1965)

Debois Landscape Survey Group, 'Burton Pynsent, a history of the landscape' (February 2002)

Thompson, Mark S., 'The rise of the scientific soldier as seen through the performance of the corps of Royal Engineers during the early 19th century' (PhD, University of Sunderland, 2009)

Secondary Sources

Alexander, Marc, *Gibraltar: conquered by no enemy* (Stroud, 2008) [ebook]

Ashbourne, Lord, *Pitt: some chapters of his life and times* (London, 1898)

Bailey, D.W., *British Board of Ordnance small arms contractors 1689–1840* (Rhyl, 1999)

Baring, Mrs Henry (ed.), *The diary of the Rt. Hon. William Windham, 1784 to 1810* (London, 1866)

Bell, James, *The history of Gibraltar, from the earliest period . . .* (London, 1845)

Benady, Sam G., *Sir George Don and the dawn of Gibraltarian identity* (Gibraltar, 2006)

Benady, Tito, *Essays on the history of Gibraltar* (Gibraltar, 2014)

Bew, John, *Castlereagh* (London, 2011)

Birdwood, Vere, *So dearly loved, so much admired* (London, 1994)

Black, Jeremy, *British foreign policy in an age of revolutions, 1783–93* (Cambridge, 1994)

Bloomfield, Peter, *Kent and the Napoleonic Wars* (London, 1987)

Bond, Gordon, *The Grand Expedition* (Athens, GA, 1971)

Burne, Alfred H., *The Noble Duke of York: the military life of Frederick Duke of York and Albany* (London, 1949)

Cannon, Richard, *Historical record of the 4th or King's Own Regiment of Foot* (London, 1839)

Carr, Raymond, *Spain, 1808–1939* (Oxford, 1966)

Clarke, Butler, *Modern Spain, 1815–98* (Cambridge, 1906)

Clements, W.H., *Towers of strength: Martello towers worldwide* (Barnsley, 1999) [ebook]

BIBLIOGRAPHY

Cleveland, Duchess of (ed.), *The life and letters of Lady Hester Stanhope* (London, 1914)

Clode, Charles M., *The military forces of the crown: their administration and government*, 2 vols (London, 1869)

Cole, Gareth, *Arming the Royal Navy, 1793–1815* (London, 2012) [ebook]

Colenbrander, H.T., *Gedenkstukken der Algemeene Geschiedenis van Nederland van 1795 tot 1840 . . .*, 10 vols (The Hague, 1905–22)

Colville, Quintin, and James Davey (eds), *Nelson, Navy and Nation: the Royal Navy and the British people 1688–1815* (London, 2013)

Constantine, Stephen, *Community and identity: the making of modern Gibraltar since 1704* (Manchester, 2009)

Cookson, J.E., *The British Armed Nation, 1793–1815* (Oxford, 1997)

Coupland, R., *The Quebec Act* (Oxford, 1925)

Cowper, L., *The King's Own: the story of a regiment*, 3 vols (Oxford, 1939)

Crook, Malcolm, *Toulon in war and revolution: from the ancien regime to the Restoration, 1750–1820* (Manchester, 1991)

Davies, D.W., *Sir John Moore's Peninsular Campaign, 1808–9* (The Hague, 1974) [ebook]

Duffy, Michael, *Soldiers, sugar, and seapower: the British expeditions to the West Indies and the war against Revolutionary France* (Oxford, 1987)

Duffy, Michael, *The Younger Pitt* (London, 2000)

Duffy, Michael and Roger Morriss (eds), *The Glorious First of June 1794: a naval battle and its aftermath* (Exeter, 2001)

Duncan, Francis, *History of the Royal Regiment of Artillery*, 2 vols (London, 1879)

Duncan, Jonathan, *The history of Guernsey, with occasional notices of Jersey, Alderney, and Sark . . .* (London, 1841)

Dunfermline, James, Lord, *Sir Ralph Abercromby, KB, 1793–1801: a memoir by his son* (London, 1861)

Ehrman, John, *The Younger Pitt: The years of acclaim* (London, 1969)

Ehrman, John, *The Younger Pitt: The reluctant transition* (Stanford, CA, 1983)

Ehrman, John, *The Younger Pitt: The consuming struggle* (Stanford, CA, 1996)

El Mansour, Mohamed, *Morocco in the reign of Mawlay Sulayman* (Wisbech, 1990)

Esdaile, Charles J., *Spain in the liberal age: from constitution to civil war, 1808–1939* (Oxford, 2000)

Fedorak, Charles John, *Henry Addington, Prime Minister, 1801–4: peace, war and parliamentary politics* (Akron, OH, 2002)

Finlayson, T.J., *Gibraltar: military fortress or commercial colony?* (Gibraltar, 2011)

Fleischman, Théo, *L'expedition Anglaise sur le continent en 1809* (Mouscron, 1973)

Forbes, General A., *A history of the Army Ordnance Services*, 3 vols (London, 1929)

Fortescue, J.W., *A History of the British Army*, 13 vols (London, 1899–1930

Foster, R.F., *Modern Ireland, 1600–1972* (London, 1990)

Gardiner, Leslie, *The British Admiralty* (London, 1968)

Gardyne, C.G., *The life of a regiment: the history of the Gordon Highlanders from its formation in 1794 to 1826* (Edinburgh, 1901)

Gash, Norman, *Lord Liverpool* (London, 1984)

Gee, Austin, *The British Volunteer Movement, 1794–1814* (Oxford, 2003)

Geoghegan, Patrick M., *The Irish Act of Union* (Dublin, 1999)

Glover, Richard, *Peninsular preparation: The reform of the British Army, 1795–1809* (Cambridge, 1963)

Glover, Richard, *Britain at bay: defence against Bonaparte, 1803–14* (London, 1973)

Government of Gibraltar, *Census of Gibraltar, 2012* (Gibraltar, 2012)

Gray, Denis, *Spencer Perceval: The Evangelical Prime Minister* (Manchester, 1963)

Gregory, Desmond, *Sicily: the insecure base* (London, 1988)

Hague, William, *William Pitt the Younger* (London, 2004)

Harling, Philip, *The waning of 'Old Corruption'* (Oxford, 1996)

Harvey, A.D., *Britain in the early nineteenth century* (New York, NY, 1978)

Harvey, Robert, *The war of wars: the epic struggle between Britain and France, 1789–1815* (London, 2007)

Hayter, Tony (ed.), *An eighteenth-century Secretary-at-War: The papers of William, Viscount Barrington* (London, 1988)

Hill, J.R. (ed.), *The Oxford Illustrated History of the Royal Navy* (Oxford, 1995)

Hills, George, *Rock of contention: a history of Gibraltar* (London, 1974)

Hinde, Wendy, *George Canning* (New York, NY, 1974)

Hinde, Wendy, *Castlereagh* (London, 1981)

Hogg, O.F.G., *The Royal Arsenal: its background, origin, and subsequent history*, 2 vols (London, 1963)

Home, William Douglas (ed.), *The Prime Ministers* (London, 1987)

Howard, Martin R., *Walcheren 1809: the scandalous destruction of a British army* (Barnsley, 2012)

Howarth, David, *The invention of Spain: cultural relations between Britain and Spain, 1770–1870* (Manchester, 2007)

Humphreys, A.L., *Lyme Regis: a retrospect* (London, 1922)

Ireland, Bernard, *The fall of Toulon: the last opportunity to defeat the French Revolution* (London, 2006)

Jackson, William G.F., *The Rock of the Gibraltarians: a history of Gibraltar* (Gibraltar, 1990)

Jennings, Louis J. (ed.), *The correspondence and diaries of John Wilson Croker*, 2 vols (London, 1884)

Julien, Charles-André, trans. John Petrie, *History of North Africa* (London, 1970)

Jupp, Peter, *Lord Grenville* (Oxford, 1985)

Knight, Roger, *Britain against Napoleon: the organization of victory, 1793–1815* (London, 2013)

Lanctot, Gustave, *Canada and the American Revolution* (London, 1967)

Laughton, Sir John Knox (ed.), *The Naval Miscellany*, 2 vols (London, 1902)

Laughton, Sir John Knox (ed.), *Letters and Papers of Charles, Lord Barham*, 3 vols (London, 1907)

Lavery, Brian, *Nelson's navy: the ships, men and organisation* (London, 2012)

Lever, Sir Tresham, *The House of Pitt* (London, 1947)

Mackesy, Piers, *Statesmen at war: the strategy of overthrow, 1798–9* (London, 1974)

Mackesy, Piers, *War without victory: the downfall of Pitt, 1799–1802* (Oxford, 1984)

Martin, R. Montgomery, *History of the British Colonies*, 5 vols (London, 1835)

Matheson, Cyril, *Henry Dundas, Viscount Melville* (London, 1933)

BIBLIOGRAPHY

Maurice-Jones, Lt Col. K.W., *The history of Coast Artillery in the British Army* (Uckfield, 2012)

Miller, Maj. D.M.O., *The Master-General of the Ordnance: a short history of the office* ([n.p.], [1973/4])

Muir, Rory, *Britain and the defeat of Napoleon, 1807–15* (London, 1996)

Muir, Rory, *Wellington: the path to victory, 1769–1814* (New Haven, CT, 2013)

Muir, Rory, *Wellington: Waterloo and the fortunes of peace, 1814–1852* (New Haven, CT, 2015)

Nelson, Paul David, *General Sir Guy Carleton, Lord Dorchester* (Madison, NJ, 2000)

Olson, Alison Gilbert, *The Radical Duke: the career and correspondence of Charles Lennox, 3rd Duke of Richmond* (Oxford, 1961)

Pellew, George, *Life of Henry Addington, 1st Viscount Sidmouth*, 3 vols (London, 1847)

Pennell, C.R., *Morocco since 1830* (London, 2000)

Peters, Marie, *The Elder Pitt* (London, 1998)

Petersen, Thomas Munch, *Defying Napoleon: how Britain bombaded Copenhagen and seized the Danish fleet in 1807* (Stroud, 2007)

Popham, Hugh, *A damned cunning fellow: the eventful life of rear-admiral Sir Home Popham 1762–1820* (Tywardreath, 1991)

Reynolds, Paul R., *Guy Carleton: a biography* (Toronto, 1980)

Roberts, Michael, *The Whig Party, 1807–12* (London, 1962)

Rodger, A.B., *The war of the Second Coalition, 1798 to 1801* (Oxford, 1964)

Rodger, N.A.M., *The Admiralty* (Lavenham, 1979)

Rodger, N.A.M., *The command of the ocean: A naval history of Britain, 1649–1815* (London, 2004)

Rogerson, Barnaby, *North Africa: a history from the Mediterranean shore to the Sahara* (London, 2012)

Rosado, Pepe, *The Convent: an illustrated guide-book* (Gibraltar, 2012)

Rose, J.H., *William Pitt and national revival* (London, 1909)

Schama, Simon, *Patriots and liberators: revolution in the Netherlands, 1780–1813* (London, 1992)

Skentelbery, Norman, *Arrows to atom bombs: a history of the Ordnance Board* (London, 1975)

Stanhope, Ghita, *The life of Charles, 3rd Earl Stanhope* (London, 1914)

Stanhope, Philip Henry, *Life of the Right Honourable William Pitt*, 4 vols (London, 1861–2)

Talbott, John E., *The Pen & ink Sailor: Charles Middleton and the King's Navy, 1778–1813* (London, 1998)

Thompson, Canon, *A history of Hayes in the County of Kent* (London, 1935)

Tomlinson, H.C., *Guns and government: the Ordnance Office under the later Stuarts* (London, 1979)

Tunstall, Brian, *William Pitt, Earl of Chatham* (London, 1938)

Twiss, Horace, *The life of Lord Eldon*, 3 vols (London, 1844)

Valensi, Lucette, *On the eve of colonialism: North Africa before the French conquest* (London, 1977)

West, Jenny, *Gunpowder, government and war in the mid-18th Century* (Woodbridge, 1991)

Wheeler, H.F.B. and A.M. Broadley, *Napoleon and the invasion of England: the story of the Great Terror*, 2 vols (London, 1908)

Wilkinson, Clive, *The British navy and the state in the 18th century* (Woodbridge, 2004)

Wilkinson, David, *The Duke of Portland: politics and party in the age of George III* (London, 2003)

Williams, Basil, *The life of William Pitt, Earl of Chatham*, 2 vols (London, 1915)

Willis, Sam, *The Glorious First of June: fleet battle in the reign of terror* (London, 2011)

Ziegler, Philip, *Addington: a life of Henry Addington, First Viscount Sidmouth* (New York, NY, 1965)

Index